Phenomenology and Existentialism

Phenomenology and Existentialism

Richard M. Zaner and Don Ihde

FOUNDED 1838

GPPS

Capricorn Books

G. P. Putnam's Sons, New York

Contents

Phenomenology and Existentialism

I

Introduction

I

Both phenomenology and existentialism have already had a marked impact in the Anglo-American community—not only in philosophy, but in numerous other disciplines, such as the social, biological and natural sciences and the fields of theology, psychiatry, and educational theory. Our effort has been to present pertinent and understandable material bearing (1) on the basic character of these philosophical movements, (2) on some of their central themes, and (3) on the concrete fruits which have emerged from actual studies of specific and major issues. That the largest number of essays is found in the last indicates the editors' conviction that these two types of philosophy are best understood when seen, so to speak, "at work." Much has been said in the literature about "description"; it is our conviction that actual instances of it will speak more relevantly and clearly than mere "talk" about it. Finally, the editors believe that phenomenology and existential philosophy are of critical significance for a vast range of pressing issues today. The present volume, and especially the last part, will hopefully demonstrate that significance.

II

Every philosophical movement arises out of specific historical circumstances. Although one cannot reduce the former to the latter, it is nevertheless true that even genuinely original ideas cannot be critically understood without appreciating their historical matrix. Thus, while we have drawn these selections solely from contemporary sources, we by no means want to underplay the significance of the historical setting from which phenomenology and existential philosophy emerge and to

11

which they frequently address themselves (both positively and negatively). This history is extraordinarily complex and hence open to a variety of interpretations. Any effort to unravel even a piece of the cloth is thus in part a function of who is doing the unraveling and from which point he begins, and is unavoidably open to continual critical questioning. With this open admission of the complexities and controversial character of the historical explication, we propose to introduce this volume by treating some of the prominent features of the historical background, dealing first with phenomenology and then with existential philosophy.

Viewed from any perspective, the historical context of concerns and ideas which lead to the phenomenological philosophy of Edmund Husserl—the inaugurator and still the seminal figure of this movement—is very difficult to analyze. Even a full-length study of it would face many almost insuperable problems. It will be appreciated, then, that a brief portrait such as is necessary here can be little more than a mere hint of a slight scratch at the surface of what are in truth profound historical foundations of phenomenology.

These difficulties themselves are instructive as warnings for the avoidance of misleading interpretations, which can too easily be made. In part, they stem from the fact that Husserl and other phenomenologists following him make use of a number of terms which have been used many times in the past but whose sense is fundamentally altered by Husserl. Thus, for instance, both he and Kant use such terms as "synthesis," "transcendent," "transcendental," "intuition," and "idealism." As Aron Gurwitsch has shown, however, such notions do not mean the same for the two philosophers, even though there are many similarities in other respects.[1] Similarly, even though Husserl frequently refers to Descartes and uses some of his terminology, it is quite clear that Husserl cannot be taken to be merely one more Cartesian.[2]

Another, more crucial case concerns what is undoubtedly the central idea in phenomenology—that of "intentiveness" (*Intentionalität*). It is commonplace to note Husserl's indebtedness to one of his teachers,

[1] Aron Gurwitsch, "The Kantian and Husserlian Conceptions of Consciousness," in his *Studies in Phenomenology and Psychology* (Evanston, Northwestern University Press, 1966), pp. 148-74.

[2] *Cf.* Edmund Husserl, *Cartesian Meditations* (The Hague, Martinus Nijhoff, 1960), esp. Meditation I.

Franz Brentano, for this idea. Since Brentano himself had referred, in the now classic passage of his *Psychologie vom empirischen Standpunkt*,[3] to "the Scholastics of the Middle Ages" as having used the notion of "the intentional (or sometimes the mental) inexistence of an object," some interpreters have thought that the Husserlian concept of intentiveness can be traced back to a Thomistic conception. And since everyone knows the Aristotelian background of Thomism, Aristotle has come in for his share of credit for this central concept. A careful study of the pertinent texts shows, however, that these are mistaken. First, as Herbert Spiegelberg has made brilliantly clear, Brentano's usage (which is always adjectival) is quite original with him. In fact, he shows that it is precisely the Thomistic conception of *"intentio"* which Brentano *does not share* at all.[4] A second point is also important. However original Brentano was in his conception, it was closely tied in with other facets of his "psychology," which were utterly unacceptable to Husserl. More to the point, Husserl *fundamentally transformed* the concept of intentiveness itself, to the point where it can only be seriously misleading to interpret it in the same way as had Brentano. Hence, one can say only that Brentano's originality is matched by an equal originality by Husserl.[5]

Other examples could be pointed to—among them the very term "phenomenology," which has had wide currency in the nineteenth and twentieth centuries—but few of them are remotely close to Husserl's special use. Such "negative history," however instructive, does not speak to the positive context of historical ideas which have helped shape the sense of phenomenology. But with this, we encounter still further and more complex difficulties of interpretation. These can be expressed rather simply. Although Husserl himself frequently mentions Descartes, Hume and Kant as "foreshadowing" the basic thrust of his

---

[3] Franz Brentano, *Psychologie vom empirischen Standpunkt,* I, *Buch* II, ed. and intro. Oskar Kraus (Hamburg, Felix Meiner, 1955, first published 1874), *Kapital* I, pp. 125 f.

[4] Herbert Spiegelberg, *The Phenomenological Movement: An Historical Introduction,* Vol. I, *Phaenomenologica* 5 (The Hague, Martinus Nijhoff, 1960), esp. pp. 39-41, and in particular footnote 2 to p. 40; also see his *"Der Begriff der Intentionalität in der Scholastik, bei Brentano und bei Husserl,"* in *Philosophische Hefte,* ed. Maximilian Beck, V (1936), pp. 72-91.

[5] See Richard M. Zaner, *The Way of Phenomenology: Criticism as a Philosophical Discipline* (New York, Pegasus Press, 1970), esp. pp. 125-32.

phenomenology, it is by no means easy to determine precisely which features of their respective ideas are really on the "verge" of being phenomenological in his sense. To complicate matters, he is just as often severely critical of these same thinkers. And, beyond these, Husserl did not have a wide knowledge of the history of philosophy, or even, it could be argued, of the works of the thinkers he mentions. Despite that circumstance, so curious to many current philosophers who insist on the thorough study of the history of philosophy, Husserl had a remarkable sense for the core issues and "spirit" of those thinkers he mentions and did indeed have a thorough knowledge especially of British empiricism from Locke onward. In fact, it seems clear that the latter, especially Hume, were most influential on his phenomenology—despite his own emphasis both on their mistakes and on his own effort to develop a genuinely "transcendental" philosophy (so antithetical to empiricism). Hence, although some features of Descartes' and Kant's ideas play their role in Husserl's transcendental philosophy, the main historical setting for phenomenology is empiricism.

The principal idea behind Husserl's mixture of negative criticism and positive admiration for empiricism, as well as for Descartes and Kant, is found in that now familiar complication running throughout modern philosophy: the turn to subjectivity (mind, mental life, or consciousness) and, on the other hand, the turn to experience.[6] While insisting that Descartes' and Kant's turn to mind is *necessary*, Husserl as well emphasizes that Locke's or Hume's insistence that every claim to knowledge be grounded on experience is *equally necessary*. The difficulty with the first is that they were not truly radical (*i.e.,* foundational) in their respective turns to subjectivity; the difficulty with the second is that they conceived experience so narrowly as practically to rule out the bulk of human life and thus invariably distorted it and the genuine sense of epistemic claims.

Thus Descartes' "methodic doubt," while initially in the right direction, founders because he did not appreciate its fundamental sense and internal requirements. Rather than disclosing the "ego cogito" as that by means of which alone we are at all aware of anything, Descartes winds up with what Husserl calls a "little tag-end of the world." Descartes' doubt leads him to a "cogito" which at one and the same time is a *part* of the world and yet functions as the purported *ground* of

[6] These themes are treated masterfully by Dorion Cairns, "An Approach to Husserlian Phenomenology," below, pp. 31-46.

knowledge and experience of the world. In slightly different terms, Descartes' dualism is an absurdity on at least three counts. First, one substance (*res cogitans*) is supposed to be a part of an indubitable ground for everything yet is set alongside another equally absolute and coordinate substance (*res extensa*). Second, Descartes introduces the divine veracity of God as a kind of epistemological underwriter who must be called in *ab extra* to guarantee the legitimacy of the only genuine knowledge obtainable by the mind (clear and distinct ideas). But he fails to see that the status of such a guarantor is essentially different from the ways in which the ego experiences the world. Third, Descartes' "doubt" itself is misconceived in his execution of it, for he moves illegitimately from the supposed *sometimes* deceptiveness of sense experience to the *in principle* possibility of doubt. His famous doubt turns out to be just the opposite: rather than "holding judgments about the world in abeyance," he tries to *posit* the world's nonexistence on the basis of a supposed in principle possibility of deceptiveness. Rather than "doubting," then, he in truth engages in *positing merely another thesis* in place of the thesis that the world exists.

Still, for all that Husserl finds wrong in Descartes, there are certain strands in his work which do find their way into phenomenology. Perhaps the most striking is one to which very little serious attention has been given but is part of the core of what Husserl means by "radical criticism." Descartes insists in many places, but especially in the "Preface" to his *Meditations,* that the character of his undertaking is such that others who are willing and able to think along with him do so, and that they then will "see for themselves" the affairs he believes he has found. Indeed, he regards such co-meditative thinking as quite essential to philosophy itself. He openly invites others to correct, modify, even to reject whatever deserves it. Indicatively, his *Meditations* were sent out to others for their study and criticism before publication; and he then insisted that no one should make any critical claims until one had read the entire text, the *Meditations, Responses* and *Replies*. This appeal to others to engage in co-meditative dialogue is no mere gesturing; it is rather an essential ingredient in phenomenology, conceived as the autonomous discipline of philosophical criticism and self-criticism. It is, in other words, essential to that central philosophical activity, seeking and claiming to find knowledge, that these claims be open to the "testing" of others.

As for Kant, Husserl also entertains serious reservations. Indeed, it is clear that Husserl grew increasingly restive with Kant. He believed that Kant's transcendental philosophy, for all its merits, fell short of being truly transcendental in at least three basic ways. First, although Kant devotes much attention to the conditions for the possibility of synthetic a priori judgments, the analytic a priori is simply left hanging. It is neither itself critically grounded nor even seen to pose a critical-transcendental problem. The analytic a priori principles, not to mention his primal categories of the understanding, are just posited as self-evidently "there," taken over uncritically from tradition. That these a prioris are themselves the "objects" (in a broader than usual sense, of course, but objects nonetheless) of specific acts of consciousness, that the former require delineation and critical explication *as strict correlates of* the latter, and thus that these acts of consciousness cannot be ignored—these issues never seem to have been appreciated by Kant. And that fact is the second discontent Husserl has with him. For Kant, any reference to acts of consciousness (*i.e.,* subjectivity in general) through which alone are we at all cognizant of any object what-soever—including analytic as well as synthetic a prioris—is anathema; it is for Kant strictly a piece of empirical psychology, incapable of having anything to say about a priori principles. But this attitude, Husserl argues, simply shows that Kant did not appreciate either the need for a critical grounding and explication of psychology or that not every in-quiry focusing on the "psychical" (subjectivity) is *eo ipso* an empirical psychological task. Hence, for Husserl, Kant just did not have an ade-quate understanding of subjective acts of consciousness, in terms of which alone not only a psychology but an adequate theory of con-sciousness is at all possible.

A third quarrel against Kant is really a cluster of reservations regard-ing some of Kant's central assumptions. Kant assumes that the concept of a "thing-in-itself" is a *legitimate* one. He assumes, moreover, *that there are* such "things-in-themselves" (noumena) as opposed to "things-as-they-appear-to-us" (phenomena). On both scores, Husserl fun-damentally disagrees, for two basic reasons. One, the concept of a thing-in-itself depends on a still more basic and unwarranted assump-tion concerning the nature of sensuous perception (*Sinnlichkeit*), taken over uncritically from tradition (especially from Hume). It says that perception is a passivity, or pure receptivity (a "taking-in-by-the-senses," or *aisthesis*), which is dependent on the causal efficacy of a presupposed but in principle unknowable "x." Sense material is "formed" (by space and time) only on condition that a "material con-tent" is imposed or impressed on the senses. But that assumption is illegitimate precisely because it not only is not descriptively true of perception, but is circular: Kant needs that presupposed "x" to "cause" a material content to arise for sense perception; yet he uses this notion of sense perception to warrant, in part, the assumption of this "x" as a "thing-in-itself." Such a position is nothing but Hume's theory of perception, with the sole exception that while Hume was unwilling to say what are the "deep, dark causes" of our sense impressions, Kant posits these explicitly—yet they are posited as "unknowable." Such a theory of sense perception is little different from that of a traditional empiricist theory and harbors all the essential difficulties and absurdities of these.[7]

The second reason Husserl disagrees with these assumptions is that at no point do they recognize the essential feature of consciousness—namely, intentiveness. Without going into this topic here—since it is treated in detail in many of the selections included herein—suffice it to say that the supposition of an in principle unknowable, inexperienceable thing-in-itself can be only an evident absurdity. Like Descartes' divine veracity, it functions in the same way: a notion brought in *ab extra* to legitimate a theory whose possibility depends on something external to and unjustifiable by that very theory. And, for Husserl, a prime critical requirement for *any philosophical theory is that it be able, minimally, to account for its own possibility.*

There are other quarrels Husserl has with Kant. But it is important to realize that there are certain features of Kant's work which are crucial for Husserl's. One is obvious to even the casual reader: Kant, after all, did clearly formulate the necessity for a prime transcendental problematic—the inquiry into the conditions for the possibility of experience and knowledge. Although Husserl does modify the conception somewhat and refuses to accept Kant's purely formal principle of selfhood (the transcendental unity of apperception), the kind of transcendental turn exemplified in his work is a positive advance, for Husserl, toward a genuine critical philosophy. And even though Husserl rejects the Kantian thesis that there is both a noumenal and a phenomenal "self," Kant's turn to the subject (however inadequate) as the locus for the legitimating of experience and knowledge of the world is also an important thesis for Husserl.

[7] For further details on this, see Aron Gurwitsch, *Field of Consciousness* (Pittsburgh, Duquesne University Press, 1964), esp. Parts I and II; and Richard M. Zaner, *The Way of Phenomenology, op. cit.,* pp. 51-71.

Perhaps a more interesting historical connection, however, is one never made explicit by Husserl. This is the recurrent, apparently purely operative use by Kant of a special method of inquiry. In many places, Kant mentions that he is "abstractively isolating" or "dissecting out" distinguishable but inseparable components of human experience and knowledge. So doing, he believes he has detected or *made explicit* what is all along merely implicit in human life. This "making explicit" (formal explication) becomes, in Husserl's hands, a major component of what he designates as "phenomenological description." The basic aim of the latter is precisely to ferret out the taken for granted, the hidden, the latent, the obscure, the recondite—as regards every region of human engagement. Kant began this type of inquiry self-consciously, but never seemed either to have been consistent in his use of it or to have critically grounded it *as such*. Husserl, then, can be seen as bringing to fruition and formally grounding this component of critical philosophy—one of whose prime characteristics, as Cairns shows in the selection below, is the strictly coordinate nature of "method" and "epistemic claim."

Both Descartes and Kant, then, despite their many mistakes (as Husserl sees it), are on the very brink of entering that veritable continent of radically new and demanding themes and issues which lies open to phenomenology. Still, as was mentioned, it is Hume—even, empiricism more generally—who was most influential on Husserl. This is all the more curious, to be sure, in view of the many definitive rejections Husserl makes concerning Hume's and other empiricists' theories. Since the brilliant essay by Cairns in the opening section below shows this succinctly, we need not focus on that here. Nor is it really necessary to do more than mention his devastating critiques of the empiricists' theories of perception, consciousness, abstraction, and the inevitable skeptical relativism which comes to fruition in Hume.[8] What is important to bring out are some of the themes in empiricism which seem to have impressed him so much. Besides their contention that every claim to knowledge must be justified by experience—taking into account that Husserl's concept of experience is vastly richer and broader—there are at least three such relevant themes.

---

[8] See Husserl, *Logical Investigations,* trans. by J. N. Findlay (New York, Humanities Press, 1970), Volume I, Prolegomena to Pure Logic, and Investigation II; and his *Crisis of European Sciences and Transcendental Phenomenology,* trans. by David Carr (Evanston, Northwestern University Press, 1970), esp. pp. 84-90.

First, Locke is almost alone in holding that, although our knowledge of the so-called external world must be mediated by "ideas" internal to the experiencing subject ("ideas" which function as curious epistemic entrepreneurs), our knowledge of our own minds is not so mediated.[9] Rather, we are able to have immediate awareness of them and their various activities. Indeed, it is clear from Locke's great work on the understanding that the prime problem in solving all epistemological questions is the delineation of the nature of the mind or understanding itself. To extrapolate somewhat, one can say that Locke's thesis is that every judgment about the mind must be grounded on a direct encounter with the mind itself—and this we have in our own case, that is, our own mind itself. But he emphasizes that the only way open for us to do this inquiry is to "distance" ourselves from our own minds; only thereby is it at all possible to disclose what the mind truly is. In brief, both of these points are already quite close to Husserl's theory of evidence and his method of "epoche and reduction" (Locke's "distancing").[10] Such points of convergence pertain, of course, to the *kind* of inquiry seen as necessary by Locke and Husserl; what Locke then claims to find thereby is quite another story, to be submitted to a separate criticism.

Second, as Husserl makes clear in one of the passages included here[11] and elsewhere,[12] Hume was the first philosopher "*to treat seriously the Cartesian focusing purely on what lies inside.*" He was the first to see the necessity to inquire into the entire region of objectivity as being strictly a product of the subject's activities—such as the "associative principles," "custom and habit," and "belief." Whatever is an "object" or "reality" is understood by Hume as having its genesis in purely subjective activity, and in this respect the region of objects or real things becomes a problem for him in an entirely new sense. Precisely in this, Husserl claims, lies Hume's as yet still unrecognized greatness. For Hume focuses on the mind purely as a field of impressions and ideas and attempts to show how objectivities arise for the mind strictly from these origins. In this, Hume was the first to hit upon

---

[9] The place of "ideas," it should be mentioned, is quite ambiguous; they are at once properties of objects (*e.g.*, the color brown) and internal components of mind. It is thanks to Husserl that this deep ambiguity is clarified.

[10] *Cf.* Zaner, *op. cit.*, pp. 197-202; and the selection from Husserl's *Formal and Transcendental Logic*, below, pp. 120-47.

[11] See below, pp. 140-42.

[12] See Husserl, *Crisis of European Sciences and Transcendental Phenomenology, op. cit.*, pp. 88-90.

the radical *transcendental problematic*. Nevertheless, Husserl is quick
to stress that Hume himself did not consciously recognize either the
sense of his own discovery or the fundamental feature of mental
life—intentiveness. Hume's naturalistic sensualism, in the end, not only
prevented that critical recognition but as well led him into his well-
known skeptical agonies. Rather than seeing his own discovery, he instead *laments* that everything seems to arise from purely subjective
sources and thus feels that we have no choice but between a false reason
and no reason at all—for these purely subjective sources, he believes,
can give no guarantees whatever for knowledge. Kant *begins* the freeing
of this critical range of transcendental themes, but as was indicated, because of his dependence on Hume, Kant did not free himself sufficiently
from that fundamental obstacle to full transcendental philosophy—namely, the sensualistic theory of perception and its coordinate
assumption of a "thing-in-itself."

Nevertheless, in Hume's very failure can be found the third basic
theme in empiricism. Setting out, as Hume's metaphor puts it, to capture the very castle of knowledge itself, the nature of the understanding
itself, and not be bothered with taking a mere outlying village here and
there, Hume eventually concludes that all objects and all relations
among them (as also among the various impressions and ideas of the
mind itself) are ultimately due to "mere belief." The associative principles which are responsible for connection, regularity, and unity (subjective and objective) never yield real, but only *apparent* such relations.
The latter are, in Santayana's succinct phrase, a function of "animal
faith" (Hume's "belief") and thus are taken as inevitably leading to a
radical skepticism of the passing moment in which the mind appears as
a mere mosaic of unrelated, unconnected, atomistic bits and fragments
of "experience" (impressions and ideas). Yet, remarkably enough,
Hume recognizes that, thanks to the very vagaries of everyday life (the
"vulgar"), none of his philosophical skepticism matters one whit
anyway. We go right on believing in real objects, real subjects, and real
connections, because of the almost magical "inadvertence" in our
lifeworldly experiences. At just this juncture, though, Hume's skepticism again rears its pointed head. For, rather than seeing in precisely
this strange inadvertence a prime philosophical region of inquiry, seeing
it itself as a theme demanding to be accounted for, Hume gives up and
despairs. What, in truth, Hume hit upon there, as becomes clear in
Husserl's, Schutz's and others' works, is precisely one of the fundamental issues in phenomenology or critical philosophy: namely, the

structures and workings of the lifeworld (*Lebenswelt*) itself. The appeals to "experiences" and to the purely subjective workings of the mind set in clear relief the problem of determining how it is that "everydayness" has such a profound and effective force, to be capable of rendering Hume's skepticism (wrongheaded as it is anyway) so irrelevant.

But with a new look at Hume and empiricism in general, thanks to discoveries made in phenomenological inquiry, not only can this important issue be freed from empiricistic prejudices, but as well the genuinely transcendental status of Hume's own discovery becomes freed. And by noting carefully the "way" (method) of such "freeing"—where this is done as regards Descartes and Kant as well—Husserl is able to set out the principal grounds of that autonomous discipline of philosophical criticism and radical self-criticism—namely, phenomenology in its psychological, philosophical, and transcendental senses.

III

Husserl himself hoped that the turn to the subject, the examination of the experiential grounds of knowledge and the thematizing of the lifeworld would result in a radical reformation of the sciences. He hoped that a growing community of philosophers engaged in the ongoing investigation of the infinite field open to phenomenology would produce a whole new set of sciences. But the first historical result of the turn toward experience was to make possible the philosophical grounding of what is known today as *existential* philosophy.

Existentialism *as philosophy* is very easily misunderstood. This is precisely because its impact on various aspects of contemporary thought has been so broad. Literature, drama, theology, psychology, and, somewhat more slowly on the Anglo-American scene, philosophy, all felt the impact of existentialism. Moreover, in our native setting existentialism became popular before the later arrival of phenomenology even if, in fact, it was phenomenology which made *philosophical* existentialism possible.

The problem is that as a movement too much was passed off as "existential," so that only recently have the philosophically significant issues begun to emerge. Existential philosophy, as we treat it in this volume, is that style of philosophy which links certain central concerns and problems revolving around man's situation in existence with the explicit methodological foundations provided by transcendental phenomenology. We direct ourselves to existential phenomenology.

This is not to deny that precontemporary thinkers were progenitors of existentialism proper. The main ancestors in this lineage are clearly Søren Kierkegaard and Friedrich Nietzsche. These "proto-exittentialists"[13] posed the root questions for what later became an existentialism turned phenomenological. Compared with the mainstream of philosophy, both Kierkegaard and Nietzsche must be seen as rebels and detractors from the dominant trends of their times. Both railed against the "sterility" of academic philosophy; both called for a return to life themes and an emphasis on the existing, concrete individual; both were highly critical of the prevailing notions of rationality; and both led scathing attacks on the directions of their surrounding cultures.

In return for these critical attacks Kierkegaard and Nietzsche were branded, particularly by the academic philosophers, as "irrationalists." Some of their followers then and now willingly accepted the term and used it as a battle cry against the times. However, what passes as irrationality can also be the herald of a different and sometimes higher rationality. To decide important issues of cosmology by appealing to specks of light seen through a telescope appeared as the epitome of irrationality to the critics of Galileo. What these critics did not understand was the emergence of a quite different criterion for truth in the application of geometrical measurements to observed phenomena. Only after the ultimately successful emergence of Galilean science could its rationality be fully appreciated and the extent of its new reach of the understanding into the spaces of the universe be fathomed.

At first such a parallel claim concerning the aim and impact of existential phenomenology might seem too strong. Certainly in its proto-existentialist form the implicit rationality had not yet taken shape. The protests of Kierkegaard and Nietzsche, however, were not merely negative. They were also affirmations. It is from these implicit affirmations that the later marriage of phenomenological reflection and criticism to the proto-existentialist themes came to seem natural.

For example, one persistent theme in Kierkegaard was the turn to subjectivity. "That the knowing spirit is an existing individual spirit,

[13] The term distinguishes forerunners from existentialism proper precisely because neither had the transcendental method of phenomenology at their disposal.

and that every human being is such an entity existing for himself, is a truth I cannot too often repeat; for the fantastic neglect of this is responsible for much confusion."[14] What Kierkegaard was reacting against was the philosophical tendency to take the subject as a mere instance of a class and moreover to regard the subject as a mere cognizing subject. For Kierkegaard, "because abstract thought is *sub specie aeterni* it ignores the concrete and the temporal, the existential process, the predicament of the existing individual. . . ."[15] The fullness of human existence, if it is to be comprehended philosophically, calls for a way to examine concreteness, temporality, the expressive and the emotive, in short, the whole range of actual experience. Kierkegaard's reversal of the Neo-Hegelianism of his day finds echo in Husserl's "to the things themselves." "Only with the concrete does becoming enter in, and it is from the concrete that abstract thought abstracts."[16]

Phenomenology, as the twentieth-century existential philosophers soon saw, provided not only the means for getting at these existential problems, but a way to lay bare the existential structures of previously obscure phenomena. Sartre was able, with the help of phenomenological analyses, to deal with the structures of the imagination;[17] Heidegger was able to show the integral involvement of mood and the substructure of emotive involvements with the most abstract of knowledge acts;[18] and from the emphasis on human finitude and concreteness emerged the existential notions of embodiment, of the lived body, taken up by Marcel and Merleau-Ponty.[19]

The same relation of critical protest to latent affirmation, later to find a grounding in phenomenology, can be seen in Nietzsche's guiding themes. One of those central themes was the concern for man's immersion in historical existence. The metaphorical pronouncement that

[14] Søren Kierkegaard, *Concluding Unscientific Postscript*, trans. by David F. Swenson and Walter Lowrie (Princeton University Press, 1968), p. 169.

[15] *Ibid.*, p. 169.

[16] *Ibid.*, p. 170.

[17] Jean-Paul Sartre, *The Psychology of the Imagination*, trans. by Bernard Frechtman (Washington Square Press, 1968).

[18] Martin Heidegger, *Being and Time*, trans. by John Macquarrie and Edward Robinson (Harper and Row, 1962).

[19] Gabriel Marcel, *The Mystery of Being* (Henry Regnery Co., 1950) and Maurice Merleau-Ponty, *The Phenomenology of Perception*, trans. by Colin Smith (Routledge and Kegan Paul, 1962).

"God is dead," its interpretation as the coming of nihilism, the announcement of the Overman who is to overcome present, or "the last man" in *Thus Spoke Zarathustra* is both the struggle to recognize our inherence in historical being and the attempt to discover the ways in which man transcends his past history.

In *Thus Spoke Zarathustra* Nietzsche outlines three stages of the human spirit in relation to its history. The three metamorphoses are metaphors for the radical shift in perspectives that can happen in the death of an era and the birth of a new era. The spirit as a camel is spirit under the reign and acceptance of tradition. Although even existence under a tradition may be difficult, the goal and meaning of life are considered clear and even self-evident. But under this load and entering a desert, the camel may metamorphose into the lion who is the preliminary figure saying no to a past become burdensome or empty. The criticism of the lion, his revolt against his burden, is not able to create new values, "but the creation of freedom for oneself for new creation—that is within the power of the lion."[20] The lion is only the preparatory "nihilism" which precedes the emergence of the child who sees anew. The child "forgets" the way things have always been seen and is able to utter a "sacred yes" in a change of view which opens a new way to view the world. "He who has been lost to the world now conquers his own world."[21]

With the emergence of phenomenology these metamorphoses which occur in human history are given shape. Through Heidegger, who retraces the exodus of our history of thought through his "destruction of the history of ontology," to the parallel development in Husserl's attempt to describe the development of the *telos* of Western rationality, phenomenology addresses itself to historicality as a structure of human existence.

Through the phenomenological *epoche,* elaborated explicitly by Husserl and presupposed by Heidegger, precisely those aspects of our taken-for-granted beliefs are lifted out of their functioning roles and made thematic. The taken-for-granted, the mundane, thus becomes a theme for phenomenological description. It is to be examined for both its structural characteristics and its dynamics of development.

Thus both sides of the Nietzschean question are addressed. Struc-

[20] Friedrich Nietzsche, *Thus Spoke Zarathustra,* trans. by Walter Kaufmann (Viking Press, 1966), p. 27.
[21] *Ibid.,* p. 27.

turally, the question is one of recognizing the function and role of the mundane. Epoche, by purposely disjointing our usual engagements in the surrounding world, thematizes our beliefs in terms of their layered "sedimentations." Once these complex layers of belief are examined, however, a second task is called for. That is the need to describe the process of sedimentation. For while there is a structure to the lifeworld—all forms of it will display layers of beliefs and at its core will lie precisely that layer which we take for granted as "obviously the case"—there are also changes in the contents of the lifeworld.

What was once a matter of struggle for attainment may become, in the next epoch, that which is taken for granted which is ready to use. This is the import of the role of mathematics in its present shape in technological society. Mathematical techniques and thinking are readily available now; they are taken for granted. But their self-evidence was not always so available, as Husserl shows in his "Origins of Geometry." So also Heidegger, in his program of the "destruction of the history of ontology," notes that historicality as tradition not only reveals what we take the world to be, but also covers over certain possibilities. His excurses into the history of thought thus serve to reopen that history to new possibilities not previously noted.

It is not accidental, then, that phenomenology and existentialism belong together. Existential philosophy is the first and most obvious extension of phenomenological inquiry. The turn to the subject both in its proto-existentialist forms and later in the systematic development made possible by existential phenomenology is that turn which opens the whole range of studies addressed to comprehending man's experience in his world. It is a turn which potentially holds great import for all the human sciences.

And although that is where we stand today, the first word of phenomenology linked as it has been historically with existentialism need not be the last word. In this introductory anthology we have emphasized the main thrusts of phenomenology and existentialism as they have addressed the issues of the self, sociality, and historicality, all domains of the first order of human experience. But this is not the exclusive thrust of phenomenology or its only possibility. If Husserl's program is to be followed, there must also be phenomenologically oriented philosophies of the natural sciences, and other dimensions of human life and disciplines of human knowledge and inquiry. Not until the whole of human experience and knowledge has been investigated and criticized through phenomenology can phenomenologists rest satisfied.

We have left much unsaid, but perhaps through this preliminary opening to phenomenology and existentialism the implications for the philosophical future of these growing movements may become clear. It is our conviction that we stand at the beginning.

II

Phenomenology and Existentialism

Phenomenology is a search for radical beginnings within the long development of Western philosophy. Thus the question "What is phenomenology?" belongs to the very center of phenomenology itself. Thinking seriously about the character, scope and presuppositions of one's own philosophical activity and results—philosophical criticism and self-criticism—is inherent to this philosophy. Husserl, in the books published during his lifetime, conceived of his writings as attempts to introduce, to begin phenomenology. Following Husserl, most of the major thinkers in this style rephrased the same question each in their own way.

Merleau-Ponty saw in phenomenology a fulfillment by way of an opening to an existential philosophy. This beginning was to root philosophy in the implicit sense of existence experienced by man immersed in an already present lifeworld. Thus on one side phenomenology stands in a long tradition of self-conscious philosophies with a "problem to be solved and a hope to be realized." It is an identifiable "manner or style of thinking" which is latent in many earlier philosophers. Husserl noted a "deep yearning" in the works of Descartes, Hume and Kant for what was to become phenomenology. Merleau-Ponty sees the same need in the writings of Hegel, Marx, and others.

First the transcendental and later the existential phenomenologists see phenomenology bringing to fruition and systematic expression the hitherto scattered insights of philosophers into the necessity for developing such a critical stance, of the need for a radical and autonomous discipline of philosophical criticism.

On the other side, particularly in the later Husserl and clearly in the existential phenomenologists, there was the strong conviction that a critical philosophy remained tied to the earth, the lifeworld of experience with all its ramifications. Phenomenology must always keep measure of the distance between our explicit assumptions and those

29

silent and implicit presuppositions which operate subtly within daily life and practice.

In the selections of this first section of readings, the outline, the reasons and the directions of the question "What is phenomenology?" take shape. Both in the originary Husserlian and the later existential forms there may be seen a "common style" of thinking with its thematic concern for the history of philosophy, the nature and scope of phenomenology, and the sense of openness to its implicit directions. Dorion Cairns provides a clear introduction to Husserlian phenomenology. Then, in a new translation of the famous article "Phenomenology," Husserl outlines his program for philosophy. Merleau-Ponty shows the implicit existentialism of this style of thought, and Paul Ricoeur places both the transcendental and existential versions of phenomenology into perspective.

A. What Is Phenomenology?

DORION CAIRNS (1901-   )

Born on the Fourth of July, 1901, in Vermont, Dorion Cairns studied with Husserl in Freiburg during the 1924-26 and 1931-32 terms. Cairns' dissertation, "The Philosophy of Edmund Husserl" (Harvard, 1933), was one of the early works on Husserl in America. Cairns has become known as a respected phenomenologist, well-known interpreter of Husserl, and was regarded by Husserl as one of his most penetrating students. Cairns is the translator of Husserl's *Cartesian Meditations, Formal and Transcendental Logic* and is the author of a forthcoming *Guide to Translating Husserl*, as well as numerous articles on Husserl and phenomenology.

AN APPROACH TO HUSSERLIAN PHENOMENOLOGY*[1]

The peculiar character of Husserlian phenomenology lies not in its content but in the way the latter is attained. Whatever its sense, an account is phenomenological in the Husserlian sense if, and only if, it is produced "phenomenologically." Mere acquaintance with the doctrines of Husserlian phenomenologists is therefore not acquaintance with Husserlian phenomenology as such. To be acquainted with an account as phenomenological in the Husserlian sense, one must also know Husserlian phenomenological method.

The theory of this method is itself phenomenological in the

* By permission of Martinus Nijhoff. From Fred Kersten and Richard M. Zaner, eds., *Criticism and Continuation: Essays in Honor of Dorian Cairns*, Martinus Nijhoff, Gravenhage, The Netherlands, 1972.

Husserlian sense—and this indicates that Husserlian phenomenological method, in some form, is prior to Husserlian phenomenological methodology as well as to the rest of Husserlian phenomenological theory. Nevertheless, methodological knowledge is an instrument for improving method deliberately; and improved method leads to improved theory in general and improved methodology in particular. In view of these facts, there is a reason for making Husserlian phenomenological method the central theme of an essay addressed partly to non-phenomenologists, and there is also a reason for not beginning such an essay with an exposition of Husserlian phenomenological methodology in its more developed form. The latter can be understood only after the method in its rudimentary form, and certain results of rudimentary method, have been grasped.

To be sure, an adequate understanding of any purposely employed method includes an understanding of what the one using the method sets up as the thing to be actualized by its means. The goal of Husserlian phenomenological activity is always knowledge, but the initial conception of knowledge—like the initial method and the theory of method—undergoes a change, because of cognitional results actually attained. There is, therefore, an analogous reason for not attempting to state the specifically Husserlian phenomenological ideal of knowledge at the beginning of the present essay.

I

The fundamental methodological principle of Husserlian phenomenology may, I think, be initially formulated as follows: *No opinion is to be accepted as philosophical knowledge unless it is seen to be adequately established by observation of what is seen as itself given "in person." Any belief seen to be incompatible with what is seen to be itself given is to be rejected. Toward opinions that fall in neither class—whether they be one's own or another's—one is to adopt an "official" philosophical attitude of neutrality.*

When this principle is first presented, or adopted either implicitly in practice or explicitly as a maxim, its sense derives not only from an already acquired familiarity with the difference between awareness of something as itself given and awareness of something as not itself given, but also from accepted traditional theories. Perhaps the most striking instance of this difference, and surely the instance most emphasized by current traditions, is the difference between sensuously perceiving a thing and being aware of a thing—otherwise, e.g., in remembering or expecting it, or in sensuously perceiving or imagining something *else* as depicting or as symbolizing it. Obviously, the sense of the principle also derives at first from a like familiarity with the difference between an opinion that merely formulates what one grasps as itself given and an opinion that goes beyond, or conflicts with, what one grasps as actually given "in person." And here too the accepted tradition plays its role.

But vague familiarity and traditional concepts do not provide the principle with such clarity and definiteness as are necessary if it is to be applied to all opinions with certainty and precision. It might be expected that this defect should be remedied by contriving a set of defining postulates or rules of procedure. The principle itself demands, however, that traditional and habitual opinions about self-giveness and the other matters referred to in it be tested and, if necessary, corrected by *original observation*.

II

Something like the Husserlian phenomenologist's fundamental maxim, as initially stated, would probably be acknowledged by empiricists, at least qua empiricists. But empiricism imposes a restriction. The empiricist, as such, accepts a belief as philosophical knowledge only when it is somehow known to be adequately established by observation of *individual* affairs. Indeed, some empiricists give the maxim an even more restrictive interpretation, in accordance with which they refuse to accept "the perception of the operations of our own minds within us" as a form of observation by which genuine knowledge may be established. To them, only opinions known to be adequately established on the basis of "sensation" of sensuous perceiving are officially acceptable, "scientific" knowledge.

The Husserlian phenomenologist asserts that any empiristic restriction of his fundamental principle leads one to ignore or "officially" reject matters of which one is in fact aware as themselves given "in person," matters that are 'data" in the very sense that spatiotemporally individuated matters (including those sensuously perceived) are data. He contends, furthermore, that this assertion of his can be verified according to the above-stated methodological principle, and that therefore any statement to the effect that only individual things are observable (as themselves given) is a statement observably *incompatible* with what is itself given—a stated opinion that must be rejected in accordance with his fundamental principle. Such opinions, far from being based on original observation, not only go beyond but actually conflict with observable data.

Sensuous perceivedness, to consider it first, is indeed contrasted, as a form of "original self-giveness," with, e.g., the "meantness" of a physical thing as represented by a (perceived, remembered, or imagined) picture or symbol, or even as directly meant in a clear recollecting of a physical thing itself as past-perceived. More than that, it is (in a quite precise sense) the "basis" for all other types of givenness. Still it is, in itself, only that manner of original self-givenness *peculiar* to individual objects of a certain kind, e.g., to individual physical things, their individual shapes, individual colors, etc., and to their individual durations and changes in worldly space-time. One can be, and often is, aware of things of *other* kinds as themselves given—in other manners, to be sure, but "given" in precisely the same sense.

The Husserlian phenomenologist finds not only that non-sensible things and their determinations may be themselves given and grasped but also that the self-givenness of a self-given thing may be itself given and seized upon—moreover, that the generic similarity of the specific sorts of self-givenness peculiar respectively to sensuous data and data of other kinds is likewise something that may be itself given and observed. Thus, when he speaks of them all as "data," as "given," or even as "seen" or "perceived," he is—at least in his own opinion—indulging in no mere metaphors.

In short, the fundamental maxim of Husserlian phenomenology requires that empiristic restrictions be rejected because they conflict with or lead one to ignore strictly self-given, observable, and—as we shall see—intersubjectively verifiable "matters themselves." It is not perchance in the name of an alleged but unobservable Absolute nor even in the name of alleged necessary conditions for the possibility of experience or knowledge, conditions that allegedly cannot themselves be experienced "data," that the Husserlian phenomenologist rejects empiricism. Rather is it solely in the name of matters whose self-givenness the empiricist overlooks or resolves officially to ignore.

Although Husserlian phenomenology differs thus from empiricism, it differs more profoundly from any philosophy that first sets up formal definitions and postulates, or material hypotheses, and proceeds by a method of formal deduction—supplemented perhaps by material interpretation and "verification"—more or less according to the example of an incompletely understood mathematics or mathematico-empirical physics. To take conceptual stuff already on hand and fashion a cloak of theory for things *in absentia,* then call them in for a partial fitting—that is at best only a way to botch together another ingenious misfit to hang away with how many others in the lumber-room of history. The matters judged about must themselves be present from the start, and throughout the entire theorizing process they must never be out of sight. They must be observed and explicated in their self-given intrinsic sense; and judgments must be produced that derive their entire content immediately and continuously from them.

In their communicative function, Husserlian phenomenological statements are intended to help the person addressed to bring to self-givenness for himself, to seize upon, explicate, and compare the very matters in question, to attach to the words a signification deriving solely from his own observations, and to see the statements as evidently confirmed (or cancelled) by the matters themselves. Whatever verbal definitions or deductive arguments may be contained in a Husserlian phenomenological discourse are quite ancillary to this purpose—or out of place. Statements that are strictly phenomenological in the Husserlian sense are to be used as guides for observation, much as one might use a previous observer's description of a landscape as an aid in distinguishing its features while all the time it lies before one's eyes. In other words, their purpose is to assist the reader to knowledge that fulfills the Husserlian phenomenologist's own criterion. Assistance is useful not only because some observations are intrinsically difficult but also because prejudices are likely to induce one to overlook or explain away what is actually there to be seen. The Husserlian phenomenologist's appeal to "immediate" inspection is not made on the assumption that a Husserlian phenomenological proposition need only be understood for its truth to become evident forthwith. The truth of an opinion is seen "immediately" only when its coincidence with a given fact, as judged on the basis of the very matters entering into it, is seen. And often it is a long and hard road to a position from which one *can* see the truth of an opinion—"immediately."

III

Not all empiricists would restrict the sphere of philosophically acceptable self-givenness to what is given sensuously. Locke spoke, as a matter of course, about perceiving such "actions of our own minds" as "perception, thinking, doubting, believing, reasoning, knowing, [and] willing.'' He did not consider it incumbent on him to vindicate the existence of ''reflection,'' ''that notice which the mind takes of its own operations and the manner of them.'' In recent years, however, it has become important to defend the view that such mental processes as Locke enumerated are indeed perceptually self-given and that processes of reflecting, in which these ''actions'' are perceived, are themselves given reflectively.

Locke apparently thought of reflection only as a perceptual process, in our terminology a process in which one is aware of something as itself given ''in person.'' But not every awareness of something as one's own mental process is an awareness of it as thus perceptually given. For example, one may not only perceive but also remember, expect, or phantasy something as one's own mental process. The Husserlian phenomenologist, imitating Husserl's terminology, applies the name ''reflection'' to any awareness of something as one's own mental process or as a determination thereof. He accordingly speaks not only of reflective perceiving but of reflective expecting, judging, etc., just as he speaks of non-reflective or ''straightforward'' perceiving, expecting, etc. Reflective and straightforward perceivings are both called ''perceivings'' because the original self-givenness of a mental process seized upon reflectively is, as such, observably like the original self-givenness of a thing seized upon straightforwardly, though their specific manners of original self-givenness are observably different.

But those who imitate Husserl's usage do not restrict the name ''reflection'' to awareness of one's mental processes and their really immanent determinations. The name, as they employ it, also covers awareness of something *as* an object of one's mental life. Usually one is busied with things not *as* objects of one's mental life but only as things. If a thing is itself given, one is usually busied with it not *as* something given but as having certain thing-determinations. As I look about, I see physical things, their shapes, colors, etc., and usually occupy myself—cognitively, aesthetically, practically—with physical things only as having physical thing-determinations, not as things believed in, seen, liked, etc. Sometimes, however, one does pay attention to things *as* believed, *as* things given, *as* liked—in brief, *as* intended to in one's awareness of them. And this paying of attention to the usually ignored status of things *as* intended to is contrasted terminologically as ''reflection'' with one's usual ''straightforward'' paying attention only to things.

The deliberate application of the fundamental principle of Husserlian phenomenological method requires paying attention not to things simpliciter *but to things as intended to* and, more particularly, to their self-givenness or non-self-givenness. That is to say, it requires reflective rather than straightforward observation. To be sure, one can and frequently does establish one's beliefs by straightforward observation of what is itself given, without making its givenness one's theme. But straightforward observation, even when it does not in fact go beyond what is itself given, is not "phenomenological" in a Husserlian sense of the word. The exclusively reflective character of all Husserlian phenomenological inquiry deserves emphasis, if only because, according to a perhaps more common usage, pure straightforward descriptions (without construction or explanation) are also called "phenomenological." There is an important difference, however, between simply describing a thing and describing the sense that a thing is intended to as having—between ascribing to an (in fact presented) thing certain (in fact presented) thing-determinations and saying that a thing is presented as having certain determinations that are also presented. Husserl sometimes expressed the difference by saying, in effect, that straightforward description is description of things *per se* whereas his phenomenological description is description of *intentional objects*. Once the difference itself has been grasped, this convenient manner of speaking should not be misleading. It is apt to mislead, however, if one fails to see that the terms "thing *per se*" (or "thing *simpliciter*") and "intentional object" are names for one and the same thing, only paid attention to in different manners. In the straightforward attitude one ignores the thing's being intended to, being believed in (or believed), etc., being paid attention to, etc., and lives in one's intending to, one's believing in (or believing) the thing *per se*; in the reflective attitude one pays attention to *the same thing's* being intended to.

No matter how one may be busied straightforwardly—believing, doubting, denying; liking or fearing; perceiving, phantasying, willing—no matter what the object of one's concern is meant as being—a stone, an atom, an adjective, an angel, space or time, or even the world itself as a concrete whole—always one can adopt a reflective attitude and concern oneself with the thing *as* what one is, or was, busied with straightforwardly, *as* what remains intended to in this manner or that, as having such and such thing-determinations. When one does so, one is attending the "intentional object," the same thing qua object of one's mental process.

From this it should be clear that the dual terminology does not indicate an epistemological dualism. Intentional objects are not things somehow "in one's mind," nor are they intermediaries between mental processes and the things themselves. They are the things one's mental processes intend to, the things with which one perhaps deals cognitively, emotionally, volitionally; they include all the things that one correctly means as existing in the real, intersubjectively accessible world. Things *per se*, things pure and simple, are, on the other hand, not alleged things transcendent of the realm of intentional objects, but these same intentional objects as they are meant straightforwardly, without regarding their being intended to.

Our usual attitudes and mental activities are not reflective, but that does not mean that reflection is practiced only by Husserlian phenomenologists. Reflection, and even reflective perceiving, are the occasional practices of everyone, including those whose historically understandable prejudices make them oblivious to reflection and its data as soon as they adopt a theoretical attitude. And from this it follows that reflection, though essential to Husserlian phenomenologizing, is not its sufficient differentia.

IV

We have seen that the fundamental principle of Husserlian phenomenological method requires that one's mental processes, as themselves given in reflective perceivings, be acknowledged as genuine data. We have seen also that, to apply that principle, one must regard all things reflectively as intentional objects, i.e., consider them in their status as somehow intended to in one's mental processes. Any thing of which he is aware serves the Husserlian phenomenologist as a clue to the mental processes in which it is intended to. Following this clue, he attempts to bring to clear self-givenness the really immanent determinations of the process and correlatively the manner of givenness—perhaps self-givenness—of the thing *as* intended to in that process. In this attempt he is applying his fundamental principle—and doing so in the only manner that can bring to original self-givenness the matters of which the principle speaks, and thus lead to its original clarification.

So far, we have centered our attention on individual matters: primarily on things intended to as individuals and on individual processes intending to them. But it is to be observed that some things are straightforwardly meant as not being individuals. Indeed, they are not only meant but sometimes themselves given and grasped as such. An individual thing is intended to not merely in its individuality, as having individual parts and standing in individual relationships to other individual things. It is also intended to and may be explicitly seized upon *as* an individual (an instance of that *category*), as an instance of a *specific sort* of individuals, as having parts of *specific sorts,* etc. Furthermore, these "categories" and "specific sorts" may be not only thus co-intended to but also directly paid attention to for their own sakes and grasped in their original self-givenness on the basis of a clear perceiving or phantasying of at least possible instances. Thus, e.g., a thing may be intended to and clearly given as a possible, and perhaps an actual, instance of *color in general*, as having a quality that is an individual instance of *brightness in general,* and as standing in an individual relationship, that is an instance of *similarity in general,* to other individual instances of color. And color, brightness, similarity—these general kinds—may themselves be presented and seized upon. Indeed, it is only on the basis of the original givenness and seizedness of the kind as well as the individual that one can judge "with original insight": This is an instance of color; this has a brightness; this is similar to that in brightness; this instance of color belongs to this instance of surface; etc. And only when one has thus judged with original insight can one seize upon, as originally self-given, the state of affairs itself: that this is a color, that it is bright, etc. Moreover, general kinds themselves can be judged *about* just as individuals can—they can be identified, distinguished, named, and, in short, "treated" in all the manners necessary to justify one in calling them "things," despite their non-individuality.

Straightforward seizing upon, observing, and judging about generic and specific things that are themselves given are not, however, Husserlian phenomenological activities. The Husserlian phenomenologist as such observes and describes color in general *as* intended to, *as* seized upon, in its manner of being given, etc., not color in general *simpliciter*. And, correlatively, he describes the mental processes in which color in general is variously intended to, seized upon, judged about, etc. He observes that the generic and specific pure "essences" instanced by individuals straightforwardly intended to are, in a strict sense, themselves given; he describes the manner of their straightforward givenness, and the straightforward method of seizing upon them and judging with evidence about them. But he himself, qua Husserlian phenomenologist, practices the observation of only such generic and specific pure essences as are instanced by *reflectively* given individuals, i.e., by his own mental processes and their intentional objects. Reflectively seized upon individual processes of sensuous perceiving provide him with the basis for seizing upon the specific pure essence instanced by any sensuous perceiving as such; processes of visual perceiving function as a basis for seizing upon the more specific pure essence instanced by any visual perceiving; and processes of seizing upon individual things as themselves given, whether sensuously or nonsensuously, function as a basis for seizing upon the generic pure essence instanced by any perceiving. The same is true, *mutatis mutandis,* for reflectively seized upon mental processes of whatever kind. Similarly, the intentional object as such, in its sense for the mental process, in its manner of being given, believed, doubted, valued, etc., is a basis for seizing upon the generic or specific pure essences instanced by any intentional object, any givenness, any objective sense, any intentional object intended to as an individual thing, etc.

Though other egos cannot directly examine my individual mental processes, each of them can examine his own and confirm or refute my statements about the generic pure essence of any mental process, etc. If there is anyone who has anything like what I have and call "perceiving," it is *ipso facto* an instance of the genus of which my perceiving is an instance, and he can seize upon that *same* genus on the basis of his processes even as I seize upon it on the basis of mine.

Active seizing upon generic pure essences, whether they be instanced by straightforwardly or by reflectively seized upon individual processes, is at first practiced naïvely. But when it has been practiced, individual mental processes may be themselves seized upon reflectively and used as a basis for grasping their specific pure essence and, correlatively, the pure essence of the self-givenness peculiar to things seized upon as specific pure essences. On the basis of such an original seizing upon the pure essence of the process and the pure essence of what it accomplishes as an original seizing upon essences, one then may practice it not naïvely but as a deliberate and critically justified method.

Thus, as deliberately practiced and critically justified, it presupposes reflective inquiry. But as a naïve "method" it has always been practiced by everyone. To paraphrase Locke's aphorism: God has not been so sparing to men to make them barely able to seize upon individuals and left it to Husserl to make them able to seize upon pure essences. It should be emphasized that, according to the Husserlian phenomenologist, reflection and the observing of pure essences are not his prerogatives but the *de facto* practices even of the narrowest empiricist.

But it would not be correct to say that *all* judgments based on the observation of pure essences exemplified by reflectively given matters are phenomenological in the Husserlian sense. Indeed, it would not be correct even to say, conversely, that *all* judgments that are strictly phenomenological in the Husserlian sense are based on observation of pure essences. The observation of one's individual mental life provides a basis not only for seizing upon the generic pure essence it exemplifies but also for making Husserlian phenomenological judgments of existence, most notably, the judgment that this individual mental life itself is not only essentially possible but also exists as an actual instance of mental life. And this turns out to be anything but trivial, since it is the basis for every other Husserlian phenomenological judgment of existence.[2]

V

The present flux of mental life, as reflectively observed, is not simply a process of being actually busied now with this thing, now with that. The intentional objects of my actual believings, valuings, and willings are singled out from an intentionally objective background that is all the while meant as there, to be paid attention to.

No matter how intendings to things may vary, as I live actually now in perceiving, now in remembering, in judging, liking, willing—straightforwardly or reflectively—always there goes on, at least automatically, a continuous simple believing-intending to "the world" as the concrete individual nexus in which all particular individuals intended to are intended to as having their actual or possible being. The course of mental life may bring doubting or disbelieving of some previously believed in detail in the objective sense of this world, but the latter as a whole is still simply believed in—only as somehow otherwise, or perhaps otherwise, than was previously believed. If I am busied with matters that have the sense of not being temporally individuated, still the individual world is at least automatically co-intended to and itself given—though incompletely, as having more to it than presents itself—and, by their sense, these non-individual things have their varied types of "ideal" being, essentially in relation to the individual world of individuals, e.g., as pure essences *exemplified* by actual or possible world-individuals, as facts ultimately "about" world-individuals, as cultural affairs ultimately "embodied" in individual physical things or processes in the world. Thus, in a broad sense, they too are all intended to and perchance originally given, as worldly things.

In particular, when I busy myself reflectively with this mental life, it is at least co-intended to, like any individual process to which I pay straightforward attention, as a process in the world; and when I seize upon the pure essence exemplified by this mental life, it is at least automatically intended to as the pure essence exemplified by an individual process possible in the world. Indeed, even when I am not busied with this mental life or its intentional objects as such, but paying attention straightforwardly to "outside" affairs—still there goes on an intending to this intending to the world as an intending itself *in the world,* as an actually existing part of the actually existing individual nexus in which all actually existing particular individuals occur.

The "being in the world" that this mental life always automatically accepts itself as having is a determination that is always at least partially self-given and capable of being seized upon whenever I advert to it. Thus, e.g., causal-functional relationships between straightforwardly perceived changes in this physical organism and reflectively perceived changes in mental processes are continuously given and belong to the familiar, simply believed-in style of the world that is intended to and partially itself given.

However, even in this, its original self-givenness, the sense of this mental life as "in the world" is a sense it has *only by virtue of its essential character as intentive to the world.* It is, as it were, a necessary *reflex* effect on this mental life produced by its own essential nature as intentive to the world. Its given status as intentive to the world is in this way *fundamental* to its given status as in the world, to which it is intentive.

The Husserlian phenomenologist, as I have seen, is always reflectively orientated toward this mental life and toward things to which it is intentive *as* things to which it is intentive. In order to seize upon the above-stated intentional structure clearly, the reflecting Husserlian phenomenologist adopts as his fixed policy an attitude of neutrality, or self-restraint, vis-à-vis his own continuous believing in, and otherwise taking a position toward particular intramundane things intended to and toward the world as a whole.

This means, in the first place, not only that he seizes reflectively upon the believedness, etc., of what he is actually busied with but also that, for purposes of investigation, he "officially" dissociates himself from his actual positions and regards their intentional objects *purely* as "what I believe in," "what I see," etc. In the second place, it means not only that he makes explicit and seizes upon the believedness of the continuously, even if "only tacitly," automatically, believed-in intentionally objective world as a whole, but also that he actively dissociates himself from this fundamental and continuously validated belief. Thus the world and *all* intra-worldly things, in the broadest sense, are regarded purely as "what is believed-in," "what is meant," etc. This fixed policy of dissociation from all believing, valuing and willing—automatic as well as actional—is then maintained *in his reflective seizing upon mental processes*. That is to say, reflectively he not only makes explicit and seizes upon the continuously believed-in, self-given sense of mental processes as "in the world," but he also regards this sense of these mental processes *purely* as part of "what is believed in," "what is itself given." Thus, e.g., the experienced status of these mental processes as in causal-functional relations with this physical organism, and, more fundamentally, as a process in world space-time, are regarded by the Husserlian phenomenologist purely as "what is experienced."

If I am successful in maintaining this attitude, I *find*, over against the whole world, including this mental life as a process in it, this mental life in its more fundamental status purely as this continuous process of believing in the world and in this believing as itself a process in the world. In its status "apart" from its essentially necessary being in the world, this mental life is, if you will, an "abstraction," but not in the sense of being an abstract *part of the world* that now I merely think of and seize upon "regardless" of everything *else* in the world—perhaps as evidently existing even if nothing else "in the world" exists.

When the Husserlian phenomenologist applies the epithet "transcendental" to this mental life purely as a process of intending to and "having" the world, and speaks of this mental life in its status as *also* in the world as "phenomenal," he must exercise vigilance not to be seduced by the habitual associations of such language, not to mean by the different words something more—or other—than the difference in "status" that is actually itself given and grasped in reflection. In particular he must be careful not to think of "transcendental" mental life as, so to speak, existing in an "other world," or as a realm concretely apart from the world. He must not be misled by the traditional associations of the word "phenomenal," as applied by him to himself and this mental life as in the world, and to the whole world and all other intramundane things. He must reject any suggested contrast of phenomenon with noumenon, with its relegation of the experienced world to the status of an appearance relative to some alleged unexperienced reality.

A further pitfall, not easily avoided at the outset, is the tendency to think still of the "relationship" of transcendental mental life to the world as analogous to the real relationship of phenomenal mental life to other processes in the world—to think, let us say, of the intentional "relationship" between, on the one hand, a transcendental process of perceiving a physical thing and, on the other hand, the physical thing itself, as analogous to the real relationship between the "same" process, as an event in the world, and the physical thing. The difficulty has its roots in the fact that, in the world, perceiving and perceived are not only "related" *as* perceiving and perceived but also as realities in space-time, with real spatiotemporal relations. There is some sense in asking how soon after a change takes place in the perceived physical thing a change in the perceiving (as an event in the world) takes place. The question would, however, be absurd if asked concerning the perceiving as transcendental and the thing as phenomenal. The "relationship" of mental life *purely* as intending and things *purely* as intended to is utterly *sui generis*; it has no real analogue. Mental life as in the world not only has this "relationship" to the world but also has real relationships to other things in it, and this is a chief source of the confused strife among the various types of idealism and realism. Only after the peculiar dual status of mental life as pure transcendental intending (to the world) and as phenomenal mental life (in and intentive to the world) has been clearly seen, can the confusion be dissipated and the historic enigma solved.

The general structure of mental life as itself given in reflection *to one who dissociates himself from his own believing in the world and in the status of mental life as itself in the world* may be said to be the first theme of strictly Husserlian phenomenological inquiry. The "transcendental" possibility of the reflexionally given mental life as a clearly possible instance of the pure essence, transcendental mental life, is, at first, simply accepted as itself given. And this is the *only* "assumption" of Husserlian phenomenology, even at the outset, since the being intended-to, the givenness, etc., of the world qua phenomenon is implicit in the essential nature of transcendental mental life, even though the world intended to is not itself a really immanent part there of. In analyzing this transcendental mental life as intentive to the world and the world as something to which this transcendental mental life is essentially intentive, Husserlian phenomenology is presupposing neither the existence nor the possibility of the world, as every other philosophical inquiry must do, at least tacitly.

* * *

Thus, in attempting to carry out the fundamental methodological principle stated at the beginning of this essay, the Husserlian phenomenologist comes upon a self-givenness that, in a clear but not easily expressed sense, is "prior" to every other self-givenness, and is able to discover and verify by direct observation the fundamental presuppositions of all natural inquiry—without involving himself in the otherwise inevitable circularity of assuming their validity as its own basis and as the justification of the method itself.

It is at this point that a genuinely philosophical inquiry can really *begin*: as a "transcendental phenomenology." As its inquiry progresses, it develops its own peculiar problems and method, in accordance with the gradually discovered nature of "the matters themselves"—always following the maxim that only what is seen to be itself given is to be accepted as genuine knowledge.

FOOTNOTES

[1]Published under the title, "An Approach to Phenomenology," in *Philosophical Essays in Memory of Edmund Husserl,* edited by Marvin Farber (Cambridge, Mass., Harvard University Press, 1940). What I publish here is not a reprint. I have corrected a few orthographical, punctuational, or stylistic errori; I have deleted the translation of two sentences in Husserl's *Ideen* . . . , I. Bd., sec. 22—two sentences to which Husserl himself objected and one sentence of mine; I have appended this footnote and one other new one; I have, above all, altered the terminology again and again, to make it more nearly in accordance with my present (and, I believe, greatly improved) usage. But I have changed neither the essay's structure nor its sense, though today (thirty years later) a few opinions expressed in the essay are opinions to which I no longer adhere unqualifiedly.

[2]*Footnote appended in November, 1970, to the passage beginning*: "Indeed, it would not be correct even to say . . .": According to Husserl's *Ideas*. . . , "Introduction" and "Book I," what I wrote in these sentences is terminologically incorrect. Fully expressed, the title of that work would be: *Ideen zu einer <rein deskriptiven, rein eidetis-*

chen, transzendental-> reinen <oder transzendentalen< Phänomenologie und <zu einer transzendental-> reinen <oder transzendental-phänomenologischen Philosophie [Ideas Pertaining to a <Purely Descriptive, Purely Eidetic, Transcendentally> Pure <or Transcendental<Phenomenology and <to a Transcendentally>Pure <or Transcendental-> Phenomenological Philosophy]. None of the judgments of existence referred to in the sentences to which this footnote is appended would belong in a Husserlian phenomenology itself as Husserl conceived such a discipline when he was writing his *Ideas. . .*, "Introduction" and "Book I." Each of them would belong rather in some other philosophical discipline, *founded on* such a *Husserlian phenomenology.*

description, not analysis—
attack on the rational

EDMUND HUSSERL (1859-1938)

Edmund Husserl was born in 1859 in Prossnitz, Czechoslovakia. Between 1876 and 1878 he studied mathematics, physics and astronomy at the University of Leipzig and attended Wilhelm Wundt's lectures in philosophy. In 1878 he moved to the University of Berlin to continue his mathematical studies, moving again to the University of Vienna to receive his PhD in mathematics in 1883. There he remained to study philosophy and psychology with Franz Brentano from 1884 to 1886, the period which was to prove decisive for the beginnings of phenomenology. Among his major works are: *Logical Investigations* (1900-1), *Ideas* (1913), *Formal and Transcendental Logic* (1928), *Cartesian Meditations* (1931), and *The Crisis of European Sciences and Transcendental Phenomenology* (1936). Other important works are included in the Husserliana series directed by Father H. L. Van Breda, published by Martinus Nijhoff.

"PHENOMENOLOGY," EDMUND HUSSERL'S ARTICLE FOR THE *ENCYCLOPAEDIA BRITANNICA* (1927): NEW COMPLETE TRANSLATION BY RICHARD E. PALMER*

Introduction

I. Pure psychology: Its field of experience, its method and its function.

A. *Pure natural science and pure psychology.*

B. *The purely psychic element in self-experience and community experience. The universal description of intentional experiences.*

C. *The self-contained field of the purely psychical.—Phenomenological reduction and true inner experience.*

D. *Eidetic reduction and phenomenological psychology as an eidetic science.*

E. *The fundamental function of pure phenomenological psychology for an exact empirical psychology.*

II. Phenomenological psychology and transcendental phenomenology.

A. *Descartes' transcendental turn and Locke's psychologism.*

B. *The transcendental problem.*

C. *The solution by psychologism as a transcendental circle.*

D. *The transcendental-phenomenological reduction and the illusion of transcendental duplication.*

E. *Pure psychology as a propaedeutic to transcendental phenomenology.*

*We are grateful to Martinus Nijhoff N. V., The Hague, the publisher, for permission to publish a translation. Reprinted here by permission of the publisher and the translator. (Eds.)

III. Transcendental phenomenology and philosophy as universal science with absolute foundations

    A. Transcendental phenomenology as ontology.

    B. Phenomenology and the crisis in the foundations of the exact sciences.

    C. The phenomenological grounding of the factual sciences in relation to empirical phenomenology.

    D. Complete phenomenology as all-embracing philosophy.

    E. The "ultimate and highest" problems as phenomenological.

    F. The phenomenological resolution of all philosophical antitheses.

Introduction

The term "phenomenology" designates two things: a new kind of descriptive method which made a breakthrough in philosophy at the turn of the century, and an *a priori* science derived from it; a science which is intended to supply the basic instrument (*Organon*) for a rigorously scientific philosophy and, in its consequent application, to make possible a methodical reform of all the sciences. Together with this philosophical phenomenology, but not yet separated from it, however, there also came into being a new psychological discipline parallel to it in method and content: the *a priori* pure or "phenomenological" psychology, which raises the reformational claim to being the basic methodological foundation on which alone a scientifically rigorous empirical psychology can be established. An outline of this psychological phenomenology, standing nearer to our natural thinking, is well suited to serve as a preliminary step that will lead up to an understanding of philosophical phenomenology.

I. Pure psychology: Its field of experience,
its method, and its function

A. *Pure natural science and pure psychology.*

Modern psychology is the science dealing with the "psychical" in concrete relationship to spatiotemporal realities. In other words, it deals with the relationship of what occurs in nature as egoical, with all that inseparably belongs to it as psychic processes like experiencing, thinking, feeling, willing, as capacity, and as *habitus*. Experience presents the psychical as merely a stratum of human and animal being. Accordingly, psychology is seen as a branch of the more concrete science of anthropology, or rather zoology. Animal realities are first of all, at the most basic stratum, physical realities. As such, they belong in the closed nexus of relationships in physical nature, in Nature meant in the highest and most pregnant sense as the universal theme of a pure natural science; that is to say, an objective science of nature which in deliberate one-sidedness excludes all extra-physical predications of reality. The scientific investigation of the bodies of animals fits within this area. By contrast, however if the psychic aspect of the animal world is to become the topic of investigation, the first thing we have to ask is how far, in parallel with the pure science of nature, a pure psychology is possible. Obviously, purely psychological research can be done to a certain extent. To it we owe the basic concepts of the psychical in its most essential properties. These concepts must be incorporated into the others, into the psychophysical foundational concepts of psychology.

It is by no means clear from the very outset, however, how far the idea of a pure psychology—as a psychological discipline sharply separate in itself and as a real parallel to the pure physical science of nature—has a meaning that is legitimate and necessary of realization.

B. *The purely psychic element in self-experience and community experience. The universal description of intentional experiences.*

To establish and unfold this guiding idea, the first thing that is necessary is a clarification of what is peculiar to experience, and especially to the pure experience of the psychical—and specifically the purely psychical that experience reveals, which is to become the theme of a pure psychology. It is natural and appropriate that precedence will be accorded to the most immediate types of experience, which in each case reveal to us our own psychic being.

Focusing our experiencing gaze on our own psychic life necessarily takes place as reflection, as a turning about of a glance which had previously been directed elsewhere. Every experience can be subject to such reflection, as can indeed every manner in which we occupy ourselves with any real or ideal objects—for instance, thinking, or in the modes of feeling and will, valuing and striving. So when we are fully engaged in conscious activity, we focus exclusively on the specific thing, thoughts, values, goals, or means involved, but not on the psychical experience as such, in which these things are known *as* such. Only reflection reveals this to us. Through reflection, instead of grasping simply the matter straight-out—the values, goals, and instrumentalities—we grasp the corresponding subjective experiences in which we become "conscious" of them, in which (in the broadest sense) they "appear". For this reason, they are called "phenomena", and their most general essential character is to exist as the "consciousness-of" or "appearance-of" the specific things, thoughts (judged states of affairs, grounds, conclusions), plans, decisions, hopes, and so forth. This relatedness of the appearing to the object of appearance resides in the meaning of all expressions in the vernacular languages which relate to psychic experience—for instance, perception *of* something, recalling *of* something, thinking *of* something, hoping *for* something, fearing something, striving *for* something, deciding on something, and so on. If this realm of what we call "phenomena" proves to be the possible field for a pure psychological discipline related exclusively to phenomena, we can understand the designation of it as *phenomenological psychology*. The terminological expression, deriving from Scholasticism, for designating the basic character of being as consciousness, as consciousness of something, is *intentionality*. In unreflective holding of some object or other in consciousness, we are turned or directed towards it: our *"intentio"* goes out towards it. The phenomenological reversal of our gaze shows that this "being directed" (*Gerichtetsein*) is really an immanent essential feature of the respective experiences involved: they are "intentional" experiences.

An extremely large and variegated number of kinds of special cases fall within the general scope of this concept. Consciousness of something is not an empty holding of something; every phenomenon has its own total form of intention [*intentionale Gesamtform*], but at the same time it has a structure, which in intentional analysis leads always again to components which are themselves also intentional. So for example in starting from a perception of something (for example, a die), phenomenological reflection leads to a multiple and yet synthetically unified intentionality. There are continually varying differences in the modes of appearing of objects, which are caused by the changing of "orientation"—of right and left, nearness and farness, with the consequent differences in perspective involved. There are further differences in appearance between the "actually seen front" and the "unseeable" ("*unanschaulichen*") and relatively "undetermined" reverse side, which is nevertheless "meant along with it". Observing the flux of modes of appearing and the manner of their "synthesis", one finds that every phase and portion is already in itself "consciousness-of"—but in such a manner that there is formed within the constant emerging of new phases the synthetically unified awareness that this is one and the same object. The intentional structure of any process of perception has its fixed essential type (*seine feste Wesenstypik*), which must necessarily be realized in all its extraordinary complexity just in order for a physical body simply to be perceived as such. If this same thing is intuited in other modes—for example, in the modes of recollection, fantasy or pictorial representation—to some extent the whole intentional content of the perception comes back, but all aspects peculiarly transformed to correspond to that mode. This applies similarly for every other category of psychic process: the judging, valuing, striving consciousness is not an empty having knowledge of the specific judgments, values, goals, and means. Rather, these constitute themselves, with fixed essential forms corresponding to each process, in a flowing intentionality. For psychology, the universal task presents itself: to investigate systematically the elementary intentionalities, and from out of these [unfold] the typical forms of intentional processes, their possible variants, their syntheses to new forms, their structural composition, and from this advance towards a descriptive knowledge of the totality of mental process, towards a comprehensive type of a life of the psyche (*Gesamttypus eines Lebens der Seele*). Clearly, the consistent carrying out of this task will produce knowledge which will have validity far beyond the psychologist's own particular psychic existence.

Psychic life is accessible to us not only through self-experience but also through experience of others. This novel source of experience offers us not only what matches our self-experience but also what is new, in as much as, in terms of consciousness and indeed as experience, it establishes the differences between own and other, as well as the properties peculiar to the life of a community. At just this point there arises the task of also making phenomenologically understandable the mental life of the community, with all the intentionalities that pertain to it.

> *C. The self-contained field of the purely psy-chical.—Phenomenological reduction and true inner ex-perience.*

The idea of a phenomenological psychology encompasses the whole range of tasks arising out of the experience of self and the experience of the other founded on it. But it is not yet clear whether phenomenological experience, followed through in exclusiveness and consistency, really provides us with a kind of closed-off field of being, out of which a science can grow which is exclusively focused on it and completely free of everything psychophysical. Here [in fact] difficulties do exist, which have hidden from psychologists the possibility of such a purely phenomenological psychology even after Brentano's discovery of intentionality. They are relevant already to the construction of a really pure self-experience, and therewith of a really pure psychic datum. A particular method of access is required for the pure phenomenological field: the method of "phenomenological reduction". This method of "phenomenological reduction" is thus the foundational method of pure psychology and the presupposition of all its specifically theoretical methods.

Ultimately the great difficulty rests on the way that the self-ex-perience of the psychologist is everywhere intertwined with external experience, with that of extra-psychical real things. The experienced "exterior" does not belong to one's intentional interiority, although cer-tainly the experience itself belongs to it as experience—*of* the exterior. Exactly this same thing is true of every kind of awareness directed at something out there in the world. A consistent *epoché* of the phenom-enologist is required, if he wishes to break through to his own consciousness as pure phenomenon, either in the case of individual phenomena or as the totality of his purely mental processes. This means that in the performance of phenomenological reflection he must inhibit every co-performance of objective positing operative in unreflective consciousness, and [operative also, of course] in the mode of judging, where what is posited is the world as it exists for him purely and simply. The specific experience of this house, this body, of a world as such, is and remains, however, according to its own essential content and thus inseparably, experience "*of* this house", this body, this world; this is so for every mode of consciousness which is directed towards an object. It is, after all, quite impossible to describe an intentional experience— even if illusionary, an invalid judgment, or the like—without at the same time describing the element of consciousness in it *as* such. The universal *epoché* of the world as it becomes conscious (the "putting it in brackets") shuts out from the phenomenological field the world as it simply exists; its place, however, is taken by the world as given in *consciousness* (perceived, remembered, judged, thought, valued, etc.)—the world *as such*, the "world in brackets," or in other words, the world, or rather individual things in the world, are simply replaced by the respective meaning of each *in consciousness (Bewusstseinssinn)* in its various modes (perceptual meaning, recollected meaning, and so on).

With this, we have clarified and supplemented our initial determination of the phenomenological experience and its sphere of being. In going back from the unities already given in the natural attitude to the manifold of modes of consciousness in which they appear, the unities, as inseparable from these multiplicities—but as "bracketed"—are also to be reckoned among what is purely psychical, and always specifically in the appearance-character in which they present themselves. The method of phenomenological reduction (to the pure "phenomenon", the purely psychical) accordingly consists (1) in the methodical and rigorously consistent *epoché* of every objective positing in the psychic sphere, both of the individual phenomenon and of the whole psychic field in general; and (2) in the methodically practised seizing and describing of the multiple "appearances" as appearances of their unitary objects and their unities as unities of components of meaning [or "constituted sense"] accruing to them each time in their appearances. With this is shown a two-fold direction—the *noetic* and *noematic* of phenomenological description. Phenomenological experience in the methodical form of the phenomenological reduction is the only genuine "inner experience" in the sense meant by any well-grounded science of psychology. In its own nature lies manifest the possibility of being carried out continuously *in infinitum* with methodical preservation of purity. The reductive method is transferred from self-experience to the experience of others insofar as there can be applied to the envisaged mental life of the Other the corresponding bracketing and description according to the subjective "How" ("noesis" and "noema") of its appearance and what is appearing. As a further consequence, the community that is experienced in community experience is reduced not only to the mentally particularized intentional fields but also to the unity of the community life that connects them all together, the community mental life in its phenomenological purity (intersubjective reduction). Thus results the perfect expansion of the genuine psychological concept of "inner experience".

To every mind there belongs not only the unity of its multiple *intentional life-process (intentionalen Lebens)* with all its inseparable unities of sense directed towards the "object". There is also, inseparable from this life-process, the experiencing *I-subject* as the identical *I-pole* giving a centre for all specific intentionalities, and as the carrier of all the habitualities growing out of this life-process. Likewise, then, the (phenomenologically) reduced intersubjectivity, in pure form and concretely grasped, is an acting community of pure "persons" in the intersubjective realm of the pure life of consciousness.

D. Eidetic reduction and phenomenological psychology as an eidetic science.

To what extent does the unity of the field of phenomenological experience assure the possibility of a psychology exclusively based on it, thus a pure phenomenological psychology? It does not automatically (by itself) assure an empirically pure science of *facts* from which everything psychophysical is abstracted. But this situation is quite different with an *a priori* science. In it, every self-enclosed field of possible experience permits *eo ipso* the all-embracing transition from the factual to the essential form, the *eidos*. So here, too. If the phenomenological actual fact as such becomes irrelevant; if, rather, it serves only as an example and as the foundation for a free but intuitive variation of the factual mind and communities of minds *into* the *a priori* possible (thinkable) ones; and if now the theoretical eye directs itself to the necessarily enduring invariant in the variation; then there will arise with this systematic way of proceeding a realm of its own, the realm of the *a priori*. There emerges therewith the eidetically necessary typical form, the *eidos;* this *eidos* must manifest itself throughout all the potential forms of mental being in particular cases, must be present in all the synthetic combinations and self-enclosed wholes, if it is to be at all "thinkable", that is, intuitively phantasied or objectivated. Phenomenological psychology in this manner undoubtedly must be established as an "eidetic phenomenology"; it is then exclusively directed toward the invariant essential forms [of intuition]. For instance, the phenomenology of perception of bodies will not be (simply) a report on the factually occurring perceptions or those to be expected; rather it will be the presentation of invariant structural systems without which perception of a body and a synthetically concordant multiplicity of perceptions of one and the same body as such would be unthinkable. If the phenomenological reduction contrived a means of access to the phenomenon of real and also potential inner experience, the method founded in it of "eidetic reduction" provides the means of access to the invariant essential structures of the total sphere of pure mental process.

E. The fundamental function of pure phenomenological psychology for an exact empirical psychology.

A phenomenological pure psychology is absolutely necessary as the foundation for the building up of an "exact" empirical psychology, which since its modern beginnings has been sought according to the model of the exact pure sciences of physical nature. The fundamental meaning of "exactness" in this natural science lies in its being founded on an *a priori* form-system—each part unfolded in its own region (pure geometry, a theory of pure time, theory of motion, etc.)—for a Nature conceivable in these terms. It is through the utilization of this *a priori* form-system for factual nature that the vague, inductive empirical approach attains to a share of eidetic necessity (*Wesensnotwendigkeit*) and empirical natural science itself gains a new sense—that of working out for all vague concepts and rules their indispensable basis of rational concepts and laws. As essentially differentiated as the methods of natural science and psychology may remain, there does exist a necessary common ground: that psychology, like every science, can only draw its "rigour" ("exactness") from the rationality of what "conforms to essence". The uncovering of the *a priori* set of types without which "I," "we," "consciousness," "the objectivity of consciousness," and therewith mental being as such would be inconceivable—with all the essentially necessary and essentially possible forms of synthesis which are inseparable from the idea of a whole comprised of individual and communal mental life—produces a prodigious field of exactness that can immediately (without the intervening link of *Limes-idealizing**)

* By this expression (*Limes-Idealisierung*), Husserl would seem to mean idealisation to exact (mathematical) limits. (Ed.)

be carried over into research on the psyche. Admittedly, the phenomenological *a priori* does not comprise the complete *a priori* of psychology, inasmuch as the psychophysical relationship as such has its own *a priori*. It is clear, however, that this *a priori* will presuppose that of a pure phenomenological psychology, just as on the other side it will presuppose the pure *a priori* of a physical (and specifically the organic) Nature as such.

The systematic construction of a phenomenological pure psychology demands:

(1) The description of the peculiarities universally belonging to the essence of intentional mental process, which includes the most general law of synthesis: every connection of consciousness with consciousness gives rise to consciousness.

(2) The exploration of single forms of intentional mental process which in essential necessity generally must or can present themselves in the mind; in unity with this, also the exploration of the syntheses they are members of for a typology of their essences: both those that are discrete and those continuous with others, both the finitely closed and those continuing into open infinity.

(3) The showing and eidetic description (*Wesensdeskription*) of the total structure (*Gesamtgestalt*) of mental life as such; in other words, a description of the essential character (*Wesensart*) of a universal "stream of consciousness".

(4) The term "I" designates a new direction for investigation (still in abstraction from the social sense of this word) in reference to the essence-forms of "habituality"; in other words, the "I" as subject of lasting beliefs or thought-tendencies—"persuasions"—(convictions about being, value-convictions, volitional decisions, and so on), as the personal subject of habits, of trained knowing, of certain character qualities.

Throughout all this, the "static" description of essences ultimately leads to problems of genesis, and to an all-pervasive genesis that governs the whole life and development of the personal "I" according to eidetic laws (*eidetischen Gesetzen*). So on top of the first "static phenomenology'' will be constructed in higher levels a dynamic or genetic phenomenology. As the first and founding genesis it will deal with that of passivity—genesis in which the "I" does not actively participate. Here lies the new task, an all-embracing eidetic phenomenology of association, a latter-day rehabilitation of David Hume's great discovery, involving an account of the *a priori* genesis out of which a real spatial world constitutes itself for the mind in habitual acceptance. There follows from this the eidetic theory dealing with the development of personal habituality, in which the purely mental "I" within the invariant structural forms of consciousness exists as personal "I" and is conscious of itself in habitual continuing being and as always being transformed. For further investigation, there offers itself an especially interconnected stratum at a higher level: the static and then the genetic phenomenology of reason.

II. Phenomenological psychology and transcendental phenomenology.

A. Descartes' transcendental turn and Locke's psychologism.

The idea of a purely phenomenological psychology does not have just the function described above, of reforming empirical psychology. For deeply rooted reasons, it can also serve as a preliminary step for laying open the essence of a transcendental phenomenology. Historically, this idea too did not grow out of the peculiar need of psychology proper. Its history leads us back to John Locke's notable basic work, and the significant development in Berkeley and Hume of the impetus it contained. Already Locke's restriction to the purely subjective was determined by extra-psychological interests: psychology here stood in the service of the transcendental problem awakened through Descartes. In Descartes' *Meditations,* the thought that had become the guiding one for "first philosophy" was that all of the "real," and finally the whole world of what exists and is thus and so determined *for us,* exists only as the idea content of our own objectivations, as meant through judgements and proven as evident from out of our own cognitive life. Here [in our own cognitive life] lay the motivation for all transcendental problems, genuine or false. Descartes' method of doubt was the first method of exhibiting "transcendental subjectivity," and his *ego cogito* led to its first conceptual formulation. In Locke, Descartes' transcendentally pure *mens* is changed into the "human mind," whose systematic exploration through inner experience Locke tackled out of a transcendental-philosophical interest. And so he is the founder of *psychologism*—as a transcendental philosophy derived *through* psychology *out of* inner experience. The fate of scientific philosophy hangs on the radical overcoming of every trace of psychologism, an overcoming which not only exposes the fundamental absurdity of psychologism but also does justice to its transcendentally significant kernel of truth. The sources of its continuous historical power are drawn from out of a double sense [an ambiguity] of all the concepts of the subjective, which arises as soon as the transcendental question is broached. The uncovering of this ambiguity involves [us in the need for] at once the sharp separation, and at the time the parallel treatment, of pure phenomenological psychology (as the scientifically rigorous form of a psychology purely of inner experience) and transcendental phenomenology as true transcendental philosophy. At the same time this will justify our advance discussion of psychology as the means of access to true philosophy. We will begin with a clarification of the true transcendental problem, which in the initially obscure unsteadiness of its sense makes one so very prone (and this applies already to Descartes) to shunt it off to a side track.

B. The transcendental problem.

To the essential sense of the transcendental problem belongs its all-inclusiveness, in which it places in question the world and all investigative sciences. It arises within a general reversal of that "natural attitude" in which everyday life as a whole as well as the positive sciences operate. In it [the natural attitude] the world is for us the self-evidently existing universe of realities which are continuously before us in unquestioned givenness. So this is the general field of our practical and theoretical activities. As soon as the theoretical interest abandons this natural attitude and in a general turning around of our regard directs itself to the life of consciousness—*in which* the "world" is for us precisely that, the world which is present *to us*—we find ourselves in a new cognitive attitude [or situation]. Every sense which the world has for us (this we now become aware of), both its general indeterminate sense and its sense determining itself in particular details, is, within the internality of our own perceiving, imagining, thinking, valuing life-process, a conscious sense, and a sense which is formed in subjective genesis. Every acceptance of something as validly existing is effected within us ourselves; and every evidence in experience and theory that establishes it, is operative in us ourselves, habitually and continuously motivating us. This [principle] concerns the world in every determination, even those that are self-evident: that what belongs *in and for itself* to the world, is how it is whether or not I, or whoever, become by chance aware of it or not. Once the world in this full universality has been related to the subjectivity of consciousness, in whose living consciousness it makes its appearance precisely as "the" world of the particular sense in question, then its whole manner of being acquires a dimension of unintelligibility, or rather of questionableness. This "making an appearance" [*Auftreten*], this being-for-us of the world as only subjectively having come to acceptance and only subjectively brought and to be brought to well-grounded evident presentation, requires clarification. Because of its empty generality, one's first awakening to the relatedness of the world to consciousness gives no understanding of *how* the varied life of consciousness, barely discerned and sinking back into obscurity, accomplishes such functions; how it, so to say, manages in its immanence that something which manifests itself can present itself *as* something existing in itself, and not only as something meant but as something authenticated in concordant experience. Obviously the problem extends to every kind of "ideal" world and its "being-in-itself" (for example, the world of pure numbers, or of "truths in themselves"). Unintelligibility is felt as a particularly telling affront to *our* very mode of being [as human beings]. For we are the ones (individually and in community) in whose conscious life-process the real world which is present for us as such gains sense and acceptance. As human creatures, however, we ourselves are supposed to belong to the world. When we take our bearings from our sense of the world (*weltlichen Sinn*), we are thus again referred back to ourselves and our conscious life-process as that wherein for us this sense is first formed. Is there conceivable here or anywhere another way of elucidating [it] than to interrogate consciousness itself and the "world" that becomes known in it? For it is precisely as meant by us, and from nowhere else than in us, that it has gained and can gain its sense and acceptance.

Next we take yet another important step, which will raise the "transcendental" problem (having to do with the being-sense of "transcendent" relative to consciousness) up to the final level. It consists in recognizing that the relativity of consciousness referred to just now applies not just to the brute fact of *our* world but in eidetic necessity to every conceivable world whatever. For if we vary our factual world in free fantasy, carrying it over into random conceivable worlds, we are implicitly varying *ourselves* whose environment the world is: we each change ourselves into a possible subjectivity, whose environment would always have to be a world that was thought of, as a world of its [the subjectivity's] possible experiences, possible theoretical evidences, possible practical life. But obviously this variation leaves untouched the pure ideal worlds of the kind which have their existence in eidetic universality, which are in their essence invariable; it becomes apparent, however, from the possible variability of such identical essences [*Identitäten*] in the knowing subject, that their cognizability, and thus their intentional relatedness does not simply have to do with our *de facto* subjectivity. With the eidetic formulation of the problem, the kind of research into consciousness that is demanded is the eidetic.

C. The solution by psychologism as a transcendental circle.

Our distillation of the idea of a phenomenologically pure psychology has demonstrated the possibility of uncovering by consistent phenomenological reduction what belongs to the conscious subject's own essence in eidetic, universal terms, according to all its possible forms. This includes those of reason [itself], which establishes and authenticates the lawful [*Recht*], and with this it includes all forms of potentially appearing worlds, both those validated in themselves through concordant experiences and those determined by theoretical truth. Accordingly, the systematic carrying through of this phenomenological psychology seems to comprehend in itself from the outset in foundational (precisely, eidetic) universality the whole of correlation research on being and consciousness; thus it would seem to be the [proper] locus for all transcendental elucidation. On the other hand, we must not overlook the fact that psychology in all its empirical and eidetic disciplines remains a "positive science," a science operating within the natural attitude, in which the simply present world is the thematic basis. What it wishes to explore are the psyches and communities of psyches that are [actually] to be found in the world. Phenomenological reduction serves as psychological only to the end that it achieves the psychical aspect of animal realities in its pure own essential specificity and its pure own specific essential interconnections. Even in eidetic research [then], the psyche retains the sense of being which belongs in the realm of what is present in the world; it is merely related to possible real worlds. Even as eidetic phenomenologist, the psychologist is transcendentally naïve: he takes the possible "minds" ("I"-subjects) completely according to the relative sense of the word as those men and animals, considered purely and simply as present in a possible spatial world. If, however, we allow the transcendental interest to be decisive, instead of the natural-worldly, then psychology as a whole receives the stamp of what is transcendentally problematic; and thus it can by no means supply the premises for transcendental philosophy. The subjectivity of consciousness, which, as psychic being, is its theme, cannot be that to which we go back in our questioning into the transcendental.

In order to arrive at an evident clarity at this decisive point, the thematic sense of the transcendental question is to be kept sharply in view, and we must try to judge how, in keeping with it, the regions of the problematical and unproblematical are set apart. The theme of transcendental philosophy is a concrete and systematic elucidation of those multiple intentional relationships, which in conformity with their essences belong to any possible world whatever as the surrounding world of a corresponding possible subjectivity, for which it [the world] would be the one present as practically and theoretically accessible. In regard to all the objects and structures present in the world for these subjectivities, this accessibility involves the regulations of its possible conscious life, which in their typology will have to be uncovered. Such categories are "lifeless things," but they are also man and animal with the internalities of their psychic life. From this starting point the full and complete being-sense of a possible world in general, and in regard to all its constitutive categories, shall be elucidated. Like every meaningful question, this transcendental question presupposes a ground of unquestioned being, in which all means of solution must be contained. This ground is here the subjectivity of that kind of conscious life in which a possible world, of whatever kind, is constituted as present. However, a self-evident basic requirement of any rational method is that this ground presupposed as beyond question is not confused with what the transcendental question, in its universality, puts into question. Hence the realm of this questionability includes the whole realm of the transcendentally naïve, thus every possible world as the one simply claimed in the natural attitude. Accordingly, all possible sciences, including all their various areas of objects, are transcendentally to be subjected to an *epoché*. So also psychology, and the entirety of what is considered the psychical in its sense. It would therefore be circular, a transcendental circle, to base the answer to the transcendental question on psychology, be it empirical or eidetic-phenomenological. We face at this point the paradoxical ambiguity: the subjectivity and consciousness to which the transcendental question recurs can thus really not be the subjectivity and consciousness with which psychology deals.

D. The transcendental-phenomenological reduction and the illusion of transcendental duplication.

Are we then supposed to be dual beings—psychological, as human objectivities in the world, the subjects of psychic life; and at the same time transcendental, as the subjects of a transcendental, world-constituting life-process? This duality can be clarified through being demonstrated with self-evidence. The psychic subjectivity, the concretely grasped "I" and "we" of ordinary conversation, is experienced in its pure psychic ownness through the method of phenomenological-psychological reduction. Modified into eidetic form it provides the ground for pure phenomenological psychology. Transcendental subjectivity, which is inquired into in the transcendental problem, and which subjectivity is presupposed in it as its ground of being, is none other than again "I myself" and "we ourselves"; not, however, as found in the natural attitude of every-day or of positive science; i.e., apperceived as components of the objectively present world before us, but rather as subjects of conscious life, *in* which this world and all that is present—for "us"—constitutes itself through certain apperceptions. As men, mentally as well as bodily present in the world, we are for "ourselves"; we are appearances standing within an extremely variegated intentional life-process, "our" life, *in which* this presence constitutes itself "for us" apperceptively, with its entire sense-content. The present (apperceived) I and we presuppose an (apperceiving) I and we, *for* which they are present, which, however, is not itself present again in the same sense. To this transcendental subjectivity we have direct access through a transcendental experience. Just as the psychic experience requires a reductive method for purity, so does the transcendental.

We would like to proceed here by introducing the *transcendental reduction* as built on the psychological reduction—as an additional part of the purification which can be performed on it any time, a purification that is once more by means of a certain *epoché*. This is merely a consequence of the all-embracing *epoché* which belongs to the sense of the transcendental question. If the transcendental relativity of every possible world demands an all-embracing bracketing, it also postulates the bracketing of pure psyches and the pure phenomenological psychology related to them. Through this bracketing they are transformed into transcendental phenomena. Thus, while the psychologist, operating within what for him is the naturally accepted world, reduces the subjectivity occurring there to pure psychic subjectivity (but still within the world), the transcendental phenomenologist, through his absolutely all-embracing *epoché*, reduces this psychologically pure element to transcendental pure subjectivity, [i.e.,] to that which performs and posits within itself the apperception of the world and therein the objectivating apperception of a "psyche [belonging to] animal realities". For example, my actual current mental processes of pure perception, fantasy, and so forth, are, in the attitude of positivity [as in the "positive" sciences], psychological givens [or data] of psychological inner experience. They are transmuted into my transcendental mental processes if through a radical *epoché* I posit as mere phenomena the world, including my own human existence, and now follow up the intentional life-process where in the entire apperception "of" the world, and in particular the apperception of my mind, my psychologically real perception-processes, and so forth, are formed. The content of these processes, what is included in their own essences, remains in this fully preserved, although it is now visible as the core of an apperception practised again and again psychologically but not previously considered. For the transcendental philosopher, who through a previous all-inclusive resolve of his will has instituted in himself the firm habituality of the transcendental "bracketing", this "mundanization" [*Verweltlichung*, treating everything as part of the world] of consciousness in the natural attitude is inhibited once and for all. Accordingly, the consistent reflection on consciousness yields him time after time transcendentally pure data, and more particularly it is intuitive in the mode of a new kind of experience, *transcendental "inner" experience*. Arisen out of the methodical transcendental *epoché*, this new kind of "inner" experience opens up the limitless transcendental field of being. This field of being is the parallel to the limitless psychological field, and the method of access [to its data] is the parallel to the purely psychological one: that specific to the psychological-phenomenological reduction. And again exactly the same is the case with the transcendental I [or ego] and the transcendental community of egos, conceived in the full concretion of transcendental life as the transcendental parallel to the I and we in the customary and psychological sense, again concretely conceived as mind and community of minds, with the psychological life of consciousness that pertains to them. My transcendental ego is thus evidently "different" from the natural ego, but by no means as a second, as one *separated* from it in the natural sense of the word, just as on the contrary it is by no means bound up with it or intertwined with it, in the usual sense of these words. It is just this field of transcendental self-experience (conceived in full concreteness) which in every case can, *through mere alteration of attitude,* be changed into psychological self-experience. In this transition, an identity of the I is necessarily brought about; in transcendental reflection on this transition the psychological Objectivation becomes visible as self-Objectivation of the transcendental I, and so it is as if in every moment of the natural attitude the I has charged itself with an apperception. If the parallelism of the transcendental and psychological experience-spheres has become comprehensible out of a mere alteration of attitude [from natural to transcendental], as a kind of identity which involves the complex interpenetration of senses of being, then there also becomes intelligible the consequence that results from the same parallelism and from the implicit interpenetration of transcendental and psychological phenomenology, whose whole theme is pure intersubjectivity, in both the psychological and transcendental sense. Only that in this case it has to be taken into account that the purely psychic intersubjectivity, as well as the subjectivity which has been subjected to the transcendental *epoché*, each lead to their parallel of transcendental intersubjectivity. Manifestly this parallelism spells nothing less than theoretical equivalence. Transcendental intersubjectivity is the concretely self-sufficient absolute ground of being, out of which everything transcendent (and, with it, everything of the real and what exists in the world) obtains its existential sense as the being of something that only in a relative and therewith incomplete sense is an existing thing, namely as the being of an intentional unity which in truth exists as the result of transcendental bestowal of sense, of harmonious confirmation, and from an habituality of lasting conviction that belongs to it by essential necessity.

E. *Pure psychology as a propaedeutic to transcendental phenomenology.*

Through the clarification of the essentially dual meaning [or essential ambiguity] of the subjectivity of consciousness, and also a clarification of the eidetic science to be directed to it, we begin to understand on very deep grounds the historical insurmountability of psychologism. Its power lies in an *essential transcendental illusion* which undisclosed had to remain effective. Also from the clarification we have gained we begin to understand on the one hand the independence of the idea of a transcendental phenomenology, and the systematic developing of it, from the idea of a phenomenological pure psychology; and yet on the other hand the propaedeutic usefulness of the preliminary project of a pure psychology for an ascent to transcendental phenomenology, a usefulness which has guided our present discussion here. As regards this point [i.e., the independence of the idea of transcendental phenomenology from a phenomenological pure psychology], clearly the phenomenological and eidetic reduction allows of being *immediately* connected to the disclosing of transcendental relativity, and in this way transcendental phenomenology springs directly out of the transcendental intuition. In point of fact, this direct path was the historical path it took. Pure phenomenological psychology as eidetic science in positivity was simply not available. As regards the second point, i.e., the propaedeutic preference of the indirect approach to transcendental phenomenology through pure psychology, [it must be remembered that] the transcendental attitude involves an alteration of focus from one's entire form of life-style, one which goes so completely beyond all previous experiencing of life, that it must, in virtue of its absolute strangeness, needs be difficult to understand. This is also true of a transcendental science. Phenomenological psychology, although also relatively new, and in its method of intentional analysis completely novel, still has the accessibility which is possessed by all positive sciences. If this psychology has once at least become clear in accordance with the very sharply defined idea [we have been discussing], then only the clarification of the true sense of the transcendental-philosophical field of problems and of the transcendental reduction is required in order for it to come into possession of transcendental phenomenology as a mere reversal of its doctrinal content into transcendental terms. The basic difficulties for penetrating into the terrain of the new phenomenology fall into two stages, namely that of understanding the true method of "inner experience", which already belongs to making possible an "exact" psychology as rational science of facts, and that of understanding the distinctive character of the transcendental methods and questioning. True, simply regarded in itself, an interest in the transcendental is the highest and ultimate scientific interest, and so it is entirely the right thing (it has been so historically and should continue) for transcendental theories to be cultivated in the autonomous, absolute system of transcendental philosophy; and for it in itself, through showing the characteristic way of the natural in contrast to the transcendental attitude, to place before us the possibility of reinterpreting all transcendental phenomenological doctrine [or theory] into doctrine [or theory] in the realm of natural positivity.

III. Transcendental phenomenology and philosophy as universal science with absolute foundations.

A. Transcendental phenomenology as ontology

Remarkable consequences arise when one weighs the significance of transcendental phenomenology. In its systematic development, it brings to realization the Leibnizian idea of a universal ontology as the systematic unity of all conceivable *a priori* sciences, but on a new foundation which overcomes "dogmatism" through the use of the transcendental phenomenological method. Phenomenology as the science of all conceivable transcendental phenomena and especially the synthetic total structures in which alone they are concretely possible—those of the transcendental single subjects bound to communities of subjects—is *eo ipso* the *a priori* science of all conceivable existent beings. But [it is the science] then not merely of the Totality of objectively existing beings, and certainly not in an attitude of natural positivity; rather, in the full concretion of that being in general which derives its sense of being and its validity from the correlative intentional constitution. This also comprises the being of transcendental subjectivity itself, whose nature it is demonstrably to be constituted transcendentally in and for itself. Accordingly, a phenomenology properly carried through is the truly universal ontology, as over against the only illusory all-embracing ontology in positivity—and precisely for this reason it overcomes the dogmatic one-sidedness and hence unintelligibility of the latter, while at the same time it comprises within itself the truly legitimate content [of an ontology in positivity] as grounded primordially in intentional constitution.

B. *Phenomenology and the crisis in the foundations of the exact sciences.*

If we consider the how of this [transcendental] inclusion, we find that what is meant is that every *a priori* is ultimately prescribed in its validity of being precisely *as* a transcendental achievement; *i.e.,* it is at one with the essential structures of its constitution, with the kinds and levels of its givenness and confirmation of itself [in objects], and with the appertaining habitualities. This implies two important points: (1) that in and through the establishment of the *a priori* the subjective *method* of this establishing is itself made transparent and (2) that for the *a priori* disciplines which are founded within phenomenology (for example, as mathematical sciences) there can be no "paradoxes" and no "foundation crises." The consequence that arises [from all this] with reference to the *a priori* sciences that have come into being historically and in transcendental naïveté is that only a radical, phenomenological grounding can transform them into true, methodical, fully self-justifying sciences. But precisely by this they will cease to be positive (dogmatic) sciences and become dependent branches of the one phenomenology as all-encompassing eidetic ontology.

C. *The phenomenological grounding of the factual sciences in relation to empirical phenomenology.*

The unending task of presenting the complete universe of the *a priori* in its transcendental relatedness-back-to-itself [or self-reference] and thus in its independence and perfect methodological clarity, is itself a function of the method for realization of an all-embracing and hence fully grounded science of empirical fact. Within [the realm of] positivity, genuine (relatively genuine) empirical science demands the methodical establishing-of-a-foundation [*Fundamentierung*] through a corresponding *a priori* science. If we take the universe of all possible empirical sciences whatever and demand a *radical* grounding that will be free from all "foundation crises," then we are led to the all-embracing *a priori* of the radical and that is [and must be] *phenomenological* grounding. The genuine form of an all-embracing science of fact is thus the phenomenological [form], and as this it is the universal science of the factual transcendental intersubjectivity, [resting] on the methodical foundation of eidetic phenomenology as knowledge applying to any possible transcendental subjectivity whatever. Hence *the idea of an empirical phenomenology* which follows after the eidetic is understood and justified. It is identical with the complete systematic universe of the positive sciences, provided that we think of them from the beginning as absolutely grounded methodologically through eidetic phenomenology.

D. Complete phenomenology as all-embracing philosophy.

Precisely through this [return to *a priori* foundations]—based on radical self-justification—is restored the most primordial concept of philosophy—as all-embracing science, which is alone [truly] science in the ancient Platonic and again in the Cartesian sense. Phenomenology rigorously and systematically carried out, phenomenology in the broadened sense [which we have explained] above, is identical with this philosophy which encompasses all genuine knowledge. It is divided into eidetic phenomenology (or all-embracing ontology) as *first philosophy,* and as *second philosophy,* [it is] the science of the universe of *facta,* or of the transcendental intersubjectivity that synthetically comprises all *facta.* First philosophy is the universe of methods for the second, and is related back into itself for its methodological grounding.

E. The "ultimate and highest" problems as phenomenological.

In phenomenology all rational problems have their place, and thus also those that traditionally are in some special sense or other philosophically significant. For out of the absolute sources of transcendental experience, or eidetic intuiting, they first [are able to] obtain their genuine formulation and feasible means for their solution. In its universal relatedness-back-to-itself, phenomenology recognizes its particular function within a possible life for man [*Menschheitsleben*] at the transcendental level. It recognizes the absolute norms which are to be picked out intuitively from it [life for man], and also its primordial teleological-tendential structure in a directedness towards disclosure of these norms and their conscious practical operation. It recognizes itself as a function of the all-embracing self-examination of (transcendental) humanity, [a self-examination] in the service of an all-inclusive praxis of reason; that is, in the service of striving towards the universal ideal of absolute perfection which lies in infinity, [a striving] which becomes free through [the process of] disclosure. Or, in different words it is a striving in the direction of the idea (lying in infinity) of a humanness which in action and throughout would live and move [be, exist] in truth and genuineness. It recognizes its meditative function [of self-examination] for the [albeit] relative realization of the correlative practical idea of a genuine human life [*Menchheitsleben*] in the second sense (whose structural forms of being and whose practical norms it is to investigate), namely as one [that is] consciously and purposively directed towards this absolute idea. In short, the metaphysically teleological, the ethical, and the problems of philosophy of history, no less than, obviously, the problems of judging reason, lie within its boundary, no differently from all significant problems whatever, and all [of them] in their inmost synthetic unity and order as [being] of transcendental spirit-quality [*Geistigkeit,* spirituality, intellectuality].

F. The phenomenological resolution of all philosophical antitheses.

In the systematic work of phenomenology, which progresses from intuitively given [concrete] data to heights of abstraction, the old traditional ambiguous antitheses of the philosophical standpoint are resolved—by themselves and without the arts of an argumentative dialectic, and without weak efforts and compromises: oppositions such as between rationalism (Platonism) and empiricism, relativism and absolutism, subjectivism and objectivism, ontologism and transcendentalism, psychologism and antipsychologism, positivism and metaphysics, or the teleological versus the causal interpretation of the world. Throughout all of these, [one finds] justified motives, but throughout also half-truths or impermissible absolutizing of only relatively and abstractively legitimate one-sidednesses.

Subjectivism can only be overcome by the most all-embracing and consistent subjectivism (the transcendental). In this [latter] form it is at the same time objectivism [of a deeper sort], in that it represents the claims of whatever objectivity is to be demonstrated through concordant experience, but admittedly [this is an objectivism which] also brings out its full and genuine sense, against which [sense] the supposedly realistic objectivism sins by its failure to understand transcendental constitution. *Relativism* can only be overcome through the most all-embracing relativism, that of transcendental phenomenology, which makes intelligible the relativity of all "objective" being [or existence] as transcendentally constituted; but at one with this [it makes intelligible] the most radical relativity, the relatedness of the transcendental subjectivity to itself. But just this [relatedness, subjectivity] proves its identity to be the only possible sense of [the term] "absolute" being—over against all "objective" being that is relative to it—namely, as the "for-itself"—being of transcendental subjectivity. Likewise: *Empiricism* can only be overcome by the most universal and consistent empiricism, which puts in place of the restricted [term] "experience" of the empiricists the necessarily broadened concept of experience [inclusive] of intuition which offers original data, an intuition which in all its forms (intuition of *eidos,* apodictic self-evidence, phenomenological intuition of essence, etc.) shows the manner and form of its legitimation through phenomenological clarification. Phenomenology as eidetic is, on the other hand, rationalistic: it overcomes restrictive and dogmatic rationalism, however, through the most universal rationalism of inquiry into essences, which is related uniformly to transcendental subjectivity, to the I, consciousness, and conscious objectivity. And it is the same in reference to the other antitheses bound up with them. The tracing back of all being to the transcendental subjectivity and its constitutive intentional functions leaves open, to mention one more thing, no other way of contemplating the world than the *teleological.* And yet phenomenology also acknowledges a kernel of truth in naturalism (or rather sensationism). That is, by revealing associations as intentional phenomena, indeed as a whole basic typology of forms of passive intentional synthesis with transcendental and purely passive genesis based on essential laws, phenomenology shows Humean fictionalism to contain anticipatory discoveries; particularly in his doctrine of the origin of the fictions thing, persisting existence, causality—anticipatory discoveries all shrouded in absurd theories.

Phenomenological philosophy regards itself in its whole method as a pure outcome of methodical intentions which already animated Greek philosophy from its beginnings; above all, however, [it continues] the still vital intentions which reach, in the two lines of rationalism and empiricism, from Descartes through Kant and German idealism into our confused present day. A pure outcome of methodical intentions means real method which allows the problems to be taken in hand and completed. In the way of true science this path is endless. Accordingly, phenomenology demands that the phenomenologist foreswear the ideal of a philosophic system and yet as a humble worker in community with others, live for a perennial philosophy [*philosophia perennis*].

Translator's Note: The translator gratefully acknowledges the help in the initial stages of this project by Mrs. Gisela Hess, a colleague in the German Department of MacMurray College. The manuscript has undergone two revisions. After attempting an initial draft of the whole article, the translator carefully revised his translation using a manuscript copy of Cairns *Guide to Translating Husserl*. This revision was in turn read through by Professor Spiegelberg, whose many valuable suggestions and answers to queries are gratefully acknowledged. He has also been kind enough to add an introductory article. [Not included in the present version. (Eds.)]

B. The Existential Turn

MAURICE MERLEAU-PONTY (1908-61)

Maurice Merleau-Ponty was born in France in 1908. He followed successfully the traditional French route of education through the Ecole Normale Supérieure and became a professor of psychology at the Sorbonne in 1950. Two years later he was appointed to the Collège de France. Merleau-Ponty first became interested in phenomenology through his close friend, Jean-Paul Sartre, who on returning from Berlin in 1935 brought Husserl's works to Merleau-Ponty's notice. Merleau-Ponty soon saw the implications of phenomenology for his own existentialist positions. Among his most important contributions are: *Structure of Behavior* (1942), *Phenomenology of Perception* (1945), and the posthumously published *The Visible and the Invisible* (1964).

PREFACE TO PHENOMENOLOGY OF PERCEPTION*

What is phenomenology? It may seem strange that this question has still to be asked half a century after the first works of Husserl. The fact remains that it has by no means been answered. Phenomenology is the study of essences; and according to it, all problems amount to finding definitions of essences; the essence of perception, or the essence of consciousness, for example. But phenomenology is also a philosophy which puts essences back into existence, and does not expect to arrive at an understanding of man and the world from any starting point other than that of their 'facticity'. It is a transcendental philosophy which places in abeyance the assertions arising out of the natural attitude, the better to understand them; but it is also a philosophy for which the world is always 'already there' before reflection begins—as an inalienable presence; and all its efforts are concentrated upon re-achieving a direct and primitive contact with the world, and endowing that contact with a philosophical status. It is the search for a philosophy which shall be a 'rigorous science', but it also offers an account of space, time and the world as we 'live' them. It tries to give a direct description of our experience as it is, without taking account of its psychological origin and the causal explanations which the scientist, the historian or the sociologist may be able to provide. Yet Husserl in his last works mentions a 'genetic phenomenology',[1] and even a 'constructive phenomenology'.[2] One may try to do away with these contradictions by making a distinction between Husserl's and Heidegger's phenomenologies; yet the whole of *Sein und Zeit* springs from an indication given by Husserl and amounts to no more than an explicit account of the 'natürlicher Weltbegriff' or the 'Lebenswelt' which Husserl, towards the end of his life, identified as the central theme of phenomenology, with the result that the contradiction reappears in Husserl's own philosophy. The reader pressed for time will be inclined to give up the idea of covering a doctrine which says everything, and will wonder whether a philosophy which cannot define its scope deserves all the discussion which has gone on around it, and whether he is not faced rather by a myth or a fashion.

Even if this were the case, there would still be a need to understand

* By permission of Humanities Press Inc. From Maurice Merleau-Ponty, *Phenomenology of Perception*, Humanities Press, Inc., New York, New York. Also by permission of Routledge & Kegan Paul, Ltd., London, England.

[1] *Méditations cartésiennes*, pp. 120 ff.

[2] See the unpublished *6th Méditation cartésienne*, edited by Eugen Fink, to which G. Berger has kindly referred us.

the prestige of the myth and the origin of the fashion, and the opinion of
the responsible philosopher must be that *phenomenology can be practised and identified as a manner or style of thinking, that it existed as a
movement before arriving at complete awareness of itself as a philosophy.* It has been long on the way, and its adherents have discovered it in
every quarter, certainly in Hegel and Kierkegaard, but equally in Marx,
Nietzsche and Freud. A purely linguistic examination of the texts in
question would yield no proof; we find in texts only what we put into
them, and if ever any kind of history has suggested the interpretations
which should be put on it, it is the history of philosophy. We shall find
in ourselves, and nowhere else, the unity and true meaning of
phenomenology. It is less a question of counting up quotations than of
determining and expressing in concrete form this *phenomenology for
ourselves* which has given a number of present-day readers the impression, on reading Husserl or Heidegger, not so much of encountering
a new philosophy as of recognizing what they had been waiting for.
Phenomenology is accessible only through a phenomenological method.
Let us, therefore, try systematically to bring together the celebrated
phenomenological themes as they have grown spontaneously together in
life. Perhaps we shall then understand why phenomenology has for so
long remained at an initial stage, as a problem to be solved and a hope
to be realized.

It is a matter of describing, not of explaining or analysing. Husserl's
first directive to phenomenology, in its early stages, to be a 'descriptive
psychology', or to return to the 'things themselves', is from the start a
rejection of science. I am not the outcome or the meeting-point of
numerous causal agencies which determine my bodily or psychological
make-up. I cannot conceive myself as nothing but a bit of the world, a
mere object of biological, psychological or sociological investigation. I
cannot shut myself up within the realm of science. All my knowledge of
the world, even my scientific knowledge, is gained from my own particular point of view, or from some experience of the world without
which the symbols of science would be meaningless. The whole universe
of science is built upon the world as directly experienced, and if we
want to subject science itself to rigorous scrutiny and arrive at a precise
assessment of its meaning and scope, we must begin by reawakening the
basic experience of the world of which science is the second-order expression. Science has not and never will have, by its nature, the same
significance *qua* form of being as the world which we perceive, for the

simple reason that it is a rationale or explanation of that world. I am, not a 'living creature' nor even a 'man', nor again even 'a consciousness' endowed with all the characteristics which zoology, social anatomy or inductive psychology recognize in these various products of the natural or historical process—I am the absolute source, my existence does not stem from my antecedents, from my physical and social environment; instead it moves out towards them and sustains them, for I alone bring into being for myself (and therefore into being in the only sense that the word can have for me) the tradition which I elect to carry on, or the horizon whose distance from me would be abolished—since that distance is not one of its properties—if I were not there to scan it with my gaze. Scientific points of view, according to which my existence is a moment of the world's, are always both naïve and at the same time dishonest, because they take for granted, without explicitly mentioning it, the other point of view, namely that of consciousness, through which from the outset a world forms itself round me and begins to exist for me. To return to things themselves is to return to that world which precedes knowledge, of which knowledge always *speaks*, and in relation to which every scientific schematization is an abstract and derivative sign-language, as is geography in relation to the countryside in which we have learnt beforehand what a forest, a prairie or a river is.

This move is absolutely distinct from the idealist return to consciousness, and the demand for a pure description excludes equally the procedure of analytical reflection on the one hand, and that of scientific explanation on the other. Descartes and particularly Kant *detached* the subject, or consciousness, by showing that I could not possibly apprehend anything as existing unless I first of all experienced myself as existing in the act of apprehending it. They presented consciousness, the absolute certainty of my existence for myself, as the condition of there being anything at all; and the act of relating as the basis of relatedness. It is true that the act of relating is nothing if divorced from the spectacle of the world in which relations are found; the unity of consciousness in Kant is achieved simultaneously with that of the world. And in Descartes methodical doubt does not deprive us of anything, since the whole world, at least in so far as we experience it, is reinstated in the *Cogito*, enjoying equal certainty, and simply labelled "thought about. . ." . But the relations between subject and world are not strictly bilateral: if they were, the certainty of the world would, in Descartes, be immediately given with that of the *Cogito*, and Kant would not have talked about his 'Copernican revolution'. Analytical reflection starts from our experience of the world and goes back to the subject as to a condition of possibility distinct from that experience, revealing the all-embracing synthesis as that without which there would be no world. To this extent it ceases to remain part of our experience and offers, in place of an account, a reconstruction. It is understandable, in view of this, that Husserl, having accused Kant of adopting a 'faculty psychologism',[1] should have urged, in place of a noetic analysis which bases the world on the synthesizing activity of the subject, his own '*noematic reflection*' which remains within the object and, instead of begetting it, brings to light its fundamental unity.

The world is there before any possible analysis of mine, and it would be artificial to make it the outcome of a series of syntheses which link, in the first place sensations, then aspects of the object corresponding to different perspectives, when both are nothing but products of analysis, with no sort of prior reality. Analytical reflection believes that it can trace back the course followed by a prior constituting act and arrive, in the 'inner man'—to use Saint Augustine's expression—at a constituting power which has always been identical with that inner self. Thus reflection itself is carried away and transplanted in an impregnable subjectivity, as yet untouched by being and time. But this is very ingenuous, or at least it is an incomplete form of reflection which loses sight of its own beginning. When I begin to reflect my reflection bears upon an unreflective experience; moreover my reflection cannot be unaware of itself as an event, and so it appears to itself in the light of a truly creative act, of a changed structure of consciousness, and yet it has to recognize, as having priority over its own operations, the world which is given to the subject, because the subject is given to himself. The real has to be described, not constructed or formed. Which means that I cannot put perception into the same category as the syntheses represented by judgements, acts or predications. My field of perception is constantly filled with a play of colours, noises and fleeting tactile sensations which I cannot relate precisely to the context of my clearly perceived world, yet which I nevertheless immediately 'place' in the world, without ever confusing them with my daydreams. Equally constantly I weave dreams round things. I imagine people and things whose presence is not incompatible with the context, yet who are not in fact involved in it: they are ahead of reality, in the realm of the imaginary. If the reality of my perception were based solely on the intrinsic coherence of 'represen-

[1] *Logische Untersuchungen, Prolegomena zur reinen Logik*, p. 93.

tations', it ought to be for ever hesitant and, being wrapped up in my conjectures on probabilities, I ought to be ceaselessly taking apart misleading syntheses, and reinstating in reality stray phenomena which I had excluded in the first place. But this does not happen. The real is a closely woven fabric. It does not await our judgement before incorporating the most surprising phenomena, or before rejecting the most plausible figments of our imagination. Perception is not a science of the world, it is not even an act, a deliberate taking up of a position; it is the background from which all acts stand out, and is presupposed by them. The world is not an object such that I have in my possession the law of its making; it is the natural setting of, and field for, all my thoughts and all my explicit perceptions. Truth does not 'inhabit' only 'the inner man', [1] or more accurately, there is no inner man, man is in the world, and only in the world does he know himself. When I return to myself from an excursion into the realm of dogmatic common sense or of science, I find, not a source of intrinsic truth, but a subject destined to be in the world.

All of which reveals the true meaning of the famous phenomenological reduction. There is probably no question over which Husserl has spent more time—or to which he has more often returned, since the 'problematic of reduction' occupies an important place in his unpublished work. For a long time, and even in recent texts, the reduction is presented as the return to a transcendental consciousness before which the world is spread out and completely transparent, quickened through and through by a series of apperceptions which it is the philosopher's task to reconstitute on the basis of their outcome. Thus my sensation of redness is *perceived as* the manifestation of a certain redness experienced, this in turn as the manifestation of a red surface, which is the manifestation of a piece of red cardboard, and this finally is the manifestation or outline of a red thing, namely this book. We are to understand, then, that it is the apprehension of a certain *hylè*, as indicating a phenomenon of a higher degree, the *Sinngebung,* or active meaning-giving operation which may be said to define consciousness, so that the world is nothing but 'world-as-meaning', and the phenomenological-reduction is idealistic, in the sense that there is here a transcendental idealism which treats the world as an indivisible unity of value shared by Peter and Paul, in which their perspectives blend.

---

[1] In te redi; in interiore homine habitat veritas (Saint Augustine).

'Peter's consciousness' and 'Paul's consciousness' are in communication, the perception of the world 'by Peter' is not Peter's doing any more than its perception 'by Paul' is Paul's doing; in each case it is the doing of pre-personal forms of consciousness, whose communication raises no problem, since it is demanded by the very definition of consciousness, meaning or truth. In so far as I am a consciousness, that is, in so far as something has meaning for me, I am neither here nor there, neither Peter nor Paul; I am in no way distinguishable from an 'other' consciousness, since we are immediately in touch with the world and since the world is, by definition, unique, being the system in which all truths cohere. A logically consistent transcendental idealism rids the world of its opacity and its transcendence. The world is precisely that thing of which we form a representation, not as men or as empirical subjects, but in so far as we are all one light and participate in the One without destroying its unity. Analytical reflection knows nothing of the problem of other minds, or of that of the world, because it insists that with the first glimmer of consciousness there appears in me theoretically the power of reaching some universal truth, and that the other person, being equally without thisness, location or body, the Alter and the Ego are one and the same in the true world which is the unifier of minds. There is no difficulty in understanding how *I* can conceive the Other, because the I and consequently the Other are not conceived as part of the woven stuff of phenomena; they have validity rather than existence. There is nothing hidden behind these faces and gestures, no domain to which I have no access, merely a little shadow which owes its very existence to the light. For Husserl, on the contrary, it is well known that there is a problem of other people, and the *alter ego* is a paradox. If the other is truly for himself alone, beyond his being for me, and if we are for each other and not both for God, we must necessarily have some appearance for each other. He must and I must have an outer appearance, and there must be, besides the perspective of the For Oneself—my view of myself and the other's of himself—a perspective of For Others—my view of others and theirs of me. Of course, these two perspectives, in each one of us, cannot be simply juxtaposed, *for in that case it is not I that the other would see, nor he that I should see.* I must be the exterior that I present to others, and the body of the other must be the other himself. This paradox and the dialectic of the Ego and the Alter are possible only provided that the Ego and the Alter Ego are defined by their situation and are not freed from all inherence; that is, provided that philosophy does not culminate in a return to the self, and that I discover by reflection not only my presence to myself, but also the possibility of an 'outside spectator'; that is, again, provided that at the very moment when I experience my existence—at the ultimate extremity of reflec-tion—I fall short of the ultimate density which would place me outside time, and that I discover within myself a kind of internal weakness standing in the way of my being totally individualized: a weakness which exposes me to the gaze of others as a man among men or at least as a consciousness among consciousnesses. Hitherto the *Cogito* depre-ciated the perception of others, teaching me as it did that the I is ac-cessible only to itself, since it defined *me* as the thought which I have of myself, and which clearly I am alone in having, at least in this ultimate sense. For the 'other' to be more than an empty word, it is necessary that my existence should never be reduced to my bare awareness of ex-isting, but that it should take in also the awareness that *one* may have of it, and thus include my incarnation in some nature and the possibility, at least, of a historical situation. The *Cogito* must reveal me in a situation, and it is on this condition alone that transcendental subjectivity can, as Husserl puts it,[1] *be* an intersubjectivity. As a meditating Ego, I can clearly distinguish from myself the world and things, since I certainly do not exist in the way in which things exist. I must even set aside from myself my body understood as a thing among things, as a collection of physico-chemical processes. But even if the *cogitatio,* which I thus discover, is without location in objective time and space, it is not without place in the phenomenological world. The world, which I dis-tinguished from myself as the totality of things or of processes linked by causal relationships, I rediscover 'in me' as the permanent horizon of all my *cogitationes* and as a dimension in relation to which I am constantly situating myself. The true *Cogito* does not define the subject's existence in terms of the thought he has of existing, and furthermore does not convert the indubitability of the world into the indubitability of thought about the world, nor finally does it replace the world itself by the world as meaning. On the contrary it recognizes my thought itself as an inalienable fact, and does away with any kind of idealism in revealing me as 'being-in-the-world'.

It is because we are through and through compounded of relation-ships with the world that for us the only way to become aware of the fact is to suspend the resultant activity, to refuse it our complicity (to

[1] *Die Krisis der europäischen Wissenschaften und die transzendentale Phänomenologie,* III (unpublished).

look at it *ohne mitzumachen,* as Husserl often says), or yet again, to put it 'out of play'. Not because we reject the certainties of common sense and a natural attitude to things—they are, on the contrary, the constant theme of philosophy—but because, being the presupposed basis of any thought, they are taken for granted, and go unnoticed, and because in order to arouse them and bring them to view, we have to suspend for a moment our recognition of them. The best formulation of the reduction is probably that given by Eugen Fink, Husserl's assistant, when he spoke of 'wonder' in the face of the world.[1] Reflection does not withdraw from the world towards the unity of consciousness as the world's basis; it steps back to watch the forms of transcendence fly up like sparks from a fire; it slackens the intentional threads which attach us to the world and thus brings them to our notice; it alone is consciousness of the world because it reveals that world as strange and paradoxical. Husserl's transcendental is not Kant's and Husserl accuses Kant's philosophy of being 'worldly', because it *makes use* of our relation to the world, which is the motive force of the transcendental deduction, and makes the world immanent in the subject, instead of *being filled with wonder* at it and conceiving the subject as a process of transcendence towards the world. All the misunderstandings with his interpreters, with the existentialist 'dissidents' and finally with himself, have arisen from the fact that in order to see the world and grasp it as paradoxical, we must break with our familiar acceptance of it and, also, from the fact that from this break we can learn nothing but the unmotivated upsurge of the world. The most important lesson which the reduction teaches us is the impossibility of a complete reduction. This is why Husserl is constantly re-examining the possibility of the reduction. If we were absolute mind, the reduction would present no problem. But since, on the contrary, we are in the world, since indeed our reflections are carried out in the temporal flux on to which we are trying to seize (since they *sich einströmen,* as Husserl says), there is no thought which embraces all our thought. The philosopher, as the unpublished works declare, is a perpetual beginner, which means that he takes for granted nothing that men, learned or otherwise, believe they know. It means also that philosophy itself must not take itself for granted, in so far as it may have managed to say something true; that it is an ever-renewed experiment in making its own beginning; that it consists wholly in the description of

---

[1] *Die phänomenologische Philosophie Edmund Husserls in der gegenwärtigen Kritik,* pp. 331 and ff.

this beginning, and finally, that radical reflection amounts to a consciousness of its own dependence on an unreflective life which is its initial situation, unchanging, given once and for all. Far from being, as has been thought, a procedure of idealistic philosophy, phenomenological reduction belongs to existential philosophy: Heidegger's 'being-in-the-world' appears only against the background of the phenomenological reduction.

A misunderstanding of a similar kind confuses the notion of the 'essences' in Husserl. Every reduction, says Husserl, as well as being transcendental is necessarily eidetic. That means that we cannot subject our perception of the world to philosophical scrutiny without ceasing to be identified with that act of positing the world, with that interest in it which delimits us, without drawing back from our commitment which is itself thus made to appear as a spectacle, without passing from the *fact* of our existence to its *nature*, from the Dasein to the Wesen. But it is clear that the essence is here not the end, but a means, that our effective involvement in the world is precisely what has to be understood and made amenable to conceptualization, for it is what polarizes all our conceptual particularizations. The need to proceed by way of essences does not mean that philosophy takes them as its object, but, on the contrary, that our existence is too tightly held in the world to be able to know itself as such at the moment of its involvement, and that it requires the field of ideality in order to become acquainted with and to prevail over its facticity. The Vienna Circle, as is well known, lays it down categorically that we can enter into relations only with meanings. For example, 'consciousness' is not for the Vienna Circle identifiable with what we are. It is a complex meaning which has developed late in time, which should be handled with care, and only after the many meanings which have contributed, throughout the word's semantic development, to the formation of its present one have been made explicit. Logical positivism of this kind is the antithesis of Husserl's thought. Whatever the subtle changes of meaning which have ultimately brought us, as a linguistic acquisition, the word and concept of consciousness, we enjoy direct access to what it designates. For we have the experience of ourselves, of that consciousness which we are, and it is on the basis of this experience that all linguistic connotations are assessed, and precisely through it that language comes to have any meaning at all for us. 'It is that as yet dumb experience . . . which we are concerned to lead to the pure expression of its own meaning.'[1] Husserl's essences are destined to bring back all the living relationships of experience, as the fisherman's net draws up from the depths of the ocean quivering fish and seaweed. Jean Wahl is therefore wrong in saying that 'Husserl separates essences from existence'.[2] The separated essences are those of language. It is the office of language to cause essences to exist in a state of separation which is in fact merely apparent, since through language they still rest upon the ante-predicative life of consciousness. In the silence of primary consciousness can be seen appearing not only what words mean, but also what things mean: the core of primary meaning round which the acts of naming and expression take shape.

Seeking the essence of consciousness will therefore not consist in developing the *Wortbedeutung* of consciousness and escaping from existence into the universe of things said; it will consist in rediscovering my actual presence to myself, the fact of my consciousness which is in the last resort what the word and the concept of consciousness mean. Looking for the world's essence is not looking for what it is as an idea once it has been reduced to a theme of discourse; it is looking for what it is as a fact for us, before any thematization. Sensationalism 'reduces' the world by noticing that after all we never experience anything but states of ourselves. Transcendental idealism too 'reduces' the world since, in so far as it guarantees the world, it does so by regarding it as thought or consciousness of the world, and as the mere correlative of our knowledge, with the result that it becomes immanent in consciousness and the aseity of things is thereby done away with. The eidetic reduction is, on the other hand, the determination to bring the world to light as it is before any falling back on ourselves has occurred, it is the ambition to make reflection emulate the unreflective life of consciousness. I aim at and perceive a world. If I said, as do the sensationalists, that we have here only 'states of consciousness', and if I tried to distinguish my perceptions from my dreams with the aid of 'criteria', I should overlook the phenomenon of the world. For if I am able to talk about 'dreams' and 'reality', to bother my head about the distinction between imaginary and real, and cast doubt upon the 'real', it is because this distinction is already made by me before any analysis; it is because I have an experience of the real as of the imaginary, and the problem then becomes one not of asking how critical thought can provide for it-

[1] *Méditations cartésiennes*, pp. 33.
[2] *Réalisme, dialectique et mystère, l'Arbalète*, Autumn, 1942, unpaginated.

self secondary equivalents of this distinction, but of making explicit our primordial knowledge of the 'real', of describing our perception of the world as that upon which our idea of truth is for ever based. We must not, therefore, wonder whether we really perceive a world, we must instead say: the world is what we perceive. In more general terms we must not wonder whether our self-evident truths are real truths, or whether, through some perversity inherent in our minds, that which is self-evident for us might not be illusory in relation to some truth in itself. For in so far as we talk about illusion, it is because we have identified illusions, and done so solely in the light of some perception which at the same time gave assurance of its own truth. It follows that doubt, or the fear of being mistaken, testifies as soon as it arises to our power of unmasking error, and that it could never finally tear us away from truth. We are in the realm of truth and it is 'the experience of truth' which is self-evident.[1] To seek the essence of perception is to declare that perception is, not presumed true, but defined as access to truth. So, if I now wanted, according to idealistic principles, to base this *de facto* self-evident truth, this irresistible belief, on some absolute self-evident truth, that is, on the absolute clarity which my thoughts have for me; if I tried to find in myself a creative thought which bodied forth the framework of the world or illumined it through and through, I should once more prove unfaithful to my experience of the world, and should be looking for what makes that experience possible instead of looking for what it is. The self-evidence of perception is not adequate thought or apodeictic self-evidence.[2] The world is not what I think, but what I live through. I am open to the world, I have no doubt that I am in communication with it, but I do not possess it; it is inexhaustible. 'There is a world', or rather: 'There is the world'; I can never completely account for this ever-reiterated assertion in my life. This facticity of the world is what constitutes the *Weltlichkeit der Welt,* what causes the world to be the world; just as the facticity of the *cogito* is not an imperfection in itself, but rather what assures me of my existence. The eidetic method is the method of a phenomenological positivism which bases the possible on the real.

---

[1] *Das Erlebnis der Wahrheit (Logische Untersuchungen, Prolegomena zur reinen Logik)* p. 190.

[2] There is no apodeictic self-evidence, the *Formale und transzendentale Logik* (p. 142) says in effect.

We can now consider the notion of intentionality, too often cited as the main discovery of phenomenology, whereas it is understandable only through the reduction. 'All consciousness is consciousness of something'; there is nothing new in that. Kant showed, in the *Refutation of Idealism,* that inner perception is impossible without outer perception, that the world, as a collection of connected phenomena, is anticipated in the consciousness of my unity, and is the means whereby I come into being as a consciousness. What distinguishes intentionality from the Kantian relation to a possible object is that the unity of the world, before being posited by knowledge in a specific act of identification, is 'lived' as ready-made or already there. Kant himself shows in the *Critique of Judgement* that there exists a unity of the imagination and the understanding and a unity of subjects *before the object,* and that, in experiencing the beautiful, for example, I am aware of a harmony between sensation and concept, between myself and others, which is itself without any concept. Here the subject is no longer the universal thinker of a system of objects rigorously interrelated, the positing power who subjects the manifold to the law of the understanding, in so far as he is to be able to put together a world—he discovers and enjoys his own nature as spontaneously in harmony with the law of the understanding. But if the subject has a nature, then the hidden art of the imagination must condition the categorial activity. It is no longer merely the aesthetic judgement, but knowledge too which rests upon this art, an art which forms the basis of the unity of consciousness and of consciousnesses.

Husserl takes up again the *Critique of Judgement* when he talks about a teleology of consciousness. It is not a matter of duplicating human consciousness with some absolute thought which, from outside, is imagined as assigning to it its aims. It is a question of recognizing consciousness itself as a project of the world, meant for a world which it neither embraces nor possesses, but towards which it is perpetually directed—and the world as this pre-objective individual whose imperious unity decrees what knowledge shall take as its goal. This is why Husserl distinguishes between intentionality of act, which is that of our judgements and of those occasions when we voluntarily take up a position—the only intentionality discussed in the *Critique of Pure Reason*—and operative intentionality (*fungierende Intentionalität*), or that which produces the natural and antepredicative unity of the world and of our life, being apparent in our desires, our evaluations and in the landscape we see, more clearly than in objective knowledge, and furnishing the text which our knowledge tries to translate into precise language. Our relationship to the world, as it is untiringly enunciated within us, is not a thing which can be any further clarified by analysis; philosophy can only place it once more before our eyes and present it for our ratification.

Through this broadened notion of intentionality, phenomenological 'comprehension' is distinguished from traditional 'intellection', which is confined to 'true and immutable natures', and so phenomenology can become a phenomenology of origins. Whether we are concerned with a thing perceived, a historical event or a doctrine, to 'understand' is to take in the total intention—not only what these things are for representation (the 'properties' of the thing perceived, the mass of 'historical facts', the 'ideas' introduced by the doctrine)—but the unique mode of existing expressed in the properties of the pebble, the glass or the piece of wax, in all the events of a revolution, in all the thoughts of a philosopher. It is a matter, in the case of each civilization, of finding the Idea in the Hegelian sense, that is, not a law of the physico-mathematical type, discoverable by objective thought, but that formula which sums up some unique manner of behaviour towards others, towards Nature, time and death: a certain way of patterning the world which the historian should be capable of seizing upon and making his own. These are the *dimensions* of history. In this context there is not a human word, not a gesture, even one which is the outcome of habit or absent-mindedness, which has not some meaning. For example, I may have been under the impression that I lapsed into silence through weariness, or some minister may have thought he had uttered merely an appropriate platitude, yet my silence or his words immediately take on a significance, because my fatigue or his falling back upon a ready-made formula are not accidental, for they express a certain lack of interest, and hence some degree of adoption of a definite position in relation to the situation.

When an event is considered at close quarters, at the moment when it is lived through, everything seems subject to chance: one man's ambition, some lucky encounter, some local circumstance or other appears to have been decisive. But chance happenings offset each other, and facts in their multiplicity coalesce and show up a certain way of taking a stand in relation to the human situation, reveal in fact an *event* which has its definite outline and about which we can talk. Should the starting-point for the understanding of history be ideology, or politics, or religion, or economics? Should we try to understand a doctrine from its overt content, or from the psychological make-up and the biography of its author? We must seek an understanding from all these angles simultaneously, everything has meaning, and we shall find this same structure of being underlying all relationships. All these views are true provided that they are not isolated, that we delve deeply into history and reach the unique core of existential meaning which emerges in each perspective. It is true, as Marx says, that history does not walk on its head, but it is also true that it does not think with its feet. Or one should say rather that it is neither its 'head' nor its 'feet' that we have to worry about, but its body. All economic and psychological explanations of a doctrine are true, since the thinker never thinks from any starting-point but the one constituted by what he is. Reflection even on a doctrine will be complete only if it succeeds in linking up with the doctrine's history and the extraneous explanations of it, and in putting back the causes and meaning of the doctrine in an existential structure. There is, as Husserl says, a 'genesis of meaning' (*Sinngenesis*),[1] which alone, in the last resort, teaches us what the doctrine 'means.' Like understanding, criticism must be pursued at all levels, and naturally, it will be insufficient, for the refutation of a doctrine, to relate it to some accidental event in the author's life: its significance goes beyond, and there is no pure accident in existence or in coexistence, since both absorb random events and transmute them into the rational.

Finally, as it is indivisible in the present, history is equally so in its sequences. Considered in the light of its fundamental dimensions, all periods of history appear as manifestations of a single existence, or as episodes in a single drama—without our knowing whether it has an ending. Because we are in the world, we are *condemned to meaning,* and we cannot do or say anything without its acquiring a name in history.

Probably the chief gain from phenomenology is to have united extreme subjectivism and extreme objectivism in its notion of the world or of rationality. Rationality is precisely measured by the experiences in which it is disclosed. To say that there exists rationality is to say that perspectives blend, perceptions confirm each other, a meaning emerges. But it should not be set in a realm apart, transposed into absolute Spirit, or into a world in the realist sense. The phenomenological world is not

[1] The usual term in the unpublished writings. The idea is already to be found in the *Formale und transzendentale Logik,* pp. 184 and ff.

pure being, but the sense which is revealed where the paths of my various experiences intersect, and also where my own and other people's intersect and engage each other like gears. It is thus inseparable from subjectivity and intersubjectivity, which find their unity when I either take up my past experiences in those of the present, or other people's in my own. For the first time the philosopher's thinking is sufficiently conscious not to anticipate itself and endow its own results with reified form in the world. The philosopher tries to conceive the world, others and himself and their interrelations. But the meditating Ego, the 'impartial spectator' (*uninteressierter Zuschauer*)[1] do not rediscover an already given rationality, they 'establish themselves',[2] and establish it, by an act of initiative which has no guarantee in being, its justification resting entirely on the effective power which it confers on us of taking our own history upon ourselves.

The phenomenological world is not the bringing to explicit expression of a pre-existing being, but the laying down of being. Philosophy is not the reflection of a pre-existing truth, but, like art, the act of bringing truth into being. One may well ask how this creation is *possible*, and if it does not recapture in things a pre-existing Reason. The answer is that the only pre-existent Logos is the world itself, and that the philosophy which brings it into visible existence does not begin by being *possible*; it is actual or real like the world of which it is a part, and no explanatory hypothesis is clearer than the act whereby we take up this unfinished world in an effort to complete and conceive it. Rationality is not a *problem*. There is behind it no unknown quantity which has to be determined by deduction, or, beginning with it, demonstrated inductively. We witness every minute the miracle of related experiences, and yet nobody knows better than we do how this miracle is worked, for we are ourselves this network of relationships. The world and reason are not problematical. We may say, if we wish, that they are mysterious, but their mystery defines them: there can be no question of dispelling it by some 'solution', it is on the hither side of all solutions. True philosophy consists in relearning to look at the world, and in this sense a historical account can give meaning to the world quite as 'deeply' as a philosophical treatise. We take our fate in our hands, we become responsible for our history through reflection, but equally by a

---

[1] *6th Méditation cartésienne* (unpublished).
[2] Ibid.

decision on which we stake our life, and in both cases what is involved is a violent act which is validated by being performed.

Phenomenology, as a disclosure of the world, rests on itself, or rather provides its own foundation.[1] All knowledge is sustained by a 'ground' of postulates and finally by our communication with the world as primary embodiment of rationality. Philosophy, as radical reflection, dispenses in principle with this resource. As, however, it too is in history, it too exploits the world and constituted reason. It must therefore put to itself the question which it puts to all branches of knowledge, and so duplicate itself infinitely, being, as Husserl says, a dialogue or infinite meditation, and, in so far as it remains faithful to its intention, never knowing where it is going. The unfinished nature of phenomenology and the inchoative atmosphere which has surrounded it are not to be taken as a sign of failure, they were inevitable because phenomenology's task was to reveal the mystery of the world and of reason.[2] If phenomenology was a movement before becoming a doctrine or a philosophical system, this was attributable neither to accident, nor to fraudulent intent. It is as painstaking as the works of Balzac, Proust, Valéry or Cézanne—by reason of the same kind of attentiveness and wonder, the same demand for awareness, the same will to seize the meaning of the world or of history as that meaning comes into being. In this way it merges into the general effort of modern thought.

PAUL RICOEUR (1913-)

Paul Ricoeur was born in France in 1913 and today remains one of France's most prolific phenomenological philosophers. Ricoeur studied with Gabriel Marcel but early began studies of Husserl as well. Ricoeur has held appointments at the University of Strasbourg, the Sorbonne, and also in the United States, chiefly at the University of Chicago. His main contribution to phenomenology has been a philosophy of the will: *Freedom and Nature* (1950), *Fallible Man* (1960), and *The Symbolism of Evil* (1960).

[1] 'Rückbeziehung der Phänomenologie auf sich selbst,' say the unpublished writings.

[2] We are indebted for this last expression to G. Gusdorf, who may well have used it in another sense.

EXISTENTIAL PHENOMENOLOGY*

Taken alone the term "phenomenology" is not very illuminating. The word means science of appearances or of appearings. Thus, any inquiry or any work devoted to the way anything whatsoever appears is already phenomenology. The way in which things, animate beings, or human beings show themselves could be described. Thus, the phenomenology of a "region" of reality, the region thing, the region animal, the region man could be produced. Likewise, the phenomenology of a feeling (e.g., fear, if one describes the way in which fear, the thing feared, and the world under the sign of fear show themselves) and in general the phenomenology of any subjective process of consciousness could be elaborated. In this diluted sense the word "phenomenology" covers every sort of popular presentation of appearances. The term is a long way from a disciplined limitation of its usage.

Phenomenology becomes strict when the status of the appearing of things (in the broadest sense of the term) becomes problematical. In short, it becomes strict when this question is raised: What does "appearing" signify for a thing, for an animate being, for a person, for a conscious experience, for a feeling, for an image, and the like? How do the "regions" of reality (thing, animal, man, etc.) relate to the subjective processes of consciousness (perceiving, imagining, positing an abstraction, judging, etc.)? In this strict sense the question of being, the ontological question, is excluded in advance from phenomenology, either provisionally or definitely. The question of knowing that which *is* in an absolute sense is placed "between parentheses," and the manner of appearing is treated as an autonomous problem. Phenomenology in the strict sense begins as soon as this distinction is reflected upon for its own sake, whatever the final result may be. On the other hand, whenever the act of birth, which brings appearing to emergence at the expense of being or against the background of being, is no longer perceived and systematized, then phenomenology ceases to be a philosophical discipline and falls back to the level of ordinary and popular description.

If what is implied in this first strict determination of the notion of phenomenology is developed and if one calls "transcendental" any attempt at relating the conditions of the appearance of things to the structure of human subjectivity, in short to the very life of the subject to whom and for whom things appear, then it will be said that all phenomenology is transcendental. Long before Husserl, Kant and Hegel understood the word "phenomenology" in this way. If this is how things stand, how can we speak of "existential" phenomenology? Is it another branch alongside transcendental phenomenology? But how could there be another branch if all phenomenology is transcendental? We shall show that the phenomenology termed "existential" is not another division juxtaposed to "transcendental phenomenology"; rather, this phenomenology becomes a method and is placed in the service of a dominating problem-set, viz., the problems concerning existence.

Phenomenology of the existential sort brings together investigations and writings from several sources: (1) Under this rubric the last investigations of the founder of contemporary phenomenology, Edmund Husserl, can be placed. In these researches we can observe "transcendental" phenomenology turning toward an investigation of the various aspects of man's insertion in the world. (2) In addition, we must draw out the whole function of the rigorous description incorporated in the great philosophies which proceeded from Kierkegaard and Nietzsche in France and Germany (and also from the Hegel of the *Phenomenology of the Spirit*, not to mention that species of phenomenology of economic existence which can be discerned in the work of Marx). These existential descriptions constitute an original source of contemporary phenomenology. In comparison with these philosophies born of the opposition to Hegel's *Logic,* in which classical philosophy is brought to its completion, Husserl's work seems to stand closer to certain currents of Neo-Kantianism than their author believed. (3) A third cycle of existential phenomenology is constituted by the works, particularly the French ones, which are situated at the confluence of the phenomenological method deriving from Husserl and the existential problem-set received from post-Hegelian philosophy. These works best merit the title "existential phenomenology."

[I] The "Existential" Turn of "Transcendental" Phenomenology

Husserlian phenomenology became more and more existential to the degree that the problem of perception took precedence over all other problems. This development deserves an explanation. In Husserl's first works, from the *Logical Investigations* to the *Cartesian Meditations,* consciousness is defined not by perception, that is to say, by its very presence to things, but rather by its distance and its absence. This distance and this absence are the power of signifying, of meaning. The intending of signifying can be empty (and even incapable of fulfillment, as in the case with absurd propositions). Then perception is only a privileged mode of fulfillment by intuition. Thus, consciousness is doubly intentional, in the first instance by virtue of being a signification and in the second instance by virtue of being an intuitive fulfilling. In short, in the first works, consciousness is at once speech (*la parole*) and perception.

It is in the works and manuscripts of the last ten years that perception is described as the initial basis and genetic origin of all operations of consciousness. This is the consciousness which gives, which sees, which effects presences, and it supports and founds the consciousness which signifies, which judges, and which speaks. This shift in accent marks the passage to existential phenomenology. In fact, the sense of the existence of things and that of the existence of the subject are revealed simultaneously in perception thus reinterpreted.

From its encounter with the Platonic and then with the Galilean tradition, which suppose that the true reality is not what one perceives but what one conceives and measures, the "thing" acquires transcendence in relation to consciousness. This transcendence certainly is not the absolute transcendence of an "in-itself" which could do without any conscious witness but is the relative transcendence of an object (*un vis-à-vis*) into which consciousness comes to transcend itself (*se dépasser*). Consciousness defined by its intentionality is outside, beyond. It ties its own wandering to the "things" to which it can apply its consideration, its desire, its action. Correlatively, the world is "world-for-my-life," environment of the "living ego." And it has this sense only with reference to the "living present," where the pact between daily living and every revealed presence is continuously renewed. Retained and anticipated, time is once more, as Kant said of the imagination, "the art hidden in nature" thanks to which the living present never ceases to move beyond itself into the project of a total world.

Yet, in becoming more and more existential the phenomenology of the late Husserl became more and more empirical, for the whole order of the understanding—predicative judgment, affirmation and negation, activity of synthesis and consecution—henceforth proceeds from "passive synthesis'' initiated on the very level of perception. Thereafter it is clear that this progression toward an ever more originary original destroys every claim of constituting the world ''in'' consciousness or ''beginning from'' consciousness. The idealistic tendency of transcendental phenomenology is thus compensated for by the progressive discovery that one does not constitute the originary but only all that one can derive from it. The originary is just what could neither be constituted nor reduced.

The ''world'' consequently, is not what Kant said it was, viz., the Idea of reason, which commands us to unify scientific experience. For this cosmological Idea there is substituted the altogether existential notion of the horizon of subjective life. The ''world'' is prior to every ''object.'' It is not only presupposed in the intellectualistic sense of a condition for possibilities, it is pre-given in the sense that every present activity surges into a world already there. Moreover, this world is the totality which, not being composed from parts and by means of addition, is inaccessible to doubt. It is the ''passive pre-given universal of all judgmental activity,'' the ''one basis of belief upon which every experience of particular objects is erected.''

[II] The Implicit Phenomenology of the Philosophy of Existence

(1) Not all of existential phenomenology is in Husserl—far from it. This is the place to recall that Hegel's first great work is called *The Phenomenology of Spirit*. Now this great book nourished the most determined opponents of Hegelianism more than they believed, particularly the opponents of Hegel's *Logic*. It is one of the sources of the philosophy of existence.

In this book philosophy, passing from consciousness to self-consciousness, incorporated for the first time the most dramatic experiences of humanity which previously had yielded only to poetic, dramatic, or religious expression and not to essays having an economic, political, or historical turn. The pages on the desire of a desire which would be another self, on the struggle for recognition through the dialectic of master and slave, on stoicism and skepticism, on unhappy consciousness, and the like—today all of these pages are well-known. Hegel's concern to let human experience appear and speak for itself in its integrity is quite comparable to Husserl's precept: ''Back to the things themselves.'' But at the same time Hegel introduced into the field of phenomenological analysis the ''negative'' experiences of disappearance, contradiction, struggle, and frustration which impart the tragic tone to his phenomenology. This tone is utterly foreign to Husserl's works which never drew on the "work of the negative"—as Hegel terms it—in the explication of self-consciousness.

This difference is fundamental. At the very moment that it promises an immense enrichment of the description, properly so-called, of human experience, this promotion of the "negative" paradoxically announces the end of phenomenology. In fact, these experiences of the negative are intended to assure the "transitions" from one form to another, and by that very fact to give a systematic cohesion which the old logic of identity and noncontradiction was quite incapable of introducing into the profusion of human experience. The "negative" is the possibility of a system no longer of the analytical type, after the fashion of the Leibnizian combinatorial logic, but of the dialectical type in which the "negative" mediates the becoming of spirit through its forms. Thus, phenomenology discovers the "negative." This negative brought in the new logic, and this logic eliminated phenomenology. This is why the philosophy of existence, though it may elaborate one or another of the Hegelian analyses taken in isolation, is set up over against the Hegelian system and against Logic, where tragedy is swallowed up.

(2) The term "existence," in the sense given it by contemporary philosophy, comes from Kierkegaard. The existent par excellence is the individual who emerges in sadness and solitude, in doubt and exaltation—and in passion—this is the individual whom the System does not include. This strange and irrational birth to itself of the existential thinker initially escapes every methodological concern; hence, it is beyond phenomenology—if its strict character as the science of phenomena be emphasized.

Nevertheless, in two respects Kierkegaard's thought contains the outlines of a quite strict phenomenology. In the first place, his almost sickly concern for self-justification initiates one of the most extraordinary apparatuses for the description of subjectivity ever constructed. For example, the description of "stages of life's way" is set out in an unusual key, one in which the intimacy of the most individual confession coincides with the generality of the barest abstraction. In the same way a vertiginous dread, even fear of the vertigo, which grasps freedom when confronted with the infinity of its possibilities and the finitude of its engagements and under the goad of the forbidden—a dread in which innocence turns aside to sin—elicits a description whose subtlety mobilizes the resources of a casuistical psychology, of dramatic art, and of theological anthropology. In short, the *Concept of Dread* is, properly speaking, already a phenomenology of freedom.

Beyond this concern for justification which generates a pitiless lucidity, Kierkegaard's work conceals within its irrationality a second motive for rigor. In fact, as against Hegel, it was a matter of framing the charter of the anti-system and thus little by little of rendering the opposition to the System coherent. The *Philosophical Fragments* and the *Postscript* develop this methodology of the anti-system by elaborating actual "categories" of the individual over against those of logic: the instant in place of the eternity of logic, the individual in place of the whole, paradox in place of mediation, and existence in place of the System. With the same stroke—and not without contradiction—the existential thinking tends toward a strict elaboration of the "concepts" of the anti-system and thus toward a phenomenology, which, unlike Hegel's, will never be swallowed up in logic. In these two ways, Kierkegaard is at the origin of existential phenomenology.

(3) But Nietzsche is also one of its fathers. He also used strict description, though for other than Kierkegaard's reasons. To be sure an aphoristic form and a symbolic, even mythological, construction belong to the essence of his thinking; an attempt to find a system in it would prove vain. But strict description is required by Nietzsche's plan just as it was by Kierkegaard's. It is set in motion not by concern for self-justification and for setting up a sort of indirect communication with the Other, but rather by the pitiless taste for unmasking the moral and spiritual falsehoods on which our culture is built. Nietzsche's work—at least the negative, nihilistic, side of it—is an enormous enterprise of methodical disillusionment. The *Genealogy of Morals*—did Husserl not call one of his last works a "genealogy of logic"?— is a genuine phenomenology, at once reductive and genetic, applied to the totality of moral phenomena.

A powerful and wily instinct for dissimulation is discovered at the center of human existence, which philosophy vows to track down, to denounce, and to destroy. Thus, long before the Husserlian phenomenology issued from the technique of reduction, the philosopher of "suspicion" followed the path from the derived to the originary. It matters little to us that he mixed in with this technique of truth a dogmatism of instinct and an evolutionistic scientism which are antiquated today. It even matters little that Nietzsche should have lost himself in his destructive passion. The fact remains that he is the first to have practiced what Jean-Paul Sartre later called "existential psychoanalysis.'' The genesis of the spirit of humility from the will to power and of the demonic form from the project of saintliness are the most remarkable, and in certain respects the most frightening, examples of this critical phenomenology, a phenomenology noticeably more inclusive than the phenomenology of cognition to which the greatest part of Husserl's work had to be limited. This phenomenology includes both a critique of the self by the self, a coming to awareness of the sense of the times, and a recapitulation of Western history in its totality.

[III] Existential Phenomenology

It is now possible to distinguish the main themes of contemporary existential phenomenology deriving from the conjunction of Husserlian phenomenology and the philosophy of existence. But these descriptive themes cannot be torn out of their philosophical context without injury. Even when they are elaborated by the same method and at times in the same terms by different philosophers, they are each traversed by a different intention which profoundly alters the sense. Existential phenomenology never describes merely for the pleasure of describing. The examples of Hegel, Kierkegaard, and Nietzsche are sufficient indication that description is effective only in the service of a great plan: to denounce an alienation, to rediscover the place of man in the world, or, on the other hand, to recover his metaphysical dimension, and so on. For each of these senses given to man's existence, there are so many descriptive styles in existential phenomenology. Let us take as examples three themes which are like the three melodic lines of existential phenomenology:

(1) First, the example of the "owned body." In Gabriel Marcel this theme has a function of break and recovery: on the one hand, break with the idolatry of the anonymous epistemological subject which is without situation, unmenaced, inaccessible to drama and to personal death, and, on the other hand, recovery of the concrete, restoration of an experience at once personal and integral which extends between the two poles of the carnal and the mysterious. This dual path, both critical and restorative, orients the patient, subtle, and sometimes evasive descriptions of the "owned body." It oscillates between being and having (I am it, and I have it), between the organ and the instrument, between the same and the different. Thought, misled by the object, works to restore the complete sense of "I exist." But at the very moment when this existential phenomenology seems to be identified with a philosophy

of incarnation, it escapes this philosophy and repays it with an investigation of experiences which can be called ontological because they reveal the insertion of my being into being: fidelity, hope, etc. Existential phenomenology then signifies the "positing and concrete approach to the ontological mystery." In other words, the phenomenology of the "owned body" plays the equivocal role of a rerooting in the concrete and of a counterpole to the ontological mystery.

In Merleau-Ponty, on the other hand, the description of the owned body is entirely in the service of a philosophy of finitude or of an exorcism of standpointless thinking; ultimately it is in the service of a philosophy without an absolute. The *Phenomenology of Perception* should be followed from one end to the other without reference to the true object, seen from nowhere, which would justify the possibility of perception, even without ever denying the inherence of consciousness in a point of view. To be sure, this program assumes that the other operations of consciousness—principally science and also that is amenable to speech and to the λόγος —bear the same fundamental structures, "the same syntheses of transition, the same sort of horizon" as perceptual experience; in short, it assumes that "every consciousness is perceptual, even the consciousness of ourselves." Thus, the first pact concluded between cognition and finitude orients the whole phenomenology of perception. The description of the "owned body" is its touchstone. This description, just as in both Husserl and Gabriel Marcel, goes hand in hand with a critique of sensation as reconstructed by psycho-physiology, i.e., as the simple effect of a physical stimulus. Phenomenology calls description from the sensation, from that late developed object of scientific consciousness, to perception, just as it is given. This perception is given as at once significational, in contrast to the pretended sensation of sensualism, but not intelligible, in contrast to the judgment of experience according to the intellectualist tradition which runs from Lachelier and Lagneau to Alain and Brunschvicg.

The theory of the "owned body" is then the critical point where the breakdown of objective thinking is consummated and where the perspectivist doctrine of perception is established. Neither the psychic, according to reflective philosophy, nor the "physiological," according to scientific thinking, accounts for the owned body. For it is the movement of being-in-the-world (*être au monde*), indivisibly voluntary and involuntary, as projected and as given. Beginning at this point, every analysis of behavior is conducted in such a way as to avoid the alternatives of automatism and abstract intelligence. The "owned body" is the locus of all ambiguities between the nascent sense and facticity, between the enacted and reflected. Merleau-Ponty's existential phenomenology thus represents the strictest disagreement with the Platonic conversion of the here-below to the beyond. Placed in the service of a reconversion from reflection to the pre-reflective, existential phenomenology becomes identified with the justification of being-in-the-world. One can only wonder, though, how the moment of reflection on the unreflected, how the devotion to universality and to truth, and finally how the philosophical act itself are possible if man is so completely identified with his insertion into his field of perception, action, and life.

(2) The theme of freedom gives rise to contrasts even greater than those of the "owned body" and confirms the subordination of the descriptive method to the existential intention in this sector of phenomenology. The reason is clear: in the case of freedom the ontological status of man is in question. Heidegger had already placed phenomenology in the service of a fundamental ontology where the explication of the being of man was to open the horizon to a theory of being qua being. Thereafter, it is not surprising that a phenomenology of freedom, such as is at the center of Jean-Paul Sartre's work, should carry an ontological title—*Being and Nothingness*—and a subtitle which combines phenomenology and ontology. Even so, we have scarcely left the field of existential phenomenology, for with freedom, the existential and the ontological become synonymous. The being of man consists in existing, in the emphatic sense which Kierkegaard has conferred on this word.

The overthrow which Sartre introduced into the problem-set of freedom consists precisely in having inverted the ontological index of freedom. Did we just say that the being of man consists in existing? Let us rather say that existing consists in being its own nothingness. Here is where phenomenology comes into play, for it has the function of collecting the experiences where I discover my freedom in the negative style of absence, of rapture, of distance, of failure to cohere, and of constancy, of anguish, of rejection, in short, where freedom is revealed as the nihilation of the past, of the completed, in a word, of being. Evidently it is presupposed that being was previously reduced to the being of a thing, to thinghood. It is then clear that the abandonment of the great metaphysical tradition, whereby being is act par excellence, is what directs this phenomenology of nihilating acts. Moreover, this phenomenology manifests an abundance, a perspicacity, and a force

rarely equaled. The "sense of the negative" of which Hegel took possession on behalf of philosophy (and to which, as we have seen, Husserl
lost the key), re-emerges in contemporary philosophy with Sartre. This
dialectical sense is enriched along the way with the Kierkegaardian and
Marxian themes of anxiety and conflict. In addition, Sartre uses an agile
imagination of concrete situations which as philosopher he takes over
from the playwright. Finally, Husserl's concept of intentionality takes
on a new look after this bath in negativity. It becomes the original
distance, the stepping away of the self from itself, the nothing which
separates existence from its having-been. But the step which carries this
phenomenology of nihilating acts to the level of an ontology of nothingness is made by the philosopher, not by the phenomenologist.

Yet the same patience, the same descriptive strictness can serve an
entirely different purpose, for one can describe, with Gabriel Marcel,
another level of freedom, which consists less in tearing oneself away
from oneself, in annulling every datum in-itself and beyond oneself,
than in letting oneself be opened up by a liberating presence. A
phenomenology of liberation, which describes the passage of unavailability to availability (*disponibilité*), from avarice to generosity,
here becomes the harbinger of a quite different ontology, one where the
main accent is on participation in being rather than on the nihilation of
being. But this descriptive spirit is not what makes for the difference between the two phenomenologies. The difference lies rather in the sense
of the word "being," which for one signifies act, the giving of existence,
and for the other signifies the brute datum or dead thing.

In Merleau-Ponty the phenomenology of freedom can also take form
within the phenomenology of the "owned body" which, as we have
seen, joins the ego to the world instead of completing the break between
the "for-itself" and the "in-itself." If in fact the body is the movement of
my being-in-the-world, if it is a spontaneity which offers itself to a situation in order to form it, then the decisive experience of freedom is to
be sought not in the dramatic moment of breaking away but rather in
the moment of engagement which includes the whole involvement in situation. To project our past, our future, our human milieu around ourselves is precisely to situate ourselves. Henceforth, concrete freedom is
not to be sought elsewhere than in this general power to place oneself in
situation. And the all or nothing of Sartrean freedom appears to have no
measure in common with actual experience, which does not know the
sovereign "in-itself" and never encounters anything but a relative
freedom which incessantly "busies itself in taking up some proposition

about the world.'' The phenomenology of freedom follows up the meta-physics of finitude which the theory of the owned body began.

(3) The theme of the Other supports our analysis of the relations be-tween the phenomenological method and the ontological intention in ex-istential phenomenology. Jean-Paul Sartre initiates his analysis of the existence of the Other with the experience of being seen, of being caught by a gaze which freezes me in my tracks, reduces me to the condition of an object, steals my world from me, and takes away my freedom along with my subject position. The existence of the Other thus constitutes my ''original fall,'' that is to say, the movement by which I fall into the world and am condemned to parry and thrust, i.e., to the struggle which is pursued in incipient or indirect ways even in sexual activity. But the choice of this glance that encroaches, fixes, determines, this glance which menaces because it is menaced, this freezing gaze—this choice comes to phenomenology from far away. If the Other appears to me by primordial right as power of encroachment (d'empiètement) and of theft, is this not because freedom itself has been described without the experience of generosity or of giving? Is it not only in a foregone project of unavailability, as Emmanuel Mounier says somewhere, that the Other's gaze is a gaze that petrifies and not instead a gaze that over-throws?

However such things stand, when it is a question of the Other, just as when it is a question of freedom or of the owned body, the field of ex-istential phenomenology is an oriented field. One does not describe just anything simply for the pleasure of making brilliant analyses. The privilege accorded to misunderstanding, to conflict, to encounter, to reciprocity, to the collaboration of a teammate or of a galley slave betrays a different ontological style, according to whether being renders the constitution of a *we* possible or not, wherein the difference and the distance between me and the Other would somehow be overcome.

Thus, existential phenomenology makes the transition between transcendental phenomenology, born of the reduction of every thing to its appearing to me, and ontology, which restores the question of the sense of being for all that is said to "exist."

III

Main Directions

Out of the question "What is phenomenology?" can now be seen to have arisen a number of basic and prevalent themes of phenomenology and existential philosophies. The study of "essences" or "structures," the rigorous development of a "descriptive" orientation, the nature of perceptual life and the role of the constantly presupposed lifeworld begin to emerge as large central issues. At the same time the fundamental and inseparable connection of such themes and directions with a "way" or method of proceeding was also indicated through the phenomenological "epoche." Moreover, whether in the form of Husserl's *ego-cogito-cogitatum* or in the existential version of it as *being-in-the-world,* the phenomenological-existential philosophies remain philosophies of correlation of man with his environment.

Without trying to preempt the question concerning which issues are predominant in the whole of the literature, the section on main directions addresses itself to some of these larger issues. The name for the phenomenological correlation itself, the "intentionality of consciousness," is indisputably central to the entire movement. This beginning in and with experience leads to the reexamination of the significance and structure of perceptual life (Merleau-Ponty), the locus of existence and language (Heidegger), and the question of the nature of intentionality with its implications for a theory of evidence (Husserl and Gurwitsch). Each of these larger issues is a focal concern of the following essays.

At the same time it will become clearer that in the efforts to reach an authentically fundamental philosophical criticism which remains in touch with the human situation different directions are taken. "Consciousness" as intentionality stands central to the transcendentally oriented philosophies of Gurwitsch and Husserl. Merleau-Ponty locates consciousness within the "primacy" of perception. And Heidegger roots human existence within the sense of "being-in" to be found eminently in the essence of language. Not only are these different thrusts, but under way the basic understandings of consciousness and experience, of sense perception, of language begin to receive new understandings out of the perspectives opened by these returns to such perennial philosophical problems.

101

ARON GURWITSCH (1901-   )

Born January 17, 1901, in Vilna, Lithuania, Aron Gurwitsch studied science, psychology and philosophy, later going to Freiburg to study under Husserl. He received his degree from the University of Göttingen summa cum laude in 1928. He teaches at the New School for Social Research in New York. His principal works are: *Theory of the Field of Consciousness* (1958) and *Studies in Phenomenology and Psychology* (1970).

ON THE INTENTIONALITY OF CONSCIOUSNESS*[1]

The intentionality of consciousness may be defined as a relation which all, or at least certain, acts bear to an object. In this manner, Brentano introduced the notion into contemporary philosophy. Seeking to account for the difference between what he calls "physical phenomena" and what he calls "psychical phenomena," Brentano found, among other characteristics, that the latter are distinguished by a relation to, or a direction towards, an object.[2] This directedness of psychical phenomena is interpreted by Brentano as their containing within themselves an "immanent" object-like entity. Although Husserl takes over Brentano's notion of intentionality, he raises some objections

* By permission of Northwestern University Press. From Aron Gurwitsch, *Studies in Phenomenology and Psychology*, Northwestern University Press, Evanston, Illinois, 1966.

[1] This article was originally published in *Philosophical Essays in Memory of Edmund Husserl*, ed. M. Farber (Cambridge, Mass.: Harvard University Press, 1940). Copyright © 1940 by the President and Fellows of Harvard College. Reprinted by permission of the publishers.

[2] F. Brentano, *Psychologie vom empirischen Standpunkt*, ed. O. Kraus (Leipzig, 1924), Book II, chap. I, para. 5.

against this interpretation.[3] His examination of Brentano's conception of intentionality finally leads him to abandon it completely; but he agrees with Brentano in acknowledging the existence of a highly important class of mental facts—for which Husserl reserves the title of acts—which have the peculiarity of presenting an object to the subject.[4] Experiencing an act, the subject is aware of an object, so that the act may be characterized, as Husserl shows, as a *consciousness of* an object whether real or ideal, whether existent or imaginary.

This peculiarity, however, ought not to be considered as a real quality or as a real property of acts, such, for example, as intensity, which is held by many psychologists to be a real property common to all sense data. In fact, one would be bestowing on an act a magic or at least mysterious power were one to ascribe to the act, under the heading of intentionality, a real quality which makes it transcend itself to seize an object belonging, as is the case in the perception of a real thing, to a universe external to the sphere of consciousness, to which the act, though endowed with the transcending quality, nevertheless remains tied. Conscious acts confront us with objects; experiencing such an act, the subject is aware of an object, and he is so aware owing to the reference that act bears in itself to the object. The objectivating function of consciousness is, however, a problem rather than a simple datum which one could content himself to take notice of. In fact, the objectivating function involves a whole complex set of problems. Out of these we choose the most elementary one. *To be aware of an object means that, in the present experience, one is aware of the object as being the same as that which one was aware of in the past experience, as the same as that which, generally speaking, one may be aware of in an indefinite number of presentative acts.* Identity in this sense is, no doubt, constitutive of objectivity (*Gegenständlichkeit*). But, even if considered on the most elementary level, the identity of objects, inasmuch as it is a conscious fact—and it is only for this reason that we have any knowledge of it and may talk of it—turns out to be an insoluble prob-

---

[3] E. Husserl, *Logische Untersuchungen* (Halle, 1913), II, v, secs. 9-11; Husserl, *Ideen zu einer reinen Phänomenologie und phänomenologischen Philosophie* (Halle, 1929), sec. 90. Lack of space forbids us to summarize Husserl's criticism of Brentano's doctrine; some essential differences between Brentano's and Husserl's conceptions are emphasized by L. Landgrebe, "Husserl's Phänomenologie und die Motive zu ihrer Umbildung," in *Revue Internationale de Philosophie*, I.

[4] Husserl, *Logische Untersuchungen*, II, p. 378.

lem for the traditional conception of consciousness. We shall go on to show, if possible, that the treatment of this problem leads to a new conception of consciousness that is radically opposed to the traditional one.

[I] The Problem of Identity as Stated by Hume

Let us consider the problem of identity in its most accentuated form, as stated by Hume concerning perceptible things.

Following Locke and Berkeley, Hume asserts "that our ideas of bodies are nothing but collections formed by the mind of the ideas of the several distinct sensible qualities, of which objects are composed, and which we find to have a constant union with each other."[5] Now the "sensible qualities" in question are identified, by Hume as well as by his predecessors, with the sensations which are produced in the mind when a perceptual act is experienced; these "sensible qualities" are taken for real elements, of which the perceptual experience is composed; consequently they pass for real elements of consciousness itself, i.e., for elements existing within consciousness. Hence the object, being composed of the same data which figure in the perceptual experience, turns out to be a real element of this experience and to coincide with it; at any rate, the object itself is also conceived to exist within consciousness and to be a content of it. This thesis is indeed defended by Hume. "Those very sensations, which enter by the eye or ear, are . . . the true objects . . . there is only a single existence, which I shall call indifferently *object* or *perception* . . . understanding by both of them what any common man means by a hat, or shoe, or stone, or any other impression conveyed to him by his senses."[6] This thesis is presented by Hume not as a result of philosophical inquiry but as the opinion of the "vulgar," i.e., the opinion of all of us, when, without philosophizing, we live in the natural attitude and are concerned with any things we find in our surroundings.

Nevertheless, a problem inevitably arises in this connection. Taking up again the observation of a thing we have already observed some time

[5] D. Hume, *A Treatise of Human Nature*, ed. T. H. Green and T. H. Grose (London, 1890), I, pp. 505-6. Cf. J. Locke, *An Essay Concerning Human Understanding*, Book II, chap. XXIII, especially secs. 6, 14; G. Berkeley, *A Treatise Concerning the Principles of Human Knowledge*, in *Works*, ed. A. C. Fraser, Vol. I (Oxford, 1901), p. 258.

[6] Hume, *A Treatise of Human Nature*, I, p. 491.

ago, as, for example, shutting and opening our eyes alternately, we obtain a set of sense data. The latter may resemble one another to a very high degree, yet they remain distinct from one another and do not fuse, in any manner whatever, into a single one. We can enumerate these multiple sense data by means of the perceptual acts which we experience successively and to which the data belong respectively. Nevertheless we believe—we do so as the "vulgar"—that we are in the presence not of a set of objects, however much they resemble one another, but of one single object appearing as identically the same in every one of the successive experiences. In the very face of the multiplicity of sense data, the identity of the object and our belief in it must be accounted for, without forgetting that the object is conceived as a complex composed of sense data. In these terms Hume stated the problem, and the solution he adduced for it is well known.[7] Because of the resemblance among the sense data, the mind passes so smoothly and so easily from one to another that it is scarcely aware of the transition. This resemblance puts the mind in a state similar to that in which it is when it surveys, without interruption, an unchangeable object for some time; this latter state gives rise to the idea of identity.[8] Thus, on account of the double resemblance, the mind mistakes similarity for identity. . . . The belief in the singleness of the perceived object rests on confounding resembling, yet distinct, sense data with identical ones.[9]

The mere presence to the mind of sensuous data composing an object is not sufficient for giving rise to the idea of its identity. Hume is perfectly right in emphasizing that the notion of identity needs that of time.[10] This means, in the case under discussion, that the object perceived now, after opening the eyes again, is held to be the same as that which appeared before shutting the eyes. Perceiving the object, the mind must recall previous perceptions; the impressions which are now present to the mind must be attended with ideas, which, although resembling the former at all points, differ from them, according to

[7] *Ibid.*, p. 493: "The very image, which is present to the sense, is with us the real body; and 'tis to these interrupted images we ascribe a perfect identity"; cf. pp. 491-94.

[8] We shall come back later to the identity of an object observed uninterruptedly for some time.

[9] Cf. Hume, *A Treatise of Human Nature*, I, p. 535.

[10] *Ibid.*, pp. 489-90.

Hume's doctrine, with respect to force and vividness. In order to conceive identity, the mind must confront itself with a plurality of items. But as soon as it has done so, it must overlook not only the differences as to intensity but also, and chiefly, the fact that it has presented to itself a plurality of items. Since identity consists in the illusion of holding the resembling but distinct items to be a single one, the function of the imagination in producing this illusion is such as to abolish the condition that is indispensable to put the imagination into function.[11]

This illusion therefore can subsist only as long as the subject is inattentive to what really happens in his mind. The contradiction, however, between the experienced succession of sense data and the irresistible propensity created by imagination to mistake them for a single and identical one is too striking to be overlooked. To disentangle itself from this contradiction, the imagination devises the further fiction of a "continued existence" ascribed to the "broken and interrupted appearances."[12] But this new fiction cannot help Hume, since only in case the identity of the object, perceived after the interruption with that perceived before it, has been established may the question be raised as to the existence of the object during the interruption.

The case is the same with the identity of an object observed for some time without interruption.[13] Under these circumstances, identity means "*invariableness* and *uninterruptedness* of any object, through a supposed variation of time." Variation of time implies succession and change, if not in the object in question, which is supposed to be permanent and unaltered, then in the co-existent objects. Nevertheless, the

---

[11] In the excellent analysis which J. Laporte ("Le scepticisme de Hume," in the *Revue Philosophique de la France et de l'Etranger,* CXV [1933], pp. 92-101) gives of the passages of the *Treatise* referred to here, he emphasizes the stress Hume laid on the "operation" of the mind in producing the illusion of identity. Laporte's analysis, however, renders the more obvious the contradiction upon which we insist. The operation of the mind does not consist in making something out of the materials for which this operation is employed, as is the case when objects are united into an ensemble, when they are numbered, when a perceived matter of fact enters into a judgment and undergoes categorial formation, and so on. Here, on the contrary, the operation, as it were, has to make disappear, before the mind, the materials necessary to set it going.

[12] Hume, *A Treatise of Human Nature,* I, pp. 494-97. We must disregard here Hume's account of continuous existence.

[13] *Ibid.,* pp. 489-90.

unchangeable object is imagined to participate in these changes, without suffering, in itself, any modification whatever.[14] Again, on the one hand, succession and variation of time must not only happen in fact but must also be experienced by consciousness, for otherwise there would be only a single permanent object, and the mind would be given the idea, not of identity, but of unity. On the other hand, the transition from one moment to another, which constitutes duration and variation of time, must scarcely be felt, no other perception or idea must be brought into play, in order that the disposition of the mind might be such as to continue surveying one permanent, unchangeable, identical object.[15] Variation of time must be felt, but not enough to produce any alteration in the mind's activity. Once more the operation of imagination is in contradiction to the very condition of this operation.

If Hume's explanation of identity is untenable, it is not because identity is held to be a "fiction," i.e., a creation of imagination. Had Hume contented himself with asserting that identity is no matter of sensibility but results from another mental faculty—namely, imagination—he would have advanced a two-factor theory of perception. Such a theory is, no doubt, open to criticism, but it cannot be rejected as inconsistent, the main objection which, it seems, is to be made against Hume's theory. His task is to account for the fact that the perceiving subject, experiencing these impressions and by means of them, is aware of something identical, despite impressions being "internal and perishing existences," subject to variation of time, so that none of them when once passed can ever return.[16] But there is no room in Hume's doctrine both for *identity* and for *temporality*. It is highly significant that Hume talks of our tending to "disguise, as much as possible, the interruption," to "remove the seeming interruption by feigning a continued being."[17] If we could sacrifice either identity or temporality, we would get rid of the irreconcilable contradiction in which these principles stand to each other; but we cannot, because of the irresistible tendency created by the imagination to ascribe identity to resembling per-

---

[14] It will be shown later that the "participation" of an object which stands before consciousness for some time, and which during this time is given as permanent and identical, in those changes which constitute its presence-time and its duration, is not a "fiction" but an immediately experienced fact.

[15] Hume, *A Treatise of Human Nature*, I, p. 492.

[16] *Ibid.*, p. 483.

[17] *Ibid.*, pp. 488, 496.

ceptions, on the one hand, and because, on the other hand, the interruptions of these perceptions are too striking to be overlooked.[18] *Identity and temporality turn out then, for Hume, not only to oppose but even to exclude each other.* . . . Philosophical reflection comes to show the falsehood of this belief, without, however, being able to shake it seriously.[19] According to whether we adopt the attitude of practical life or the philosophical one, we waver from instinctive and natural opinion to "studied reflections," without ever gaining a conclusive solution of the problem.[20] Thus Hume fails to account for a very simple fact, familiar to the "vulgar" in their everyday lives, the fact formulated by saying: The thing I see now, I saw some time ago, and tomorrow I shall take up its observation. In a case like this, identity as well as temporality stand before the subject's mind, whether his attention bears upon the one or upon the other.

The ultimate reason for Hume's failure is to be sought, I submit, in his general conception of consciousness. ". . . the true idea of the human mind," he says, "is to consider it as a system of different perceptions or different existences, which . . . mutually produce, destroy, influence, and modify each other. . . . One thought chases another, and draws after it a third, by which it is expelled in its turn."[21] *Consciousness is then conceived as a unidimensional sphere of being, whose fundamental structure consists only and exclusively in temporality.* What constitutes the mind "are the successive perceptions only," the mind being "nothing but a bundle or collection of different perceptions which succeed each other with an inconceivable rapidity, and are in a perpetual flux and movement."[22] Hume expressly likens consciousness to a theatre; but it is, so to speak, a theatre without a stage. In modern terminology, one could compare consciousness with a perpetual succession of cinematographic pictures.

Whatever differences may exist among the different kinds of perceptions, "primary qualities," "secondary qualities," passions, affections, and so on, insofar as they are perceptions, i.e., contents of consciousness, they must be taken to be on the same footing and to have the

[18] *Ibid.*, p. 494.
[19] Cf. *ibid.*, pp. 497-98, 501-5.
[20] *Ibid.*, pp. 535-36.
[21] *Ibid.*, pp. 541-42.
[22] *Ibid.*, pp. 534-35.

same manner of existence.[23] That is to say, all of them are real events happening in the stream of consciousness; they appear and disappear, and every one of them has its place in this stream with relation to other events belonging to the same stream. Nothing can ever be found in consciousness but such an event, one picture among others which precede or succeed it and which in their succession constitute the conscious life.[24] Being aware of an object is reduced to the mere presence in consciousness of a real content.[25] Hence the identification mentioned above of sensible qualities with sensations, through which the former appear, both designated, as a rule, by the same terms, as color, smoothness, raggedness, and so on.[26] After all, the object as composed of real contents of consciousness must itself become a real element in the conscious stream. For consciousness conceived in this way there can indeed exist nothing identical.[27]

Though formulated by Hume in the most explicit manner, this conception of consciousness as a unidimensional sphere constituted by the mere succession of real events was already effective with Locke and with Berkeley and—as far as I can see—it has been embraced more or less explicitly by all philosophers up to the present day. With regard to the problem under discussion, it makes no great difference whether the perceptions are considered, with Hume, as distinguishable and separable from one another[28] or whether, like James[29] and Bergson, one lays stress upon the continuity of the stream of consciousness and upon the interpenetration of the mental states, so that demarcations may no longer be drawn to separate them from one

[23] Cf., *ibid.*, pp. 480, 482-83.

[24] Cf., *ibid*, p. 487: ". . . nothing is ever really present to the mind, besides its own perceptions."

[25] Cf., *ibid.*, p. 483: ". . . every thing which appears to the mind is nothing but a perception, and is interrupted, and dependent on the mind."

[26] See Husserl's criticism of this confusion in *Logische Untersuchungen*, II, v, sec. 2, and *Ideen,* sec. 41.

[27] It is worth noting that even the identity of objects undergoing a real change, by the addition or diminution of parts, is explained by Hume in some cases by inattention. The essential condition of ascribing identity in such cases is that the changes be insignificant enough not to strike the mind. (*A Treatise of Human Nature*, I, pp. 537-38.)

[28] *Ibid.*, p. 495.

[29] W. James, *The Principles of Psychology* (London, 1908), I, pp. 237-43.

another.[30] This conception constitutes the ultimate sense of what Husserl calls *psychologism*.[31] What is true for perceptible objects belonging to the real world holds good also for mathematical entities, for significations, propositions, and for all kinds of products of logical thinking. Reduced to the real elements and contents which constitute the acts of awareness of them, none of these objects can ever be apprehended as the same, in an indefinite number of acts. Since objectivity is to be defined by this sameness of the object as opposed to the multiple acts, whether they be experienced by one person or by different persons, on the basis of the conception of consciousness under discussion there can be no objects at all, of any kind whatever.

[II] Husserl's Noesis-Noema Doctrine

The preceding discussion leaves us with the problem of how identical and identifiable objects may exist for, and stand before, a consciousness whose acts perpetually succeed one another; every one of these acts, in addition to their succeeding one another, incessantly undergoing temporal variations. For what is meant by James's "stream of thought" and by Bergson's *durée* does express an experienced reality, of which we may become conscious at any moment, if we are attentive to what happens in our conscious lives.

A solution has been given to this problem by Husserl by means of his theory of intentionality; and as far as I know, it is the only one that exists. Lack of space prevents me from studying the growth of this theory throughout Husserl's writings. When in the *Logische Untersuchungen* he tackled intentionality for the first time, Husserl was not yet dealing with the problem we have emphasized. His theory of intentionality gradually got a reference to this problem, and though this reference did not become manifest until the *Formale und transzendentale Logik,* it seems to us that the form in which intentionality is advanced in the *Ideen,* chiefly in the *noesis-noema doctrine,* already constitutes an answer to our problem. Taking the noesis-noema doctrine into consideration from this point of view, we shall proceed beyond what was explicitly formulated by Husserl himself.

When an object is perceived, there is, on the one hand, the act with its elements, whatever they may be: the act as a real event in psychical life,

---

[30] H. Bergson, *Essai sur les données immediates de la conscience,* chap. II.

[31] Cf. *Formale und transzendentale Logik* (Halle, 1929), secs. 56-58, 62, 65.

happening at a certain moment of phenomenal time, appearing, lasting, disappearing, and, when it has disappeared, never returning. On the other hand, there is what, in this concrete act, stands before the perceiving subject's mind.[32] Let the thing perceived be a tree. This tree, at any rate, presents itself in a well-determined manner: it shows itself from this side rather than from that; it stands straight before the observer or occupies a rather lateral position; it is near the perceiving subject or removed from him at a considerable distance, and so on.[33] Finally, it offers itself with a certain prospect, e.g., as giving shade, or, when the subject perceiving the tree recalls to his mind his past life, the tree perceived appears in the light of this or that scene of his youth. What has been described by these allusions is the *noema of perception*—namely, the object just (exactly so and only so) as the perceiving subject is aware of it, as he intends it in this concrete experienced mental state. It is with respect to the noema that the given perception is not only a perception of this determined object but is also that awareness of the object rather than another; that is to say, the subject experiencing the act in question, the *noesis,* finds himself confronted with a certain object appearing from such a side, in the orientation it has, in a certain aspect, and so on. Hence the noema may also be designated as the perceptual sense.

The noema is to be distinguished from the real object.[34] The latter, the tree for instance, as a real thing appears now in this determined manner; but it may offer itself from a different side, at another distance, in a different orientation and aspect; and it does so in fact when the subject goes around it. It shows itself in a multiplicity of perceptions, through all of which the same real tree presents itself; but the "perceived tree as such" varies according to the standpoint, the orientation, the attitude, etc., of the perceiving subject, as when for instance he looks at the tree from above or at another time perceives it while in the garden. Indeed, a real thing may not present itself as such except by means of a series of perceptions succeeding one another.[35] These perceptions enter into a synthesis of identification with one another, and it is by, and in, this synthesis and the parallel synthesis among the cor-

[32] Husserl, *Ideen,* sec. 88.
[33] E. Husserl, *Cartesian Meditations,* trans. D. Cairns (The Hague, 1960), pp. 39f.
[34] Husserl, *Ideen,* secs. 89-90.
[35] *Ibid.,* secs. 42, 44, 143.

responding noemata that what appears successively constitutes itself, for consciousness, into this real thing which it is, one and identical as opposed to the multiple perceptions and also to the multiple noemata.[36] Hence problems arise as to the relation of the act and its noema to the real thing perceived through the act and, further, as to what relations the noemata uniting themselves by the synthesis of identification bear to one another.[37] At any rate, it is obvious that the real object ought not to be confounded with a single noema.

On the other hand, the noema is distinct from the act in the sense that it does not constitute a part, an element, a factor of the act and does not really exist within consciousness, as the act does.[38] When, looking at a thing, we alternately shut and open our eyes again, without any change in the position of our body or in the direction of the glance, we experience a number of perceptual acts, all different from one another. Through every one of these acts, however, not only does the same object offer itself, but it appears also in the same aspect and orientation, from the same side, at the same distance, and so on. The tree presents itself now in exactly the same manner as it did a moment ago, as it did yesterday, as it is expected to do tomorrow. The "perceived tree as such" is identically the same, notwithstanding the variety of the acts to which it corresponds. *In the noema,* then, *we have something identical* which, for this very reason, ought not to be mistaken for an element of the corresponding act. Were it such an element, it would appear and disappear with the act, and it would be tied up, as the act is, to the place the latter occupies in phenomenal time.

The noema, as distinct from the real object as well as from the act, turns out to be an irreal or ideal entity which belongs to the same sphere as meanings or significations. This is the sphere of sense (*Sinn*).[39] The irreality of entities belonging to this sphere lies, first of all, in their atemporality, i.e., in a certain independence of the concrete act by which they are actualized, in the sense that every one of them may correspond, as identically the same, to another act, and even to an indefinite number of acts. Noemata are not to be found in perceptual life alone. There is a noema corresponding to every act of memory, expecta-

---

[36] *Ibid.,* secs. 41, 86, 135, 145, 150; Husserl, *Cartesian Meditations,* secs. 17-18.

[37] Husserl, *Ideen,* secs. 98, 128-31.

[38] *Ibid.,* sec. 97.

[39] *Ibid.,* sec. 133.

tion, representation, imagination, thinking, judging, volition, and so on.[40] In all these cases, the object, matter of fact, etc., in itself, towards which the subject directs himself through the act, is to be distinguished from the object just, exactly just, as the subject has it in view, as, through the act, the object stands before the subject's mind. With regard to judging, the difference is between *objects about which* and *that which is judged as such.*[41] It is worth noting that somehow James anticipated Husserl's notion of the noema of thinking and judging.[42]

Husserl's noesis-noema doctrine, which we must content ourselves with summarizing briefly, far from being a constructive or explanatory theory, is simply a descriptive statement of an objectivating mental state, i.e., of a mental state through which the experiencing subject is confronted with an object. Every mental state of this kind must then be accounted for in terms of identity as well as of temporality. The traditional conception of consciousness, in which emphasis is placed upon temporality, the succession of acts and the variations each act undergoes by its duration, is certainly not false, since the fact emphasized is a real fact of consciousness. But this conception is incomplete and unilateral. No mental state is to be conceived only and exclusively as a real and temporal event in the stream of consciousness, without any reference to a sense. This reference is overlooked in the traditional conception. *Identity is to be acknowledged as a fact irreducible to any other; it turns out to be a fact of consciousness, no less authentic and no less fundamental than temporality is.* Thus we are led to a duality. And it must be stressed that this duality holds good even for the most elementary level of consciousness, where the question concerns the repeated appearance of an object in the same manner of presentation, without there being a need for going on to consider the appearance of an object one time in perception, another time in memory, representation, etc., and, still more, to take into consideration the successive presentations of an object, appearing as identically the same, from various sides and in the most different aspects.

[III] Temporality and Identity

Before setting out the general conception of consciousness implied in,

[40] *Ibid.,* sec. 91, 93-95.
[41] Husserl, *Formale und transzendentale Logik,* secs. 42, 44-45, 48.
[42] James, *The Principles of Psychology,* I, pp. 275-76.

and following from, the noesis-noema doctrine, let us look at the nature of this duality and at the relation between the terms composing it.

That identity is a fundamental fact in conscious life does not signify a permanent explicit awareness of it. In all perceiving, thinking, judging, and so on, in all theoretical and practical life, we make use of the identity of the objects we deal with. When perceiving a thing, for instance, we take it for the same as that perceived some time ago, or when thinking of a proposition, we hold it to be the same as the one which we demonstrated yesterday, and then go on to verify this demonstration (the same as that performed yesterday) or to reason further upon the basis of this proposition. So we may behave and so we do behave, without necessarily grasping identity in an explicit way, although all of our behavior is constantly guided by it. The object with which we are concerned is our theme, and our only one; as a rule, the identity of this object does not constitute a secondary theme accompanying the former. But, of course, identity may be rendered explicit to the subject's mind and may be taken as a theme. How then does it become so? In what way do we get an originary awareness of identity?

A perceived object offers itself in a certain manner of presentation. Experiencing such a perception, we are free to remember past perceptions and to look forward to future perceptions, so that to all these mental states, past as well as future ones, there corresponds the same noema as that corresponding to the present experienced perception. Thus we become aware in an originary way of the noema and of its identity, as distinct from, and opposed to, the multiple acts to which it corresponds. It is of no importance if the past experiences are recalled with a more or less exact temporal determination or if the moment at which the future acts are expected to happen may be foreseen with some exactness. It is not even necessary that the acts taken into consideration be recalled perceptions—i.e., appear as having been present at a past moment—or that the experiences considered as future be expected really to happen. For our present purposes, it will be quite sufficient to conceive acts as possible or potential, as differing from one another and also from the present perception, and yet as actualizing the same noema. Acts through which the same object appears and offers itself in the same manner of presentation can differ from one another only as to the moments in conscious time at which each of them takes place. At any rate, *we may not render identity of the noema explicit and ascertain it by an originary experience unless we also become aware of the temporality of consciousness.*

Noematic identity may be brought up to explicitness, even without taking into consideration acts different from the present experienced one, on the condition that there be reflection upon the duration of the latter. Duration consists in, and manifests itself for consciousness by, an incessant transformation of every "actual now" into a "having just been an actual now." When time is elapsing, the present moment does not sink into the past, so that it could not be recalled again to the mind, except by reproduction; on the contrary, the present moment, ceasing to be present, is yet retained in "primary memory" and takes the form of "having just been present."[43] At once what has just been present, relative to the actual now, when transformed in the manner mentioned, undergoes a transformation in its turn, passing into a "retention of a retention"; it is then removed still more from the occasional actual now, until it disappears from immediate memory, no longer being retained.[44] Thus reflecting on what really happens in consciousness, at every moment we find a continuous variation and transformation: a continuous passing of the present phase into a retained one and then of a phase given in a retention of any degree into a retention of a higher degree, a continuous iteration of this transformation.[45] Upon these incessant variations is based the stream-character of consciousness, which, owing to their continuity, is experienced as a unidimensional order.[46] What is involved in these transformations is, however, not the object perceived or its manner of presentation but only its temporal orientation, its temporal modes of appearance.[47] In other words: what is concerned is the act rather than its noema, the fact that a perceived object as such stands before consciousness rather than the perceived object as such itself. Looking at the stream elapsing, we become explicitly aware of the fact that the perceived object as such has already appeared for a long time, or that it has just begun to appear, and—if we also allow for protentions—that we expect it to continue appearing, or that we foresee interruption of its appearance, and so on. Once more, *explicit awareness of identity requires that of temporality* and, in the

[43] As to the difference between "primary memory" (retention) and "secondary memory" (reproduction), see E. Husserl, *Vorlesungen zur Phänomenologie des inneren Zeitbewusstseins* (Halle, 1928), sec. 19.

[44] *Ibid.*, secs. 8, 10.

[45] *Ibid.*, sec. 39 and Supplement I.

[46] *Ibid.*, sec. 36 and pp. 466-67.

[47] *Ibid.*, secs. 30-31 and Supplement IV.

case just analyzed, even of *intrinsic temporality*. Hume was then perfectly right in referring to temporality when he sought to account for identity.

On the other hand, were there nothing identical standing before consciousness, awareness of temporality would no longer be possible. With this hypothesis, retentional modifications could no longer be variations in the temporal orientations of something which may successively assume different temporal orientations. The very reality of conscious life, when an act is an enduring one, is a phase of present actuality most intimately connected with a whole continuity of phases retained (in retentions of various degrees), all these phases being related to one another and the phase of present actuality constituting a limit of this continuity.[48] With identity hypothetically omitted, however, instead of this continuity of phases there could be only a set of punctiform act-impulses among which one would bear the character of actual presence, whereas the others would be given characters different from one another as well as from that of the former. All these act-impulses, though simultaneously given, would still remain in isolation from one another; at any rate, they would lack the intrinsic relationship to connect them into a unitary act—for the unity of an enduring act is possible only with regard to something identical whose appearance may assume different temporal phases.[49] Conscious life being in incessant variation, at every moment one set of such act-impulses would be displaced by another one, without any intrinsic reference between them; for such a reference supposes the same to pass from one temporal phase into another. At every moment, then, the unity and the continuity of conscious life would be broken off. Experienced time consists just in the progressive removal either of a certain phase of an act or of the act in its entirety from the actual now, in such a way that what is being removed appears as having been, a moment ago, nearer to the actual now than it is at present. Therefore a consciousness for which nothing was identical, as in the hypothesis under discussion, could not become aware of time. Consequently for such a consciousness time would not exist at all.[50]

It is then by way of the very same reflection that the subject, in an

---

[48] *Ibid.*, sec. 16. For the sake of brevity we confine the discussion to the intrinsic temporality of an enduring act.

[49] *Ibid.*, Supplement XI.

[50] *Ibid.*, pp. 376-77.

originary way, ascertains the identity of the object offering itself in a certain manner of presentation, of the noema, as well as the temporality of the noema's appearance, the duration of its appearance, and all changes the duration carries with itself. Temporality and identity are, no doubt, poles opposed to each other. As against Hume, however, *they are poles which do not exclude but require each other. Temporality and identity are related to each other like the terms of a correlation.* This is indeed the nature of the duality to which Husserl's noesis-noema doctrine leads.

[IV] The Correlation Conception of Consciousness

To each act there corresponds a noema—namely, an object just, exactly and only just, as the subject is aware of it and has it in view, when he is experiencing the act in question. *Consciousness* is not to be mistaken for a mere unidimensional sphere composed of acts, as real psychical events, which co-exist with and succeed one another. Rather, it ought to be considered as a *correlation, or correspondence, or parallelism between the plane of acts, psychical events, noeses, and a second plane which is that of sense (noemata).* This correlation is such that corresponding to each act is its noema, but the same noema may correspond to an indefinite number of acts. It is then not a one-to-one correspondence.

The noetico-noematic correlation is what the term intentionality must signify. In this light the formula consciousness *of* something is to be understood: a conscious act is an act of awareness, presenting to the subject who experiences it a sense, an ideal atemporal unity, identical, i.e., identifiable.[51] It is not by virtue of favorable circumstances calling for an explanation and for a reduction to more elementary facts but by virtue of what constitutes the nature of consciousness itself that an experienced act bears a reference to a sense. Consciousness is to be defined by its bearing reference to a sphere of sense, so that *to experience an act is the same thing as to actualize a sense.* Hence every fact of consciousness must be treated in terms of the relation *cogito-cogitatum qua cogitatum,* and no mental state may be accounted for except with regard to the objective sense (*gegenständlicher Sinn*), of

[51] Husserl, *Cartesian Meditations*, p. 33.

which the experiencing subject becomes aware through this act.[52]

Intentionality means the objectivating function of consciousness. In its most elementary form, this function consists in confronting the subject with senses, ideal unities, to which, as identical ones, he is free to revert an indefinite number of times. No sooner than this elementary structure of the objectivating function has been established, problems may be tackled as to higher structures of intentionality, concerning, for instance, syntheses by means of which particular perceptual senses are united into systems which are the real perceptual things, concerning categorial forms bestowed upon the perceptual data in thinking, concerning syntactical operations by which, in apophantics, more and more complicated meanings and significations are constructed from simpler ones, and so on.[53] All structures of intentionality rest upon the neotico-noematic correlation, which, for this reason, is the most elementary structure. But it is, at the same time, also the most fundamental and the most universal one, since every sense entity, of whatever kind and of whatever degree of complication, is an identical and identifiable unity, to which the subject may come back again and again. Thus the noetico-noematic parallelism enters into all forms of mental activity; and it is to it that one is led by the basic problems of logic.[54]

The objectivating function belongs to an act, but not as taken in itself and as isolated from other mental states. On the contrary, this function is possessed by an act even when the latter has the distinctive character of evidence or self-presentation, on account of its being inserted into the whole of the experiencing life and only with regard to this whole.[55] Objectivity is identifiableness, i.e., the possibility of reverting again and again to what, through the present experienced act, is offered to consciousness and the possibility of so doing whether in the same or in any

[52] *Ibid.*, p. 36; Husserl, *Formale und transzendentale Logik*, p. 120; Husserl, "Nachwort zu meinen 'Ideen zu einer reinen Phänomenologie und phänomenologischen Philosophie,' " in *Jahrbuch für Philosophie und phänomenologische Forschung* (Halle, 1930), XI, 6.

[53] Husserl, *Logische Untersuchungen*, II, vi, chap. VI; II, iv, sec. 3; Husserl, *Formale und transzendentale Logik*, sec. 13.

[54] Husserl, *Formale und transzendentale Logik*, sec. 73.

[55] *Ibid.*, pp. 142-43.

other mode of awareness.[56] This holds good for real as well as ideal objects.[57] It holds good also for "inner perception." When a present experienced mental state is grasped by an act of reflection and is thus made the object of this act of inner perception, the latter possesses the character of evidence, since the apprehended act is offered directly, immediately, and bodily, not by memory or in any symbolic manner. Nevertheless, it is not on this account that the act of inner perception is objectivating; it is so only because what appears through it, although its self-presentation never can be actualized again, may yet be recalled later and may be so an indefinite number of times.[58] Objectivity and identity, then, have sense with regard to a multiplicity of acts—that is to say, with reference to the temporality of conscious life. These analyses of Husserl concerning objectivity, by which he has cleared up the ultimate meaning of his struggle against psychologism,[59] throw a new light upon the correlation conception of consciousness advanced here.

Though never formulated by Husserl in quite explicit terms, this conception seems to be at the root of a large part of his theories, and, when his work is considered in its growth, this conception reveals itself, I submit, to be one of the teleological goals towards which phenomenology is tending.

[56] *Ibid.*, p. 139.
[57] *Ibid.*, secs. 61-62.
[58] *Ibid.*, pp. 140-41 and sec. 107b.
[59] *Ibid.*, secs. 56-57, 65, 67.

TRANSCENDENTAL PHENOMENOLOGY AND INTENTIONAL PSYCHOLOGY. THE PROBLEM OF TRANSCENDENTAL PSYCHOLOGISM.*

EDMUND HUSSERL

Sec. 94. Every Existent Constituted in the Subjectivity of Consciousness.

Let us make clear to ourselves the sense of transcendental problems. Every science has its province, and aims at the theory of its province. In that theory it has its result. But scientific reason is what makes those results; and experiential reason is what makes the province. This is true in the case of formal logic, with its higher-level relation to something existent and perhaps to any possible world; this is true in the case of its theory, as having a higher-level universality relating likewise to all particular theories. Something existent, theory, reason—these do not come together accidentally; and they must not be presupposed as a trio assembled accidentally, even though "with unconditional universality and necessity". This very necessity and universality must be examined, as pertaining to the logically thinking subject, to *me* as a subject who can submit himself only to a logic that he himself thinks through, and has thought through, with insight.—To me, because at first here no reference is made to any other reason than mine, nor to any other experience or theory than mine, nor to any other existent than an existent that I legitimate by experience, and that, as something somehow meant or supposed, must be in my field of consciousness if I am to produce a theory with it, in my theoretic acting, in my evidence.

As in everyday life, so too in science (unless, under the misguidance of "realistic" epistemology, it misinterprets its own doing) experience is the consciousness of being with the matters themselves, of seizing upon and having them quite directly. But experience is not an opening through which a world, existing prior to all experience, shines into a room of consciousness; it is not a mere taking of something alien to consciousness into consciousness. For how could I make a rational state-

---

* By permission of Martinus Nijhoff. From Edmund Husserl, *Formal and Transcendental Logic*, Martinus Nijhoff, Gravenhage, The Netherlands, 1927. This selection is from chapter 6.

ment to that effect, without seeing such a state-of-affairs and therefore seeing not only consciousness but also the something alien to consciousness—that is: *experiencing* the alien affair? And how could I objectivate such a state-of-affairs as at least a conceivability? Would that not be immersing myself intuitively in such a countersensical experiencing of something alien to experience? Experience is the performance in which for me, the experiencer, experienced being "is there", and is there *as what* it is, with the whole content and the mode of being that experience itself, by the performance going on in its intentionality, attributes to it. If what is experienced has the sense of *"transcendent" being,* then it is the experiencing that constitutes this sense, and does so either by itself or in the whole motivational nexus pertaining to it and helping to make up its intentionality. If an experience is *imperfect*, if it makes the intrinsically existent object appear only one-sidedly, only in a distant perspective, or the like, then the experience itself, as this current mode of consciousness, is that which, on being consulted, tells me so; it tells me: Here, in this consciousness, something is given as it itself; but it is more than what is actually itself grasped; there is more of the same object to be experienced. Thus the object is transcendent; and also in that, as experience further teaches me, it could have been an illusion, though it presented itself as actual and as itself seized upon. Moreover, it is again experience that says: These physical things, this world, is utterly transcendent of me, of my own being. It is an "Objective" world, experienceable and experienced, as the same world by others too. Actuality becomes warranted, illusion rectified, in my concourse with others—who likewise are, for me, data of actual and possible experience. Experience is what tells me here: I have experience of myself with primary originality; of others, of another's psychic life, with a merely secondary originality, since another's psychic life is essentially inaccessible to me in direct perception. The currently experienced (physical things, I myself, others, and so forth), the current More that could be experienced, the self-identity with which the experienced extends throughout manifold experiences, the pointing ahead by every sort of experience on the different levels of originality to new possible experiences of the same (first of all, possible experiences of my own and, at a higher level, possible experiences belonging to others), to the style of progressive experience, and to what this would bring out as existing and being thus and so—each and all of these are included intentionally in the consciousness itself, as this actual and potential intentionality, whose structure I can at any time *consult.*

structures of consciousness can be found.

And I *must* consult it, if I intend to understand what is actually the case here: that nothing exists for me otherwise than by virtue of the *actual and potential performance of my own consciousness*. Here the potential performance is the certainty of "I can" or "I could", which is predelineated in the sphere itself of my consciousness, starting from the actually present intentionality—the certainty, namely, that I could bring into play synthetically connected sequences of consciousness, with the unitary effect that I should continue to be conscious of the same object. In particular that includes, a priori, the potentiality of intuitions actualizable by me—experiences, evidences—in which this same object would show itself, and become determined, in continuous harmony: thereby continuously confirming its actual being. *That* this object is not only accepted as existent by me but also actually existent for me because of "good", because of "indubitable" reasons; and *what* it is for me already, and what it still leaves open for me: all this indicates certain performances, which cohere synthetically thus and so, which are consciously predelineated, which I can explicate, and which I can also freely bring about. In other words: No being nor being-thus for me, whether as actuality or as possibility, but as *accepted by me* [*mir geltend*]. This acceptance by me is precisely a name for a multiplicity of my actual and possible performances, with essentially predelineated ideas of harmony *in infinitum* and of definitive being—not a multiplicity demanded or postulated from some superior standpoint, but one that, although hidden at first, can be uncovered. Whatever I encounter as an existing object is something that (as I must recognize when I systematically explicate my own conscious life, as a life of acceptance [*Geltungsleben*]) has received its *whole* being-sense for me from my effective intentionality; not a shadow of that sense remains excluded from my effective intentionality. Precisely this I must consult, I must explicate systematically, if I intend to understand that sense and consequently to understand also what I am allowed, and what I am not allowed, to attribute to an object—whether with formal universality or with regard to it as an object belonging to its own category of being—according to the constituting intentionality from which, as just now said, its whole sense has originated. To explicate this intentionality itself is to make the sense itself understandable from the originality of the sense-constituting performance.

So it must be when I philosophize. For when I am not philosophizing, when I live naïvely, there is no danger. The living intentionality carries me along; it predelineates; it determines me practically in my whole procedure, including the procedure of my natural thinking, whether this yields being or illusion. The living intentionality does all that, even though, as actually functioning, it may be non-thematic, undisclosed, and thus beyond my ken.

I said *illusion* as well as *being*. For naturally it is characteristic of the performance-of-consciousness effected by experience itself that, on the one hand, only harmonious experience has the style of performance predelineated as normal for experience and that, on the other hand, its harmony can be broken, that experiencing can fall to pieces in *conflict*, and that the initially simple certainty of experience can end in doubt, in deeming possible, in deeming likely, in negation (nullity-qualification)—all this under definitely requisite structural conditions, which are precisely what must be explored. Exploration must then be extended to why, after all, the open possibility of deception—that is: the non-being of what is experienced—does not abolish the universal presumption of normal harmony and to why a universe of being at all times remains for me beyond all doubt: a universe of being that I miss, and can miss, only occasionally and in details.

Needless to say, something similar applies in the case of *each and every consciousness,* in the case of every manner in which something existent, possible, senseful, or countersensical, is for us what it is for us; and every *question about legitimacy* that is, or could be, asked receives from the pertinent intentionality itself of consciousness a predelineation of sense and of the way leading to legitimation. Throughout all the continuities of consciousness that pertain to the legitimation and, in favorable cases, terminate in an evidence, there runs an identity of the supposed and eventually legitimated existent—the same that, from first to last, is an intentional pole of identity: *There is no conceivable place where the life of consciousness is broken through, or could be broken through,* and we might come upon a transcendency that possibly had any sense other than that of an intentional unity making its appearance in the subjectivity itself of consciousness.

Sec. 95. Necessity of starting,
each from his own subjectivity.

To be correct, however, I must say expressly *in the first place*: *I myself* am this subjectivity, I who carry on sense-investigation concerning what exists for me and is accepted by me and who now, qua logician, am carrying on sense-investigation with regard to the presupposed existing world and the logical principles related to it. In the first place, then, it is always I and I again: purely as Ego of that life of consciousness by which everything receives being-sense for me.

But still (we must not pass over this as quickly as in the preceding section) the world is the world *for us all*; as an Objective world it has, in its own sense, the *categorial form, "once for all truly existing"*, not only for me but *for everyone*: For what we asserted[1] as a logical characteristic of predicational truth is manifestly a characteristic also of the world of experience, prior to the truth and the science that explicate this world predicatively. *World-experience,* as constitutive, signifies, not just my quite private experience, but *community-experience*: The world itself, according to its sense, is the one identical world, to which all of *us* necessarily have experiential access, and about which all of *us* by "exchanging" our experiences—that is: by making them common—, can reach a common understanding; just as "Objective" legitimation depends on mutual assent and its criticism.

Despite all this, and no matter how prodigious the difficulties that may be encountered in actually uncovering effective intentionality and, quite especially, in distinguishing between the effective intentionality that is originally one's own and the effective intentionality that belongs to others—or the difficulties that may be encountered in clarifying just *that* intersubjectivity which functions as sense-constituting for the Objective world—what was said stands fast in the first place, with an insuperable necessity. First of all, before everything else conceivable, *I* am. This "I am" is for me, the subject who says it, and says it in the right sense, the *primitive intentional basis for my world*; and, at the same time, it must not be overlooked that likewise the "Objective" world, the "world for all of us" as accepted with this sense by me, is also "my" world. But "I am" is the primitive intentional basis, not only for "the" world, the one I consider real, but also for any "ideal world" that I accept; and this holds, without exception, for anything and everything of which I am conscious as something existent in any sense whatever that I understand or accept—for everything that I show, sometimes legitimately, sometimes illegitimately, to be existent—including me myself, my life, my believing, and all this consciousness-of. Whether convenient or inconvenient, and even though (because of no matter what prejudices) it may sound monstrous to me, it is the *primal matter-of-fact to which I must hold fast,* which I, as a

---

[1] *Author's note:* See sec. 77, pp. 193ff.

philosopher, must not disregard for a single instant. For children in philosophy, this may be the dark corner haunted by the spectres of solipsism and, perhaps, of psychologism, of relativism. The true philosopher, instead of running away, will prefer to fill the dark corner with light.

Sec. 96. The transcendental problems of intersubjectivity and of the intersubjective world.

a. Intersubjectivity and the world of pure experience.

Even the world for everyone, then, is something of which *I* am conscious, something accepted by *me* as the world for everyone; in my intentionality it is legitimated, it receives its content and its being-sense. Naturally the world for everyone presupposes that, in my ego—the ego who says, with the universality in question here, *ego cogito,* and includes in his actual and possible *cogitata* everything actual and possible for him—it presupposes, I say, that, in this ego, every other ego receives sense and acceptance *as* an other ego. Someone "else", others—these have an original relation to me who experience them and am conscious of them in other manners. —With everything, naturally, that belongs to their sense (their sense for me): Such as that someone else is here "facing me", bodily and with his own life, and has me now, in like fashion, as *his* vis-à-vis; that I—with my whole life, with all my modes of consciousness and all my accepted objects—am *alter ego for him,* as he is for me; and, in like fashion, everyone else for everyone else; so that "everyone" receives its sense; and, in like fashion, we and I (as "one among others") as included in "everyone".

* * *

When, within the universality of my *ego-cogito,* I find myself as a psychophysical being, a unity constituted in my *ego-cogito,* and find related to this unity, in the form "others", psychophysical beings opposite me, who, as such, are likewise constituted in multiplicities belonging to my intentional life, I become aware of great difficulties—in the first place, even concerning myself. I, the "transcendental ego," am the ego who "precedes" everything worldly: as the Ego, that is to say, in whose life of consciousness the world, as an intentional unity, is constituted to begin with. Therefore I, the constituting Ego, am not identical with the Ego who is already worldly, not identical with myself as a psychophysical reality; and my psychic life, the psychophysical and worldly life of consciousness, is not identical with my transcendental ego, in which the world, with everything physical and psychic that belongs to it, is constituted for me.

But do I not say I in both cases: whether, in natural living, I experience myself qua human being in the world, or, in the philosophical attitude, starting from the world and myself qua human being, I go back and ask about the multiplicities of constituting "appearances", meanings, modes of consciousness, and so forth, doing so in such a manner that, taking everything Objective purely as a "phenomenon", as an intentionally constituted unity, I now find myself qua transcendental ego? And do I not find then that my transcendental life and my psychic, my worldly, life have, in each and every respect, a like content? How can it be understood that the "ego" has constituted in himself the whole of what belongs to his own peculiar essence as, at the same time, "his psyche", psychophysically Objectivated in connexion with "his" bodily organism and as thus woven into the spatial Nature constituted in him qua ego?

Furthermore, if someone "else", as is obvious, is constituted with a sense that points back to me myself, qua human Ego—in particular, his organism, as "another's", pointing back to my own; his psychic life, as "another's" psychic life, pointing back to my own—how can this constitution of the new being-sense, his sense as someone "*other*", be understood? If even the self-constitution of the ego as a spatialized, a psychophysical, being is a very obscure matter, then it is much more obscure, and a downright tormenting enigma, how, in the ego, an *other psychophysical Ego* with an *other psyche* can be constituted; since his sense as "other" involves the essential impossibility of my experiencing his own essential psychic contents with actual originality, as I do my own. Essentially, therefore, the constitution of others must be different from that of my own psychophysical Ego.

Moreover it must be made understandable that I necessarily ascribe to someone else (in his mental processes, his experiences and the rest, which I attribute to him as processes other than mine), not a merely analogous experienced world, but the *same* world that I experience; likewise, that I mean him as experiencing me in the world and, moreover, experiencing me as related to the same experienced world to which he is related; and so forth.

If it is certain to me and, thanks to transcendental clarification, already understandable that my psyche is a self-Objectivation of my transcendental ego, then the other psyche also points back to a transcendental ego, but, in this case, *another's*, as the ego that someone else, for his part, starting from the world given him beforehand in his experience and going back to ask about the ultimate constitutive life, would have to grasp in his "phenomenological reduction". Consequently the problem of "others" takes also the following form:

To understand how my transcendental ego, the primitive basis for everything that I accept as existent, can constitute within himself another transcendental ego, and then too an open plurality of such egos—"other" egos, absolutely inaccessible to my ego in their original being, and yet cognizable (for me) as existing and as being thus and so.

* * *

Let us start from the fact that for us—stated more distinctly: for *me* qua ego—the world is constituted as "Objective" (in the above-stated sense: there for everyone), showing itself to be the way it is; in an intersubjective cognitive community. It follows that a sense of "everyone" must already be constituted, relative to which an Objective world can be Objective. This implies that the *first* and fundamental *sense of "everyone"* (and therefore of "*others*") cannot be the usual, the higher-level, sense: namely the sense "every human being", which refers to something real in the Objective world and therefore already presupposes the constitution of that world.

Now someone else on the constitutionally lower level points back, by his sense, to me myself, but, as we were saying, not as a transcendental ego but as my *psychophysical Ego*. Similarly, then, *this* psychophysical Ego *cannot yet be I, the human being* in the Objective world, in the world whose Objectivity must first be made constitutionally possible by the psychophysical Ego here in question.

This, in turn, points back to the fact that my *bodily organism*, which is, according to its sense, spatial and a member of an environment made up of spatial bodies, a Nature (within which I encounter the bodily organism of someone else)—it points back, I say, to the fact that *none* of these can as yet have *Objective-world* significance. My intrinsically first psychophysical Ego (we are referring here to constitutional strata, not temporal genesis), relative to whom the intrinsically first someone-else must be constituted, is, we see, a member of an *intrinsically first* Nature, which is not yet Objective Nature, a Nature the spatio-temporality of which is not yet Objective spatio-temporality: in other words, a Nature that does not yet have constitutional traits coming from an already-constituted someone else. In the nexus of this first Nature, as holding sway in that body (within this Nature) which is called my bodily organism, as exercising psychophysical functions in that body in a unique manner, my psychic Ego makes his appearance, "animating" it as the unique animated body, according to original experience.

It is now understandable that this first Nature or world, this first, not yet intersubjective, Objectivity, is constituted in my ego as, in a *signal sense, my own,* since as yet it contains nothing other than my Ego's own—that is: nothing that, by a constitutional involvement of other Egos, would go beyond the sphere of actually direct, *actually original, experience* (or, correlatively, the sphere of what originates from such experience). On the other hand, it is clear that this sphere, the sphere of my transcendental ego's *primordial ownness,* must contain the *motivational foundation* for the constitution of those *transcendencies* that are *genuine,* that go beyond it, and originate first of all as "others" (other psychophysical beings and other transcendental egos), the transcendencies that, thus mediated, make possible the constitution of an Objective world in the everyday sense: a *world of the "non-Ego"*, of what is other than my Ego's own. All Objectivity, in this sense, is related back constitutionally to the *first affair that is other than my Ego's own,* the other-than-my-Ego's-own in the form, someone "else"—that is to say: the non-Ego in the form, "another Ego".

b. The illusion of transcendental solipsism.

It is hardly necessary to say that this whole many-leveled problem of the constitution of the Objective world is, at the same time, the problem of dissolving what may be called the *transcendental illusion* that from the outset misleads, and usually paralyzes, any attempt to start a consistent transcendental philosophy: the illusion that such a philosophy must lead to a *transcendental solipsism.* If everything I can ever accept as existent is constituted in my ego, then everything that exists does indeed seem to be a mere moment of my own transcendental being.

But the solution of this enigma lies, firstly, in the systematic unravelling of the constitutional problems implicit in the fact of consciousness which is the world always existing for *me,* always having and confirming its sense by *my* experience; and, secondly, in progressively advancing exhibitions that follow the hierarchical sequence of problems. The purpose of these exhibitions, however, is none other, and can be none other, than actually to disclose, as matters included in that very fact of consciousness, the actualities and potentialities (or habitualities) of life, in which the sense, world, has been, and is continually being, built up immanently. The world is continually there for us; but in the first place it is there for *me*. This fact too is there for me; otherwise there could be no sense for me in which the world is there for *us,* there as one and the same, and as a world having a particular sense—not a sense to be "postulated" as such and such (and perhaps even to be suitably "interpreted", in order to reconcile the interests of the understanding and the emotions), but a sense to be explicated in the first place, and with primary originality, out of experience itself. The first thing, therefore, is to consult the experienced world, purely as experienced. Immersing myself wholly in the flow of my world-experiencing and in all the open possibilities of its consistent fulfilment, I direct my regard to what is experienced and to its universal, eidetically apprehensible sense-structures. Guided by these, I must then turn back and seek out the configurations and contents of the actualities and potentialities that function as sense-constituting for this being-sense and for its different levels—and here too there is nothing to "postulate" or to "interpret suitably", but only something to bring to light. Thus alone can that ultimate understanding of the world be attained, behind which, since it is ultimate, there is nothing more that can be sensefully inquired for, nothing more to understand. Can the transcendental illusion of solipsism withstand this onward march of mere *concrete explication*? Is it not an illusion that can appear only *before* the explication, because, as already said, this fact—that others and the world for others have their sense in and from me myself—is a presented fact, and therefore there can be no other problem here than that of clarifying this matter-of-fact, clarifying it, that is, as what is implicit in me myself?

c. Problems at higher levels
concerning the Objective world.

Naturally the lines of work indicated above are not exhaustive. Research must go further. First of all—and the researches indicated above are concerned exclusively with this—the world of naïve experience must be apprehended purely and submitted to a constitutional clarification, in order to make possible the asking of the higher-level questions (which must be sharply distinguished from problems concerning the world of naïve experience). Among the higher questions are those concerning the constitution of what we may call a theoretical world: the world truly existing in the theoretical sense, or the world pertaining to an unconditionally and Objectively valid theoretical cognition. A particularly important and difficult problem in this connexion is that of clarifying the *idealizations* involved in the intentional sense of the sciences. With formal universality these idealizations are stated as "being in itself" and "truth in itself", in the *idealized* sense proper to formal logic and its "principles". But in their particularizations, as relating to world-regions, these idealizations become truly great problems—for example: as the idea of exact Nature (according to the "exact" natural sciences), the Nature characterized by the "ideal" space of geometry (with its ideal straight lines, circles and so forth), by a correspondingly ideal time, and the like.

d. Concluding observations.

We must rest content here with having made at least roughly understandable the confusing involved problems of intersubjectivity and worldly Objectivity.[1] Now it is clear: Only by the aforesaid uncovering of the performance that constitutes the being-sense of the given world can we avoid every countersensical absolutizing of this world's being and know, universally and in every respect, what we (as philosophers) are allowed to assign to that sense, to Nature, to space, to space-time, to causality, and in what sense we can legitimately understand the exactnesses of geometry, mathematical physics, and so forth —to say nothing of corresponding, but specifically different, problems concerning the moral sciences.

---

[1] *Author's note:* The chief points for the solution of the problem of intersubjectivity and for the overcoming of transcendental solipsism were already developed in lectures that I gave at Göttingen during the winter semester of 1910-11. But the actual carrying out required further difficult single investigations, which did not reach their conclusion until much later. A short exposition of the theory itself will be presented soon in my *Cartesianische Meditationen* [*cf.* p. 7 n., *supra,* and *op. cit.,* "*V. Meditation*"]. I hope that, within the next year, I shall be able to publish the pertinent explicit investigations. [This hope was not fulfilled.]

* * *

Sec. 97. Universal philosophic significance
of the method that consists in uncovering
constitution in consciousness.

No philosopher can be spared the path of thorny investigations that we have tried to open. That *absolutely everything* of which an Ego can think is related to his life of consciousness has, to be sure, been generally recognized, since Descartes, as a fact that is fundamental for philosophy; and, particularly in recent times, it has again become the theme of much discussion. But there is no use in philosophizing about it from on high and veiling it even in the finest-spun thoughts, instead of forcing one's way into its huge concretenesses and making it actually fruitful philosophically. He who philosophizes must make clear to himself from the beginning what we, with good reason, have emphasized so strongly and so often: Anything that can exist, and be this or that, for him (accordingly, that can have sense for him and be accepted by him as existent and as being this or that) must be something of which he has consciousness in the shape of an appertinent intentional performance, which *corresponds to the particularity* of that existent; it must be something of which he is conscious by virtue of an appertinent *"sense-bestowing [Sinngebung]"*, as I expressed it in my *Ideen*. He must not stop short with the empty generality of the word consciousness, nor with the empty words experience, judgment, and so forth, treating the rest as though it were philosophically irrelevant and leaving it to psychology, this psychology whose heritage is blindness to intentionality as the own-essentiality of the life of consciousness or, in any case, blindness to intentionality as a teleological function—that is: a constitutive performance. Consciousness can be methodically uncovered in such fashion that one can directly "see" it in its performing, whereby sense is bestowed and is produced with modalities of being. One can follow the way in which an object-sense, the particular *cogitatum* of the *cogitationes* in question, becomes fashioned into a new sense in the changing flow of these *cogitationes* with its functioning motivational coherence; one can see how what is already at hand has been previously fashioned out of a foundational sense, which originated from an earlier performance. . . .

To be sure, the method of intentional explication had first to be developed, owing to the remarkable fact that Brentano's discovery of intentionality never led to seeing in it a complex of performances, which are included as *sedimented history* in the currently constituted intentional unity and its current manners of givenness—a history *that one can always uncover by following a strict method*. In consequence of this fundamental cognition, every sort of intentional unity becomes a *"transcendental clue"* to guide constitutional "analyses" and these acquire a wholly unique character: They are *not analyses in the usual sense* (analyses into really immanent parts), but *uncoverings of intentional implications* (advancing, perhaps, from an experience to the system of experiences that are *predelineated* as possible).

Sec. 98. Constitutional investigations as a priori.

But that fundamental insight would nevertheless have remained comparatively sterile, were it not for the cognition, already mentioned occasionally, that, in constitutional investigations, *inductive empirical inquiry is not one of the first things,* but rather becomes so much as possible only by virtue of an antecedent *inquiry into essences*. The truly fundamental cognition in this connexion—a cognition foreign to all previous psychology and all previous transcendental philosophy—is that *any straightforwardly constituted objectivity* (for example: an Object belonging to Nature) *points back, according to its essential sort* (for example: physical thing *in specie*), to a *correlative essential form of* manifold, actual and possible, *intentionality* (in our example, an infinite intentionality), *which is constitutive for that objectivity*. The multiplicity of possible perceptions, memories, and, indeed, intentional processes of whatever sort, that relate, or can relate, "harmoniously" to one and the same physical thing has (in all its tremendous complication) a quite definite *essential style,* which is identical in the case of any physical thing whatever and is particularized only according to the different individual things constituted in different cases. In the same fashion, the modes of consciousness that can make one aware of some ideal objectivity or other, and can become united as a synthetic consciousness of it, have a definite style, essential to *this* sort of objectivity. As my entire life of consciousness—even in its entirety, and without prejudice to all the manifold separate objectivities that become constituted in it—is an all-embracing unity of effective life, with a unitary performance, the *whole life of consciousness is governed by a universal constitutional Apriori, embracing all intentionalities*—an Apriori that, on account of the intrinsic nature of the intersubjectivity constituted in the ego, becomes extended as an *Apriori pertaining to intersubjective intentionality* and its production of intersubjective unities and "worlds". Exploration of this entire Apriori is an exceedingly great task, but is by no means unassailable or incapable of progressive, step by step, accomplishment. It is the *task of transcendental phenomenology*.

In that connexion, one must bear in mind that *effective subjectivity is necessarily more* than *actual* intentional life, with its in fact coordinating intentional processes; it consists also, and continually, in its *abilities*. These are not, perchance, hypothetical explanatory constructs; on the contrary, they can be brought to light, in single pulses of "I can" and "I do", as continually productive factors. And, going on from there, one can likewise bring to light all the universal abilities, single-subjective and intersubjective. It should be expressly emphasized that they too fall within the scope of the phenomenological Apriori, as drawn from corresponding intuitions of essences—such a source being universally implicit in the sense of phenomenology.

For the sake of a better understanding of the *method of inquiry into essences,* let us add the following brief indications.

Everything that we have stated in our observations concerning constitution can, in the first place, be made a matter of insight on the basis of no matter what *examples* of no matter what sorts of already-given objects—that is: in a reflective explication of the intentionality in which we simply and straightforwardly "have" a real or an ideal objectivity. We have made a significant advance when we recognize that what obviously holds good for *de facto* single cases of actuality or possibility still holds good necessarily when we vary our examples *quite as we please* and then inquire retrogressively for the correlatively varying "objectivations"—that is: the constituting mental processes—[and] for the "subjective" manners of givenness, which change, sometimes continuously and sometimes discretely. Primarily we must inquire here for the manners of "appearance" that are constitutive in the *pregnant* sense, the ones that are *experiences* of the exemplary objects in question or of their variants; and we must look for the *manners in which* the objects take shape as synthetic unities in the mode "they themselves", in those experiences. That, however, is nothing other than inquiring for the systematic universe of possible experiences, possible evidences; or for the *idea* of a complete synthesis of possible harmonious experiences, as whose synthetic product the object in question would be intentional as itself absolutely given and absolutely verified, "all-sidedly", with the totality of determinations belonging to it: In this inquiry, the variation of the necessary initial example is the performance in which the "eidos" should emerge and by means of which the evidence of the indissoluble eidetic correlation between constitution and constituted should also emerge. If it is to have these effects, it must be understood, not as an *empirical variation,* but as a variation carried on with the freedom of pure phantasy and with the consciousness of its purely optional charac-ter—the consciousness of the "pure" Any Whatever. Thus understood, the variation extends into an open horizon of endlessly manifold free possibilities of more and more variants. Now, in such a fully free varia-tion, released from all restrictions to facts accepted beforehand, all the variants belonging to the openly infinite sphere—which includes the [initial] example itself, as "optional" and freed of all its fac-tualness—stand in a relationship of synthetic interrelatedness and in-tegral connectedness; more particularly, they stand in a continuous and all-inclusive synthesis of "coincidence in conflict". But, precisely with this coinciding, what necessarily persists throughout this free and al-ways-repeatable variation comes to the fore: the *invariant,* the in-dissolubly identical in the different and ever-again different, the *essence* common to all, the universal essence by which all "imaginable" variants of the example, and all variants of any such variant, are restricted. This invariant is the ontic essential form (apriori form), the *eidos,* cor-responding to the example, in place of which any variant of the example could have served equally well.[1]

But, when one turns one's regard reflectively from the ontic essential form (highest of them all, the "category") to the possible experiences that do the constituting, the possible manners of appearance, one sees that these necessarily vary concomitantly [with the constituted ob-jects], and in such a fashion that now an essential form with two cor-relative sides shows itself as invariant. Thus it becomes evident that an ontic Apriori is possible, as a concretely full possibility, only as the cor-relate of a constitutional Apriori that is concretely united with it, con-cretely inseparable from it. . . .

Finally, ascending to the broadest, the analytico-formal universali-ties, one sees that any object (no matter how indeterminately it is thought of, nay, even if it be conceived as void of content), any object

---

[1] *Author's note:* It should be noted here that object [*Gegenstand*] is always understood by me in the broadest sense, which comprehends likewise all syn-tactical objectivities. Accordingly, the concept *eidos* is also given a maximally broad sense. At the same time, this sense defines the only concept belonging to the multisignificant expression, *a priori,* that I recognize philosophically. That concept alone is meant wherever the locution *a priori* occurs in my writings.

thought of as a "wholly optional" Anything Whatever, is thinkable only as the correlate of an intentional constitution inseparable from it. This constitution is indeterminately empty, and yet it is not variable without restriction; that is to say: with each particularization of "Something", and with each ontic category thus substituted (the eidos that can be brought out by ontic variation of a suitable example), the constitution must become correlatively particularized. Accordingly, any intentional and constitutional analysis performable on the basis of factual data is to be looked upon from the start as an analysis of examples, even though the analyst does not understand it in that manner. All its results, when freed from factualness and thereby transposed into the realm of free phantasy-variation, become eidetic, become results that (as is apodictically evident) govern a universe of conceivability (a "pure" allness), in such a manner that the negation of any result is equivalent to an intuitable eidetic impossibility, an inconceivability. Accordingly that applies in particular to all the observations conducted just now. They have themselves been conducted as eidetic. To explicate the eidetic method is not to describe an empirical fact, a method that can, as a matter of empirical fact, be repeatedly followed at will. The universal validity of the eidetic method is unconditionally necessary; it is a method that can be followed, no matter what conceivable object is taken as an initial example; and that is the sense in which we meant it. Only in eidetic intuition can the essence of eidetic intuition become clarified.

*   *   *

Though the constitutional problems pertaining to all regions of objectivity open up vast fields here of apriori and the same time subjective research, we can already foresee that the fields for such research must be even more extensive than those included at first in the scope of methodical analysis. That is to say: if everything subjective that is factual has its genesis in immanent time, it is to be expected that this genesis also has its Apriori. In that case, [inquiry into] the *"static" constitution* of objects, which relates to an already-"developed" subjectivity, has its counterpart in [an inquiry into] *apriori genetic constitution*, [a subsequent inquiry,] based on [the results of] the former, which necessarily precedes it. Only by virtue of this genetic Apriori does what was already said in advance[1] become evident (and evident in its profounder sense): that, in what analysis uncovers as intentionally implicit in the 'iving sense-constitution, there lies a sedimented *"history"*.

---

[1] *Author's note: See* sec. 97 [pp. 13f., *supra*].

Sec. 99. Psychological and transcendental subjectivity.
The problem of transcendental psychologism.

Neither a world nor any other existent of any conceivable sort comes "from outdoors [θύραθεν]" into my ego, my life of consciousness. Everything outside is what it is in this inside, and gets its *true being* from the givings of it itself, and from the verifications, within this inside—its true being, which for that very reason is something that itself belongs to this inside: as a *pole of unity* in my (and then, intersubjectively, in our) actual and possible multiplicities, with [their] possibilities as [my (and our)] abilities: as "I can go there", "I could perform syntactical operations", and so forth. Whatever the modalizations of being that may also come and go here, they too belong in this interior, where everything constituted therein is not only an end but also a beginning, perhaps a thematic end that also functions for a new thematizing. And, above all, it is thus with respect to the *ideas* constituted in the ego—for example: the idea of the *absolutely existing* Object belonging to Nature and the idea of the absolute *"truths in themselves"* about that Object. In connexion with the constituted relativities, the constituted unities at a lower level, such ideas have a "regulative significance".

The relation of my consciousness to a *world* is not a matter of fact imposed on me either by a God, who adventitiously decides it thus, or by a world accidentally existing beforehand, and a causal regularity belonging thereto. On the contrary, the subjective Apriori precedes the being of God and world, the being of everything, individually and collectively, for me, the thinking subject. Even God is for me what he is, in consequence of my own productivity of consciousness; here too I must not look aside lest I commit a supposed blasphemy, rather I must see the problem. Here too, as in the case of the other ego, productivity of consciousness will hardly signify that I invent and make this highest transcendency.

The like is true of the world and of all worldly causation. Certainly I am in psychophysical causal connexion with the outside world—that is to say: I, this human being, a man among men and brutes, among other realities too, all going together to make up the world. But the world with all its realities, including my human real being, is a universe of constituted transcendencies—constituted in mental processes and abilities of my ego (and, only through the mediation of mine, in mental processes and abilities belonging to the intersubjectivity that exists for me); accordingly, this constituted world is preceded by my ego, as the ultimately constitutive subjectivity. The world's transcendence is a transcendence relative to this Ego and, by virtue of this Ego, a transcendence relative to the open community of Egos as this Ego's community. There comes to light in this connexion the difference already descried by Descartes, despite all the obscurity: that *this* Ego—that I, understood as the ultimately constitutive subjectivity, *exist for myself with apodictic necessity* (without prejudice to my infinite horizons of undisclosed and unknown determinations); whereas the world constituted in me, though it always exists for me in the stream of my harmonious experience, and exists quite without doubt (I could never summon up a doubt, where every new experience confirms existence),—this world, I say, has and, by essential necessity, retains the sense of only a *presumptive existence.* The real world exists, only on the continually delineated presumption that experience will go on continually in the same constitutional style.

It may be that profound and difficult investigations are necessary here, in order to attain perfect clarity. But there is no need of them in order to convince oneself that this difference emerges, which we turned to legitimate account earlier and which ranks as the most fundamental difference of all for the theory of cognition, the difference namely between—

Firstly, *transcendental-phenomenological subjectivity* (seen, through *my* transcendental subjectivity, as transcendental intersubjectivity), with its constitutive life of consciousness and its transcendental abilities, and—

Secondly, *psychological or psychophysical subjectivity,* the human psyche, the human person and community of persons with their psychic mental processes (in the psychological sense), component parts of the Objective world, in psychophysical, inductively determined, connexion with physical organisms, which are also parts of the world.

It was because of this difference that all attempts to establish the existence of an Objective world by causal inferences from an ego given in the first place all by himself (in the first place as *solus ipse*) were characterized by us as involving a countersensical confounding of psychophysical causation, occurring in the world, with the correlation, occurring in transcendental subjectivity, between constitutive consciousness and the world constituted in consciousness. For [an understanding of] the true and genuine sense of transcendental philosophy it is decisively important to lay hold of the fact that *human being,* and not only *human organism* but also *human psyche* (no matter how purely the human psyche may be apprehended by internal experience), are *worldly* concepts and, as worldly, [apply only to] objectivities of a *transcendent apperception,* which therefore are included, as constitutional problems, within the universal transcendental problem, the problem of the transcendental constitution of all transcendencies, nay, all objectivities of whatever sort.

The radical separation of psychological from transcendental subjectivity (in which the former becomes constituted as having a worldly and therefore transcendent sense-content) signifies a *radical separation of psychology from transcendental philosophy*—in especial: from the transcendental theory of transcendent cognition. It will not do to engage in any shifting of the concept of psychology, in spite of what may be called the essentially rooted temptations implicit in the circumstance that a pure analysis of consciousness, even though made in the first place as psychological, can be turned into a transcendental analysis, without altering any of its own essential contents.

It must never be lost sight of: that the only sense that *psychology* has now, or has ever had, is that of being a *branch of "anthropology"*, a positive worldly science; that, in psychology, "psychic phenomena"—more precisely, psychological Data: the mental processes and the dispositions (abilities)—are Data within the already-given world; that "internal experience" is a species of worldly, "Objective", experience, as truly as any experience of others, or any experience of something physical; and that it is a *falsifying dislocation,* if one mistakes this psychological internal experience for the internal experience relied on transcendentally as an evidential experiencing of ego-cogito. To be sure, it is a falsification that could not become noticeable before the rise of transcendental phenomenology.

We by no means deny that every mode of intentionality, including every mode of evidence and every mode of the fulfilling of meanings by evidence, can be found by experience *also when one takes the psychological attitude,* and can be treated psychologically. We do not deny that *all our intentional analyses, whether carried out or merely indicated, are valid also when intentional life is apperceived psychologically*; but we do contend that psychological apperception is a particular worldly apperception, and that only a parenthesizing of it yields the concretions of transcendental subjectivity and their concrete parallels. Psychological theory of cognition has a legitimate sense— when understood simply as a name for work done on the manifold problems that cognizing, as a function in human psychic life, sets for psychology as the science of this psychic life. Such a theory of cognition becomes a countersense, only if it is expected to perform the transcendental tasks. . . .

And yet it can be said that, if this psychology of cognition had ever gone to work with a consciousness of its aim and had consequently been successful, its results would also have been work accomplished directly for the philosophic theory of cognition. All insights into structure that had been acquired for the psychology of cognition would also have benefited transcendental philosophy. . . . The interpenetration that is decisive here, and that necessarily remains hidden at first, is the very thing that causes such great difficulty—and defines the *transcendental problem of psychologism*.

And here attention must be paid to the following, as a misleading moment connected with the peculiar nature of so-called "descriptive" psychology—the psychology that considers the psyche abstractly, purely in and by itself, and is based on a correspondingly purified experiencing of it: *Pure psychology* (as had already become evident from the case of the *Logische Untersuchungen*) can be developed as *apriori,* just as transcendental phenomenology can be so developed. The restriction of psychological judging to intentional mental processes (those given in pure "internal" experience), to their essential forms (which become themselves-given in internal eidetic universalization), and likewise to purely psychic abilities,—this restriction yields a *psychologico-phenomenological* judging. It may even be said that the result is a self-contained *psychological phenomenology,* having the same method of intentional "analysis" that is used in transcendental phenomenology. . . . Insight into this parallelism between purely immanental and apriori psychology (psychological phenomenology), on the one hand, and transcendental phenomenology, on the other, and the showing of its essential necessity are the radically ultimate clarification of the problem of transcendental psychologism and, at the same time, its solution.

Sec. 100. Historico-critical remarks on the development of
transcendental philosophy and, in particular, on
transcendental inquiry concerning formal logic.

The way leading to the whole inquiry concerning origins, an inquiry that must be taken collaterally, as belonging to pure psychology and transcendental philosophy, and includes, in its essential universality, all possible worlds with all their essential regions of real and ideal objectivities and all their world-strata (therefore, in particular, the world of ideal senses, of truths, theories, sciences, the idealities of every culture, of every socio-historical world)—that way remained for centuries untrod. This was an entirely understandable consequence of naturalistic and sensualistic aberration on the part of all modern psychology based on internal experience. This aberration not only drove the transcendental philosophy of English empiricism into that well-known development which made it end in countersensical fictionalism; it also arrested the transcendental philosophy of Kant's Copernican revolution short of full effectuation, so that the Kantian philosophy could never force its way through to the point where the ultimately necessary aims and methods can be adopted. If the *pure* concrete ego, in whom all the objectivities and worlds accepted by him are subjectively constituted, is only a senseless bundle or collection of Data—which come and perish, cast together now in this way and now in that, according to a senselessly accidental regularity analogous to that of mechanics (the sort of regularity ascribed to association as it was then interpreted),—the result is that only surreptitious reasons can explain how even as much as the illusion of a real world could arise. Yet Hume professed to make it *understandable* that, by a blind matter-of-fact regularity, purely in the mind, particular types of fictions having the names "objects with continued existence", "identical persons", and so forth, arise for us. Now illusions, fictions, are produced *sense-formations*; the constituting of them takes place as intentionality; they are *cogitata* of *cogitationes*; and only from intentionality can a new intentionality arise. Fictions have their own sort of being, which points back to actualities, to what is existent in the normal sense. Once productive intentionality has been discovered, everything, being as well as illusion, becomes understandable in its essential Objective possibility; the subjectiveness of anything is then for us its constitutedness. And that is not the bad subjectivizing that, in Hume's case, turns both being and illusion into a solipsistic illusion; rather it is a transcendental subjectivizing, which is not merely compatible with genuine Objectivity but the apriori other side of genuine Objectivity.

Hume's greatness (a greatness still unrecognized in this, its most important aspect) lies in the fact that, despite all that, he was the first to grasp the universal *concrete problem* of transcendental philosophy. In the concreteness of purely egological internality, as he saw, everything Objective becomes intended to (and, in favorable cases, perceived), thanks to a subjective genesis. Hume was the first to see the necessity of investigating the Objective itself as a product of its genesis from that concreteness, in order to make the legitimate being-sense of everything that exists for us intelligible through its ultimate origins. Stated more precisely: The real world and the categories of reality, which are its fundamental forms, became for him a problem in a new fashion. He was the first to *treat seriously the Cartesian focusing purely on what lies inside*: in that he began by freeing the soul radically from everything that gives it the significance of a reality in the world, and then presupposed the soul purely as a field of "perceptions" ("impressions" and "ideas"), such as it is qua datum of a suitably purified internal experience. Within this "phenomenological" realm, he outlined for the first time what we call "constitutional" problems; for he recognized the necessity of making it possible to understand how it happens that, purely within this phenomenologically reduced subjectivity and its immanent genesis, this same subjectivity can find, in a supposed "experience", transcendent Objectivities—realities with the ontological forms (space, time, continuum, physical thing, personality) that we already take for granted.

Such a description of Hume's general intention can be made with assurance from the position attained by present-day phenomenology. We must add, however, that by no means did Hume consciously practise—to say nothing of thinking out radically—the method of phenomenological reduction, which prepares the ground for phenomenology; furthermore, that he, the first discoverer of constitutional problems, completely *overlooked the fundamentally essential property of mental life* as a life of consciousness, the very property to which those problems relate; and that consequently he overlooked the method appropriate to them as problems concerning intentionality, a method that, on being carried out, immediately confirms its own power of actual clarification. Because of his naturalistic sensualism, which could see only a collection of data floating in an unsubstantial void and was blind to the Objectivating function of intentional synthesis, Hume fell into the countersense of a "philosophy of as-if".

As for *Kant*, on the other hand: With the dependence on Hume implicit in his reaction against that philosopher, Kant took over the constitutional problem, at least so far as it concerns Nature; but without the full sense of even the problem of Nature, as only one component in the universal complex of constitutional problems to which Hume's reconception of the Cartesian *ego-cogito,* as a concrete "mental" being, had pointed. Kant did not set up a genuine intentional psychology, in opposition to *sensualistic* "psychology" (which, as we have said, was in truth a transcendental phenomenology in Hume's case, even though its sensualism made it countersensical); *a fortiori,* he did not set up such a psychology as, in our sense, an apriori eidetic theory. He never submitted the psychology of Locke and his school to a radical criticism, one that would affect the underlying sense of that psychology's sensualism. His own dependence on Lockean psychology was still too great. And, connected with this dependence, there is the additional fact that he never worked out the profound sense of the difference between *pure psychology* (solely on the basis of "internal experience") and *transcendental phenomenology* (on the basis of transcendental experience, which originates from "transcendental-phenomenological reduction") and therefore did not work out the deepest sense of the transcendental problem of *"psychologism"*. And yet one must say that his doctrine of synthesis and of transcendental abilities—that *all of his theories* relating to the Humean problem—are *implicitly theories of intentional constitution*; only they are not erected on the ultimate basis nor developed from there by a radical method.

* * *

We shall emphasize here some of the chief moments that throw light on the historical development. Let us return to Hume, who demands our attention not only because of the intrinsic significance that, as already indicated, we ascribe to him but also because of his effect on Kant.

Hume did not raise, along with the transcendental problem of the constitution of the world, the transcendental problem of the *constitution of ideal objectivities*; thus he failed to raise, in particular, the transcendental problem of the constitution of logical idealities, of the categorial formations, the judgments, that make up the theme of logic. It ought to have been raised in connexion with those *"relations of ideas"* that, as the sphere of "reason" in the pregnant sense, play so great a rôle for Hume. Those relations *take the place of* the ideal eidetic relationships and laws. But neither these relationships and laws themselves nor any other ideal objectivities were introduced—not even as de facto data of a *supposed "experience"* or of some similar consciousness *supposedly giving objects themselves,* in the way that the data belonging to "Objective" Nature were introduced, as given in the experiencing of Nature. Accordingly, the corresponding Humean problem is missing; and also the corresponding theory, with the function of "explaining" the "experience" of such supposed ideal objects as being likewise an internal producing of mere fictions.

As a substitute, to some extent, for the transcendental problem of ideal objectivities, we have Hume's famous section dealing with *abstraction*. There, as we were saying, it is not a matter of converting abstract ideas, as the data of an experience, into fictions by showing that, although "perceptions" that we always consider to be an experience of them are indeed encountered, nevertheless, as psychological analysis teaches, these perceptions have only the value of pseudo-experiences—as Hume tried to show with respect to external experience and its datum. Rather the aim of that section is to show that we have no abstract "perceptions" at all, that abstract "ideas", as data of some "experience" or other, are not encountered at all; but only particular individual ideas and the attendant habits, by which our general thinking is supposed to be explained as merely a thinking upon individual ideas.

Thus *Kant's position regarding logic* also becomes understandable. *According to the words,* beginning with the definition and throughout the exposition, Kant's logic is presented as a science directed to the subjective—a science of thinking, which is nevertheless distinguished, as apriori, from the empirical psychology of thinking. But *actually,* according to its sense, Kant's purely formal logic concerns the ideal formations produced by thinking. And, concerning them, Kant fails to ask properly transcendental questions of the possibility of cognition. How does it happen that he regards a formal logic, with its apriority, as self-sufficiently grounded? How is it comprehensible that he never thought of asking transcendental questions about the sphere of formal logic, taken as a sphere in and for itself?

That can be understood as a consequence of the above-mentioned *dependence on Hume implicit in Kant's reaction* against him. Hume directed his criticism to experience and the experienced world, but accepted the unassailableness of the relations of ideas (which Kant conceived as the analytic Apriori). Kant did the same with his counterproblem: He did not make his analytic Apriori a problem.

For the succeeding age this meant, however, that *those investigations in the psychology of cognition, or rather those transcendental phenomenological investigations, that are the thing actually needed for a full and, therefore, two-sided logic were never seriously undertaken.* But that was because no one ventured, or had the courage to venture, to take the *ideality of the formations with which logic is concerned* as the characteristic of a separate, self-contained, *"world" of ideal Objects* and, in so doing, to come face to face with the painful question of how subjectivity can in itself bring forth, purely from sources appertaining to its own spontaneity, formations that can be rightly accounted as ideal *Objects* in an ideal "world".—And then (on a higher level) the question of how these idealities can take on spatio-temporally restricted *existence,* in the cultural world (which must surely be considered as real, as included in the spatio-temporal universe), real existence, in the form of historical temporality, as theories and sciences. Naturally this question becomes universalized to concern idealities of every sort.

As for Kant himself: clearly as he recognized (in the nuclear components of the Aristotelian tradition) the apriori character of logic, its purity from everything pertaining to empirical psychology, and the wrongness of including logic in a theory of experience, he still did not grasp the peculiar sense in which logic is ideal. Otherwise that sense would surely have given him a motive for asking transcendental questions.

The overlooking of the objectivity of the ideal, in all its forms, has had its effect, beginning with Locke, in the theory of cognition—which was originally intended as a substitute for the disdained traditional logic—and, to state matters more precisely, its effect, beginning with Hume, in the famous *problem of judgment* and the attendant judgment-theories, which at bottom have never changed their style. What a genuine, clear-purposed, judgment-theory must perform we have already attempted to set forth in detail. Here, with a critical consideration of history, the contrasting theory first comes into view.

The psychological naturalism that became generally dominant and that, beginning with Locke, was looking for describable psychic "Data", in which the origin of all concepts was supposed to lie, saw the describable essence of the judgment in "belief"—a psychic Datum, not differing as such from any Datum of sensation, a red-Datum or sound-Datum. But is it not peculiar that, after this discovery, Hume and, later, Mill speak in words of emotion about the enigmas of belief? What sort of enigmas can a Datum have? Why is it, then, that red and the other Data of sensation present no enigmas?

Naturally, everyone has intentionality really immanent in his mental life and has its performance before him; but, in the naturalistic attitude, one cannot lay hold of the very matter that is most important. This state of affairs was *not essentially changed even by Brentano's discovery of intentionality*. There was no consistently correlative observing of noesis and noema, *cogito* and *cogitatum qua cogitatum*. There was no unravelling of the intentionalities involved, no uncovering of the "multiplicities" in which the "unity" becomes constituted. Because this unity was not taken as the transcendental clue; because, in judgment-theory, the aim was not directed, from the very beginning, at an examination of the judgment, in the logical sense, as the *ideally identical* affair, with a view to the noetic and noematic multiplicities, which enable us to understand its original accruing to us in its ideality: the whole theory lacked a proper goal. Such a goal would have presupposed recognizing the ideal judgment as ideal and as given in tangible evidence. But the theories stuck to their psychic "Data".

. . . Intentionality is not something isolated; it can be observed only in the synthetic unity that connects every single pulse of psychic life *teleologically,* in the unity-relation to *objectivities*—or rather in the double polarity, toward Ego-pole and object-pole. The "Objectivating" performance—to which all single intentional processes at a multiplicity of levels and in relation to various objects (which nevertheless combine sensefully to make up "worlds") are subservient—makes it ultimately necessary to have the whole universality of psychic life in view, as correlated with the ontic universality (the universality of the intrinsically unitary All of the objects). This teleological structure of intentional life, as a universally Objectivating life, is indicated by the fact that object and judgment (in the widest sense) belong together, and by the universality with which we can freely submit any already-given object to our categorial actions. For that reason moreover (and this is another index of that same teleology), the predicative judgment gains universal significance for psychic life.

* * *

As we said above, the definite aim could not be attached to the obscure need for logical inquiries directed somehow to the subjective until after the ideal Objectivity of such formations had been sharply brought out and firmly acknowledged. For only then was one faced with the unintelligibility of *how ideal objectivities* that originate purely in our own subjective activities of judgment and cognition, that are there originaliter in our field of consciousness purely as formations produced by our own spontaneity, *acquire the being-sense of "Objects"*, existing in themselves over against the adventitiousness of the acts and the subjects. How does this sense "come about", how does it originate in us ourselves? And where else could we get it, if not from our own sense-constituting performance? Can what has sense for us receive sense ultimately from anywhere else than from us ourselves? These problems, once they are seen in one sort of Objects, immediately become universal: Is not each and every Objectivity, with all the sense in which it is accepted by us, an Objectivity that is winning or has won, acceptance within ourselves—as an Objectivity having the sense that we ourselves acquired for it?

Accordingly the *transcendental problem* that *Objective logic* (taken no matter how broadly or narrowly) must raise concerning its field of ideal objectivities takes a position *parallel to the transcendental problems of the sciences of realities,* the problems that must be raised concerning the regions of realities to which those sciences pertain, and, in particular, the transcendental problems concerning Nature, which were treated by Hume and Kant. It seems, then, that the immediate consequence of bringing out the world of ideas and, in particular (thanks to the effectuation of impulses received from Leibniz, Bolzano, and Lotze), the world of ideas with which pure logic is concerned, should have been an *immediate extention* of transcendental problems to this sphere.

But the historical development could not assume such a simple form. The Kantian problems and theory were fashioned as a whole, and were so rigidly closed off inside the hard shell of their systematic formation that any possible extension of them to the sphere of ideas with which logic is concerned was utterly out of the question. This was the case, then, not merely because such a thought had never occurred to Kant himself, for reasons already discussed. His transcendental problems, in their historically restricted form, are not raised—as such problems must be, in order to have ultimate clarity—within the primal realm of all transcendental research: phenomenological subjectivity. . . .

At all events, it seems certain that the historical forms of Kantian and neo-Kantian transcendental philosophy, no matter how significant as preliminary stages of a genuine transcendental philosophy, were not suited to promote the transition to a transcendental consideration of ideal worlds—in particular: the world of idealities with which logic is concerned. Nay more, it was implicit in the nature of the historical development, at the stage reached with the uncovering of the sphere belonging to logic, as a realm of ideal objectivities, that it was, as it still is, *easier* to start *from these* objectivities—constituted by spontaneous activities—and *penetrate to the pure sense of all transcendental inquiries,* than to do so by a critical reform of the Kantian modes of inquiry and starting from their particular thematic sphere. Thus it was not at all accidental that phenomenology itself, when it first arose, took the way leading, from the uncovering of the ideality of the formations with which logic is concerned, to exploration of their subjective constitution, and only from there to grasping constitutional inquiry as universal and not concerned with those formations alone.

MARTIN HEIDEGGER (1889-   )

Born in Messkirch, Germany, in 1889, Heidegger studied philosophy and theology, completing his degree at the University of Freiburg. Heidegger soon was a close friend, collaborator and later chosen successor of Husserl after Husserl's arrival at Freiburg in 1916. However, Heidegger's thought took its own directions with a primary focus on the question of Being and language. Among the many major works of Heidegger are: *Being and Time* (1927), *What Is Metaphysics?* (1929), *What Is Called Thinking?* (1954), and *The Essence of Reasons* (1957).

LETTER ON HUMANISM*[1]

Translated by Edgar Lohner

. . . Thought brings to fulfillment the relation of Being to the essence of man, it does not make or produce this relation. Thought merely offers it to Being as that which has been delivered to itself by Being. This

*By permission of William Barrett. From William Barrett and Henry D. Aiken, editors, *Philosophy in The Twentieth Century: An Anthology Volume III*, Random House, Westminster, Maryland.
[1] *Platons Lehre von der Wahrheit. Mit einin Brief uher den "Humanismus,"* pp. 53-119. A. Francke, Bern, 1947. [The letter is addressed to a French student of Heidegger's, Jean Beaufret.] Trans. by Edgar Lohner.

offering consists in this: that in thought Being is taken up in language. Language is the house of Being. In its home man dwells. Whoever thinks or creates in words is a guardian of this dwelling. As guardian, he brings to fulfillment the unhiddenness of Being insofar as he, by his speaking, takes up this unhiddenness in language and preserves it in language. Thought does not become action because an effect issues from it, or because it is applied. Thought acts in that it thinks. This is presumably the simplest and, at the same time, the highest form of action: it concerns man's relation to what is. All effecting, in the end, rests upon Being, is bent upon what is. Thought, on the other hand, lets itself be called into service by Being in order to speak the truth of Being. It is thought which accomplishes this letting be (*Lassen*). Thought is *l'engagement par l'Etre pour l'Etre*. I do not know if it is linguistically possible to express both (*"par" et "pour"*) as one, i.e. by *penser, c'est l'engagement de l'Etre*. Here the possessive form *"de l' . . ."* is meant simultaneously to express the genitive as *genitivus subiectivus* and *obiectivus*. In this, "subject" and "object" are inadequate terms of the metaphysics which, in the form of Western "logic" and "grammar," early took possession of the interpretation of language. Today we can but begin to surmise what lies hidden in this process. The freeing of language from grammar, and placing it in a more original and essential framework, is reserved for thought and poetry. Thought is not merely *l'engagement dans l'action* for and by "what is" in the sense of the actual and present situation. Thought is *l'engagement* by and for the truth of Being. Its history is never past, it is always imminent. The history of Being sustains and determines every *condition et situation humaine*. In order that we may first learn how to perceive the aforesaid essence of thinking in its pure form—and that means to fulfill it as well—we must free ourselves from the technical interpretation of thought. Its beginnings reach back to Plato and Aristotle. With them thought is valued as τέχνη, the procedure of reflection in the service of doing and making. The reflection ere is already seen from the viewpoint of πρᾶξις and ποίησις. Hence thought, when taken by itself, is not "practical." The characterization of thought as θεωρία and the determination of cognition as "theoretical" behavior occur already within the "technical" interpretation of thought. They constitute a reactive attempt of saving for thought an independence in the face of doing and acting. Ever since, "philosophy" has faced the constant distress of justifying its existence against "science." It believes it accomplishes this most securely by elevating itself to the rank of science. Yet this effort is the surrender of the essence of thought. Philosophy is haunted by the fear of losing prestige and validity, unless it becomes science. It is considered a failure equated with unscientific rigor. Being as the element of thought has been abandoned in the technical interpretation of thought. "Logic," since sophistry and Plato, is the initial sanction of this interpretation. Thought is judged by a measure inadequate to it. This judgment is like the procedure of trying to evaluate the nature and the capability of a fish by how long it is able to live on dry land. Too long, all too long, thought has been lying on dry land. Can the effort to bring thought back to its element be called "irrationalism" now?

* * *

You ask: *Comment dedonner un sens au mot "Humanisme"*? This question is asked with the intention of retaining the word "humanism." I wonder if it is necessary. Or is the harm wrought by all such terms not obvious enough yet? Of course, for some time now, "isms" have been suspect. But the market of public opinion always demands new ones. Again and again this demand is readily answered. And terms like "logic," "ethics," "physics" occur only when original thinking has stopped. The Greeks, in their great age, did their thinking without such terms. They did not even call it "philosophy." Thinking ceases when it withdraws from its element. The element is that by means of which thinking can be thinking. It is the element which is potent, which is potency.[2] It concerns itself with thought and so brings thought into its essence. Thought is, more simply, thought of Being. The genitive has two meanings. Thought is of Being, insofar as thought, eventuated by Being, belongs to Being. Thought is at the same time thought of Being insofar as thought listens to, heeds, Being. Listening to and belonging to Being, thought constitutes what it is in its essential origin. Thought is—this means, Being has always, in the manner of destiny, concerned itself about its essence, embraced it. To concern oneself about a "thing" or a

[2] This and the following passage depends essentially on a play on words though it is not just that. The verb "vermögen" means "to be able to," "to have the power to do . . . ." The noun "Vermögen" means "potency," also "wealth," "resources," "means." "Vermögend" means accordingly "potent" and also "propertied." The play lies in this that, without the prefix "ver" there is a word "mögen" meaning "to like." "Mögen" is then used here in a fusion of the two strains of meaning, potency and liking.

"person" means, to love, to like him or it. Such "liking," understood in a more original way, means: to confer essence. Such "liking origin" is the proper nature of potency (*Vermögen*), which not only can perform this or that, but which can let something be what it is as it stems from its true origin. It is the potency of this loving on the "strength of which something is in fact capable of being." This potency is the truly "possible," that whose essence rests on "Mögen." Being is capable of thought. The one makes the other possible. Being as the element is the "quiet power" of the loving potency, i.e. of the possible. Our words "possible" and "possibility," however, are, under the domination of "logic" and "metaphysics," taken only in contrast to "actuality," i.e. they are conceived with reference to a determined—viz. the metaphysical—interpretation of Being as *actus* and *potentia* the distinction of which is identified with that of *existentia* and *essentia*. When I speak of the "quiet power of the possible," I do not mean the possible of a merely represented *possibilitas,* nor the *potentia* as *essentia* of an *actus* of the *existentia,* but Being itself, which in its loving potency commands thought and thus also the essence of man, which means in turn his relationship to Being. To command something is to sustain it in its essence, to retain it in its element.

When thought comes to an end of withdrawing from its element, it replaces the loss by making its validity felt as τέχνη, as an educational instrument and therefore as a scholarly matter and later as a cultural matter. Philosophy gradually becomes a technique of explanation drawn from ultimate causes. One no longer thinks, but one occupies oneself with "philosophy." In competition such occupations publicly present themselves as "isms" and try to outdo each other. The domination achieved through such terminology does not just happen. It rests, especially in modern times, on the peculiar dictatorship of the public. So-called private existence does not mean yet, however, essentially and freely being human. It merely adheres obstinately to a negation of the public. It remains an offshoot dependent on the public and nourishes itself on its mere retreat from the public. So it is witness, against its own will, of its subjection to the public. The public itself, however, is the metaphysically conditioned—as it is derived from the domination of subjectivity—establishment and authorization of the overtness of the existent in the absolute objectivization of everything. Therefore, language falls into the service of arranging the lines of communication, on which objectification as the uniform accessibility of everything for everybody expands, disregarding all limits. So language comes under the dictatorship of the public. This public predetermines what is intelligible and what must be rejected as unintelligible. What has been said in *Sein und Zeit* (1927), secs. 27 and 35, about the word *"man"* the impersonal one) is not simply meant to furnish, in passing, a contribution to sociology. In the same way the word *man* does not simply mean the counterpart—in an ethical existential way—to a person's self-Being. What has been said contains rather an indication—thought of from the question of the truth of Being—of the original pertinence of the word Being. This relationship remains concealed under the domination of subjectivity, which is represented as the public. When, however, the truth of Being has become memorable to thought, then reflection on the essence of language must obtain a new rank. It can no longer be mere philosophy of language. And for just this reason *Sein und Zeit* (sec. 34) contains an indication of the essential dimension of language and broaches the simple question of what mode of Being the language as language from time to time is in. The ubiquitous and fast-spreading impoverishment of language does not gnaw only at aesthetic and moral responsibility in all use of language. It rises from an endangering of man's essence. A merely cultured use of language still does not demonstrate that we have as yet escaped this essential danger. Today it may rather signify that we have not yet seen the danger and cannot see it, because we have never exposed ourselves to its gaze. The decadence of language, quite recently considered though very late, is, however, not the cause but rather a consequence of the process that language under the domination of the modern metaphysics of subjectivity almost always falls out of its element. Language still denies us its essence: that it is the house of the truth of Being. Language, moreover, leaves itself to our mere willing and cultivating as an instrument of domination over beings. This itself appears as the actual in the concatenation of cause and effect. Calculating and acting we encounter beings as the actual, but also scientifically and in philosophizing with explanations and arguments. To these also belongs the assurance that something is inexplicable. Through such assertions we believe we confront the mystery. As if it were taken for granted that the truth of Being could be set up over causes and basic explanations or, what is the same, over their incomprehensibility.

If man, however, is once again to find himself in the nearness of Being, he must first learn to exist in the nameless. He must recognize the seduction of the public, as well as the impotence of the private. Man must, before he speaks, let himself first be claimed again by Being at the risk of having under this claim little or almost nothing to say. Only in this way will the preciousness of its essence be returned to the word, and to man the dwelling where he can live in the truth of Being.

* * *

But when one understands by humanism, in general, the effort of man to become free for his humanity and to find therein his dignity rather than some conceptual understanding of the "freedom" and the "nature" of man, the humanism is in each instance different. Likewise its modes of realization differ. Marx's humanism requires no return to antiquity, nor does the humanism which Sartre conceives existentialism to be. In this broad sense Christianity is also a humanism, insofar as, according to its doctrine, everything comes down to the salvation of the soul (*salus aeterna*) of man and the history of mankind appears in the frame of the history of salvation. However different these kinds of humanism may be, in regard to their aims and basis, in regard to the ways and means of their respective realizations, in regard to the form of their doctrine, all of them coincide in that the *humanitas* of the homo humanus is deter- mined from the view of an already established interpretation of nature, of history, of world, of the basis of the world (*Weltgrund*), i.e. of beings in their totality.

Every humanism is either founded in a metaphysics or is convert- ed into the basis for a metaphysics. Every determination of the es- sence of man that presupposes the interpretation of beings without asking the question of the truth of Being, be it wittingly or not, is metaphysical. Therefore, and precisely in view of the way in which the essence of man is determined, the characteristic of all meta- physics shows itself in the fact that it is "humanistic." For this reason every humanism remains metaphysical. Humanism not only does not ask, in determining the humanity of man, for the relation of Being to the essence of man, but humanism even impedes this question, since, by vir- tue of its derivation from metaphysics it neither knows nor understands it. Inversely, the necessary and the proper way of asking the question of the truth of Being, in metaphysics but forgotten by it, can only come to light, if amidst the domination of metaphysics the question is asked: "What is metaphysics?" First of all each question of "Being," even that of the truth of Being, must be presented as a "metaphysical" question.

The first humanism, the Roman, and all the humanisms that have since appeared, presupposes as self-evident the most general "essence" of man. Man is considered as the *animal rationale*. This determination is not only the Latin translation of the Greek ζῷον λόγον ἔχον but a metaphysical interpretation. This essential determination of man is not wrong, but it is conditioned by metaphysics. Its essential extraction and not merely its limit has, however, become questionable in *Sein und Zeit*. This questionableness is first of all given to thought as what has to be thought, but not in such a way as to be devoured by an empty skepticism.

Certainly metaphysics posits beings in their Being and so thinks of the Being of beings. But it does not discriminate between the two (cf. "Vom Wesen des Grundes" 1929, p. 8; *Kant und das Problem der Metaphysik*, 1929, p. 225; *Sein und Zeit*, p. 230). Metaphysics does not ask for the truth of Being itself. Nor does it ever ask, therefore, in what way the essence of man belongs to the truth of Being. This question metaphysics has not only not asked up to now, but this question cannot be treated by metaphysics as metaphysics. Being still waits for Itself to become memorable to man. However one may—in regard to the determination of the essence of man—determine the *ratio* of the animal and the reason of the living being, whether as "capacity for principles," or as "capacity for categories," or otherwise, everywhere and always the essence of reason is based upon the fact that for each perceiving of beings in their Being, Being itself is discovered and realized in its truth. In the same way, an interpretation of "life" is given in the term "animal," ζῷον, which necessarily rests on an interpretation of beings as ζωή and φύσις, within which what is living appears. Besides this, however, the question finally remains whether, originating and predetermining everything, the essence of man lies in the dimension of the *animalitas*. Are we on the right track at all to reach the essence of man, if and as long as we delimit man as a living-being amongst others, against plant, animal and God? One can so proceed, one can in such a way put man within beings as a being amongst others. Thereby one will always be able to assert what is correct about man. But one must also be clear in this regard that by this man remains cast off in the essential realm of *animalitas*, even when one does not put him on the same level as the animal, but attributes a specific difference to him. In principle one always thinks of the *homo animalis*, even when one puts *anima* as *animus sive mens* and later as subject, as person, as spirit. To put it so is the way of metaphysics. But by this the essence of man is too lightly considered and is not thought of in the light of its source, that essential source which always remains for historical humanity the essential future. Metaphysics thinks of man as arising from *animalitas* and does not think of him as pointing toward *humanitas*.

Metaphysics shuts itself off from the simple essential certitude that man is essentially only in his essence, in which he is claimed by Being. Only from this claim "has" he found wherein his essence dwells. Only from this dwelling "has" he "language" as the home which preserves the ecstatic for his essence. The standing in the clearing of Being I call the ex-sistence of man. Only man has this way to be. Ex-sistence, so understood, is not only the basis of the possibility of reason, *ratio*, but ex-sistence is that, wherein the essence of man preserves the source that determines him.

man's mode of living is radically different

Ex-sistence can only be said of the essence of man, i.e. only of the human way "to be"; for only man, as far as we know, is admitted into the destiny of ex-sistence. Thus ex-sistence can never be thought of as a specific way, amongst other ways, of a living being, so long as man is destined to think of the essence of his Being and not merely to report theories of nature and history about his composition and activity. Thus all that we attribute to man as *animalitas* in comparing him to the "animal" is grounded in the essence of ex-sistence. The body of man is something essentially different from the animal organism. The error of biologism has not yet been overcome by the fact that one affixes the soul to corporeal man and the mind to the soul and the existential to the mind, and more strongly than ever before preaches the appreciation of the mind, in order that everything may then fall back into the experience of life, with the admonitory assurance that thought will destroy by its rigid concepts the stream of life and the thought of Being will deform existence. That physiology and physiological chemistry can scientifically examine man as an organism, does not prove that in this "organic" disposition, i.e. in the body scientifically explained, the essence of man rests. This has as little value as the opinion that the essence of nature is contained in atomic energy. It may very well be that nature hides its essence in that aspect of which human technology has taken possession. As little as the essence of man consists of being an animal organism, so little can this insufficient determination of the essence of man be eliminated and compensated for by the fact that man is equipped with an immortal soul or with the capability of reason or with the character of a person. Each time the essence is overlooked and, no doubt, on the basis of the same metaphysical design.

All that man is, i.e. in the traditional language of metaphysics the "essence" of man, rests in his ex-sistence. But ex-sistence, so thought of, is not identical with the traditional concept of *existentia,* which signifies actuality in contrast to essentia as possibility. In *Sein und Zeit* (p. 42) is the sentence, italicized: "The 'essence' of being-there (*Dasein*) lies in its existence." Here, however, this is not a matter of opposing *existentia* and *essentia,* because these two metaphysical determinations of Being have not yet been placed in question, let alone their relationship. The sentence contains even less a general statement about "being-there," insofar as this term (brought into usage in the eighteenth century for the word "object") is to express the metaphysical concept of the actuality of the actual. The sentence says rather: man is essentially such that he is "Here" (*Da*), i.e. within the clearing of Being. This "Being" of the Here, and only this, has the basic trait of ex-sistence: i.e. it stands outside itself within the truth of Being. The ecstatic essence of man rests in the ex-sistence that remains different from the metaphysically conceived *existentia.* Medieval philosophy conceived this *existentia* as *actualitas.* Kant presents *existentia* as actuality in the sense of the objectivity of experience. Hegel determines *existentia* as the self-knowing idea of the absolute subjectivity. Nietzsche understands *existentia* as the eternal return of the same. Whether, however, through *existentia,* in its various interpretations as actuality, different only at first glance, the Being of the stone, or even life as the Being of plants and animals, has been sufficiently thought about, remains an open question here. In each case animals are as they are, without their standing—from their Being as such—in the truth of Being and preserving in such standing what is essentially their Being. Presumably, animals are the most difficult of all entities for us to think of, because we are, on the one hand, most akin to them and, on the other hand, they are, at the same time separated from our ex-sistential essence by an abyss. And against this it might seem that the essence of the divine is much nearer us than the strangeness of animals, nearer in an essential distance, which as distance is much more familiar to our existential essence than the barely conceivable abysmal corporeal kinship to the animal. Such reflections cast a strange light on the current and therefore still premature designation of man as an *animal rationale.* Because plants and animals, although bound to their environment, are never freely placed in the clearing of Being—and only this clearing is "world"—they have no language. But it is not because they are without language that they find themselves hanging worldless in their environment. Yet in the word "environment" is concentrated all the enigma of the animal. Language is in its essence not utterance of an organism nor is it expression of an animal. Thus it is never thought of with exactness in its symbolical or semantic character. Language is the clearing-and-concealing advent of Being itself.

Ex-sistence, ecstatically thought of, does not coincide with *existentia* either in regard to content or form. Ex-sistence means substantially the emerging into the truth of Being. *Existentia* (existence) means, however, *actualitas,* actuality in contrast to mere possibility as idea. Ex-sistence states the characteristic of man as he is in the destiny of truth. *Existentia* remains the name for the actualization of something-that-is, as an instance of its idea. The phrase, "man exists," does not answer the question of whether there are actually men or not; it answers the question of the "essence" of man. We usually put this question in an equally unsuitable way, whether we ask what man is or who he is. For, in the Who or What we are already on the lookout for something like a person or an object. Yet the personal, no less than the objective, misses and obstructs at the same time all that is essentially ex-sistence in its historical Being. Therefore, the quoted phrase in *Sein und Zeit* (p. 52) deliberately puts the word "essence" in quotation marks. This indicates that the "essence" is not now determined either from the *esse essentiae* or from the *esse existentiae,* but from the ec-static nature of "being-there." Insofar as he ex-sists, man endures the "being-there" by taking the There as the clearing of Being within his "care." The *Dasein* itself, however, is essentially the "thrown" (*geworfene*). It is essentially in the cast (*Wurf*) of Being, a destiny that destines, projects a destiny.

It would undoubtedly be the greatest error, if one were to explain the existent essence of man, as though it were the secularized translation of a thought about man by Christian theology via God (*Deus est suum esse*); for ex-sistence is neither the actualization of an essence, nor does ex-sistence itself realize and constitute the essential. If one understands the "project" (*Entwurf*), alluded to in *Sein und Zeit* as a representative concept [an idea in the mind of an agent] then one considers it as an act of subjectivity and does not think of it as one should within the realm of the "existential analysis" of the "Being-in-the-world" (*In-der-Welt-Seins*), i.e. as the ecstatic relation to the clearing of Being. The necessary and sufficiently verified comprehension of this other way of thought—the thought that abandons subjectivity—is, however, made more difficult by the fact that at the publication of *Sein und Zeit* the third section of the first part, i.e. "Time and Being," was suppressed (cf. *Sein und Zeit*, p. 39). Here the whole thing is reversed. The section in question was suppressed because the thinking failed to find language adequate to this reversal and did not succeed through the aid of the language of metaphysics. The lecture "On the Essence of Truth," which was composed and delivered in 1930, but was first printed in 1943, gives some insight into the thought of the reversal from "Being and Time" to "Time and Being". This reversal is not a change from the standpoint of *Sein und Zeit*, but in it the intended thought for the first time attains the place of the dimension from which "Being and Time" is experienced; and, indeed, experienced from the basic experience of Being.

Sartre formulates, on the other hand, the basic principle of existentialism as this: existence precedes essence, whereby he understands *existentia* and *essentia* in the sense of metaphysics, which since Plato has said *essentia* precedes *existentia*. Sartre reverses this phrasing. But the reversal of a metaphysical phrase remains a metaphysical phrase. As such it remains with metaphysics in the oblivion of the truth of Being. For though philosophy may determine the relationship between *essentia* and *existentia* in the sense of the controversy of the Middle Ages or in the sense of Leibniz or others, one must first of all ask, through what destiny of Being this difference in Being as *esse essentiae* and *esse existentiae* precedes thought. It remains to be considered why this question about the destiny of Being has never been asked and why it could never be thought. Or isn't this a sign of the oblivion of Being that there is this difference between *essentia* and *existentia*? We may suppose that this destiny does not lie in a mere neglect by human thought, let alone in an inferior capacity of earlier western thought. The difference—hidden in its essential source—between *essentia* (essentiality) and *existentia* (actuality) dominates the destiny of Western history and of all the history determined by Europe.

* * *

In order that we today, however, may arrive at the dimension of the truth of Being, we have first of all to make clear how Being concerns man and how it claims him. Such an essential experience happens to us when it dawns upon us that man is, as long as he exists. Let us say this first in the language of tradition, which says: the ex-sistence of man is his substance. For this reason in *Sein und Zeit* the following phrase often recurs: "the 'substance' of man is ex-sistence" (pp. 117, 212, 314). But "substance" is already understood according to the history of Being, the blanket translation of οὐσία, a word which designates the presence of one present and at the same time very often signifies with a mysterious ambiguity what is present (*das Anwesende*). If we think of the metaphysical term "substance" in this sense, which in *Sein und Zeit* is already suggested because of the "phenomenological destruction" realized there (cf. p. 25), then the phrase "the 'substance' of man is existence" does not say anything other than that the way in which man is essentially in his own essence moving toward Being, is that he stands outside himself within the truth of Being. Through this essential determination of man the humanistic interpretations of man as *animal rationale,* as "person," or as an intellectual, spiritual, corporeal, being, are not declared wrong, nor rejected. The only thought is rather that the highest humanistic determinations of the essence of man do not yet come to know the authentic dignity of man. In this the thinking in *Sein und Zeit* runs counter to humanism. But this opposition does not mean that such thinking would make common cause with the opposite of the human and espouse the inhuman, defend inhumanity and degrade the dignity of man. Humanism is opposed because it does not set the *humanitas* of man high enough. However, the essential dignity of man does not lie in the fact that he is as the "subject" of beings, their substance, so that as the despot of Being he may let the character of beings dissolve into an "objectivity" that is much too loudly praised.

Man is rather "cast" by Being itself into the truth of Being, in order that he, ex-sisting thus, may guard the truth of Being; in order that in the light of Being, beings as beings may appear as what it is. Whether and how it appears, whether and how God and the gods, history and nature, enter, presenting and absenting themselves in the clearing of Being, is not determined by man. The advent of beings rests in the destiny of Being. For man, however, the question remains whether he finds what is appropriate to his essence to correspond to his destiny; according to this, as an ex-sisting person, he has to guard the truth of Being. Man is the guardian of Being. The thinking in *Sein und Zeit* proceeds towards this, when ecstatic existence only is experienced as "care" (cf. sec. 44a, p. 226 ff.).

Yet Being—what is Being? It is Itself. Future thought must learn to experience and to express this. "Being" is neither God nor the basis of the world. Being is further from all that is being and yet closer to man than every being, be it a rock, an animal, a work of art, a machine, be it an angel or God. Being is the closest. Yet its closeness remains farthest from man. Man first clings always and only to beings. But when thought represents beings as beings it no doubt refers to Being. Yet, in fact, it always thinks only of beings as such and never of Being as such. The "question of Being" always remains the question of beings. The question of Being still does not get at what this captious term means: the question seeking for Being. Philosophy, even when critical, as in Descartes and Kant, always follows the procedure of metaphysical representation. It thinks from beings to beings with a glance in passing at Being. For the light of Being already implies each departure from beings and each return to them.

Metaphysics, however, knows the clearing of Being as the looking toward what is present in its appearance (ἰδέα), or critically as what is seen of the external aspect of the categorical representation from the side of subjectivity. This means: the truth of Being as the clearing itself remains concealed from metaphysics. This concealment, however, is not a defect of metaphysics, but the treasure of its own richness, which is withheld and yet held up to it. The clearing itself, however, is Being. Within the destiny of Being the clearing grants a view to metaphysics, a view from which all that is present is attained by man as he presents himself to it, so that man himself can only attain Being (θιγεῖν, Aristotle, *Metaphysics,* theta, 10) through intellection (νοεῖν). The outward view only draws upon itself. Man yields to this, when intellection has become the projection in the *perceptio* of the *res cogitans* taken as the *subiectum* of the *certitudo*.

Or to proceed in more straightforward fashion perhaps: What relation has Being to ex-sistence? Being itself is the relationship, insofar as It retains and reunites ex-sistence in its existential (i.e. ecstatic) essence—as the place of the truth of Being amidst the beings. Since man as an existing one comes to stand in this relationship which Being itself professes to be, insofar as he, man, ecstatically stands (*aussteht*) it, i.e. insofar as he, caring, takes over, he fails to recognize at first the closest and clings to the next closest. He even believes that this is the closest. Yet closer than the closest and at the same time, for ordinary thought, farther than his farthest is closensss itself: the truth of Being.

The oblivion of the truth of Being under the impact of beings, which is not considered in its essence, is the sense of "decadence" in *Sein und Zeit*. This word does not signify the fall of man, understood as in a "moral philosophy" that has been secularized; this word states an essential relationship between man and Being with the relation of Being to man's essence. In view of this, the terms "authenticity" and "unauthenticity" (*Eigentlichkeit und Uneigentlichkeit*) do not signify a moral-existential or an "anthropological" distinction, but the "ecstatic" relation of man's essence to the truth of Being, which is still to be realized and up to now has remained concealed from philosophy. But this relation, such as it is, does not derive from ex-sistence, but the essence of ex-sistence derives existential-ecstatically from the essence of the truth of Being.

The unique thought that *Sein und Zeit* attempts to express, wants to achieve, is something simple. As such, Being remains mysterious, the plain closeness of an unobtrusive rule. This closeness is essentially language itself. Yet the language is not merely language, insofar as we imagine it at the most as the unity of sound-form (script), melody and rhythm and meaning. We think of sound-form and script as the body of the word; of melody and rhythm as the soul and of meaning as the mind of language. We generally think of language as corresponding to the essence of man, insofar as this essence is represented as *animal rationale,* i.e. as the unity of body-soul-mind. But as in the *humanitas* of the *homo animalis* ex-sistence remains concealed and through this the relation of the truth of Being to man, so does the metaphysical-animal interpretation of language conceal its essence from the point of view of the history of Being. According to this, language is the house of Being, owned and pervaded by Being. Therefore, the point is to think of the essence of language in its correspondence to Being and, what is more, as this very correspondence, i.e., the dwelling of man's essence.

Man, however, is not only a living being, who besides other faculties possesses language. Language is rather the house of Being, wherein living, man ex-sists, while he, guarding it, belongs to the truth of Being.

Thus, what matters in the determination of the humanity of man as ex-sistence is not that man is the essential, but that Being is the essential as the dimension of the ecstatic of ex-sistence. This, however, is not the spatial dimension. All that is spatial and all time-space is essentially dimensional, which is what Being itself is.

Thought heeds these simple relationships. It seeks the appropriate word for them amidst the traditional language and grammar of metaphysics. Can such thought, if terminology is important at all, still be denominated as humanism? Certainly not, insofar as humanism thinks metaphysically. . . . Instead of this, if we think as in *Sein und Zeit*, we should say: *précisement nous sommes sur un plan où il y a principialement l'Etre.* But whence does *le plan* come and what is it? *L'Etre et le plan* are the same. In *Sein und Zeit* (p. 212) it is said intentionally and cautiously: *il y a l'Etre*: "it gives" (there is) Being. The *il y a* translates the "it gives" inexactly. For the "it," which here "gives," is Being itself. The "gives" names, however, the essence of Being; the giving itself and the imparting of its truth. The giving itself into the open with this self, is Being itself.

At the same time "it gives" is used in order to avoid at once the locution. "Being is"; for usually the "is" is said of what-is. This we call "the being." Being "is," however, precisely not "the being." Were the "is" said without closer interpretation of Being, then Being would all too easily be represented as a "being" in the manner of the known being, which as cause effects and as effect is effectuated. Nevertheless, Parmenides had already said in the early days of thought: ἔστιν γὰρ εἶναι, "Being is." In this utterance the original mystery of all thought is concealed. Perhaps this "is" is not and could only be appropriately said of Being, so that no being ever properly "is." But because thought should first manage to express Being in its truth, instead of explaining it as a trait of the being, it must be open to the attention of thought whether and how Being is.

The ἔστιν γὰρ εἶναι of Parmenides has as yet been given no thought. From this we can realize the state of progress in philosophy. If it considers its essence, it never progresses at all, It marks time by continually thinking the same thing. The progressing, i.e., away from this spot, is an error that follows thought as the shadow it casts. Since Being is as yet unthought of, it is said of Being in *Sein und Zeit*, "it gives." Yet one cannot speculate directly and without help upon this *il y a*. The "it gives" rules as the destiny of Being. Its history finds expression in the words of the essential thinkers. So the thought that thinks of the truth of Being thinks historically. There is no "systematic" thinking, nor is there a history of past opinions as illustration. Nor is there even, as Hegel believed, a systematics, which could deduce from the laws of its thought a law of history and at the same time reduce it to the system. There is, it was originally believed, the history of Being, to which thought belongs as the remembrance of this history, realized by itself. This remembrance is to be distinguished essentially from the posterior representation of history in the sense of the past passing. History does not at first occur as occurrence. And it is not the passing. The occurrence of history lives as the destiny of the truth of Being, and derives from it (cf. The essay on Hölderlin's Hymn "*Wie wenn am Feiertage,*" 1941, p. 31). Being comes to destiny, as It, Being, gives itself. This, however, means from the point of view of destiny that it gives itself and negates itself at the same time. Nonetheless, Hegel's determination of history as the development of the "mind" is not wrong. Nor is it neither partly right, nor partly wrong. It is as true as metaphysics is, which through Hegel for the first time absolutely expresses its essence systematically. Absolute metaphysics belongs with its inversions via Marx and Nietzsche to the history of the truth of Being. Whatever stems from it cannot be affected or done away with by refutation. It can only be appraised, as its truth is reintegrated more incipiently into Being itself and removed from the sphere of mere human opinion. To refute everything in the field of essential thought is ridiculous. A quarrel amongst thinkers is a ''lovers' quarrel'' for the thing itself. It helps them mutually in their belonging to that one and the same sphere, in which they find what is appropriate in the destiny of Being.

Granted that man is capable of thinking of the truth of Being in the future, he will think from his ex-sistence. Ex-sisting, he stands in the destiny of Being. The ex-sistence of man as ex-sistence is historical, but not primarily for that reason, or simply for that reason, because many a thing may occur with man and human affairs in the course of time. Because it is important to think of the ex-sistence of *Da-sein*, it is quite essential to the thinking in *Sein und Zeit* that the historicity of *Dasein* be grasped.

But is it not said in *Sein und Zeit* (p. 212), where the ''it gives'' finds expression that ''only as long as Dasein is, is there Being?'' Indeed, it is. This means that only as long as the clearing of Being is realized, is Being itself conveyed to man. That the ''Da'' (Here), however, the clearing of Being itself, is realized, is the destination of Being itself. This is the destiny of the clearing. The sentence, however, does not mean that the Dasein of man in the traditional sense of *existentia*, understood more recently as the actuality of the *ego cogito*, would be the existent through which alone Being is created. The sentence does not say that Being is a product of man. The introduction to *Sein und Zeit* (p. 38) states simply and clearly and even in italics that ''Being is the *transcendens* as such.'' Just as the openness of spatial nearness surpasses everything near and far, so Being is essentially broader than all the beings, because it is the clearing itself. Thus, in accordance with the next inevitable attack of the still dominant metaphysics, Being will be thought of as deriving from beings. Only from such an outlook does Being show itself in such a surpassing.

The preliminary definition of ''Being as the *transcendens* as such'' expresses simply the way in which the essence of Being has so far been cleared for man. This retrospective definition of the essence of Being out of the clearing of beings is and remains indispensable for further thinking of the question of the truth of Being. So thought attests to its historical essence. It is far from the pretension of wishing to begin from the beginning and to declare all previous philosophy wrong. Whether, however, the definition of Being as the simple *transcendens* yet expresses the simple essence of the truth of Being, this and this alone is the immediate question for the thinking that tries to think of the truth of Being. For this reason you find (on page 230) that only from "meaning," that is from the truth of Being, can one understand how Being is. Being clears itself for man in ecstatic projection. But this projection does not create Being.

Moreover, the projection is essentially a matter of being cast. What projects in the project is not man, but Being itself, which destines man to the ex-sistence which is the essence of *Dasein*. This destiny is realized as the clearing of Being. The clearing imparts the closeness to Being. In this closeness, in the clearing of the "Da" (Here), man dwells as one existing, without being capable now of properly experiencing and taking over this dwelling. The closeness of Being, which is the "Da" of *Dasein*, is thought of (from the point of view of *Sein und Zeit*) in my essay on Hölderlin's elegy *"Heimkunft"* (1943) as the "Homeland" (*Heimat*), as understood by the poet from the experience of the oblivion of Being. The word is here thought of in an essential sense, neither patriotic, nor nationalistic, but according to the history of Being. The essence of the homeland, however, is at the same time expressed with the intention of thinking of the homelessness of modern man as seen from the essence of the history of Being. The last one to experience this homelessness was Nietzsche. He was incapable of finding any other way out of metaphysics than by the reversal of metaphysics. This, however, is the height of being lost. Hölderlin, in contrast, when he writes *"Heimkunft"* is concerned that his "countrymen" find their essential home. He by no means seeks this in an egoism of his people. He sees it rather in their belonging to the destiny of the Western world. But even the Western world is not thought of regionally as the Occident in contrast to the Orient, nor merely as Europe, but in the frame of world history from the closeness to its origin. We have hardly begun to think of the mysterious relations to the East, which find expression in Hölderlin's poetry (cf. *"Der Ister"* as well as *"Die Wanderung,"* 3rd. stanza and ff.). The "German" is not said to the world so that the world may be healed thanks to the German essence, but it is said to the Germans so that they from their fateful membership amongst the nations may become with them world-historical (cf. Hölderlin's poem *"Andenken,"* *Tübinger Gedenkschrift*, 1943, v. 322). The homeland of this historical dwelling is the closeness to Being.

In this closeness the decision, if any, is reached as to whether and how God and the gods deny themselves and the night remains, whether and how the day of the Holy dawns, whether and how in the rise of the Holy an appearance of God and the gods can start anew. The Holy, however, which is only the essential space of divinity, for its part yields; but the dimension for the gods and God only comes into appearance when, first and after a long preparation, Being itself has been cleared and been experienced in its truth. Only in this way does the overcoming of homelessness start from Being, where not only man, but the essence of man, wanders about.

Homelessness, so understood, lies in beings' abandonment of Being. It is the sign of the oblivion of Being. Consequently, the truth of Being remains unthought of. The oblivion of Being is indirectly evidenced in the fact that man only considers and cultivates beings. Since he cannot help having a conception of Being it is explained as the "most general" and for that reason as what embraces beings; or as the universe of an infinite being or as the handiwork of a finite subject. At the same time "Being" stands of old for "beings" and vice-versa, both are tossed about in a strange and still thoughtless confusion.

Being as the destiny that destines truth remains concealed. But the world's destiny is proclaimed in poetry without its becoming apparent at once as the history of Being. Hölderlin's world-historical thought, which finds expression in the poem *"Andenken,"* is therefore essentially much more original and so much more appropriate to the future than the mere cosmopolitanism of Goethe. For the same reason Hölderlin's relation to the Greek world is an essentially different thing from humanism. Therefore, young Germans who knew of Hölderlin have thought and lived (in the face of death) other than what publicity proclaimed as the German attitude.

Homelessness becomes a world destiny. It is, therefore, necessary to think of this destiny from the point of view of the history of Being. What Marx, deriving from Hegel, recognized in an essential and significant sense as the alienation of man, reaches roots back into the homelessness of modern man. This is evoked—from the destiny of Being—in the form of metaphysics, strengthened by it and at the same time covered by it in its character as homelessness. Because Marx, in discovering this alienation, reaches into an essential dimension of history, the Marxist view of history excels all other history. . . .

For this it is necessary to liberate oneself from the naïve conceptions of materialism and from the cheap, supposedly effective, refutations of it. The essence of materialism does not consist of the assertion that everything is merely matter, but rather of a metaphysical determination, according to which everything being appears as the material of labor. The modern metaphysical essence of labor is anticipated in Hegel's *Phenomenology of the Spirit* as the self-establishing process of unconditional production; i.e., the objectivization of the actual through man experienced as subjectivity. The essence of materialism is concealed in the essence of technics, about which, indeed, a great deal is written, but little is thought. Technics in its essence is a destiny (in the history of Being) of the truth of Being resting in oblivion. It not only goes back in its name to the Greek τέχνη but it historically stems from τέχνη as a way of the ἀληθεύειν i.e. the making open of beings. As a form of truth technics is grounded in the history of metaphysics. This is itself an exceptional phase of the history of Being. One can take various positions in regard to the theories (and arguments) of communism, but from the point of view of the history of Being, it is indisputable that in it an elementary experience has been made manifest of what is world-historical. He who takes "communism" only as a "party" or as *"Weltanschauung,"* is thinking just as narrowly as those who by the term "Americanism" mean—and what is more in a depreciatory way—a particular mode of life. The danger into which Europe up to now has been more and more clearly pushed, probably consists of the fact that its thought, which was once its greatness, lags behind the destiny that opens for the world, a destiny which undoubtedly in the basic traits of its essential origin remains European in its determination. No metaphysics, be it idealistic, materialistic, or Christian, considering its essence and not its sporadic efforts, can, to develop itself overtake this destiny, i.e. reach it by thought and bring together what, in a complete sense of Being, now is.

In view of the essential homelessness of man the thought of the history of Being demonstrates the future destiny of man in that he investigates the truth of Being and sets out toward its discovery. Each nationalism is metaphysically an anthropologism and as such subjectivism. Nationalism is not overcome by mere internationalism, but only expanded and elevated to a system. Nationalism is far from being annulled by it or brought to *humanitas,* as individualism is by historical collectivism. This is the subjectivity of man in totality. He realizes its absolute self-assertion. This cannot be canceled. It cannot even be sufficiently experienced by one-sided thinking that tries to mediate. Everywhere man, thrust out from the truth of Being, runs around in a circle as the *animal rationale*.

The essence of man, however, consists of being more than mere man, insofar as this mere man is represented as a rational animal. "More" must not be understood here in an additive sense, as if the traditional definition of man were to remain as the basic definition, in order to undergo an expansion through an addition of the existential. The "more" means: more original and, therefore, in essence more essential. But here the mysterious is manifest: man is in his thrownness (*Geworfenheit*). This means that man is as the ex-sisting counter-throw (*Gegenwurf*) of Being even more than the *animal rationale,* insofar as he is less related to the man who is conceived from subjectivity. Man is not the master of beings. Man is the shepherd of Being. In this "less" man does not suffer any loss, but gains, because he comes into the truth of Being. He gains the essential poverty of the shepherd whose dignity rests in the fact that he was called by Being itself into the trueness of his truth. This call comes as the throw, from which stems the thrownness of the *Da-sein.* Man is in his essence (from the point of view of the history of Being) that being whose Being as ex-sistence consists of dwelling in the nearness of Being. Man is the neighbor of Being.

* * *

In *Sein und Zeit* (p. 38) it is said that all questioning of philosophy "strikes back into existence." But existence is here not the actuality of the *ego cogito.* Nor is it the actuality of subjects that act with and for each other and in this way come into their own. "Ex-sistence" is basically different from all *existentia* and "existence," the ec-static dwelling in the nearness of Being. It is the guardianship, i.e. the concern of Being. Since in this thinking something simple is to be thought, it is very difficult to represent it by traditional philosophy. Yet the difficulty does not consist of indulging in a particular profundity and of forming complex conceptions, but it conceals itself in stepping back and letting thought take up a skilful inquiry and abandon the trained opinions of philosophy.

It is everywhere believed that the effort in *Sein und Zeit* has ended up a blind alley. We won't discuss this opinion here. The thought, which in the above mentioned essay attempted a few steps, has not yet passed beyond *Sein und Zeit*. But perhaps it has in the meantime come a little bit more into its own. As long as philosophy, however, occupies itself only with constantly obstructing possibilities, with engaging in matters of thought—i.e. the truth of Being—, so long is it perfectly secure from the danger of ever breaking down at the hardness of its matter. So the "philosophizing" about the failure is separated by an abyss from a failing thought. If a man should be fortunate in this, no misfortunes would occur. For him it would be the only gift that thought could receive from Being.

Yet this too is important: the matter of thinking is not reached by talking about "the truth of Being" and of "the history of Being." Everything depends upon bringing into language the truth of Being and letting thought penetrate this language. Perhaps then language requires far less precipitate utterance than correct silence. Yet who amongst us today would like to imagine that his attempts at thought were at home on the path of silence? If it goes far enough, our thought might perhaps point to the truth of Being and to it as what is to be thought. In this way it would be more than anything else removed from mere suspicion and opinion and be allotted to the already rare handiwork of script. The matters, in which something is, even if they are not determined for eternity, come in due time.

Whether the realm of the truth of Being is a blind alley or whether it is the free dimension in which freedom saves its essence, each one may judge for himself after having tried to go his appointed way or blaze a better; that is, one in more accord with the question. On the next to the last page of *Sein und Zeit* (p. 437) are the words "the *dispute* in regard to the interpretation of Being (i.e. not of the existent, nor of the Being of man) cannot be straightened out, *because it has not even been begun*. And in the end one cannot 'pick a quarrel,' for the beginning of a dispute requires some equipment. Only towards that is the investigation aimed." These words retain their validity even after two decades. Let us also in the coming days be voyagers to the neighborhood of Being. The question which you put helps to clarify the way.

You ask: *Comment redonner un sens au mot "Humanisme"*? "How can one restore meaning to the word humanism?" Your question not only presupposes that you want to retain the word "humanism," but it also contains the admission that the word has lost its meaning.

It has lost it through the realization that the essence of humanism is metaphysical and this now means that metaphysics not only does not ask the question of the truth of Being, but even abstracts asking it, insofar as metaphysics persists in its oblivion of Being. The thought, however, that leads to this realization of the questionable essence of humanism has at the same time brought us to think of the essence of man more originally. In view of this more essential *humanitas* of the *homo humanus,* the possibility follows of restoring to the word humanism an historical meaning that is older than what "history" considers the oldest. This restoration is not to be understood as though the word humanism were without meaning at all and a mere *flatus vocis.* The *"humanum"* in the word points to the *humanitas,* the essence of man. The "ism" indicates that the essence of man would like to be understood essentially. The word "humanism" has this meaning as a word. This requires first that we experience the essence of man more originally; and then show in what degree this essence becomes in its own way a destiny. The essence of man rests in ex-sistence. This essence desires from Being itself, insofar as Being raises man as the ex-sisting one for the guardianship of the truth of Being. "Humanism" means now, should we decide to retain the word: the essence of man is essential for the truth of Being, and apart from this truth of Being man himself does not matter. So we think of a "humanism" of a strange sort. The word offers a term which is a *lucus a non lucendo.*

Should one still call "humanism" this view which speaks out against all earlier humanism, but which does not at all advocate the in-human? And this only in order to swim perhaps in the dominant currents, which are stifled in a metaphysical subjectivism and find themselves drowned in the oblivion of Being? Or should thought, resisting the word "humanism," make an effort to become more attentive to the *humanitas* of the *homo humanus* and what grounds this *humanitas*? So, if the world-historical moment has not already gone that far itself, a reflection might be awakened that would not only think of man, but of the "nature" of man, and even more than this of his nature, the original dimension in which the essence of man, determined as coming from Being itself, is at home. But perhaps we should rather suffer for a while the inevitable misinterpretations to which the way of thought that centers on Being and time has so far been exposed and let them gradually be worn out? These misinterpretations are the natural reinterpretations of what people had read or rather, what they later thought they had read, but which, in fact, was preconception. They all show the same structure and the same basis.

Because "humanism" is argued against, one fears a defense of the inhuman and a glorification of barbaric cruelty. For what is more "logical" than that for one who negates humanism only the affirmation of inhumanity can remain?

Because "logic" is argued against, one believes that we renounce the rigor of thinking and in its place enthrone the despotism of instincts and emotions, and so proclaim "irrationalism" as the truth. For what is more "logical" than that one who argues against the logical defends the a-logical?

Because "values" are argued against, one is shocked by a philosophy that allegedly dares to neglect the highest goods of humankind. For what is more "logical" than that thinking which negates values must necessarily declare everything valueless?

Because it is said that the Being of man consists of "Being-in-the-World" (*In-der-Welt-sein*), one considers man to have been degraded to the level of a mere this-worldly being, and that philosophy thereby sinks into positivism. For what is more "logical" than that one who maintains the worldliness of man only admits the this-worldly, thereby negating the other-worldly and renouncing all "transcendency"?

Because reference is made to Nietzsche's expression of "God's death," one declares such a procedure to be atheism. For what is more "logical" than that one who has experienced "God's death" is a godless person?

Because in all that has been said I have argued everywhere against what mankind values as high and holy, this philosophy therefore teaches an irresponsible and destructive "nihilism." For what is more "logical" than that one who negates everywhere what is truly being, places himself on the side of the nonbeing and with that advocates mere nothingness as the meaning of reality?

What is happening here? One hears talk of "humanism," of "logic," of "values," of "world," of "God." One hears talk of an opposition to these. One knows and takes these things as positive. What is expressed against them, one immediately takes as their negation and thus "negative" in a sense of the destructive. This is a question of what, in a certain part of *Sein und Zeit,* we called "the phenomenological destruction." One believes that with the help of logic and *ratio* [Reason] that all that is not positive is negative and so would reject reason; and therefore, deserves to be branded as an infamy. One is so full of "logic," that everything which is repugnant to the usual somnolence of opinion is immediately charged to a censurable contrariness. One casts all that does not remain in the well-known beloved positive into the prearranged pit of bare negation that negates everything and therefore ends in nothingness and so achieves nihilism. In this logical way one lets everything succumb to a nihilism that one has fabricated with the help of logic.

But is it certain that the apparition that thought brings up against common opinion necessarily points to mere negation and to the negative? This occurs only when (but then so inevitably and so definitively, that is, without a free view of other directions) one fixes beforehand what is meant by "the positive" and from this decides absolutely and negatively against the sphere of possible oppositions to it. Such a procedure hides the refusal to expose to scrutiny the preconceived "positive," together with the black and white opposition, in which it believes that it has preserved itself. Through the constant appeal to logic one produces the illusion that one has yielded to thought, while one has abjured it.

That the opposition to "humanism" by no means implies the defence of the inhuman, but opens other prospectives must have become clearer to some extent now.

"Logic" understands thought as the representation of beings in their Being, and this Being as producing this representation as a universal concept. But how is it with the consideration of Being itself, i.e., with thought that thinks of the truth of Being? Such thought reaches the original essence of the λόγος, which in Plato and Aristotle, the founder of "logic," had already been dead and buried. To think "counter to logic" does not mean to stick up for the illogical, but only means to think the *logos,* and its essence as it appeared in the early days of thought; i.e. to make an effort first of all to prepare such an act of re-flecting (*Nachdenkens*). Of what use are all such prolix systems of logic to us, when even without knowing what they are doing they immediately avoid the task of asking after the essence of the λόγος?   If one wanted to retaliate with objections, which is frankly fruitless, then one could more rightly say that irrationalism, as a renunciation of *ratio,* rules as unrecognized and undisputed master of that "logic" which believes it can avoid a consideration of the *logos* and of the essence of *ratio,* which is founded on the *logos.*

The thinking that runs counter to "values" does not state that all that one declares "values"—"culture," "art," "science," "human dignity," "world," and "God"—is worthless. One should rather come to understand that it is exactly through the characterization of something as "value," that it loses its dignity. This is to say that through the estimation of something as a value, one accepts what is evaluated only as a mere object for the appreciation of man. But what a thing is in its Being is not exhausted by its being an object, much less when the objectivity has the character of value. All valuing, even when it values positively, subjectivizes the thing. It does not let beings be, but makes them valuable as the object of its action. The extravagant effort to demonstrate the objectivity of values does not know what it is doing. When one proclaims "God" as altogether "the highest value," this is a degradation of the essence of God. Thinking in values here and in general is the greatest blasphemy that can be thought of in the face of Being. To think counter to values, therefore, does not mean to beat the drum for the worthlessness and nullity of the existent, but means to bring—against the subjectivization of the existent as mere object—the clearing of the truth of Being before thought.

To refer to "Being-in-the-World" as the basic trait of the *humanitas* of the *homo humanus* is not to claim that man is simply a secular being, in the Christian sense, and so turned away from God and devoid of "transcendency." What is meant by this last word might be more clearly called: the Transcendent. The Transcendent is the super-sensual being. This is valued as the supreme being in the sense of the first cause of every being. God is thought of as this first cause. "World," however, does not in any way signify, in the term "Being-in-the-World," the earthly being in contrast to the heavenly, nor does it mean the "secular" in contrast to the "spiritual." "World" does not signify in this determination a being at all and no realm of beings, but the openness of Being. Man is and is man insofar as he is the existing. He stands exposed to the openness of Being, an openness which is Being itself, that has projected the essence of man into "care." So thrown, man stands "in" the openness of Being. "World" is the clearing of Being, wherein man stands out from his thrown essence. "Being-in-the-World" names the essence of ex-sistence in relation to the cleared dimension out of which the "ex" of the ex-sistence essentially arises. Thought of from the point of view of ex-sistence, "world" is in a way transcendence within and for existence. Man is never this-worldly and of the world as a "subject," whether this "subject" be understood as "I" or as "We." He is also not essentially a subject who is also always in reference to an object, so that his essence lies in the subject-object relation. Man is rather in his essence ex-sistent in the openness of Being; this Open only clears the "between," within which the "relation" between subject and object can "be."

The statement that the essence of man rests in Being-in-the-World contains no resolution about whether man is in the theological-metaphysical sense a mere this-worldly creature or an other-worldly one.

Therefore, with the existential determination of the essence of man nothing has yet been decided about the "existence" or "non-existence" of God, not about the possibility or impossibility of God. It is thus not only precipitate but erroneous to assert that the interpretation of the essence of man in its relation to the truth of Being is atheism. This arbitrary classification, besides everything else, lacks carefulness in reading. One ignores the fact that since 1929 the following statement could be found in the work *Vom Wesen des Grundes* (p. 28, fn. 1): "Through the word "God" is to signify. Or must we not first be able to under- neither a positive nor a negative resolution of a possible Being-towards-God. However, through the elucidation of the transcendency there is first obtained *an adequate concept of Dasein,* in consideration of which one may now ask what exactly is, ontologically, the relationship between God and *Dasein."* Now when this observation, too, is, as usual, taken too narrowly, one is likely to say that this philosophy makes no decision either for or against the existence of God. It remains indifferent. Thus, the religious question does not concern it. Such "indifferentism" must surely turn into nihilism.

But does the quoted remark really teach indifferentism? Why, then, are some words, and not others, printed in italics in the footnotes? Only to indicate, surely, that thought that thinks from the question of the truth of Being questions more originally than metaphysics can. Only from the truth of Being can the essence of the holy be thought. Only from the essence of the holy can the essence of divinity be thought. Only in the light of the essence of divinity can it be thought and said what the word "God" is to signify. Or must we not first be able to understand and hear these words carefully if we as men, i.e., as existing beings, are to have the privilege of experiencing a relation of God to man? How, then, is the man of the present epoch even to be able to ask seriously and firmly whether God approaches or withdraws when man omits the primary step of thinking deeply in the one dimension where this question can be asked: that is, the dimension of the holy, which, even as dimension, remains closed unless the openness of Being is cleared and in its clearing is close to man. Perhaps the distinction of this age consists in the fact that the dimension of grace has been closed. Perhaps this is its unique dis-grace.

But with this indication, which points to the truth of Being as what-has-to-be-thought, this thought would in no way wish to have declared itself for theism. It can no more be theistic than it can be atheistic. This, however, is not because of any indifferent attitude but out of respect for the limits which have been set upon thought as thought, and precisely through which it is understood as that which has-to-be-thought, through the truth of Being. In so far as thought does not exceed the limits of its task, at the moment of present world destiny it gives man an indication of the original dimension of his historical abode. In so far as thought expresses in this way the truth of Being, it has entrusted itself to what is more essential than all values and all beings. Thought does not overcome metaphysics by surpassing and cancelling it in some direction or other and ascending ever higher: it descends into the nearness of the nearest. The descent, especially where man has ascended too far into subjectivity, is more difficult and more dangerous than the ascent. The descent leads to the poverty of the ex-sistence of the *homo humanus*. In ex-sistence, the sphere of the *homo animalis* of metaphysics is abandoned. The domination of this sphere is the indirect and very old reason for the delusion and arbitrariness of what is denominated as biologism, but also for what is known as pragmatism. To think of the truth of Being means at the same time to think of the *humanitas* of the *homo humanus*. What is at stake is *humanitas,* in the service of the truth of Being but without humanism in the metaphysical sense.

But if the thought of Being is so essentially focused on humanitas, must ontology then not be completed by "ethics"? . . .

Shortly after *Sein und Zeit* appeared, a young friend asked me, "When are you going to write an ethics?" Where the essence of man is thought of so essentially, i.e., only from the question of the truth of Being, but without raising man to the center of beings, there the desire must arise for personally relevant directives and rules that tell how man, having gathered from his ex-sistence experience for Being, is to live "fatefully." The wish for an ethics needs to be fulfilled, all the more urgently, because the overt no less than the concealed, perplexity of man increases to immeasurable dimensions. Every care must be given to ties to ethics, in an age of technology when the individual, subject to the nature of a mass society, can be brought to a dependable steadfastness only by means of ordering and gathering his plans and actions as a whole in a way that corresponds to a technological age.

Who can ignore this crisis? Should we not preserve and secure the ties we now have, even if they only hold human beings together precariously and in mere immediacy? Certainly. But does this crisis ever absolve thought of the responsibility of thinking of that which primarily remains to-be-thought and, as Being, remains the guarantee and truth prior to every being? Can thought continue to retreat from the thought of Being after this has lain so long hidden in oblivion and at the same time announces itself at this very moment of world history through the uprooting of every being?

Before we attempt to determine more precisely the relationship between "ontology" and "ethics," we must ask what "ontology" and "ethics" themselves are. It is necessary to consider whether what can be designated by these terms still remains adequate and close to what has been assigned to thought, which as thought has to think before all else of the truth of Being.

Should, however, "ontology" as well as "ethics" and all thinking in disciplines become untenable and our thinking thereby become more disciplined, what happens then to the question of the relationship between these two disciplines of philosophy?

Ethics appeared for the first time, along with logic and physics in the school of Plato. These disciplines were born at a time that converted thought into "philosophy," but philosophy into *episteme* (science) and science itself into a matter for schools and school administrations. In passing through philosophy, so understood, science was born and thought [*Denken*] vanished. Thinkers up to then had known neither a "logic," nor an "ethics," nor a "physics." Yet their thinking is neither illogical nor immoral. But their conception of *physis* had a profundity and breadth which all the later "physics" was never again able to attain. The tragedies of Sophocles, if such a comparison can be made at all, hold the ethics more originally concealed in their telling than Aristotle's lecture on "ethics." A saying of Heraclitus that only consists of three words says something so simple that from it the essence of the *ethos* immediately comes to light.

The saying of Heraclitus goes (frag.): ἦθος ἀνθρώπῳ δαίμων. This is usually translated as: "A man's character is his daimon." This translation is modern but not Greek thinking, ἦθος means an abode, place of dwelling. The word designates the open sphere in which man dwells. The openness of his abode allows that to appear which approaches toward the essence of man and so arriving abides near him. The abode of man contains and maintains the advent of that to which man in essence belongs. This, according to Heraclitus' saying, is δαίμων, God. The fragment says: Man, insofar as he is man, dwells in the nearness of God. A story that Aristotle relates (de part. anim. A 5, 645 a 17) coincides with this saying of Heraclitus. It runs: "An anecdote tells of an explanation that Heraclitus is said to have given strangers who wanted to approach him. Upon approaching they found him warming himself at a stove. They stopped surprised and all the more so because as they hesitated he encouraged them and bade them come in with the words: 'For here too there are Gods present.' "

The story speaks for itself, yet some aspects should be stressed.

The group of unknown visitors in its inquisitive curiosity about the thinker is disappointed and puzzled at first by his abode. It believes that it must find the thinker in conditions which, contrary to man's usual way of living, show everywhere traits of the exceptional and the rare, and, therefore, the sensational. The group hopes to find through its visit with the thinker things which, at least for a time, will provide material for entertaining small talk. The strangers who wish to visit the thinker hope to see him perhaps precisely at the moment when, sunk in profound meditation, he is thinking. The visitors wish to experience this, not in order to be affected by his thinking, but merely so that they will be able to say that they have seen and heard one who is reputed to be a thinker.

Instead, the inquisitive ones find Heraclitus at a stove. This is a pretty ordinary and insignificant place. True enough, bread is baked there. But Heraclitus is not even busy with baking at the stove. He is there only to warm himself, and so he betrays the whole poverty of his life at this spot which is in itself prosaic. The glimpse of a freezing thinker offers little of interest. And so the inquisitive ones at this disappointing sight immediately lose their desire to come any closer. What are they to do there? This ordinary dull event of someone cold and standing by the stove one can find any time in his own home. Then, why look up a thinker? The visitors are about to leave again. Heraclitus reads the disappointed curiosity in their faces. He realizes that with the crowd the mere absence of an expected sensation is enough to make those who have just come leave. Therefore, he heartens them. He especially urges them to enter the words εἶναι γὰρ καὶ ἐνταῦθα θέους. There are Gods present even here."

This statement puts the abode (ἦθος) of the thinker and his doing in a different light. Whether the visitors have understood the statement immediately or at all and then seen everything in this different light, the story does not tell. But that the story was told and transmitted to us today, is due to the fact that what it reports is of the bearing of this thinker and characterizes it. καὶ ἐνταῦθα. "Even here," at the baking oven, at this common place, where all things and every condition, each act and thought, are familiar and current, i.e., securer, "even there" in the sphere of the secure εἶναι θεούς it is so "that even there there are gods present."

ἦθος ἀνθρώπῳ δαίμων   Heraclitus says: "The (secure) abode for man is the open quality of the presence (*Anwesung*) of God" (of the insecure, the strange) (*des Un-geheuren*).

If now, in accord with the basic meaning of the word ἦθος, ethics dwells in the abode of man, then that thought which thinks the truth of Being as the original element of man as existing is already in itself at the source of ethics. But then this kind of thinking is not ethics, either, because it is ontology. For ontology always thinks only the being (ὄν) in its Being. As long as the truth of Being, however, is not thought, all ontology remains without its base. Hence the thought, which with *Sein und Zeit* tried to think forward into the truth of Being, called itself fundamental ontology. It attempts to go back to the basic essence, from which the thought of the truth of Being derives. The formulation of different questions removes this thinking from the "ontology" of metaphysics (including that of Kant). The reason, however, why "ontology," be it transcendental or precritical, is not subject to criticism is not that it thinks the Being of beings and thereby forces Being into a concept, but that it does not think the truth of Being and so fails to realize the fact that there is a mode of thinking more rigorous than the conceptual. Thinking which tries to think forward into the truth of Being in the struggle of the first breakthrough expresses only a small part of this entirely different dimension. And the latter is further distorted in that it no longer retains the essential health of phenomenological vision and has not yet abandoned its inadequate pretensions toward "science" and "research." In order to make this attempt of thinking recognizable and understandable within philosophy, it was possible at first to speak only within the horizon of the existing philosophy and within the usage of the terms familiar to it.

In the meantime I have come to be convinced that even these terms must immediately and inevitably lead astray. For the terms and their corresponding conceptual language were not rethought by the readers from the thing which had-to-be-thought first; instead, this thing was imagined through terms maintained in their usual signification. Thinking that seeks for the truth of Being and thereby determines the essential abode of man from Being is neither ethics nor ontology. Therefore, the question of the relationship of the two to each other has no longer any basis in this sphere. Nevertheless your question, if it be thought more originally, continues to make sense and be of essential importance.

One must, of course, ask: If thought, considering the truth of Being, determines the essence of the *humanitas* as ex-sistence from its pertinence to Being, does this thought only remain a theoretical imagining of Being and of man, or is it possible to extract from knowledge directives for action and put them to use for life?

The answer is that such thinking is neither theoretical nor practical. It occurs before such a differentiation. This thinking is, insofar as it is, the recollection of Being and nothing else. Belonging to Being, because it is thrown by being into the trueness of its truth and claims for it, it thinks Being. Such thinking results in nothing. It has no effect. It suffices its own essence, in that it is. But it is, in that it expresses its matter. At each epoch of history one thing only is important to it: that it be in accord with its matter. Its material relevance is essentially superior to the validity of science, because it is freer. For it lets Being—be.

Thinking works at building the house of Being; in which house Being joins and as such the joining of Being enjoins that man, according to destiny, dwell in the truth of Being. This dwelling is the essence of "Being-in-the-World" (cf. *Sein und Zeit*). The reference there to the "in-Being" (*In-Sein*) as "dwelling" is no etymological game. The reference in the essay of 1936 to Hölderlin's phrase, "Laboring, yet poetically man dwells on this earth" is no mere gilding of a thought that abandoning science, takes refuge in poetry. To talk of the house of Being is not to transfer the image of "house" to Being, but from the materially understood essence of Being we shall some day be more easily able to think what "house" and "dwelling" are.

Nonetheless, thought never creates the house of Being. Thought accompanies historical existence, i.e., the *humanitas* of the *homo humanus,* to the domain where grace arises.

With grace, evil appears in the clearing of Being. The essence of evil does not consist in pure wickedness of human action, but in the malice of anger. Both grace and anger can, however, essentially only be in Being, insofar as Being itself is what is disputed. In it is hidden the essential source of nihilation (*das Nichten*). What nihilates, is manifest as the nothing-like (*das Nichthafte*). This can be approached in the "No." The "Not" does not arise from the Nay-saying of negation. Each "No" which is not misinterpreted as a self-willed insistence on the positing power of subjectivity (but remains letting-be of ex-sistence) answers the claim of the manifest nihilation. Every "No" is only the affirmation of the "Not." Every affirmation rests in recognition. This lets that towards which it goes approach it. It is believed that nihilation cannot be found anywhere in beings themselves. This is true as long as one seeks for nihilation as something that is being, as an existing quality of the existent. But that is not the place to seek for nihilation. Being is no existing quality which characterizes the being. Nevertheless, Being is being more than any actual being. Because nihilation is essentially in Being itself, we can never become aware of it as something that is being in the existent. But this impossibility does not prove that the source of the Not is from Nay-saying. This proof only seems conclusive if one posits the existent as the object of subjectivity. From this alternative it then follows that each Not, since it never appears as something objective, must inevitably be the product of a subjective act. Whether, however, the Nay-saying constitutes the Not as something merely thought, or whether the nihilation only demands the "No" as what-is-to-be-said in the letting-be of beings, certainly can never be distinguished from the subjective reflection of thinking, which has already been posited as subjectivity. In such a reflection, the dimension for the formulation of the questions adequate to the matter has not yet been reached. It remains to be asked, granted that thought belongs to existence, whether all "Yes" and "No" is not already existent in the truth of Being. If so, then "Yes" and "No" are already in themselves bound to Being. As bondsmen, they can never first posit that to which they themselves belong.

Nihilation is essentially in Being itself and by no means in the *Dasein* of man, insofar as this is thought as subjectivity of the *ego cogito*. The Dasein by no means nihilates, insofar as man as subject performs the nihilation in the sense of rejection, but the Da-sein nihilates, insofar as, as essence, wherein man ex-sists, it itself belongs to the essence of Being. Being nihilates—as Being. Therefore, in the absolute idealism of Hegel and Schelling, the Not appears as the negativity of the negative in the essence of Being. This, however, is thought there in the essence of absolute actuality as the unconditioned will, which wills itself and, indeed, as the will of knowledge and love. In this will, Being is still concealed as the will to power. Why, however, the negativity of the absolute subjectivity is the "dialectical" and why, through the dialectic, the nihilation is discovered, but at the same time is concealed in its essence cannot here be discussed.

The nihilating (*das Nichtende*) in Being is the essence of what I call the Nothing. Because it thinks Being, thought thinks the Nothing.

Only Being lends to grace the ascent to graciousness and to anger the push toward disgrace.

Only so far as man, ex-sisting in the truth of Being, belongs to it, can the assigning of all the directions which must become for man law and rule, come from Being itself. The verb "assign" in Greek is νόμος. The νέμειν is not only law, but more originally the assigning concealed in the destiny of Being. Only this is capable of ordering man in Being. Only such ordering is capable of bearing up and binding. Otherwise, all law remains but the handiwork of human reason. More essential than any establishment of rule is the abode in the truth of Being. Only this abode yields the experience of the tenable (*das Haltbare*). The hold (*Halt*) for all behavior (*Verhalten*) is given by the truth of Being. "Hold" in our language means "shelter." Being is the shelter that in view of its own truth shelters man in his ex-sisting essence in such a way that it lodges ex-sistence in language. Thus language is at once the house of Being and the dwelling of human beings. Only because language is the dwelling of the essence of man, can the historical ways of mankind and men not be at home in their language, so that for them it becomes the shell of their machinations.

In what relationship now does the thought of Being stand to theoretical and practical behavior? It is superior to all contemplation,. because it cares for the light in which only a seeing as theory can abide and move. Thought attends to the clearing of Being by putting its speaking of Being into language as the dwelling of existence. Thus thought is an action. But an action that is superior at the same time to all practice. Thinking surpasses doing and producing, not through the magnitude of its performance, nor through the consequences of its activity, but through the humbleness of the achievement that it accomplishes without result.

Thinking, as you know, brings into language in its saying only the unspoken word of Being.

The expression used here, "to bring into language," is now to be taken quite literally. Being, clearing itself, comes into language. It is always on its way towards it. As it arrives, it in its turn brings ex-sisting thought to language in its telling, which is thus elevated into the clearing of Being. Only thus, language *is* in its mysterious and yet humanly pervasive way. Insofar as language, thus brought fully into its essence, is historical, Being is preserved in remembering. Ex-sistence inhabits as it thinks the house of Being. In all this, it is as if nothing had happened at all through the utterance of thought.

But we have just seen an example of this insignificant act of thinking. For while we specifically think the expression "to bring to language," which was given to language, only this and nothing else, and while we retain in the observance of speaking what we have thought as something that always has-to-be-thought in the future, we have ourselves brought something essential of Being into language.

The strange thing in this thought of Being is its simplicity. This is precisely what keeps us from it. For we seek for the thought that in the name of "philosophy" has its world-historical prestige in the form of the unusual, which is only accessible to the initiate. At the same time we represent thought to ourselves in the manner of scientific knowledge and research. We measure the act against the impressive and successful achievements of practice. But the act of thinking is neither theoretical nor practical, nor is it the coupling together of both ways of behavior.

Through its simple essence the thought of Being is disguised for us. But when we become friends with the unusualness of the simple, another affliction befalls us at once. The suspicion arises that this thought of Being may lapse into the arbitrary; for it cannot cling to beings. From whence does thought derive its rule? What is the law of its action?

Here the third question of your letter must be heard: *Comment sauver l'élément d'aventure que comporte toute recherche sans faire de la philosophie une simple aventurière*? I shall mention poetry only in passing at this point. It confronts the same question in the same way as thought. But Aristotle's point in his *Poetics,* scarcely considered today, is still of value—that the making of poetry is truer than the exploration of beings.

But thought is *une aventure* not only as seeking and asking into the realm of the unthought. Thought, in its essence as thought of Being, is claimed by it. Thought is related to Being as the arriving (*l'avenant*). Thought is as thought in the advent of Being, is bound to Being as arrival. Being has already destined itself to thought. Being *is* as the destiny of thought. The destiny, however, is in itself historical. Its history has already arrived at language in the speaking of thinkers.

To express over and over again the advent of Being, permanent and in its permanence waiting for man, is the only matter for thought. That is why the essential thinkers always say the same thing. But that does not mean: the like. Yet they say this only to the one who undertakes to follow their thought. While thought, remembering historically, attends to the destiny of Being, it has already bound itself to what is according to destiny. To escape into the like is not dangerous. To venture into discord in order to say the same thing, that is the danger. Ambiguity and mere quibbling threaten.

That the speaking of Being can become the destiny of truth is the first law of thought and not the rules of logic, which can become rules only through the law of Being. To attend to the destiny of the thinking-speaking does not only include our recollecting each time *what* is to be said about Being and *how* it is to be said. It remains equally essential to consider *whether* that which has-to-be-thought may be said, to what extent, at what moment in the history of Being, in what dialogue with it, and with what claim. That threefold thing, mentioned in a previous letter, is determined in the interdependence of its parts by the law of the destiny or historical thought of Being: the rigor of reflection, the carefulness of speaking, the economy of the word.

It is about time to get rid of the habit of overestimating philosophy and thereby asking too much of it. It is necessary in the present plight of the world that there be less philosophy, but more attention to thought; less literature, but more cultivation of the letter.

Future thought is no longer philosophy, because it thinks more originally than metaphysics. But neither can future thought, as Hegel demanded, lay aside the name "love of wisdom" and become wisdom itself in the form of absolute knowledge. Thought is on its descent to the poverty of its provisional essence. Thought gathers language in simple speech. Language is thus the language of Being, as the clouds are the clouds of the sky. Thought by its speaking traces insignificant furrows in language. They seem even more insignificant than the furrows the peasant with deliberate steps traces in the field.

THE PHENOMENAL FIELD*

MAURICE MERLEAU-PONTY

'Sense experience'** has become once more a question for us. Empiricism had emptied it of all mystery by bringing it down to the possession of a quality. This had been possible only at the price of moving far from the ordinary acceptation of the word. Between sense experience and knowing, common experience establishes a difference which is not that between the quality and the concept. This rich notion of sense experience is still to be found in Romantic usage, for example in Herder. It points to an experience in which we are given not 'dead' qualities, but active ones. A wooden wheel placed on the ground is not, *for sight,* the same thing as a wheel bearing a load. A body at rest because no force is being exerted upon it is again for sight not the same thing as a body in which opposing forces are in equilibrium.[1] The light of a candle changes its appearance for a child when, after a burn, it stops attracting the child's hand and becomes literally repulsive.[2] The vision is already inhabited by a significance which gives it a function in the spectacle of the world and in our existence. The pure *quale* would be given to us only if the world were a spectacle and one's own body a mechanism with which some impartial mind made itself acquainted.[3] Sense experience, on the other hand, invests the quality with vital value, grasping it first in its meaning for us, for that heavy mass which is our body, whence it comes about that it always involves a reference to the body. The problem is to understand these strange relationships which are woven between the parts of the landscape, or between it and me as incarnate subject, and through which an object perceived can concentrate in itself a whole scene or become the *imago* of a whole segment of life. Sense experience is that vital communicaton with the world which makes it present as a familiar setting of our life. It is to it that the perceived object and the perceiving subject owe their thickness. It is the intentional tissue which the effort to know will try to take apart. With the

---

* By permission of Humanities Press, Inc. From Maurice Merleau-Ponty, *Phenomenology of Perception*, Humanities Press, Inc., New York, New York.

[1] Koffka, *Perception, an Introduction to the Gestalt Theory,* pp. 558-9.

[2] Id., *Mental Development,* p. 138.

[3] Scheler, *Die Wissenformen und die Gesellschaft,* p. 408.

** The original French word is 'le sentir' (Translator's note).

problem of sense experience, we rediscover that of association and passivity. They have ceased to be problematical because the classical philosophies put themselves either below or above them, giving them everything or nothing: sometimes association was understood as a mere *de facto* co-existence, sometimes derived from an intellectual construction; sometimes passivity was imported from things into the mind, and sometimes analytical reflection would find in it an activity of understanding. Whereas these notions take on their full meaning if sense experience is distinguished from quality: then association, or rather 'affinity', in the Kantian sense, is the central phenomenon of perceptual life, since it is the constitution, without any ideal model, of a significant grouping. The distinction between the perceptual life and the concept between passivity and spontaneity is no longer abolished by analytical reflection, since we are no longer forced by the atomism of sensation to look to some connecting activity for our principle of all co-ordination. Finally, after sense experience, understanding also needs to be redefined, since the general connective function ultimately attributed to it by Kantianism is now spread over the whole intentional life and no longer suffices to distinguish it. We shall try to bring out in relation to perception, both the instinctive substructure and the superstructures erected upon it by the exercise of intelligence. As Cassirer puts it, by mutilating perception from above, empiricism mutilated it from below too:[4] the impression is as devoid of instinctive and affective meaning as of ideal significance. One might add that mutilating perception from below, treating it immediately as knowledge and forgetting its existential content, amounts to mutilating it from above, since it involves taking for granted and passing over in silence the decisive moment in perception: the upsurge of a *true* and *accurate* world. Reflection will be sure of having precisely located the centre of the phenomenon if it is equally capable of bringing to light its vital inherence and its rational intention.

So, 'sensation' and 'judgment' have together lost their apparent clearness: we have observed that they were clear only as long as the prejudice in favour of the world was maintained. As soon as one tried by means of them, to picture consciousness in the process of perceiving, to revive the forgotten perceptual experience, and to relate them to it, they were found to be inconceivable. By dint of making these difficulties

---

[4] Cassirer, *Philosophie der symbolischen Formen*, T. III, *Phänomenologie der Erkenntnis*, pp. 77-8.

more explicit, we were drawn implicitly into a new kind of analysis, into a new dimension in which they were destined to disappear. The criticism of the constancy hypothesis and more generally the reduction of the idea of 'the world' opened up a *phenomenal field* which now has to be more accurately circumscribed, and suggested the rediscovery of a direct experience which must be, at least provisionally, assigned its place in relation to scientific knowledge, psychological and philosophical reflection.

Science and philosophy have for centuries been sustained by unquestioning faith in perception. Perception opens a window on to things. This means that it is directed, quasi-teleologically, towards a *truth in itself* in which the reason underlying all appearances is to be found. The tacit assumption of perception is that at every instant experience can be co-ordinated with that of the previous instant and that of the following, and my perspective with that of other consciousnesses—that all contradictions can be removed, that monadic and intersubjective experience is one unbroken text—that what is now indeterminate for me could become determinate for a more complete knowledge, which is as it were realized in advance in the thing, or rather which is the thing itself. Science has first been merely the sequel or amplification of the process which constitutes perceived things. Just as the thing is the invariant of all sensory fields and of all individual perceptual fields, so the scientific concept is the means of fixing and objectifying phenomena. Science defined a theoretical state of bodies not subject to the action of any force, and *ipso facto* defined force, reconstituting with the aid of these ideal components the processes actually observed. It established statistically the chemical properties of pure bodies, deducing from these those of empirical bodies, and seeming thus to hold the plan of creation or in any case to have found a reason immanent in the world. The notion of geometrical space, indifferent to its contents, that of pure movement which does not by itself affect the properties of the object, provided phenomena with a setting of inert existence in which each event could be related to physical conditions responsible for the changes occurring, and therefore contributed to this freezing of being which appeared to be the task of physics. In thus developing the concept of the thing, scientific knowledge was not aware that it was working on a presupposition. Precisely because perception, in its vital implications and prior to any theoretical thought, is presented as perception of a being, it was not considered necessary for reflection to undertake a genealogy of being, and it was therefore confined to seeking the conditions which make being possible. Even if one took account of the transformations of determinant consciousness,[5] even if it were conceded that the constitution of the object is never completed, there was nothing to add to what science said of it; the natural object remained an ideal unity for us and, in the famous words of Lachelier, a network of general properties. It was no use denying any ontological value to the principles of science and leaving them with only a methodical value,[6] for this reservation made no essential change as far as philosophy was concerned, since the sole conceivable being remained defined by scientific method. The living body, under these circumstances, could not escape the determinations which alone made the object into an object and without which it would have had no place in the system of experience. The value predicates which the reflecting judgement confers upon it had to be sustained, in being, by a foundation of physico-chemical properties. In ordinary experience we find a fittingness and a meaningful relationship between the gesture, the smile and the tone of a speaker. But this reciprocal relationship of expression which presents the human body as the outward manifestation of a certain manner of being-in-the-world, had, for mechanistic physiology, to be resolved into a series of causal relations.

It was necessary to link to centripetal conditions the centrifugal phenomenon of expression, reduce to third person processes that particular way of dealing with the world which we know as behaviour, bring experience down to the level of physical nature and convert the living body into an interiorless thing. The emotional and practical attitudes of the living subject in relation to the world were, then, incorporated into a psycho-physiological mechanism. Every evaluation had to be the outcome of a transfer whereby complex situations became capable of awakening elementary impressions of pleasure and pain, impressions bound up, in turn, with nervous processes. The impelling intentions of the living creature were converted into objective movements: to the will only an instantaneous fiat was allowed, the execution of the act being entirely given over to a nervous mechanism. Sense experience, thus detached from the affective and motor functions, became the mere reception of a quality, and physiologists thought they could follow, from the point of reception to the nervous centres, the projection of the external world in the living body. The latter, thus transformed, ceased

[5] As L. Brunschvicg does.
[6] Cf. for example, *L'Expérience humaine et la Causalité physique,* p. 536.

to be my body, the visible expression of a concrete Ego, and became one object among all others. Conversely, the body of another person could not appear to me as encasing another Ego. It was merely a machine, and the perception of the other could not really be *of the other,* since it resulted from an inference and therefore placed behind the automaton no more than a consciousness in general, a transcendent cause and not an inhabitant of his movements. So we no longer had a grouping of factors constituting the self co-existing in a world. The whole concrete content of 'psychic states' resulting, according to the laws of psychophysiology and psychology, from a universal determinism, was integrated into the *in-itself.* There was no longer any real *for-itself* other than the thought of the scientist which perceives the system and which alone ceases to occupy any place in it. Thus, while the living body became an exterior without interior, subjectivity became an interior without exterior, an impartial spectator. The naturalism of science and the spiritualism of the universal constituting subject, to which reflection on science led, had this in common, that they levelled out experience: in face of the constituting I, the empirical selves are objects. The empirical Self is a hybrid notion, a mixture of in-itself and for-itself, to which reflective philosophy could give no status. In so far as it has a concrete content it is inserted in the system of experience and is therefore not a subject; in so far as it *is* a subject, it is empty and resolves itself into the transcendental subject. The ideality of the object, the objectification of the living body, the placing of spirit in an axiological dimension having no common measure with nature, such is the transparent philosophy arrived at by pushing further along the route of knowledge opened up by perception. It could be held that perception is an incipient science, science a methodical and complete perception,[7] since science was merely following uncritically the ideal of knowledge set up by the perceived thing.

Now this philosophy is collapsing before our eyes. The natural object was the first to disappear and physics has itself recognized the limits of its categories by demanding a recasting and blending of the pure concepts which it had adopted. For its part the organism presents physico-chemical analysis not with the practical difficulties of a complex object,

---

[7] Cf. for example Alain, *Quatre-vingt-un chapitres sur l'Esprit et les Passions,* p. 19, and Brunschvicg, *L'Expérience humaine et la Causalité physique,* p. 468.

but with the theoretical difficulty of a meaningful being.[8] In more general terms the idea of a universe of thought or a universe of values, in which all thinking lives come into contact and are reconciled, is called into question. Nature is *not* in itself geometrical, and it appears so only to a careful observer who contents himself with macrocosmic data. Human society is *not* a community of reasonable minds, and only in fortunate countries where a biological and economic balance has locally and temporarily been struck has such a conception of it been possible. The experience of chaos, both on the speculative and the other level, prompts us to see rationalism in a historical perspective which it set itself on principle to avoid, to seek a philosophy which explains the upsurge of reason in a world not of its making and to prepare the substructure of living experience without which reason and liberty are emptied of their content and wither away. We shall no longer hold that perception is incipient science, but conversely that classical science is a form of perception which loses sight of its origins and believes itself complete. The first philosophical act would appear to be to return to the world of actual experience which is prior to the objective world, since it is in it that we shall be able to grasp the theoretical basis no less than the limits of that objective world, restore to things their concrete physiognomy, to organisms their individual ways of dealing with the world, and to subjectivity its inherence in history. Our task will be, moreover, to rediscover phenomena, the layer of living experience through which other people and things are first given to us, the system 'Self-others-things' as it comes into being; to reawaken perception and foil its trick of allowing us to forget it as a fact and as perception in the interest of the object which it presents to us and of the rational tradition to which it gives rise.

This phenomenal field is not an 'inner world', the 'phenomenon' is not a 'state of consciousness', or a 'mental fact', and the experience of phenomena is not an act of introspection or an intuition in Bergson's sense. It has long been the practice to define the object of psychology by saying that it was 'without extension' and 'accessible to one person only', with the result that this peculiar object could be grasped only by means of a special kind of act, 'internal perception' or introspection, in which subject and object were mingled and knowledge achieved by an act of coinciding. The return to the 'immediate data of consciousness'

---

[8] Cf. *La Structure du Comportement*.

became therefore a hopeless enterprise since the philosophical scrutiny was trying to *be* what it could not, in principle, *see*. The difficulty was not only to destroy the prejudice of the exterior, as all philosophies urge the beginner to do, or to describe the mind in a language made for representing things. It was much more fundamental, since interiority, defined by the impression, by its nature evaded every attempt to express it. It was not only the imparting of philosophical intuitions to others which became difficult—or rather reduced itself to a sort of incantation designed to induce in them experiences comparable to the philosopher's—but the philosopher himself could not be clearly aware of *what* he saw in the instant, since he would have had to think it, that is fix and distort it. The immediate was therefore a lonely, blind and mute life. The return to the phenomenal presents none of these pecularities. The sensible configuration of an object or a gesture, which the criticism of the constancy hypothesis brings before our eyes, is not grasped in some inexpressible coincidence, it 'is understood' through a sort of act of appropriation which we all experience when we say that we have 'found' the rabbit in the foliage of a puzzle, or that we have 'caught' a slight gesture. Once the prejudice of sensation has been banished, a face, a signature, a form of behaviour cease to be mere 'visual data' whose psychological meaning is to be sought in our inner experience, and the mental life of others becomes an immediate object, a whole charged with immanent meaning. More generally it is the very notion of the immediate which is transformed: henceforth the immediate is no longer the impression, the object which is one with the subject, but the meaning, the structure, the spontaneous arrangement of parts. My own 'mental life' is given to me in precisely the same way, since the criticism of the constancy hypothesis teaches me to recognize the articulation and melodic unity of my behaviour as original data of inner experience, and since introspection, when brought down to its positive content, consists equally in making the immanent meaning of any behaviour explicit. Thus what we discover by going beyond the prejudice of the objective world is not an occult inner world. Nor is this world of living experience completely closed to naïve consciousness, as is Bergson's interiority. In criticizing the constancy hypothesis and in laying bare phenomena, the psychologist, it is true, runs counter to the natural direction of the process of knowing, which goes blindly through the operations of perception straight on to their teleological results. Nothing is more difficult than to know precisely *what we see*. 'There is in natural intuition a sort of "cryptomechanism" which we have to break in order to reach phenomenal being'[9] or again a dialectic whereby perception hides it-self from itself. But although it is of the essence of consciousness to forget its own phenomena thus enabling 'things' to be constituted, this forgetfulness is not mere absence, it is the absence of something which consciousness could bring into its presence: in other words conscious-ness can forget phenomena only because it can recall them, it neg-lects them in favour of things only because they are the cradle of things. For example they are never completely unknown to scientific consciousness which simply borrows all its models from the structures of living experience; it does not 'thematize' them, or make explicit the horizons of perceptual consciousness which surround it and to the con-crete relationships of which it tries to give objective expression. Ex-perience of phenomena is not, then, like Bergsonian intuition, that of a reality of which we are ignorant and leading to which there is no me-thodical bridge—it is the making explicit or bringing to light of the prescientific life of consciousness which alone endows scientific opera-tions with meaning and to which these latter always refer back. It is not an irrational conversion, but an intentional analysis.

If, as we see, phenomenological psychology is distinguished in all its characteristics from introspective psychology, it is because it is different in basic principle. Introspective psychology detected, on the perimeter of the physical world, a zone of consciousness in which physical con-cepts are no longer valid, but the psychologist still believed conscious-ness to be no more than a sector of being, and he decided to explore this sector as the physicist explores his. He tried to describe the data of consciousness but without questioning the absolute existence of the world surrounding it. In company with the scientist and common sense, he presupposed the objective world as the logical framework of all his descriptions, and as the setting of his thought. He was unaware that this presupposition dominated the meaning given to the word 'being', forcing it to bring consciousness into existence under the name of 'psychic fact', and thus diverting it from a true grasp of consciousness or from truly immediate experience, and stultifying the many pre-cautions taken to avoid distorting the 'interior'. This is what happened to empiricism when it replaced the physical world by a world of inner events. It is again what happens to Bergson precisely when he contrasts 'multiplicity of fusion' and 'multiplicity of juxtaposition'. For it is here still a question of two modes of being. All that has happened is that me-

[9] Scheler, *Idole der Selbsterkenntnis*, p. 106.

chanical energy has been replaced by spiritual, the discontinuous being of empiricism by being of a fluid kind, but of which we can say that *it* flows, describing it in the third person. By taking the *Gestalt* as the theme of his reflection, the psychologist breaks with psychologism, since the meaning, connection and 'truth' of the percept no longer arise from the fortuitous coming together of our sensations as they are given to us by our psycho-physiological nature, but determine the spatial and qualitative values of these sensations, and *are* their irreducible configuration.[10] It follows that the transcendental attitude is already implied in the descriptions of the psychologist, in so far as they are faithful ones. Consciousness as an object of study presents the peculiarity of not being analysable, even naïvely, without carrying us beyond common sense postulates. If, for example, we set out to create a positive psychology of perception, while still allowing consciousness to be enclosed in the body, and through it suffer the action of a world in itself, we are led to describe the object and the world as they appear to consciousness, and in this way to inquire whether this immediately present world, the only one we know, may not also be the only one of which there is reason to speak. A psychology is always brought face to face with the problem of the constitution of the world.

Psychological reflection, once begun, then, outruns itself through its own momentum. Having recognized the originality of phenomena in relation to the objective world, since it is through them that the objective world is known to us, it is led to integrate with them every possible object and to try to find out how that object is constituted through them. At the same time the phenomenal field becomes a transcendental field. Since it is now the universal focus of knowledge, consciousness definitely ceases to be a particular region of being, a certain collection of 'mental' contents; it no longer resides or is no longer confined within the domain of 'forms' which psychological reflection had first recognized, but the forms, like all things, exist for it. It can no longer be a question of describing the world of living experience which it carries within itself like some opaque datum, it has to be constituted. The process of making explicit, which had laid bare the 'lived-through' world which is prior to the objective one, is put into operation upon the 'lived-through' world itself, thus revealing, prior to the phenomenal field, the transcendental field. The system 'self-others-world' is in its turn taken as an object of analysis and it is now a matter of awakening the thoughts

[10] Cf. *La Structure du Comportement*, pp. 106-19 and 261.

which constitute other people, myself as individual subject and the world as a pole of my perception. This new 'reduction' would then recognize only one true subject, the thinking Ego. This move from *naturata* to *naturans,* from constituted to constituting, would complete the discovery of positing reality begun by psychology and would leave nothing implicit or tacitly accepted in my knowledge. It would enable me to take complete possession of my experience, thus equating thinking and thought. Such is the ordinary perspective of a transcendental philosophy, and also, to all appearances at least, the programme of a transcendental phenomenology.[11] Now the phenomenal field as we have revealed it in this chapter, places a fundamental difficulty in the way of any attempt to make experience directly and totally explicit. It is true that psychologism has been left behind, that the meaning and structure of the percept are for us no longer the mere outcome of psycho-physiological events, that rationality is no longer a fortunate accident bringing together dispersed sensations, and that the Gestalt is recognized as primary. But although the Gestalt may be expressible in terms of some internal law, this law must not be considered as a model on which the phenomena of structure are built up. Their appearance is not the external unfolding of a pre-existing reason. It is not *because* the 'form' produces a certain state of equilibrium, solving a problem of maximum coherence and, in the Kantian sense, making a world possible, that it enjoys a privileged place in our perception; it is the very appearance of the world and not the condition of its possibility; it is the birth of a norm and is not realized according to a norm; it is the identity of the external and the internal and not the projection of the internal in the external. Although, then, it is not the outcome of some circulation of mental states in themselves, neither is it an idea. The Gestalt of a circle is not its mathematical law but its physiognomy. The recognition of phenomena as an original order is a condemnation of empiricism as an *explanation* of order and reason in terms of a coming together of facts and of natural accidents, but it leaves reason and order themselves with the character of facticity. If a universal constituting consciousness were possible, the opacity of the fact would disappear. If then we want reflection to maintain, in the object on which it bears, its descriptive characteristics, and thoroughly to understand that object, we must not consider it as a mere return to a universal reason and see it as an-

---

[11] It is set forth in these terms in most of Husserl's works, even in those published during his last period.

ticipated in unreflective experience, we must regard it as a creative operation which itself participates in the facticity of that experience. That is why phenomenology, alone of all philosophies, talks about a transcendental *field*. This word indicates that reflection never holds, arrayed and objectified before its gaze, the whole world and the plurality of nomads, and that its view is never other than partial and of limited power. It is also why phenomenology is phenomenology, that is, a study of the *advent* of being into consciousness, instead of presuming its possibility as given in advance. It is striking how transcendental philosophies of the classical type never consider the possibility of effecting the complete disclosure which they always assume *done somewhere*. It is enough for them that it should be necessary, and in this way they judge what is by what ought to be, by what the idea of knowledge requires. In fact, the thinking Ego can never abolish its inherence in an individual subject, which knows all things in a particular perspective. Reflection can never make me stop seeing the sun two hundred yards away on a misty day, or seeing it 'rise' and 'set', or thinking with the cultural apparatus with which my education, my previous efforts, my personal history, have provided me. I never actually collect together, or call up simultaneously, all the primary thoughts which contribute to my perception or to my present conviction. A philosophy such as the critical attaches in the last analysis no importance to this resistance offered by passivity, as if it were not necessary to become the transcendental subject in order to have the right to affirm it. It tacitly assumes, consequently, that the philosopher's thinking is not conditioned by any situation. Starting from the spectacle of the world, which is that of nature open to a plurality of thinking subjects, it looks for the conditions which make possible this unique world presented to a number of empirical selves, and finds it in a transcendental ego in which they participate without dividing it up, because it is not a Being, but a Unity or a Value. This is why the problem of the knowledge of other people is never posed in Kantian philosophy: the transcendental ego which it discusses is just as much other people's as mine, analysis is from the start located outside me, and has nothing to do but to determine the general conditions which make possible a world for an ego— myself or others equally—and so it never comes up against the question: *who is thinking?* If on the other hand contemporary philosophy takes this as its main theme, and if other people become a problem for it, it is because it is trying to achieve a more radical self-discovery. Reflection cannot be thorough-going, or bring a complete elucidation of its object, if it does not arrive at awareness of itself as well as of its results. We must not only adopt a reflective attitude in an impregnable *Cogito*, but furthermore reflect on this reflection, understand the natural situation which it is conscious of succeeding and which is therefore part of its definition; not merely practise philosophy, but realize the transformation which it brings with it in the spectacle of the world and in our existence. Only on this condition can philosophical knowledge become absolute knowledge and cease to be a speciality or a technique. So there will be no assertion of an absolute Unity, all the less doubtful for not having to come into Being. The core of philosophy is no longer an autonomous transcendental subjectivity, to be found everywhere and nowhere: it lies in the perpetual beginning of reflection, at the point where the individual life begins to reflect on itself. Reflection is truly reflection only if it is not carried outside itself, only if it knows itself as reflection-on-an-unreflective-experience, and consequently as a change in structure of our existence. We earlier attacked Bergsonian intuitionism and introspection for seeking to know by coinciding. But at the opposite extremity of philosophy, in the notion of a universal constituting consciousness, we encounter an exactly corresponding mistake. Bergson's mistake consists in believing that the thinking subject can become fused with the object thought about, and that knowledge can swell and be incorporated into being. The mistake of reflective philosophies is to believe that the thinking subject can absorb into its thinking or appropriate without remainder the object of its thought, that our being can be brought down to our knowledge. As thinking subject we are never the unreflective subject that we seek to know; but neither can we become wholly consciousness, or make ourselves into the transcendental consciousness. If we were consciousness, we would have to have before us the world, our history and perceived objects in their uniqueness as systems of transparent relationships. Now even when we are not dealing with psychology, when we try to comprehend, in direct reflection and without the help of the varied associations of inductive thought, what a perceived movement, or a circle, are, we can elucidate this singular fact only by varying it somewhat through the agency of imagination, and then fastening our thought upon the invariable element of this mental experience. We can get through to the individual only by the hybrid procedure of finding an *example*, that is, by stripping it of its facticity. Thus it is questionable whether thought can ever quite cease to be inductive, and whether it can assimilate any experience to the point of taking up and appropriating its whole texture.

A philosophy becomes transcendental, or radical, not by taking its place in absolute consciousness without mentioning the ways by which this is reached, but by considering itself as a problem; not by postulating a knowledge rendered totally explicit, but by recognizing as the fundamental philosophic problem this *presumption* on reason's part.

That is why we had to begin our examination of perception with psychological considerations. If we had not done so, we would not have understood the whole meaning of the transcendental problem, since we would not, starting from the natural attitude, have methodically followed the procedures which lead to it. We had to frequent the phenomenal field and become acquainted, through psychological descriptions, with the subject of phenomena, if we were to avoid placing ourselves from the start, as does reflective philosophy, in a transcendental dimension assumed to be eternally given, thus by-passing the whole problem of constitution. We had to avoid, however, beginning our psychological description without suggesting that once purged of all psychologism it can become a philosophical method. In order to revive perceptual experience buried under its own results, it would not have been enough to present descriptions of them which might possibly not have been understood, we had to establish by philosophical references and anticipations the point of view from which they might appear true. Thus we could begin neither without psychology nor with psychology alone. Experience anticipates a philosophy and philosophy is merely an elucidated experience. But now that the phenomenal field has been sufficiently circumscribed, let us enter this ambiguous domain and let us make sure of our first steps as far as the psychologist is concerned, until the psychologist's self-scrutiny leads us, by way of a second-order reflection, to the phenomenon of the phenomenon, and decisively transforms the phenomenal field into a transcendental one.

IV

Descriptions

The results of the phenomenological-existential philosophies are to be found in the vast number of descriptive analyses already performed and still being produced. From the outset the sheer number of specific issues and areas ranged over both traditional and new philosophical problems. Husserl dealt not only with the structures of consciousness, but with the problems of essence, perception, judgment, evidence. He opened the areas of inner-time sense, intersubjectivity and embodiment.

The existentialist followers of phenomenology pursued pathways into the theory of value, of aesthetics, of religion, of psychology and of the social world. There is no way to include all these themes which cover the areas philosophers of every persuasion have also addressed; but in order to give an adequate sense of the issues and the way they have been treated without compromising the integrity of individual analyses, three main clusters of problems have been chosen:

"The Embodied Self" deals with what would often be called the "body-mind" problem. It shows the emergent sense of embodiment central to phenomenological-existential treatments of the self—"I am my body" (Marcel). The examination of the experience of the self, its possibilities (Ortega y Gasset), and the concrete orientation within the world down to the "upright posture" (Straus) is traced in this section.

The experience and meaning of others deal with social relations and "other minds" in the section on "Sociality." The appearance of the other poses the focus of conflict (Sartre), of ethics (Levinas), and of the relation between our social experience and the social sciences (Schutz).

Finally, the sense of being in a cultural world, already *Ideenkleid*, clothed with ideas, as Husserl put it, is posed in the section on "Historicality." Here the genetic and hermeneutical implications of phenomenology and existentialism begin to show themselves. The rooting of geometry in the very history of experience (Husserl) and of thinking in the oldest layers of Western thought (Heidegger), with the subsequent implications for a philosophy of language (Ricoeur), closes the group of readings for this collection.

And although these descriptions are focused—as in much of the literature—on the human world, these descriptions are not to be understood as the final development of phenomenology and existentialism. Rather, they are the beginnings which lie closest to the reexamination of human experience and thought. They are in this wise a revivification of the Socratic traditions in the present.

A. The Embodied Self

GABRIEL MARCEL (1889-   )

Gabriel Marcel is a highly individualistic philosopher who has not held a major teaching position. His personal contacts both with the major thinkers in Europe and with his students are hallmarks of his own philosophical style. His most influential writings are: *Metaphysical Journal* (1927), *Being and Having* (1935), and *The Mystery of Being* (1951).

PRIMARY AND SECONDARY REFLECTION

THE EXISTENTIAL FULCRUM*

. . . If I take experience as merely a sort of passive recording of impressions, I shall never manage to understand how the reflective process could be integrated with experience. On the other hand, the more we grasp the notion of experience in its proper complexity, in its active and I would even dare to say in its dialectical aspects, the better we shall understand how experience cannot fail to transform itself into reflection, and we shall even have the right to say that the more richly it is ex-

* By permission of Henry Regnery Company. From Gabriel Marcel, *The Mystery of Being*, Volume I, Chapter V, Henry Regnery Company, Chicago, Illinois, 1960.

perience, the more, also, it is reflection. But we must, at this point, take one step more and grasp the fact that reflection itself can manifest itself at various levels; there is primary reflection, and there is also what I shall call secondary reflection; this secondary reflection has, in fact, been very often at work during these early lectures, and I dare to hope that as our task proceeds it will appear more and more clearly as the special high instrument of philosophical research. Roughly, we can say that where primary reflection tends to dissolve the unity of experience which is first put before it, the function of secondary reflection is essentially recuperative; it reconquers that unity. But how is such a reconquest possible? The possibility is what we are going to try to show by means of the quite general, the (in the parliamentary sense) privileged, example on which we must now concentrate our attention. We shall soon see that what we have to deal with here is not merely, in fact, an illustration or an example, but an actual way of access to a realm that is assuredly as near to us as can be, but that nevertheless, by a fatality (a perfectly explicable fatality, however), has been, through the influence of modern thought, set at a greater and greater distance from us; so that the realm has become more and more of a problematic realm, and we are forced to call its very existence into queston. I am talking about the self, about that reality of the self, with which we have already come in contact so often, but always to be struck by its disquieting ambiguity.

We are now embarking upon the question on which, really, all the other questions hang: it is the question I put when I ask myself who I am and, more deeply still, when I probe into my meaning in asking myself that question.

There is a remark which, in such a setting, may appear trifling and even farcical; yet it is interesting, one must say it, at this point to remind ourselves of how very often nowadays we are called upon to fill in forms establishing what is called our identity. The multiplication of such forms today is significant, and its causes should be looked into; it is tied up, of course, with that growth of bureaucracy we have already spoken of. That growth has a sinister, metaphysical significance, though that significance, apart from such a writer as Kafka and his more thoughtful readers, is not yet generally recognized. My point now is that when one fills in such a form one has a silly feeling—as if one were putting on fancy dress, not to go to a costume ball, but to set about one's daily labours. The most precise fashion in which I can express this feeling in general terms is as follows: I have not a consciousness of *being* the person who is entered under the various headings thus: *son of, born at, occupation,* and so on. Yet everything I enter under these headings is strictly true; I should be guilty of telling a lie if I varied the entries from form to form, and, besides that, I would be risking serious trouble. If this form-filling is a game, it is a game I am forced to play. But what is really remarkable is that the filling in of any such form whatsoever would give me the same silly feeling, unless, for a single moment, I could exercise my creative faculty by inventing an identity of my own choice; only the strange thing is that after a short time this invented identity, if I were forced to stick to it, would give me a feeling of peculiar, intimate disgust—like some shabby garment, not my own, that I was forced to drag around with me everywhere. It is, in fact, against the existence of such garments that I have to protest: *I* am not this garment. . . . A mental specialist might say that we are here on a dangerous path that can lead to mythomania or even actual insanity. But such a remark has a merely practical value, and is irrelevant to our present speculative discussion. The point I want to make now is that this feeling about identity forms that I have been talking about is no doubt completely foreign to many people: but why? Must we say that such people quite lack the sense of fantasy? I think we can go further and say that the absence of this uneasiness must be linked to a total deficiency as far as the faculty of creation is concerned. Later on, we shall see more clearly why this is so.

Let us try to imagine, now, the sheer dumbfoundedness of the civil servant who, on asking me, 'So you are Mr. So-and-so?' received the curt reply 'Certainly not'. He would arrive at only one of two conclusions: either this person is insane, or he is passing under a false identity. But what is quite certain is that he would never begin to suspect that for me and him the verb 'to be' in that sentence—'*Are* you Mr. So-and-so?'—has a quite different meaning. If I am a person of common sense, therefore, I shall try not to step outside the very narrow limits in which what such a creature calls his mind functions, and to stick loyally to his categories, to the headings on the form which he wishes me to fill up, however rudimentary these categories may appear to me to be.

But in compensation there is nothing to stop me personally from facing up to the strange duality which seems to be implied in the uneasiness with which I regard an identity form, and asking myself certain direct questions: if I cannot satisfy myself by saying, 'I am Mr. So-and-so, the son of Mr. So-and-So, living in Paris or wherever it may be', what then is the urgent inner need which makes me aware of this dissatisfaction? *Really,* who am I?

I should like to observe, in the first place, that the question put by the civil servant—'So you', let us say, 'are Mr. So-and-so, and these are your particulars?'—has to do with somebody or other, or rather with some one definite somebody, of whom one might say that he springs to attention, as a soldier does, when his number is called out. It is just as if somebody had said to me: 'State the identity of Number 98', and as if I had the job of answering for this unfortunate Number 98—as if Number 98 were illiterate for instance, and so could not fill in the form, or were deaf, and so could not hear the question. But I, who am forced to answer for Number 98, who am I, really? The real fact, the thing that complicates the whole business, that is, the truth of it, is that I am myself and not somebody else; if I were somebody else, the question would be put again, when my turn came up, but it would still be exactly the same sort of question. There is thus, or so it seems to me, a sense in which I am not a definite somebody; from the moment when I start to reflect, I am bound to appear to myself as a, as it were, non-somebody linked in a profoundly obscure fashion, with a somebody about whom I am being questioned and about whom I am certainly not free to answer just what I like at the moment when I am being questioned.

These are the conclusions at which we can arrive after a first examination of our topic. We shall certainly have to go beyond them. Nevertheless, they throw some light on an aspect of the situation which we cannot pass over without some further comment.

It is only in so far as I assert myself to be, in one sense, not merely a somebody, that I can acknowledge two facts; firstly, that there is another sense in which I *am* a somebody, a particular individual (though not merely that), and secondly that other somebodies, other particular individuals, also exist. Let us point out that a solipsistic type of idealism would never be able to grasp the fact of my existence, in so far as it is a somebody's existence, neither do I possess any particular ontological privilege in relation to all the other somebodies; indeed, one may go further, it is obvious that if I am a somebody, a particular individual, I am only so at once in connection with and in opposition to an indefinite number of other somebodies; and this enables us to solve *a priori*, and without any trouble at all, a problem which the philosophers of the past have woven into wantonly intricate tangles: the problem of how I can be certain that anybody, or anything, other than myself, exists.

In compensation, we have still a paradox of our own to play with, the central fact that I appear to myself both as a somebody and not a somebody, a particular individual and not a particular individual, and at this point we must probe a little more deeply into that paradox. Can we get a closer grip on this experience of the self as not being a somebody? Can we assign a positive character to this experience? The experience consists, it seems to me, in recognizing that the definite characteristics that constitute the self in so far as I grasp it as a particular individual, a somebody, have a contingent character—but contingent in relation to what? Can I really truthfully say that, at the same time as I grasp myself as a somebody, I also grasp myself as universal mind? In spite of some testimonies, like those of Amiel in his *Journal,* it would, I think, be rash to claim this. This mysterious reality in relation to which I see the definite characteristics of my particular individuality as contingent is not really an object for me—or if it is an object, it is one completely hidden by a veil, which seems self-contradictory, for it is part of the notion of an object that it is at least partly unveiled. I shall feel tempted to say, therefore, that it is in relation to myself as subject that these definite characteristics of my particular individuality are felt to be, and acknowledged to be, contingent. But will the introduction of the term 'subject' get us out of the wood here? In what sense can I grasp myself as a subject without, to the very degree that I do grasp myself, turning myself into an object? But we should not allow ourselves to be halted here by difficulties which arise, in the last analysis, from an attempt to interpret philosophical thought as springing from the grammatical structure of language; the accusative case being linked, in that structure, to the object, and to the process of objectivization. One, in fact, of the most serious weaknesses of philosophy up to our own times seems to me to have consisted in an outrageous over-simplification (I have already made such a point and we shall have to go into the whole topic much more closely) of the relationships that bind me to myself, a failure to see that an indefinite, perhaps an infinite, number of such relationships can be specified; for I can behave to myself as a master, as a friend, as an antagonist, and so on . . . I can treat myself as a stranger and, on the other hand, as somebody with whom I am intimate. But to treat myself as somebody with whom I am intimate is to be in touch with myself as a subject. That feeling, which has always been so strong, not only among Christian mystics, but in, for instance, a Stoic like Marcus Aurelius, of a certain sacred reality in the self cannot be separated from an apprehension of the self in its subjectivity.

Nevertheless, if we push our analysis a little further, we cannot fail to strike upon a disconcerting fact. Of this self, felt and recognized as *not* being the self of some particular individual, can we strictly say that it exists? Of course, the answer will be that it primarily depends upon what one means by 'exists'; nevertheless, I am forced to take account of very numerous cases in which I do not hesitate to say, without running any risk of contradiction, that somebody or something exists; the real question is whether the current use of the verb 'to exist' (quite apart from all the notional elaborations of the idea of existence in recent philosophy) permits us to say that this 'veiled reality' also exists. I have no doubt about the answer: it is in the negative. In the usual sense of the verb 'to exist', a sense, of course, which we shall have to define by and by, this reality, taken in isolation, does not exist—which does not necessarily mean that it is imaginary, for there is no *a priori* reason for postulating a relationship between the actual and the imaginary, such that what is not actual must be imaginary, and what is not imaginary must be actual.

But we must now ask ourselves, still holding back from any attempt to define the notion of existence, if there is any touchstone of existence, or rather any existence that will itself serve as a touchstone, that we can put a name to: to be as precise as possible, do I know of an existence such that, if I were to deny it, any assertion by me that anything else at all existed would become quite inconceivable? Let us notice that we are here at the level of phenomenology and not of ontology; in the old-fashioned terms, of appearance and not reality, of manifestation and not ground. The question I am asking myself is by no means a question of the following order: whether in the hierarchy of being there is an absolute existent—which could only, of course, be God—such that it confers existence, that the derivative existence of everything else proceeds from it. No, I am talking merely about myself, in so far as I make a judgment that something or other exists, and I am asking myself whether there is some central significance of existence, or some centrally significant existence in relation to which all these judgments are arrayed and organized. If there is, I would call it an existential indubitable. Now this centrally significant existence, my denial of which entails the inconceivability of my asserting any other existence, is simply, of course, myself, in so far as I feel sure that I exist. But the exact implications of that statement must be carefully elicited; for I risk, at this point, a head-on collision with total or modified scepticism.

Total scepticism would consist in saying: 'I am not sure either that something exists or what sort of a something it would be that could exist'. But to assert, in this way, that perhaps nothing exists implies the previous taking up of two positions; firstly, I lay down a criterion, no doubt a vague, inexplicit criterion, failing to satisfy which nothing can be said to exist; secondly, I ask myself whether anything I am directly acquainted with satisfies that criterion, and come to the conclusion that I am not quite sure. I will risk saying that a question framed in such hazily defined terms lacks even metaphysical significance; but at the phenomenological level, at least, it is quite obviously meaningless. From our phenomenological point of view, we have only to consider that for us, in the everyday experience we start from, there is that which exists and that which does not exist, and to ask ourselves what meaning we attach to this distinction; we need not ask ourselves whether this existence of everyday experience is or is not an absolute existence, nor whether these two terms, absolute and existent, are congruous with each other, that is whether the notion of an absolute existent conveys anything to the mind. That is a problem which we must tackle much later, in the context of all our other problems.

Relative or modified scepticism, on the other hand, would consist in saying: 'Possibly I myself do not really exist, I who am asking questions about existence'. Here, I think, we do really run our heads against the existential indubitable. But we must remember that a certain caution is necessary even at this point. If, in the question, 'Do *I* exist?' I take the 'I' separately and treat it as a sort of mental object that can be isolated, a sort of 'that', and if I take the question as meaning: 'Is or is not existence something that can be predicated of this "that"?' the question does not seem to suggest any answer to itself, not even a negative answer. But this would prove simply that the question had been badly put, that it was, if I may say so, a vicious question. It was vicious for two reasons: because the 'I' cannot in any case whatsoever be treated as a 'that', because the 'I' is the very negation of the 'that', of any 'that' whatsoever and also because existence is not a predicate, as Kant seems to have established once and for all, in the *Critique of Pure Reason*.

If therefore the 'I exist' can be taken as an indubitable touchstone of existence, it is on condition that it is treated as an indissoluble unity: the 'I' cannot be considered apart from the 'exist'. It seems necessary, however, to probe more deeply still, for I think a discussion about the nature of this pure immediacy—the pure immediacy expressed by the 'I exist'—must inevitably intrude at this point. One might, in particular, be tempted to say that the self's immediate certitude of its existence pertains essentially to its sense-experience; and some modern philosophers might be tempted to substitute for the *Cogito, ergo sum* of Descartes a

Sentio, ergo sum. It would be easy, to be sure, to show that this change is a mere change in appearance; for from the moment that, in a mental process, there intervenes anything resembling the process of inference (like the *ergo* in *Sentio, ergo sum*), or rather it is itself a *cogito* in an enshrouded and indistinct state. On the other hand the *sum* itself, the affirmation, 'I exist', seems to lie at another level; above, as it were, and on the banks of every possible current of inference. This is what Claudel expresses with peculiar pungency in the opening lines of his *Tête d'Or*:

Here am I,
Weak, ignorant,
A new man in the face of unknown things,
And I turn my face to the year and the rainy
　arc, my heart is full of weariness,
I lack knowledge or force for action. What shall
　I utter, what shall I undertake? How shall I use
　these dangling hands, these feet of mine that
　draw me on like dreams?

In such lines, we are up against existence in all its nakedness. But I would rather evoke another image, that of the small child who comes up to us with shining eyes, and who seems to be saying: 'Here I am! What luck!' As I wrote a few years ago in my *Diary* (1943): 'When I say, not that I am, but that I exist. . . . I glimpse more or less obscurely the fact that my being is not only present to my own awareness but that it is a manifest being. It might be better, indeed, instead of saying, "I exist", to say, "I am manifest". The Latin prefix *ex*—meaning *out, outwards, out from*—in "exist" has the greatest importance. I exist—that is as much as to say: I have something to make myself known and recognized both by others and by myself, even if I wear borrowed plumes.' There is, to be sure, one difficulty that seems to arise in this connection; we may be tempted to make a distinction between the fact of existing and that of saying, to others or to oneself, that one does exist. But in such a context perhaps the verb 'to say' is ambiguous. To clear away that ambiguity as far as possible, let me say that this impossibility of doubting one's own existence of which we have been talking seems to be linked to a kind of exclamatory awareness of oneself; this awareness is expressed in the small child (and, indeed, perhaps already at the level of consciousness of the higher animals) by cries, by leaps, and so on, though naturally with the adult its expression is more measured and restrained—more and more so, the more, for the adult, that immediacy of self-awareness is crusted over by habits and by all the superstructures of an official, compartmentalized life; it is pretty certain, in fact, that we are all tending to become bureaucrats, and not only in our outward behaviour, but in our relations with ourselves. This is as much as to say that between ourselves and existence we are interposing thicker and thicker screens.

But even if this is the case, we must still say, quite peremptorily, that existence and the exclamatory awareness of existence cannot be really separated; the dissociation of the two can be carried out only at the cost of robbing the subject of our investigation of its proper nature; separated from that exclamatory self-awareness (the child's, 'Here I am! What luck!'), existence tends to be reduced to its own corpse; and it lies outside the power of any philosophy whatsoever to resuscitate such a corpse. But what we should specially notice here, and what cannot be too much underlined, is the massive character of this self, this existential indubitable. If we are, as I think we are, in the presence here of a key datum, or rather a datum on which everything else hinges, we should also acknowledge from the first that this datum is not transparent to itself; nothing could bear a smaller likeness to the transcendental ego, which already in a certain sense in Kant's case, but much more noticeably among his successors, had taken its stance, as it were, at the very heart and center of the philosophical arena. This nontransparency is implied in the fact, which I mentioned earlier, that I postulate myself as existing both for myself and for others; and when I do so, whatever I am asserting cannot be considered apart from the datum which is now going to take up our attention, I mean, my body; my body in so far as it is *my* body, my body in so far as it has the character, in itself so mysterious, which we are expressing here by saying it is something I *possess*, something that belongs to me.

Let us note at once that there could be no clearer example than that which we are now beginning to consider of the special part played in thought by secondary, by what I have called recuperative, reflection. Primary reflection, on the contrary, for its part, is forced to break the fragile link between me and my body that is constituted here by the word 'mine'. The body that I call my body is in fact only one body among many others. In relation to these other bodies, it has been endowed with no special privileges whatsoever. It is not enough to say that this is objectively true, it is the precondition of any sort of objectivity whatsoever, it is the foundation of all scientific knowledge (in the case we are thinking of, of anatomy, of physiology, and all their connected disciplines). Primary reflection is therefore forced to take up an attitude of radical detachment, of complete lack of interest, towards the fact that this particular body happens to be *mine*; primary reflection has to recall the facts that this body has just the same properties, that it is liable to suffer the same disorders, that it is fated in the end to undergo the same destruction, as any other body whatsoever. Objectively speaking, it is non-privileged; and yet spontaneous, naïvely, I do have a tendency to delude myself about it, and to attribute to it—in relation to this malady, or that—a sort of mysterious immunity; sad experience, however, in most cases dissipates such an illusion, and primary reflection forces me to acknowledge that the facts must be as I have stated them.

Let it be clearly understood that secondary reflection does not set out flatly to give the lie to these propositions; it manifests itself rather by a refusal to treat primary reflection's separation of this body, considered as just a body, a sample body, some body or other, from the self that I am, as final. Its fulcrum, or its springboard, is just that massive, indistinct sense of one's total existence which a short time ago we were trying, not exactly to define (for, as the condition which makes the defining activity possible, it seems to be prior to all definition) but to give a name to and evoke, to locate as an existential centre.

It is easy to see that the dualism of body and soul, as it is postulated, for instance, in the Cartesian philosophy, springs from primary reflection, though in one peculiarly obscure passage, indeed, Descartes was led into talking of the union of body and soul as a third substance; but what I propose to do here is not, in fact, to comment on such well-known philosophical doctrines, but to get directly to grips with that non-transparent datum, which is constituted by my body felt as *my* body, before primary reflection has performed its task of dissociating the notion of body from the notion of what is intimately mine. But how will secondary reflection proceed in this case? It can only, it might seem, get to work on the processes to which primary reflection has itself had recourse; seeking, as it were, to restore a semblance of unity to the elements which primary reflection has first severed. However, even when engaged in this attempt at unification, the reflective process would in reality still remain at the primary stage, since it would remain a prisoner in the hands of the very oppositions which it, itself, had in the first instance postulated, instead of calling the ultimate validity of these oppositions into question.

Everything, however, becomes fairly clear if we set the matter in the following perspective, keeping within the limits of that traditional logic, the logic not of the process but of the thing, which remains faithful to the age-old distinction between the subject and the predicate. With the categories of such a logic in mind, we shall be led either to consider the body and soul as two distinct things between which some determinable relationship must exist, some relationship capable of abstract formulation, or to think of the body as something of which the soul, as we improperly call it, is the predicate, or on the other hand of the soul as something of which the body, as we improperly call it, is the predicate. The arguments that tell against the two latter interpretations have been put forward so often, and besides are so obvious in themselves, that I do not think there would be any point in going over them again now. Besides, they are implied in the whole general drift of our investigation. There remains to be considered a dualism of body and soul which can, however, take extremely different forms; we can have psycho-physical parallelism, as in Spinoza, or we can have psycho-physical interactionism. But in both cases, body and soul, at least, are treated as *things,* and things, for purposes of logical discourse, become *terms,* which one imagines as strictly defined, and as linked to each other by some determinable relation. I want to show that if we reflect on what is implied by the datum of my body, by what I cannot help calling *my* body, this postulate that body and soul are *things* must be rejected; and this rejection entails consequences of the first importance.

We should notice, in the first place, that to say 'my body' is to reject psycho-physical parallelism; for it is to postulate a certain intimacy of relationship between me (whatever exactly I mean by 'me' here) and my body for which the parallelist schema has no place. I may be told that my belief in the existence of this intimacy is a simple illusion on my part, which it is the business of the philosopher, as such, to clear out of the way. But let us remember, once more, that we are proceeding, throughout the whole of this discussion, in a strictly phenomenological fashion; that is to say, we are accepting our everyday experience, and asking ourselves what implications we can draw from it. From this phenomenological point of view we have to ask ourselves where the philosopher, who is eager to clear this illusory belief out of the way, is taking his stand. He is taking his stand on some height where he has abstracted from his own experience, where he has put aside, as unworthy of consideration, the fact that he himself has this feeling of an intimate connection between himself and his body; but it is surely permissible to think, in that case, that for the richness of experience he is substituting mere abstract schemas, and that, far from transcending experience, he has not yet reached the stage of grappling with it. From my own point of view, all I have to bear in mind is that my own experience implies the possibility of behaving in a various number of definite ways towards my own body; I can yield to its whims, or on the other hand I can try to master it. It can become my tyrant, but I can also, or so it seems, make it my slave. It is only by sheer prodigies of acrobatic sophistry that I can fit these facts into the framework of the parallelist thesis; and at the point in our discussion we have now reached, I can see no worthwhile reason for trying to do so. In compensation every experience of this kind does presuppose, as its basis, that opaque datum: *my* body. What we must now see is whether an analysis of the notion of ownership in general—of whatever the 'my' of 'my body' implies—can set that datum in a clearer and more penetrating light.

Is my body *my* body, for instance, in the same sense in which I would say that my dog belongs to me? The question, let us first of all notice, of how the dog originally came into my hands is quite irrelevant here. Perhaps I found it wandering wretchedly about the streets, perhaps I bought it in a shop; I can say it is mine if nobody else puts in a claim for it—though this is still quite a negative condition of ownership. For the dog to be really, not merely nominally, mine there must exist between us a more positive set of relations. He must live, either with me, or as I, and I alone, have decided he shall live—lodged, perhaps, with a servant or a farmer; whether or not I look after him personally, I must assume the responsibility for his being looked after. And this implies something reciprocal in our relations. It is only if the dog recognizes me, obeys me, expresses by his behaviour towards me some feeling which I can interpret as affection, or at the very least, as wholesome fear, that he is really mine; I would become a laughingstock if I persisted in calling an animal that completely ignored me, that took no notice of me at all, *my* dog. And the mockery to which I would be exposed in such an instance is very significant. It is linked to a very positive idea of how things must be between my dog and me, before I can really say, 'This dog is mine'.

Let us now try to see what relationship there may be between such a mode of ownership and the link between myself and my body that makes my body mine. We are forced to recognize that the analogy is rather a full and exact one. There is first of all my indisputable claim to my body, as to my dog. I recall, in this connection, the title of a very bad novel that came out in Paris a few years ago: *My Body is My Own*. This claim, this right to one's own body, this instinctive feeling that my body belongs to me, can be held in check only under slavery. The slave's master thinks, on the contrary, that the slave's body belongs to him; because he has bought that body, or for some other reason that has to do with a particular historical situation. But it must be pointed out that even where slavery exists as a social fact, it is always more or less obscurely resented by the slave himself as essentially unjust and not to be justified, as incompatible with a human right written, as it were, into the very build of the slave's own nature; and I would even go as far as to say that a creature who had lost even the very obscurest awareness of the rape committed ón him by slavery would no longer be quite human. But that is a limit which, so long as life itself persists, can never be quite reached; the slave really cannot rid himself of the feeling that his body is his own.

When it comes to the question of looking after my dog, or my body, the analogy is still relevant. Thinking of my body, I am bound to envisage the inescapable responsibility laid upon me to provide for its subsistence. Here, too, there is a limit, though this time an upper limit, that implied by a total asceticism; but here too we are leaving life, though leaving it at a more elevated level (it is the yogi, of course, rather than the Christian Fathers of the Desert, that I have in mind). We should notice, also, that these two ideal limits, these two possibilities—that the slave might say, 'This body is not mine', and the yogi, 'Looking after this body is not my responsibility'—are in the highest degree characteristic of our situation or our condition, call it what you will. This is a fact we must never lose sight of.

Finally, what I have said about the dog's obedience applies also to my union with my body; my body is only properly mine to the degree to which I am able to control it. But here, too, there is a limit, an inner limit; if as a consequence of some serious illness, I lose all control of my body, it tends to cease to be *my* body, for the very profound reason that, as we say in the common idiom, I am 'no longer myself'. But at the other extreme, possibly as a yogi I also cease to be myself, and that for the opposite reason, because the control exercised by the yogi over his body is absolute, whereas in the mean position which is that of what we call normal life, such control is always partial, always threatened to some degree.

Having recognized the·fulness and exactness of this analogy, we must interpret it, but not without first recognizing that, in spite of its fulness and exactness, it has its specious side; my dog, like, to be sure, any other object that belongs to me, presents itself to me as something distinct from that spatio-temporal being that I am, as external to that being. Literally speaking, it does not form part of that being, though after a long association between my dog and myself a special and mysterious link may be created, something that comes very near, and in a rather precise fashion, to what we shall later call intersubjectivity.

But our central problem here has to do with the idea of *having* as such. It is not, I think, very difficult to see that my link with my body is really the model (a model not shaped, but felt) to which I relate all kinds of ownership, for instance my ownership of my dog; but it is not true that this link can *itself* be defined as a sort of ownership. In other words it is by what literally must be called a paralogism that I seek to think through my relationship with my body, starting off with my relationship with my dog. The truth is rather that *within* every ownership, every kind of ownership I exercise, there is this kernel that I feel to be there at the centre; and this kernel is nothing other than the experience—an experience which of its very nature cannot be formulated in intellectual terms—by which my body is mine.

We can throw at least a little light on our argument at this point by making the following observation. The self that owns things can never, even in thought, be reduced to a completely dematerialized ego. It seems to me impossible even to conceive how a dematerialized ego could have any claim, or any care, to possess anything; but the two notions of claiming and caring are implied, of course, in every case of something's being possessed.

In the second place—and this observation derives from, and may throw light on, that previously made—my possessions, in so far as I really hold to them, or cling to them, present themselves to me as felt additions to, or completions of, my own body. This becomes extraordinarily clear at any moment when, for whatever reason, the link between myself and my possessions is snapped or even threatened. I have at such moments a sort of *rending* feeling which seems quite on all fours with my feeling when the actual wholeness of my body is threatened in some way; and indeed such words as 'rending' or 'wrenching', which are quite commonly used to express people's feelings about losing their possessions, are themselves very significant in this connection.

I shall say once more that *having*, possessing, owning, in the strong and exact sense of the term, has to be thought of in analogy with that unity, a unity *sui generis,* which is constituted by my body in so far as it is *my* body. No doubt, as I have already said, in the case of external having, possessing, ownership, the unity is imperfect; the object that I possess can be lost, can be stolen, can be damaged or decayed—while I, the dispossessed possessor, remain. I remain, but affected by my loss, and the more affected the more deeply, the more strongly I was, if I may coin the term, a *haver*. The tragedy of all having invariably lies in our desperate efforts to make ourselves as one with something which nevertheless is not, and cannot, be identical with our beings; not even with the being of him who really does possess it. This, of course, is most strikingly so in the case where what we want to possess is another being who, just because he or she *is* a being, recoils from the idea of being possessed. That, for instance, is the point of Molière's *L'Ecole des Femmes,* a comedy which strikes us even today as one of the world's imperishable masterpieces; while the penultimate sections of Proust's great novel, with their account of Marcel's desperate attempts to hide Albertine away, and thus make himself feel sure of her inside himself, provide a tragic illustration of the same theme.

But in relation to this whole matter of possession, what is at once characteristic and exceptional about my own body is that, in this solitary instance, it does not seem that we can assert, in the case of the thing possessed, the usual relationship of independence of the being who possesses. More precisely, rather, the structure of my experience offers me no direct means of knowing what I shall still be, what I *can* still be, once the link between myself and my body is broken by what I call death. That is a point to which we must return, to deal with it at length, in my second volume; and we shall then have to ask ourselves whether there is any way of getting out of this metaphysical blind alley. But for the moment we must simply admit that, swathed up, as it were, in my situation as an incarnate being, there is this riddle, which, at a purely objective level, appears to admit of no answer at all.

To explore this situation more thoroughly, we must tackle it from yet another angle, and naturally it is still secondary reflection that we are calling on to help us.

I cannot avoid being tempted to think of my body as a kind of instrument; or, more generally speaking, as the apparatus which permits me to act upon, and even to intrude myself into, the world. It does look, for instance, as if Bergson's philosophy implied a doctrine of the body-soul relationship of this sort; though this cannot be taken as a definitive interpretation of that philosophy. What we must do in this case, however, is just what we did when we were examining the notion of having, owning, possessing; we must ask ourselves what being an instrument implies, and within what limits instrumental action is feasible.

It is obvious that every instrument is an artificial means of extending, developing, or reinforcing a pre-existing power which must be possessed by anyone who wants to make use of the instrument. This, for instance, is true of the simplest tool, for instance of the knife or the hoe. It is equally, however, true of the most complicated optical apparatus conceivable. The basis of such an apparatus is our power of seeing and the possibility of extending that. Such powers are what one might call the very notes of an organized body's activity; it might even be contended that, considered realistically—that is to say, dynamically, functionally—such a body consists merely of its assembled powers. The word 'assembled', however, seems to convey in a very inadequate fashion the *kind* of totality which we have here in mind; so it might be better to say that each of the body's powers is a specific expression of its unity—and I am thinking of the unity of an apparatus, an apparatus adaptable to many purposes, and considered, by us, from the outside. Only let us remember that it is not *a* body, but *my* body, that we are asking ourselves questions about. As soon as we get back to this perspective, our original perspective, the whole picture changes.

My body is *my* body just in so far as I do *not* consider it in this detached fashion, do not put a gap between myself and it. To put this point in another way, my body is mine in so far as for me my body is not an object but, rather, I *am* my body. Certainly, the meaning of 'am' in that sentence is, at a first glance, obscure; it is essentially, perhaps, in its implications, a negative meaning. To say that I *am* my body is to negate, to deny, to erase that gap which, on the other hand, I would be postulating as soon as I asserted that my body was merely my instrument. And we must notice at this point that if I do postulate such a gap, I am involved at once in an infinite regress. The use of any instrument whatsoever is, as we have seen, to extend the powers of the body, or in a sense to extend the body itself. If, then, we think of the body as merely an instrument, we must think of the use of the body as being the extension of the powers of some *other* body (a mental body, an astral body, or what you will); but this mental or astral body must itself be the instrument that extends the powers of some third kind of body, and so on for ever. . . . We can avoid this infinite regress, but only on one condition: we must say that this body, which, by a fiction modelled on the instruments that extend its powers of action, we can think of as itself an instrument, is nevertheless, in so far as it is *my* body, not an instrument at all. Speaking of my body is, in a certain sense, a way of speaking of myself; it places me at a point where either I have not yet reached the instrumental relationship or I have passed beyond it.

But let us walk warily at this point. There is a way of conceiving the identity of myself and my body which comes down to mere materialism, and materialism of a coarse and incoherent sort. There would be no point in asserting my identity with the body that other people can see and touch, and which for myself is something other than myself, in so far as I put it on the same level as any other body whatsoever, that is, at the level of the body as an object. The proper position to take up seems, on the contrary, to be this: I *am* my body in so far as I succeed in recognizing that this body of mine *cannot*, in the last analysis, be brought down to the level of being this object, *an* object, a something or other. It is at this point that we have to bring in the idea of the body not as an object but as a subject. It is in so far as I enter into some kind of relationship (though relationship is not an adequate term for what I have in mind) with the body, some kind of relationship which resists being made wholly objective to the mind, that I can properly assert that I am identical with my body; one should notice, also, that, like the term 'relationship', the term 'identity' is inadequate to our meaning here, for it is a term fully applicable only in a world of things or more precisely of mental abstractions from things, a world which our incarnate condition inevitably transcends. It goes without saying, by the way, that the term 'incarnation', of which I shall have to make a frequent use from now on, applies solely and exclusively in our present context to the situation of a being who appears to himself to be linked fundamentally and not accidentally to *his* or *her* body . . . In a former work of mine, my *Metaphysical Diary,* I used the phrase 'sympathetic mediation' to convey the notion of our non-instrumental communion with our bodies; I cannot say that I find the phrase wholly satisfactory, but even today, that is to say, twenty-five years later, the phrase seems to me the least inadequate way, if only that, of conveying the slippery notion. To elucidate the meaning of the phrase, we should recall the fact that my body, in so far as it is properly mine, presents itself to me in the first instance as something felt; I am my body only in so far as I am a being that has feelings. From this point of view it seems, therefore, that my body is endowed with an absolute priority in relation to everything that I can feel that is other than my body itself; but then, strictly speaking, can I really feel anything other than my body itself? Would not the case of my feeling something else be merely the case of my feeling *myself* as feeling something else, so that I would never be able to pass beyond various modifications of my own self-feeling?

But this is not the end of our difficulties: I shall be tempted to ask myself whether I am not forced to make use of my body in order to feel my body—the body being, at one and the same time, what feels and what is felt. Let us notice moreover that at this point the whole question of instrumentality intrudes itself once more surreptitiously into our argument. My postulate has been simply that feeling is a function which can be exercised only thanks to some apparatus or other—the apparatus, in fact, of my body—but by postulating this I have once more committed myself to all the contradictions, with which we are already well acquainted, of the instrumental view. Ought we not therefore to conclude from this that feeling is not really a function, that there is no instrument that enables us to feel? Was it not, really, just this fact that feeling is not instrumentally based that my rather obscure expression, 'sympathetic mediation', was intended to convey?

However that may be, we have certainly at this point laid upon ourselves the duty of enquiring into the fundamental nature of feeling. . . .

JOSÉ ORTEGA Y GASSET (1883-1955)

Born in Madrid in 1883, Ortega y Gasset became one of the intellectual leaders of the Spanish republican government, serving for a time in the Cortes. For many years he also held the chair of metaphysics at the University of Madrid. He founded the influential review *Revista de Occidente*. After the Spanish Civil War, Ortega became an exile in South America and later in Portugal. Some of his books include: *Meditations on Quixote* (1914), *The Revolt of the Masses* (1932), and the posthumously published *What Is Philosophy?* (1963).

BEING IN ONE'S SELF AND BEING BESIDE ONE'S SELF*

. . . So, once again, let us set out in search of clear ideas; that is, of truths.

Few are the peoples who in these latter days still enjoy that tranquillity which permits one to choose the truth, to abstract oneself in meditation. Almost all the world is in tumult, is beside itself, and when man is beside himself he loses his most essential attribute: the possibility of meditating, or withdrawing into himself in order to come to terms with himself and define what it is that he believes, what he truly esteems and what he truly detests. Being beside himself bemuses him, blinds him, forces him to act mechanically in a frenetic somnambulism.

Nowhere do we better see that the possibility of meditation is man's essential attribute than at the zoo, before the cages of our cousins the monkeys. The bird and the crustacean are forms of life too remote from our own for us to see, comparing them with ourselves, anything but gross, abstract differences, vague by their very extremeness. But the simian is so like ourselves that he invites us to pursue the comparison, to discover differences that are more concrete and more fertile.

If we can remain still for a time in passive contemplation of the simian scene, one of its characteristics will presently, and as if spontaneously, stand out and come to us like a ray of light. This is that the infernal little beasts are constantly on the alert, perpetually uneasy, looking and listening for all the signals that reach them from their surroundings, forever intent on their environment as if they feared some constant peril from it, to which they must automatically respond by flight or bite, the mechanical discharge of a muscular reflex. The animal, in short, lives in perpetual fear of the world, and at the same time in a perpetual hunger for the things that are in the world and appear in the world, an ungovernable hunger that also discharges itself without any possible restraint or inhibition, just as the animal's fear does. In either case it is the objects and events in its environment which govern the animal's life, which pull and push it about like a marionette. It does not rule its life, it does not live from *itself*, but is always intent on what is happening outside it, on all that is *other* than itself. The word for "other" in Spanish—*otro*—is nothing but the Latin *alter*. To say,

* By permission of W. W. Norton & Company, Inc. From José Ortega y Gasset, *Man and People*, Authorized translation from the Spanish by Willard R. Trask, Copyright © 1957 by W. W. Norton & Company, Inc., New York, New York.
Also by permission of George Allen & Unwin, Ltd., London, England.

then, that the animal lives not from *itself* but from what is *other* than it-self, pulled and pushed and tyrannized over by that *other*, is equivalent to saying that the animal is always estranged from itself, beside itself, that its life is essential *alteracíon*[1]—possession by all that is *other*.

As we contemplate this fate of unremitting disquietude, there comes a moment when we say to ourselves, "What a job!" Whereby, with complete ingenuousness and without realizing it, we set forth the most essential difference between man and animal. Because the expression means that we feel a strange weariness, a gratuitous weariness, occasioned by our simply imagining ourselves forced to live as they do, perpetually harassed by our environment and tensely attentive to it. But, you will ask, does man perchance not find himself in the same situation as the animal, a prisoner of the world, surrounded by things that terrify him, by things that enchant him, and obliged all his life, inexorably, whether he will or no, to concern himself with them? There is no doubt of it. But with this essential difference—that man can, from time to time, suspend his direct concern with things, detach himself from his surroundings, ignore them, and subjecting his faculty of attention to a radical shift—incomprehensible zoologically—turn, so to speak, his back on the world and take his stand inside himself, attend to his own inwardness or, what is the same thing, concern himself with himself and not with what is *other*, with things.

In words which, merely from having been worn by use, like old coins, are no longer able to convey their meaning to us with any force, we are accustomed to calling this operation thinking, meditation, contemplation. But these expressions hide the most surprising thing in the phenomenon: man's power of virtually and provisionally withdrawing himself from the world and taking his stand inside himself—or to use a magnificent word which exists only in Spanish, that man can *ensimismarse* ["be inside himself"].

Observe that this marvelous faculty that man possesses of temporarily freeing himself from his slavery to things implies two very dif-

---

[1] [Literally, "otheration." The Spanish word has, in addition to the meaning of English "alteration," that of "state of tumult," "being beside oneself." Throughout this chapter, the author plays on the root meanings of this and another equally untranslatable word, *ensimismamiento,* literally, "within-oneself-ness," in ordinary usage "being absorbed in thought," "meditation," "contemplation." The chapter title in Spanish is *Ensimismamiento y Alteración.—Trans.*]

ferent powers: one is his ability to ignore the world for a greater or less time without fatal risk; the other is his having somewhere to take his stand, to be, when he has virtually left the world. Baudelaire expressed this latter difficulty with romantic and mannered dandyism when, asked where he would choose to live, he answered: "Anywhere, as long as it is out of the world!" But the world is the whole of exteriority, the absolute *without*, which can have no other *without* beyond itself. The only possible without to this *without* is, precisely, a *within*, an *intus*, the inwardness of man, his *self*, which is principally made up of ideas.

Because ideas possess the most extraordinary condition of being nowhere in the world, of being outside of all places; although symbolically we situate them in our heads, as Homer's Greeks situated them in the heart or the pre-Homeric Greeks in the diaphragm or the liver. All these symbolic changes of domicile to which we subject ideas always agree in situating them in one of the viscera; that is, in the innermost part of the body, although the *within* of the body is always a merely relative *within*. In this fashion we give a materialized expression—since we can give no other—to our suspicion that ideas are in no place in space, which is pure exteriority; but that, over against the external world, they constitute another world which is not in the world: our inner world.

That is why the animal has always to be attentive to what goes on outside it, to the things around it. Because, even if the dangers and incitements of those things were to diminish, the animal would perforce continue to be governed by them, by the outward, by what is *other* than itself; because it cannot go *within itself*, since it has no *self*, no *chez soi*, where it can withdraw and rest.

The animal is pure *alteración*. It cannot be within itself. Hence when things cease to threaten it or caress it; when they give it a holiday; in short, when what is *other* ceases to move it and manage it, the poor animal has virtually to stop existing, that is, it goes to sleep. Hence the enormous capacity for somnolence that the animal exhibits, the infrahuman torpor which primitive man continues in part; and, on the other hand, the increasing insomnia of civilized man, the almost permanent, sometimes terrible and uncontrollable wakefulness which afflicts men of an intense inner life. Not many years ago my great friend Scheler—one of the most fertile minds of our time, a man whose life was an incessant radiating of ideas—died from inability to sleep.

But of course—and with this we touch for the first time upon something which will be apparent to us again and again at almost every turn and winding of this course, if each time on a deeper level and in virtue of more precise and effectual reasons (those which I now give are neither the one nor the other)—of course these two things, man's power of withdrawing himself from the world and his power of taking his stand within himself are not gifts conferred upon man. I must emphasize this for those of you who are concerned with philosophy: they are not gifts conferred upon man. *Nothing that is substantive has been conferred upon man*. He has to do everything for himself.

Hence, if man enjoys this privilege of temporarily freeing himself from things and the power to enter into himself and there rest, it is because by his effort, his toil, and his ideas he has succeeded in reacting upon things, in transforming them, and creating around himself a margin of security, which is always limited but always or almost always increasing. This specifically human creation is technology. Thanks to it, and in proportion to its progress, man can take his stand within himself. But, vice versa, man is a technician, he is also able to modify his environment in the direction of his convenience, because, seizing every moment of rest that things allowed him, he has used it to retire into himself and form ideas about this world, about these things and his relation to them, to form a plan of attack against his circumstances, in short, to create an inner world for himself. From this inner world he emerges and returns to the outer. But he returns as protagonist, he returns with a *self* which he did not possess before, with his plan of campaign—not to let himself be dominated by things, but to govern them himself, to impose his will and his design upon them, to realize his ideas in that outer world, to mould the planet after the preferences of his inmost being. Far from losing his own self in this return to the world, he carries it thither, projects it energetically and masterfully upon things, in other words, he forces the *other*—the world—little by little to become himself. Man humanizes the world, injects it, impregnates it with his own ideal substance, and it is possible to imagine that one day or another, in the far depths of time, this terrible outer world will become so saturated with man that our descendants will be able to travel through it as today we mentally travel through our own inner selves; it is possible to imagine that the world, without ceasing to be the world, will one day be changed into something like a materialized soul, and, as in

Shakespeare's *Tempest*, the winds will blow at the bidding of Ariel, the elf of Ideas.[2]

It seems to me that we can now, if only vaguely and schematically, represent to ourselves what humanity's course has been from this point of view. Let us do so in a brief statement which will at the same time serve us as a summary and a reminder of all that has so far been said.

Man, no less than the animal, finds himself consigned to the world, to the things about him, to his surroundings, his circumstance. At first his existence hardly differs from zoological existence; he too lives governed by his environment, is set among the things of the world as one of them. Yet no sooner do the beings around him give him a moment of repose than man, making a gigantic effort, achieves an instant of concentration—enters into himself, that is—by great efforts keeps his attention fixed upon the ideas that spring up within him, ideas which things have evoked and which have reference to the behavior of things, to what the philosopher will later call "the being of things." For the moment it is only a very crude idea of the world, but one that allows him to sketch a first plan of defense, a preconceived course of conduct. But the things around him neither allow him to devote much time to this concentration, nor even if they allowed it would our primigenial man be capable of prolonging this unusual twist of his attention, this fixation upon the impalpable phantoms of ideas, for more than a few seconds or minutes. This inwardly directed attention, which is being within one's self, is the most antinatural and ultrabiological of phenomena. It took man thousands upon thousands of years to educate his capacity for concentration a little—only a little. What is natural to him is to disperse himself, to divert his thought outward, like the monkey in the jungle and in his cage in the zoo.

Father Chevesta, explorer and missionary, who was the first ethnographer to specialize in the study of the pygmies, probably the old-

---

[2] I do not say that this is certain—such certainty is the exclusive possession of the *progressivist,* and I am no *progressivist,* as will appear—but I do say that it is possible.

Nor should it be assumed from what I have just said, that I am an idealist. I am *neither a progressivist nor an idealist!* On the contrary, the idea of progress, and idealism—that exquisitely and nobly proportioned name—progress and idealism are two of my *bêtes noires,* because I see in them perhaps the two greatest sins of the last two hundred years, the two greatest forms of irresponsibility. But let us leave this subject, to treat it in due season, and continue quietly along our road.

est known variety of man, and who went into the deepest of tropical jungles to find them—Father Chevesta, who knows nothing of the doctrine I am now expounding and who confines himself to describing what he sees, says in his most recent book, on the dwarfs of the Congo:[3]

"They completely lack the power of concentration. They are always absorbed by external impressions, whose continual change prevents them from withdrawing into themselves, which is the indispensable condition for any learning. To put them on a school bench would be an unbearable torture to these little men. So that the work of the missionary and the teacher becomes extremely difficult."

But even though momentary and crude, this primitive withdrawal into the self tends basically to separate human life from animal life. Because now man, our primigenial man, goes back and again submerges himself in the things of the world, but resisting them, not delivering himself wholly over to them. He has a plan against them, a project for dealing with them, for manipulating their forms, which produces a minimum transformation of his environment, just enough so that things oppress him a little less and in consequence allow him more frequent and leisurely intervals of withdrawal into himself, of meditation . . . and so on, time after time.

There are, then, three different moments, which are repeated cyclically thoughout the course of human history, in forms each time more complex and rich: 1. Man feels himself lost, shipwrecked among things; this is *alteración*. 2. Man, by an energetic effort, withdraws into himself to form ideas about things and possible ways of dominating them; this is being within one's self, *ensimismamiento*, the *vita contemplativa* of the Romans, the *theoretikos bios* of the Greeks, *theory*. 3. Man again submerges himself in the world, to act in it according to a preconceived plan; this is action, *vita activa, praxis*.

Accordingly, *it is impossible to speak of action except in so far as it will be governed by a previous contemplation; and vice versa, contemplation, or being within one's self, is nothing but a projecting of future action.*

Man's destiny, then, is primarily *action*. We do not live to think, but the other way round: we think in order that we may succeed in surviving. This is a point of capital importance, upon which, in my judgment, we must set ourselves in radical opposition to the entire philosophical tradition and make up our minds to deny that *thought*, in any sufficing

---

[3] *Bambuti, die Zwerge des Congo*, 1932.

sense of the word, was given to man once and for all, so that without further ado he finds it at his disposal as a perfect faculty or power, ready to be employed and exercised, as flight was given to the bird and swimming to the fish.

If this pertinacious doctrine were valid, it would follow that as the fish can—from the outset—swim, man could—from the outset and without further ado—think. Such a notion deplorably blinds us to perceiving the peculiar drama, the unique drama, which constitutes the very condition of man. Because if for the present, in order to understand one another at this moment, we admit the traditional idea that thought is the characteristic of man—remember "man, a rational animal"—so that to be a man would be, as our inspired forefather, Descartes, claimed, the same as to be *a thinking thing*—it would follow that man, by being endowed once and for all with *thought*, by possessing it with the certainty with which a constitutive and inalienable quality is possessed, would be sure of being man as the fish is in fact sure of being a fish. Now this is a formidable and a fatal error. Man is never sure that he will be able to exercise thought—that is, in an adequate manner; and only if it is adequate is it thought. Or, in more popular terms: man is never sure that he will be right, that he will hit the mark. Which means nothing less than the tremendous fact that, unlike all other entities in the universe, man is not and can never be sure that he is, in fact, man, as the tiger is sure of being a tiger and the fish of being a fish.

Far from thought having been bestowed upon man, the truth is—a truth which I cannot now properly support by argument but can only state—the truth is that he has continually been creating thought, making it little by little, perforce of a discipline, a culture or cultivation; a millennial, nay, multimillennial effort, without having yet succeeded—far from it!—in finishing the job. Not only was thought not given to man from the first, but even at this point in history he has only succeeded in forming a small portion and a crude form of what in the simple and ordinary sense of the word we call thought. And even the small portion gained, being an acquired and not a constitutive quality, is always in danger of being lost, and considerable quantities of it have been lost, many times in fact, in the past; and today we are on the point of losing it again. To such an extent, unlike all the other beings in the universe, is man never surely *man*; on the contrary, being *man* signifies precisely being always on the point of not being man, being a living problem, an absolute and hazardous adventure, or, as I am wont to say:

being, in essence, drama! Because there is drama only when we do not know what is going to happen, so that every instant is pure peril and shuddering risk. While the tiger cannot stop being a tiger, cannot be de-tigered, man lives in perpetual danger of being dehumanized. With him, not only is it problematic and contingent whether this or that will happen to him, as it is with the other animals, but at times what happens to man is nothing less than *ceasing to be man*. And this is true not only abstractly and generically but it holds of our own individuality. Each one of us is always in danger of not being the unique and untransferable *self* which he is. The majority of men perpetually betray this *self* which is waiting to be; and to tell the whole truth, our personal individuality is a personage which is never completely realized, a stimulating Utopia, a secret legend, which each of us guards in the depths of his heart. It is thoroughly comprehensible that Pindar summarized his heroic ethics in the well-known imperative: "Become what you are."

The condition of man, then, is essential uncertainty. Hence the cogency of the charmingly mannered *mot* of a fifteenth-century Burgundian gentleman: *"Rien ne m'est sûre que la chose incertaine,"* "I am sure of nought save the uncertain."

No human acquisition is stable. Even what appears to us most completely won and consolidated can disappear in a few generations. This thing we call "civilization"—all these physical and moral comforts, all these conveniences, all these shelters, all these virtues and disciplines which have become habit now, on which we count, and which in effect constitute a repertory or system of securities which man made for himself like a raft in the initial shipwreck which living always is—all these securities are insecure securities which in the twinkling of an eye, at the least carelessness, escape from man's hands and vanish like phantoms. History tells us of innumerable retrogressions, of decadences and degenerations. But nothing tells us that there is no possibility of much more basic retrogressions than any so far known, including the most radical of all: the total disappearance of man as man and his silent return to the animal scale, to complete and definitive *alteración*. The fate of culture, the destiny of man, depends upon our maintaining this dramatic consciousness ever alive in our inmost being, and upon our being well aware, as of a murmuring counterpoint in our entrails, that we can only be sure of insecurity.

No small part of the anguish that is today tormenting the souls of the West derives from the fact that during the past century—and perhaps for the first time in history—man reached the point of believing himself secure. Secure! For the truth is that the one and only person who ever succeeded in feeling and believing himself secure was the pharmaceutical Monsieur Homais, the net result of progressivism! The progressivist idea consists in affirming not only that humanity—an abstract, irresponsible, nonexistent entity invented at the time—that humanity progresses, which is certain, but also that it progresses of necessity. This idea anesthetized the European and the American to that basic feeling of risk which is the substance of man. Because if humanity inevitably progresses, this means that we abandon all watchfulness, stop worrying, throw off all responsibility, or, as we say in Spain, "snore away" and let humanity bear us inevitably to perfection and delight. Human history thus loses all the bone and sinew of drama and is reduced to a peaceful tourist trip, organized by some transcendent "Cook's." Traveling thus securely toward its fulfillment, the civilization in which we are embarked would be like the Phaeacian ship in Homer which sailed straight to port without a pilot. This security is what we are paying for today.[4]

[4] This is one of the reasons why I said that I am not a *progressivist*. This is why I prefer to renew in myself, at frequent intervals, the emotion aroused in me in my youth by Hegel's words at the beginning of his *Philosophy of History:* *"When we contemplate the past, that is, history,"* he says, *"the first thing we see is nothing but—ruins."*

In passing, let us seize the opportunity to see, from the altitude of this vision, the element of frivolity, and even of vulgarity, in Nietzsche's famous imperative: *"Live dangerously."* Which, furthermore, is not Nietzsche's but the exaggeration of an old Italian Renaissance saying, Aretino's famous motto: *Vivere risolutamente.* Because Nietzsche does not say *"Live on the alert,"* which would have been good, but *"Live dangerously."* And this shows that despite his genius, he did not know that the very substance of our life is danger and hence it is rather affected, and supererogatory, to propose as something new, added, and original that we should seek and collect danger. An idea, furthermore, which is typical of the period that called itself *"fin de siècle,"* a period which will remain in history—it culminated about 1900—as that in which man felt himself most secure and, at the same time—with its stiff shirts and frock coats, its *femmes fatales,* its affectation of perversity, and its Barresian cult of the "I"—as the epoch of vulgarity par excellence. In every period there are ideas that I should call "fishing" ideas, ideas that are expressed and proclaimed precisely because it is known they will not happen, that are thought only as a game, as *folie;* some years ago, for example, there was a rage in England for wolf stories, because England is a country where the last wolf was killed in 1668 and which hence has no genuine experience of wolves. In a period that has no strong experience of insecurity—such as the *fin de siècle* period—they play at the dangerous life.

Let all this be taken as going to show that thought is not a gift to man but a laborious, precarious, and volatile acquisition.

Such being my view, you will understand that I see an element of absurdity in the definition of man put forth by Linnaeus and the eighteenth century: *homo sapiens*. Because if we take this expression in good faith, it can mean only that man in fact knows—in other words, that he knows all that he needs to know. Now nothing is further from the reality. Man has never known what he needed to know. So if we understand *homo sapiens* in the sense that man knows some things, a very few things, but does not know the remainder, since this remainder is immense it would seem to me more appropriate to define him as *homo insciens, insipiens*, as man the unknowing. And certainly, if we were not now in such a hurry, we could see the good judgment with which Plato defines man precisely by his ignorance. Ignorance is, in fact, man's privilege. Neither God nor beast is ignorant—the former because he possesses all knowledge, the latter because he needs none.

It is clear, then, that man does not exercise his thought because he finds it amusing, but because, obliged as he is to live immersed in the world and to force his way among things, he finds himself under the necessity of organizing his psychic activities, which are not very different from those of the anthropoid, *in the form* of thought—which is what the animal does not do.

Man, then, rather than by what he *is*, or by what he *has*, escapes from the zoological scale by what he *does*, by his conduct. Hence it is that he must always keep watch on himself.

This is something of what I wanted to suggest in the epigram—which seems to be merely an epigram—that *we do not live in order to think* but *we think in order to succeed in subsisting or surviving*. And you see how this attributing thought to man as an innate quality—which at first seems to be a homage and even a compliment to his species—is, strictly speaking, an injustice. Because there is no such gift, no such gratuity; there is only a laborious fabrication and a conquest which, like every conquest—be it of a city or of a woman—is always unstable and fugitive.

This consideration of thought has been necessary as an aid to understanding my earlier statement that man is primarily and fundamentally action. In passing, let us do homage to the first man who thought this truth with complete clarity; it was not Kant nor Fichte, it was that inspired madman Auguste Comte.

We saw that *action* is not a random fisticuffs with the things around us or with our fellow men; this is the infrahuman, this is *alteración*. *Action* is to act upon the environment of material things or of other men in accordance with a plan preconceived in a previous period of meditation or thought. There is, then, no genuine action if there is no thought, and there is no authentic thought if it is not duly referred to action and made virile by its relation to action.

But this relation—which is the true one—between action and contemplation has been persistently ignored. When the Greeks discovered that man thought, that there existed in the universe the strange reality that is thought (until then men had not thought, or, like the *bourgeois gentilhomme*, had done so without knowing it), they felt such an enthusiasm for the charms of ideas that they conferred upon intelligence, upon the *logos*, the supreme rank in the universe. Compared with it, everything else seemed to them ancillary and contemptible. And as we tend to project into God whatever appears to us to be the best, the Greeks, with Aristotle, reached the point of maintaining that God had no other occupation but to think. And not even to think about things— that seemed to them as it were a debasement of the intellectual process. No—according to Aristotle, God does nothing but think about thought—which is to turn God into an intellectual, or, more precisely, into a modest professor of philosophy. But I repeat that, for them, this was the most sublime thing in the world and the most sublime thing that a being could do. Hence they believed that man's destiny was solely to exercise his intellect, that man had come into the world to meditate, or, in our terminology, to be himself (*ensimismarse*).

This doctrine has been given the name *"intellectualism"*—that idolatry of the intelligence which isolates thought from its setting, from its function in the general economy of human life. As if man thinks because he thinks, and not because, whether he will or no, he has to think in order to maintain himself among things! As if thought could awaken and function of its own motion, as if it began and ended in itself, and was not—as is the true state of the case—engendered by action, with its roots and its end in action! We owe innumerable things of the highest value to the Greeks, but they have put chains on us too. The man of the West still lives, to no small degree, enslaved by the preferences of the men of Greece—preferences that, operating in the subsoil of our culture, for eight centuries turned us from our proper and genuine Western vocation. The heaviest of these chains is *"intellectualism"*; and now, when it is imperative that we correct our course and find new roads—in short, succeed—it is of the greatest importance that we resolutely rid ourselves of this archaic attitude, which has been carried to its extreme during these last two centuries.

Under the name first of *raison*, then of *enlightenment*, and finally of *culture*, a radical prevarication of terms and the most indiscreet deification of intelligence were effected. Among the majority of almost all the thinkers of the period, especially among the Germans—for example, among those who were my masters at the beginning of the century— *culture, thought,* came to fill the vacant office of a God who had been put to flight. All my work, from its first stammerings, has been a battle against this attitude, which many years ago I called the *"bigotry of culture."* The bigotry of culture, because it presented us with culture, with thought, as something justified by itself, that is, which needs no justification but is valid by its own essence, whatever its concrete activity and its content may be. Human life was to put itself at the service of culture because only thus would it become filled with worthy substance. From which it would follow that human life, our pure existence, would in itself be a mean and worthless thing.

This way of reversing the true relation between *life* and *culture*, between *action* and *contemplation*, brought it about that, during the last century—hence until a very short time ago—there was an overproduction of ideas, of books and works of art, a real *cultural inflation*. The result has been what—jokingly, because I distrust "isms"—we could call a "capitalism of culture," a modern aspect of Byzantinism. There has been production for production's sake, instead of production in view of consumption, in view of the necessary ideas that the man of today needs and can absorb. And, as occurs in capitalism, the market was glutted and crisis has ensued. Let no one tell me that the greater part of the immense changes that have recently occurred has taken us by surprise. For twenty years I have been announcing them and prognosticating them. To mention no other subject than the one we are now treating, reference may be made to my essay, formally and programmatically entitled "The Reform of Intelligence."[5]

But the most dangerous aspect of the intellectual aberration that this "bigotry of culture" signifies is not this; it consists in presenting culture, withdrawal into one's self, thought, as a grace or jewel that man is to add to his life, hence as something that provisionally lies outside of his life and as if there were life without culture and thought—as if it were possible to live without withdrawing into one's self. Men were set, as it were, before a jeweler's window—were given the choice of acquiring culture or doing without it. And it is clear that, faced with such a dilemma, during the years we are now living through men have not hesitated, but have resolved to explore the second alternative to its limits and are

[5] [See *Obras completas,* Vol. IV.]

seeking to flee from all taking a stand within the self and to give themselves up to the opposite extreme. That is why Europe is in extremities today.

The intellectualist aberration, which isolates contemplation from action, was followed by the opposite aberration—the *voluntarist* aberration, which throws contemplation overboard and deifies pure action. This is the other way of wrongly interpreting the foregoing thesis, that man is primarily and fundamentally *action*. Undoubtedly every idea—even the truest—is susceptible of misinterpretation; undoubtedly every idea is dangerous; this must be admitted with all formality and once and for all, but upon condition that we add that this danger, this latent risk, is not limited to ideas but is inseparable from everything, absolutely everything, that man does. This is why I have said that the essence of man is purely and simply *danger*. Man always travels among precipices, and, whether he will or no, his truest obligation is to keep his balance.

As has happened more than once in the known past, now again—and I refer to these years, almost to this century—once again peoples are plunging into *alteración*. The same thing that happened in Rome! Europe began by letting itself be overwhelmed by pleasure, as Rome was by what Ferrero has called "luxury"—an excess, an extravagance, of commodities. Then pain and terror took their turn. As in Rome, social conflicts and the consequent wars stupefied men's souls. And stupefaction, the extreme form of *alteración*—stupefaction, when it persists, becomes stupidity. It has aroused some attention that, for quite a long time now and with the insistence of a leitmotiv, I have referred in my writings to the insufficiently recognized fact that, even in Cicero's time, the ancient world was becoming stupid. It has been said that his master Posidonius was the last man of antique civilization who was able to set himself before things and think about them effectually. The capacity to take a stand within the self, to withdraw serenely into one's incorruptible depths, was lost—as it threatens to be lost in Europe if something is not done to prevent it. Nothing is talked about but action. The demagogues, impresarios of *alteración*, who have already caused the death of several civilizations, harass men so that they shall not reflect, see to it that they are kept herded together in crowds so that they cannot reconstruct their individuality in the one place where it can be reconstructed, which is in solitude. They cry down service to truth, and in its stead offer us: *myths*. And by all these means they succeed in throwing men into a passion, in putting them, between ardors and terrors, *beside*, that is, *outside of, themselves*. And clearly, since man is the animal that has succeeded in putting himself *inside himself*, when man is *beside himself* his aspiration is to descend and he falls back into animality. Such is the spectacle—always the same—of every period in which pure action is deified. The interval is filled with crimes. Human life loses value, is no longer regarded, and all forms of violence and spoliation are practiced—especially of spoliation. Hence whenever the figure of the pure man of action rises above the horizon and becomes dominant, the first thing for us to do is to lock everything up. Anyone who would really like to learn what effects spoliation produces in a great civilization can see them set forth in the first book of major importance to be written on the Roman Empire. I refer to the book by the great Russian savant Rostovtzeff, who for many years has been teaching in the United States—*Social and Economic History of the Roman Empire*.

Torn in this way from its normal connection with contemplation, with being within one's self, *pure action* permits and produces only a chain of stupidities which we might better call "stupidity unchained." So we see today that an absurd attitude justifies the appearance of an opposing attitude no more reasonable; at least, reasonable enough, and so on indefinitely. Such is the extreme to which political affairs in the West have come!

This being the situation, it would seem sensible that, whenever circumstances give us even the slightest respite, we should attempt to break this enchanted circle of *alteración*, which hurries us from one folly to another; it would seem sensible that we should say to ourselves—as, after all, we often say to ourselves in our more ordinary life whenever our surroundings overwhelm us, when we feel lost in a whirlpool of problems—that we say to ourselves: "Quietly now!" What is the meaning of this adjuration? Simply that of inviting us to suspend for a moment the action which threatens to preoccupy us and make us lose our heads; to suspend action for a moment so that we may withdraw into ourselves, review our ideas of the circumstance in which we are placed, and work out a plan of strategy.

Hence I consider it neither extravagant nor insolent if, having come to a country that still enjoys a serene horizon,[6] I think that the most fruitful work that it can do, for itself and for the rest of mankind, is not

[6] [The reference is to Argentina, where this chapter was delivered as a lecture in 1939.—Editor's note.]

to add to the world's state of *alteración*, still less to be affected more than need be by the fact that others have succumbed to it, but to take advantage of its own fortunate situation to do what others cannot now do—to withdraw and think a little. If now, in places where it is possible, no store of new human projects—that is, of ideas—is created, we can have little confidence in the future. Half of the unhappy things that are taking place today are taking place because no such projects were in readiness, just as I prophesied that they would take place, as long ago as 1922 in the Prologue to my *Invertebrate Spain*.

Without a strategic retreat into the self, without vigilant thought, human life is impossible. Call to mind all that mankind owes to certain great withdrawals into the self! It is no chance that all the great founders of religions preceded their apostolates by famous retreats. Buddha withdraws to the forest; Mahomet withdraws to his tent, and even there he withdraws from his tent by wrapping his head in his cloak; above all, Jesus goes apart into the desert for forty days. What do we not owe to Newton! Well, when someone, amazed that he had succeeded in reducing the countless phenomena of physics to such a precise and simple system, asked him how he had succeeded in doing so, he replied ingenuously: *Nocte dieque incubando*, "turning them over day and night"—words behind which we glimpse vast and abysmal withdrawals into the self.

In the world today a great thing is dying; it is truth. Without a certain margin of tranquillity, truth succumbs. With which we now close the circle begun by our opening words. It was to give them their full meaning that I have said what I have said.

Hence, over against the incitements to *alteración* which today reach us from every point of the compass and from every angle of life, I believed that before plunging into this course of lectures, I should by way of prologue set before you a sketch of this doctrine of withdrawal into one's self—even though it has been a hurried sketch, even though I have been unable to dwell on any of its parts as I should have wished to do and have had to pass many of them over entirely. For example, I have not been able to point out that contemplation, withdrawal into one's self, like everything human, has sex, that there is a masculine form of it, and another that is feminine. Which cannot be otherwise, since woman is not *him*self but *her*self.

Similarly, the man of the East withdraws into himself in a different way from the man of the West. The Occidental does it in clarity of mind. Remember Goethe's lines:

I own allegiance to the race of those
Who from the dark aspire to clarity.

Ich bekenne mich zu dem Geschlecht
Der aus dem Dunkel ins Helle strebt.

Europe and America mean the attempt to live by clear ideas, not by myths. Because clear ideas were not to be found today, the European feels lost and demoralized.

Machiavelli—not to be confused with *Machiavellianism*—tells us that when an army is demoralized and scatters, losing its formations, there is only one salvation: *"Ritornare al segno,"* *"to return to the banner,"* to take shelter under its folds, and regroup the scattered hosts beneath that sign. Europe and America must also *"ritornare al segno"* of clear ideas. The new generations, who delight in the strong body and the pure act, must integrate themselves in the clear idea, in the strictly constructed idea, which is not redundant, which is not flabby, which is necessary to life. Let us return—I repeat—from myths to clear and distinct ideas, as they were called three centuries ago, with programmatic solemnity, by the keenest mind that the West has known: René Descartes, "that French cavalier who set out at such a good pace," as Péguy put it. I know very well that Descartes and his rationalism are completely of the past, but man is nothing positive if he is not continuity. To excel the past we must not allow ourselves to lose contact with it; on the contrary, we must feel it under our feet because we have raised ourselves upon it.

ERWIN STRAUS (1891-

Erwin Straus, born in 1891, took his MD degree at the University of Berlin. There he became a professor of psychiatry. Later, upon coming to the United States, he became a member of the staff of the Veterans Administration Hospital in Lexington, Kentucky. Straus has been a central figure in the influence of a phenomenological psychology in many disciplines. His books include: *The Primary World of the Senses* (1935) and an important collection of his essays, *Phenomenological Psychology* (1966).

THE UPRIGHT POSTURE*

Introduction

A breakdown of physical well-being is alarming; it turns our attention to functions that, on good days, we take for granted. A healthy person does not ponder about breathing, seeing, or walking. Infirmities of breath, sight, or gait startle us. Among the patients consulting a psychiatrist, there are some who can no longer master the seemingly banal arts of standing and walking. They are not paralyzed, but, under certain conditions, they cannot, or feel as if they cannot, keep themselves upright. They tremble and quiver. Incomprehensible terror takes away their strength. Sometimes, a minute change in the physiognomy of the frightful situation may restore their strength. Obviously, upright posture is not confined to the technical problems of locomotion. It contains a psychological element. It is pregnant with a meaning not exhausted by the physiological tasks of meeting the forces of gravity and maintaining equilibrium.

Language has long since taken cognizance of this fact. The ex-

---

* By permission of Basic Books, Inc. Excerpted from Chapter 7, *Phenomenological Psychology* by Erwin W. Straus, Copyright © 1966 by Erwin W. Straus, Basic Books, Inc., Publishers, New York.

Also by permission of Tavistock Publications Ltd., London, England.

pression "to be upright" has two connotations: first, to rise, to get up, and to stand on one's own feet and, second, the moral implication, not to stoop to anything, to be honest and just, to be true to friends in danger, to stand by one's convictions, and to act accordingly, even at the risk of one's life. We praise an upright man; we admire someone who stands up for his ideas of rectitude. There are good reasons to assume that the term "upright" in its moral connotation is more than a mere allegory.

The upright posture distinguishes the human genus from other living creatures. To Milton, Adam and Eve appeared as ". . . Two of far nobler shape, erect and tall, God-like erect, with native honor clad. . . ." Some biologists, however, would like to take exception to this praise, and, in slightly more prosaic statements, they indict the upright posture as a cause of hernias and flat feet. However this may be, whether the poet is right or his misanthropic opponents, whether upright posture is an excellence or not, in any case it is a distinction. It does not occur in any species other than man.[1]

Upright posture, while unique, is also essential. This is no necessary consequence. The exceptional might be nothing but a peculiarity, an accidental caprice of nature. However, there is no doubt that the shape and function of the human body are determined in almost every detail by, and for, the upright posture. The skeleton of the foot; the structure of the ankle, knee, and hip; the curvature of the vertebral column; the proportions of the limbs—all serve the same purpose. This purpose could not be accomplished if the muscles and the nervous system were not built accordingly. While all parts contribute to the upright posture, upright posture in turn permits the development of the forelimbs into

[1] F. Weidenreich (1946) discusses the relationship between man and his simian ancestors. He enumerates the main peculiarities that, compared to the condition of the apes, characterize man in his upright posture. The human leg, which he mentions among other things, "is stretched in hip and knee joints to its maximum extent and adduced toward the midline, so that the knees touch each other, while in anthropoids, even if the latter succeed in standing and walking upright, the legs remain bent in hip and knee joints and are held in abduction, so that anthropoids always stand stooped, with their knees crooked and turned outward" (p. 6). In the so-called normal attitude of man, therefore, the lines connecting the centers of hip, knee, and ankle joints are all located in the same frontal plane. The plumb line passes through this plane. Furthermore, the center of the hip joint is, for each leg, vertically above the center of the knee and ankle joints.

the human shoulders, arms, and hands and of the skull into the human skull and face.

With upright posture, the vertebral column takes on, for the first time, the architectural function of a column. The skull rests on the articular surfaces of the atlas (which here, indeed, deserves its name) like an architrave on the capitals of columns. This arrangement makes it possible and necessary for the atlanto-occipital joint to be moved forward toward the center of the base of the skull, resulting in the typical configuration of the human skull, the extension of the base, and the closing vault, which in turn provides wider space for the orbitae. The skulls of the other primates still show the shape characteristic of other quadrupeds, in which the head does not rest on the vertebral column but hangs down from it. The foramen magnum accordingly is in a more caudal position; the clivus cuts the vertical at a more obtuse angle. The other primates—as has been said—are built to stand upright but not for upright posture.[2]

Because upright posture is the leitmotiv in the formation of the human organism, an individual who has lost or is deprived of the capacity to get up and keep himself upright depends, for his survival, completely on the aid of others. Without their help, he is doomed to die. A biologically oriented psychology must not forget that upright posture is an indispensable condition of man's self-preservation. Upright we are, and we experience ourselves in this specific relation to the world.

Men and mice do not have the same environment, even if they share the same room. Environment is not a stage with the scenery set as one and the same for all actors who make their entrance. Each species has its own environment. There is a mutual interdependence between species and environment. The surrounding world is determined by the organization of the species in a process of selecting what is relevant to

---

[2] The comparison of man and other primates is a time-honored topic, widely discussed among pre-Darwinian zoologists. Most of the characteristic differences enumerated by Weidenreich (1946) were known to the anatomists of the eighteenth century, who also considered the possibility of a common origin. Daubenton published, in 1764, a paper about the different positions of the foramen magnum in man and animals (Herder, 1778). Even the sentence passed on upright posture because of its inherent evils is old enough. Moskati (1771), comparing the essential differences of man and animals, came to the conclusion that upright posture disposed heart, circulation, and intestines to many defects and diseases.

the function cycle of action and reaction (von Uexkuell, 1926). Upright posture pre-establishes a definite attitude toward the world; it is a specific mode of being-in-the-world.

Relating the basic forms of human experience to man's upright posture may well be called an anthropological approach, if that term is used with its original connotation. It was not until the middle of the nineteenth century that the meaning of "anthropology" was confined to zoological aspects, to a study of man as an animal in his evolution and history as a race. The nineteenth-century view aimed to see man exclusively and understand him completely as an animal. It was motivated by an antagonism to theology. Instead of seeing man created in the image of God, it wanted to see man as the descendant of the monkey. This antitheological view remains theological because of its concern with refutation. However, one can and should consider man in his own right without either theological or antitheological bias. Anthropology can be developed, indifferent to both the Biblical account and the evolutionary theory of genesis.

This writer's interest is in what man is and not in how he supposedly became what he is. . . . Looking from man to the hominids[3] or the other primates, we see what man no longer is. Looking from the other primates to man, we see what the other primates are not yet. Any explanation of the causes of evolution demands a knowledge of both the old and new forms. . . .

* * *

With all due respect for the accomplishments of those early ancestors, we should not forget to investigate our own situation. Man is not only the end of a long development; he also represents a new beginning. One may doubt if old rocks will reveal all the secrets of human existence.

[3] The early Darwinians were searching for the "missing link" connecting modern man with the living anthropoids. Today, the opinion prevails that the human branch parted from the modern anthropoids "much earlier than we ever dreamed." Weidenreich (1946) believed that this separation occurred in the Miocene period or not very long afterward. Portmann (1944) placed it in the late Cretaceous period. From there on, a fragmentary line of hominids, documented by fossils in Europe, Asia, and Africa, leads toward modern man. There is also another line, still more hypothetical, leading to the living anthropoids: chimpanzee, gorilla, orangutan.

Human Kinematics

Acquiring Upright Posture

Upright posture has a delayed beginning in the life of an individual. The heart of the unborn beats in the mother's womb. Breathing starts with the first cry at birth. Upright posture keeps us waiting. Even when the physiological conditions—e.g., the maturation of fibers, the development of postural reflexes, or, later, the elongation of the legs— are fulfilled, the child will not master upright posture at once. He has to learn it, to conquer it. The acquisition will pass through several phases, which, although not completely separate, are sufficiently distinct. Progress is slow; it takes a number of years. This development will be followed here from the getting up, to standing, and, finally, to walking.

The origin and the beginning of upright posture do not coincide, just as the first cry, the beginning of the functioning of breathing, does not mark the origin of breathing. The conditions surrounding the beginning of a function, whether it be breathing, speaking, or standing, do not at all give an account of the structures of breath, speech, upright posture, or of their origins. As long as one speaks about breathing and walking, the distinction appears banal and not worth mentioning. There are, however, situations where the distinction is less obvious but not less true. This writer wonders whether genetic psychologists sometimes actually do confuse beginning and origin.

Upright posture characterizes the human species. Nevertheless, each individual has to struggle in order to make it really his own. Man has to become what he is. The acquisition does not make him an "absentee landlord." While the heart continues to beat from its fetal beginning to death without our active intervention and while breathing neither demands nor tolerates our voluntary interference beyond narrow limits, upright posture remains a task throughout our lives. Before reflection or self-reflection start, but as if they were a prelude to it, work makes its appearance within the realm of the elemental biological functions of man. In getting up, in reaching the upright posture, man must oppose the forces of gravity. It seems to be his nature to oppose nature in its impersonal, fundamental aspects with natural means. However, gravity is never fully overcome; upright posture always maintains its character of counteraction. It calls for our activity and attention.

Automatic regulation alone does not suffice. An old horse may go to sleep standing on its four legs; man has to be awake to keep himself upright. Much as we are part of nature with every breath, with every bite, with every step, we first become our true selves in waking opposition to nature. In sleep, we do not withdraw our interest from the world so much as we surrender ourselves completely to it. We abandon ourselves to the world, relinquishing our individuality. We no longer hold our own in the world, opposed to it. Awakeness and the force of gravity are mutually interdependent. While awakeness is necessary for upright posture, that is, for counteracting gravity, gravity determines waking experience. The dreams of one night are not related to the dreams of another night, but days are related to one another. They form a continuum where every hour, every moment, anticipates the next and prepares for it. Held back by gravity to a precise point, we can overcome distance only in an orderly sequence. During our waking hours, sequence means consequence. Gravity, which holds us in line, imposes on waking experience a methodical proceeding. In sleep, when we no longer oppose gravity, in our weightless dreams, or in our lofty fantasies, experience becomes kaleidoscopic and finally amorphous. Sequence, then, no longer means consequence. Awakeness is no mere addendum, still less an impediment, to an otherwise happily functioning id. The waking man alone can preserve himself, and he alone can help drives to reach their goal.

. . . We can read man's natural endowment from his physique. Considering man in his upright posture, we do well to envisage the possibility that not society has first brought man into conflict with nature, but that man's natural opposition to nature enables him to produce society, history, and conventions.

The direction upward, against gravity, inscribes into space world-regions to which we attach values, such as those expressed by high and low, rise and decline, climbing and falling, superior and inferior, elevated and downcast, looking up to and despising. On Olympus, high, remote, inaccessible, and exalted, dwell the Homeric gods. On Mount Sinai, Moses receives the Ten Commandments. Below, in the depths, is Hades and the world of shadows. There, also, is the Inferno. However, such evaluations are not unequivocal. "Base" (adjective) and "base" (noun) have, in spite of their phonetic resemblance, different etymological roots and opposite meanings. "Base," the adjective, is derived from the Latin root *bassus* with the connotation "short" and, later, "low"; "base," the noun, originated in the Greek root *baino*—"walking" or "stepping." The earth that pulls us downward is also the ground that carries and gives support. The weighty man signifies, by his dignified gait, that he carries a heavy burden but sustains it well. Upright posture as counteraction cannot lack the forces against which it strives.

Standing

In getting up, man gains his standing in the world. The parents are not the only ones who greet the child's progress with joy. The child enjoys no less the triumph of his achievement. There is a forceful urge toward the goal of getting up and of resisting, in a state of dangerous balance, the downward-pulling forces. There need not be any other premium, like satisfaction of hunger, attention, or applause. The child certainly does not strive for security. Failure does not discourage him. He enjoys the freedom gained by upright posture—the freedom to stand on his own feet and the freedom to walk. Upright posture, which we learn in and through falling, remains threatened by falls throughout our lives. The natural stance of man is, therefore, "resistance." A rock reposes in its own weight. The things that surround us appear solid and safe in their quiet resting on the ground, but man's status demands endeavor. It is essentially restless. We are committed to an ever renewed exertion. Our task is not finished with getting up and standing. We have to "withstand." He who is able to accomplish this is called constant, stable.

Language expresses well the psychological meaning of standing, with all its facets. The coupling of the transitive and the intransitive meanings "to stand" and "to stand something" characterizes them as resisting and, therefore, enduring against threat, danger, and attack. The etymological root of standing—*sta*—is one of the most prolific elements not only in English but also in Greek, Latin, French, and German. It may suffice to mention only a few derivatives of an almost exhaustible store. Besides such combinations as "standing for," "standing by," and "making a stand," there are many words where the root has undergone slight changes but is still recognizable: e.g., "state," "status," "estate," "statement," "standard," "statue," "institution," "constitution," "substance," "establish," "understand," "assist," "distant." This entire family of words is kept together by one and the same principal meaning. They refer to something that is instituted, erected, constructed, and, in its dangerous equilibrium, threatened by fall and collapse. Falling is not always tragic. Clowns, modern and old, primitive and sublime, all have made use of falling as a reliable trick to stir up laughter.

With upright posture, an inescapable ambivalence penetrates and pervades all human behavior. Upright posture removes us from the ground, keeps us away from things, and holds us aloof from our fellow-men. All of these three distances can be experienced either as gain or as loss.

1. *Distance from the ground.* In getting up, we gain the freedom of motion and enjoy it, but, at the same time, we lose secure contact with the supporting ground, with Mother Earth, and we miss it. We stand alone and have to rely on our own strength and capacities. With the acquisition of upright posture, a characteristic change in language occurs. In the early years, when speaking of himself, a child uses his given name. However, when he has reached the age when he can stand firmly on his own feet, he begins to use the pronoun "I" for himself. This change marks a first gaining of independence. Among all words, "I" has a peculiar character. Everyone uses "I" to refer to himself alone. "I" is a most general world. At the same time, it has a unique meaning for every speaker. In using the word "I," I oppose myself to everyone else, who, nevertheless, is my fellow-man.

Because getting up and standing are so demanding, we enjoy resting, relaxing, yielding, lying down, and sinking back. There is the voluptuous gratification of succumbing. Sex remains a form of lying down or, as language says, of lying or sleeping with. Addicts, in their experience, behavior, and intention, reveal the double aspect of sinking back and its contrast to being upright. A *symposium* found the ancient Greeks, a *convivium* the Romans, stretched on their couches until, after many libations to Dionysus and Bacchus, they finally sank to the ground. *Symposium* means "drinking together," or "a drinking party." It could be well translated by the characteristic German word *Gelage*. Plato's dialogue first helped the word *symposium* to reach its modern connotation. The old and new are not so far apart as one might assume. Their relation can also be expressed—Plato clearly indicates this—as the difference between being upright and sinking.

2. *Distance from things.* In upright posture, the immediate contact with things is loosened. A child creeping on his hands and knees not only keeps contact with the ground but is, in his all-fours locomotion, like the quadrupeds, directed toward immediate contact with things. The length-axis of his body coincides with the direction of his motion.

With getting up, all this changes. In walking, man moves his body in a parallel transposition, the length-axis of his body at a right angle to the direction of his motion. He finds himself always "confronted" with things. Such remoteness enables him to see things, detached from the immediate contact of grasping and incorporating, in their relation to one another. Seeing is transformed into "looking at." The horizon is widened, removed; the distant becomes momentous, of great import. In the same measure, contact with near things is lost.

Thales, the philosopher and astronomer, fell into a ditch while watching the stars. A young child is close to the ground; to him the stars are far off. He does not mind picking things up from the ground; but, growing older, he will learn to accept our table manners, which remove even food to a distance. We set the table; we serve the meal; we use spoon and fork. Our feeding is regulated by a ritual, which we like to discard at a picnic. Artificiality and tools interfere with the direct satisfaction of hunger. The mouth is kept away from the plate. The hand lifts the food to the mouth. Spoon and fork do not create distance; tools can only be invented and used where distance already exists. In the early months of life, hands hold on to things in a grasping reflex. Not until the immediate contact of grasping is abandoned is the use of tools possible. This development is not simply the result of motor maturation. An imbecile may never learn and a paretic may unlearn manners, not so much because of failure of the motorium as because of the loss and lack of distance. Pointing likewise presupposes distance. It appears to be a human activity. Animals do not easily, if at all, understand pointing to distant things.[4] Pathology reveals an antagonistic relationship between grasping and pointing. There are cases where pointing is distorted while grasping either remains undamaged or is later intensified and becomes forced grasping (Goldstein, 1931).[5]

3. *Distance from fellow-men*. In upright posture, we find ourselves "face to face" with others, distant, aloof—verticals that never meet. On the horizontal plane, parallel lines converge toward a vanishing point. Theoretically, the vanishing point of parallel verticals—to which we are comparable, standing vis-à-vis—is in infinite distance. In the

---

[4] It is the hunter who understands and interprets the dog's aiming as pointing. The "point" is the natural outgrowth of the dog's pausing previous to springing the game.

[5] Experimental ablations of cortical areas indicate that grasping is under the control of Brodmann's area 6.

finiteness of seeing, however, parallel verticals do not meet. Therefore, the strict upright posture expresses austerity, inaccessibility, decisiveness, domination, majesty, mercilessness, or unapproachable remoteness, as in catatonic symmetry. Inclination first brings us closer to another. Inclination,[6] just like leaning, means literally "bending out" from the austere vertical.

Dictators, reviewing their parading troops, try to show by their rigid poses their imperturbable and unshakable wills. Formalized attitudes and pantomimic, signifying gestures follow the pattern set by spontaneous expressions. When we lower our heads or kneel in prayer, when we bow or bend our knees in greeting, the deviation from the vertical reveals the relation to it.

So it is with expressions of reverence, of asking and granting a request, and many others. The formalization and shortening of social gestures sometimes make it hard to recognize their origin; but even the stiff forms of military greeting may, with a slight courteous bending of the head, be revitalized by spontaneous expression.

There is only one vertical but many deviations from it, each one carrying a specific, expressive meaning. The sailor puts his cap askew, and his girl understands well the cocky expression and his "leanings." King Comus at the Mardi Gras may lean backward and his crown may slip off-center. However, even the disciples of informality would be seriously concerned if, on his way to his inauguration, the President should wear his silk hat (the elongation and accentuation of the vertical) aslant. There are no teachers, no textbooks, that instruct in this field. There are no pupils, either, who need instruction. Without ever being taught, we understand the rules governing this and other areas of expression. We understand them not conceptually but, it seems, by intuition. This is true for the actor as well as the onlooker.

One may argue that these are cultural patterns with which we grow up and that our final attitudes are the result of many infinitesimal steps.

---

[6] The root is Latin, *clino,* to bend. It is interesting to see how greatly language is shaped in accordance with expressive phenomena. Not only does the English language have two words of the same structure from different roots; but there is the German word *Zuneigung,* with still another etymological derivation, which, however, expresses the same meaning with the corresponding space experience. All this points to the fact that metaphors do not simply carry over a meaning from one medium to another. There is much more intimate relation—that between expressive motion and emotional attitude.

To support this view, one may point to the fact that gestures of greeting were different in the old days from ours and are different in the Occident and the Orient. Yet, in spite of their divergences, they are all modifications of the upright posture. Exceptions only confirm the rule. We give our assent by nodding the head, which is obviously also a motion that carries the head downward following gravity, away from the vertical. It has been observed that this gesture is not universal, that there are peoples to whom the same vertical motion of nodding means negation or denial. However, these two forms of expression, which indeed resemble each other, are not identical. Our mode of assertion, as well as their negation, consists of a two-phased motion—the motion downward and the movement up and backward. While in assertion the accent is on the downward motion, negation chooses the opposite direction. The head is moved from the position of inclination back to the vertical, expressing inaccessibility and denial.

Cultural patterns do not arbitrarily create forms but, within the given framework, formalize a socially accepted scheme valid only for its group and period. With upright posture counteracting gravity, the vertical, pointing upward and away from the center of gravity, becomes a natural determinant. The vertical is a constancy phenomenon. Its apparent position does not change, even if the head is tilted, and, therefore, its projection on the retina varies. At an early age, children are able to draw a vertical or a horizontal line, to copy a cross or a square, but they fail when asked to copy the same square presented as a diamond.[7]

Walking

With getting up, man is ready for walking. The precarious equilibrium reached in standing has to be risked again. A quadruped rests with relative safety on his four legs, which inscribe an appropriate base on the ground. The center of gravity does not leave its position above this base even when the animal walks or trots. The human situation is different. The center of gravity is elevated high over the small base of support. This provides for greater flexibility and variability of

[7] Gibson and Mowrer (1938) assumed that our orientation in space is determined by postural factors, while visual stimulation is of secondary importance. Asche and Witkin (1948), however, in their more recent experiments, came to the opposite conclusion.

movement, but it increases instability and the danger of falling. Man has to find a hold within himself. Standing and walking, he has to keep himself in suspension.

The legs support the body like columns; in the hip joint, the trunk rests on the femur bones as on pillars. At least, it seems to. The appearance is convincing enough for a hysterical person to use it as a model for his astasia-abasia. If one tries, however, to carry through the comparison in detail, one sees immediately the striking contrast to the architectonic principles of column and pillar. Many old temples have collapsed, leaving their columns still standing erect. The stone pillars of a bridge are constructed from the foundation upward. Each lower section really carries the upper one, which can be removed without unbalancing the lower ones. Neither the skeleton nor the legs will stand of their own power. The legs could not do it, even if the muscles could still contract and were not severed from their origin on the pelvis. The legs have to be held in suspension by the counteraction of the trunk muscles and by the counterweight of the trunk. A column, a pillar, or a tower taper off. Their bases are broader than the top. Human legs also have a conical shape, but the bulk is high. The origin of the muscles and, therefore, their main volume is on top. The muscles extend with their tendons downward from pelvis to knee and again from knee to ankle. Their contraction, however, is directed upward.

With the circumference of the thighs near the hip joint considerably larger than the circumference around the ankle, the leg resembles an inverted obelisk more than a column. This leg-obelisk cannot support itself on its tip. There is a gyrostatic system of balance, holding the legs as much as being carried by them. The old anatomical names of muscles and the traditional signification of their functions are often misleading. The biceps femoris and hamstring muscles, the so-called flexors of the leg, bend the lower leg in one position only, while in another they extend the knee and the hip. The erector trunci and the muscles of the legs cooperate—with gravity as their invisible partner—as synergists, originating in adjacent areas of the ilium and the sacrum. They act on the pelvis in opposite directions. They turn the pelvis around an axis, connecting the centers of the hip joints. There is a second balancing system between the right and left that keeps the pelvis and trunk in balance in a sagittal plane. From clinical observation of dystrophies and paralyses, we learn which individual muscles—e.g., the glutaeus maximus, the iliopsoas, the quadriceps femoris, the sacrospinalis—contribute to upright posture; from physiological experiments, we come to know how they are correlated. Through the combined work of observation and experiment, we gain information about the means of locomotion. At this point, a new horizon of problems is opened up— the question of how a being equipped with such motorium will experience the world and himself in this world.

Human bipedal gait is a rhythmical movement whereby, in a sequence of steps, the whole weight of the body rests for a short time on one leg only. The center of gravity has to be swung forward. It has to be brought from a never stable equilibrium to a still less stable balance. Support will be denied to it for a moment until the leg brought forward prevents the threatening fall. Human gait is, in fact, a continuously arrested falling. Therefore, an unforeseen obstacle or a little unevenness of the ground may precipitate a fall. Human gait is an expansive motion, performed in the expectation that the leg brought forward will ultimately find solid ground. It is motion on credit. Confidence and timidity, elation and depression, and stability and insecurity are all expressed in gait.

Bipedal gait is, in fact, a balance alternating from one leg to the other; it permits variations in length, tempo, direction, and accent. In a polka step, even the rhythmical sequence of right and left and left and right is interrupted and exchanged. The symmetry of rhythmically alternating locomotor reflexes is thereby broken. Steps varied in many ways can be united in a scheme, in a meter. It is not poetry alone that moves on "metrical feet" in an anapestic, iambic, or trochaic meter. In marching or in dancing, we perform a great variety of set patterns. "Performing" means that we follow a given form, that we are able to conduct ourselves in accordance with a scheme set beforehand, that we can use our limbs like instruments. Everyone who drives a car uses his legs and feet as tools. No one, however, outdoes the organist, who plays one pedal with his feet. Such an instrumental use of the limbs, obviously not limited to the arms and hands, demands a centralization of functions, demands a dominating hemisphere. For symmetrical alternating movements, bilateral, segmental, and suprasegmental structures may suffice. Instrumental use depends on an interruption of symmetry followed by higher integration.

A breakdown of this integration should result in kinetic apraxia of trunk and legs. There are indeed some cases recorded (Nielsen, 1946) that confirm this expectation. Their number is small. It probably would be greater if, as Sittig pointed out, more attention were given to this symptom. Even then, it might escape observation for two reasons: first, paresis may cover the apraxia of the legs; and, second, gait and other symmetrical motions may still be found intact when actions based on less symmetrical motions, such as jumping and dancing, have already failed (Kleist, 1934).

Upright Posture and the Development of the Human Hand and Arm

The Hand as a Sensory Organ and as a Tool

In upright posture, the frontal extremities are no longer asked to support and carry the body. Relieved from former duties, they are free for new tasks. The anterior limb develops into the human arm and hand and acquires multifarious new functions. For this development, upright posture is not only the genetic condition but also continues to dominate the functions of hand and arm.

Opposition of the thumb has been frequently mentioned as the most essential innovation. This statement is not completely true or completely correct. It is not correct because the hands of other than human primates are not entirely lacking in opposition of the thumb.[8] It is not completely true because one detail is singled out. With the same justification, or lack of it, the index finger has been honored as the specifically human acquisition. Those who say this think, of course, of its function of pointing. The index finger, however, could not point if the hand were not joined to the arm and if the hand and arm were not related to upright posture.

In upright posture, the hand becomes an organ of active gnostic touching—the epicritic, discriminative instrument par excellence. As such, the hand now ranks with the eye and the ear. Anatomy that describes the eye and the ear as sensory organs does not grant the same privileged status to the hand. Anatomy dissects. It divides the hand into different layers and, "in a systematic order," describes the skin as a part of the integument and places the bones in the osteological, the muscles in the myological, and the vessels in the cardiovascular system. Not to call the

---

[8] The proportions of their hands, however, especially the length of the metacarpus, prevent the formation of the finger-thumb forceps with its characteristic effect (Revesz, 1944).

hand an organ seems strange in view of the fact that "organ" originally meant "tool." For Aristotle (432a 12-4), the hand was "the tool of tools." Anatomy has good reasons for its procedure; they are not, however, simply of a pragmatic order. The hand is a tool in relation to the living, experiencing being—to the man who stretches out his hand, touches, and grasps. The anatomical description that attributes the tissues of the hand to different systems is an analysis of the dead body. The wholes that function as frames of reference differ widely.

The hand as an object of anatomy and the hand experienced as a part of my body are not exactly the same object. The moment the anatomist takes up his scalpel, he behaves, in regard to his own hand, like anyone who has no knowledge of anatomy. This change of attitude is not simply a relapse into näive, primitive, prescientific behavior, unavoidable as a kind of abbreviating procedure. The anatomist, like everyone else, does not innervate the opponens, the interossei, the flexores digitorum. He does not use *the* hand but *his* hand. The possessive relation expressed by the words "my," "yours," "his," familiar and simple as it appears, contains, in fact, one of the most difficult problems for our understanding. It indicates the transition from physiology to psychology.[9]

Anatomy and physiology relate the body as a whole and its parts to neutral space—as the frame of reference. In experience, however, I experience my hand as an organ in relation to the world. The space that surrounds me is not a piece of neutral extended manifold determined by a Cartesian system of coordinates. Experienced space is action space; it is my space of action. To it, I am related through my body, my limbs, my hands. The experience of the body as mine is the origin of possessive experience. All other connotations of possessive relations are derived from it. "Mine" is a distinction that has its place only in the experienced relation of myself and the world. Severed from this basic concept of experience psychology will lose its specific theme and content.

Discussion is necessarily discursive. Analysis cannot avoid dividing into parts that which exists as a whole. When the dissection is completed, synthesis sometimes will be found difficult. It depends on the preceding methods of dividing. They may be so radical as to prevent the restitution of the whole. Adding part to part does not give a full reintegration of the whole. The parts have to be understood from the begin-

---

[9] Sherrington (1947) emphasizes this gap between physiological and psychological approach and method. Although he does not directly mention the probblems posed by the possessive relation, he obviously is fully aware of them.

ning as parts of that specific whole to which they belong. With attention focused on details, the human arm and hand appear as just one other variation in the development of the forelegs. For every part, one can find a homologue in other species. However, "homologue" means difference as well as similarity. If one gives due respect to both and considers the arm in its entirety within the entire framework of upright posture, one can hardly deny that, through the peculiar structure and function of arm and hand, a new relation between the human organism and the world has been established.

Only in relation to action space, then, will the hand be understood as a sensory organ. It is true that the microscope does not reveal any tactile receivers specific to the skin of the hands. Meissner's corpuscles and Pacinian bodies are most numerous, but they are also found elsewhere. Their number alone would not justify our speaking of the hand as a sensory organ. There is a better reason for doing so than the mere frequency of corpuscles. It is their distribution over the multiplex, mobile structure of the fingers, which, in their diversity, form a motorsensoric unit. It is not the individual finger that, in feeling, recognizes but all the fingers together, combined in a group. It is not the resting finger that feels but the actively moved digits. Tactile impressions result from motion; nevertheless, we do not experience our motion so much as the quality of the things touched (Katz, 1925). We feel the smoothness of a surface by letting our fingers glide over it.

While motion is indispensable for tactile impressions, the impression-guided fingers function as working tools. This intimate interpenetration of sensorium and motorium is well expressed in such words as "handling," "fingering," "thumbing," "groping," each of which combines the transitive and intransitive meanings of touching into one. The hand has, it seems, an insight of its own. In an ataxia of the legs, seeing may partially compensate for the sensory deficiencies. However, in a posterior root deficit of the hands, seeing is of little help; neither is it an aid in finger agnosia and right-left disturbances.

The epicritic-discriminative functioning of the hands depends on still another condition. There is an inner distance necessary—a remoteness experienced in spite of the proximity of contact. A physician, in examining (palpating) a body, is expected to remain a neutral observer. He should be neither attracted nor disgusted by what he observes. His goal is not closeness nor unification. His action resembles that of a wine-taster who takes a sip but spits it out again, avoiding swallowing and incorporation. The gnostic function of touching depends on the upright posture, which through its permanent distances produces a hiatus in the immediateness of contact.

"Experienced distance" (Minkowski, 1930) cannot be expressed in geometrical terms. It cannot be defined as the length of a straight line connecting two points in space. The geometrical consideration of distance is completely indifferent to time. The concept of a vector adding direction, and thereby time, to distance would be more adequate. Still, it lacks any conative character. Geometrical distance relates two points in space, both detached from the observer. Experienced distance is that which unfolds between an experiencing being and another person or object. It can be experienced only by a being who aims at unification or separation. The modes of unification and separation vary. The spatial relation is only one among others. While experienced distance cannot, therefore, be expressed completely in spatial terms, it never lacks a spatial element. The space to which it is related, however, is not the conceptual homogeneous space of mathematics but perceptual space, articulated in accordance with the specific corporeal organization of the experiencing person.

The role of distance is not limited to the hand as a sensory organ. It also dominates manual expression, communication, and contact. Distance is ambivalent. Sometimes we want to preserve it; sometimes we want to eliminate it. The hand is instrumental in both cases. When our equilibrium is out of balance or disturbed, the hand grasps for a hold. In darkness, it functions as scout and sentry, warning against collision and searching for contact. Sometimes no hold is found, no contact is made. Searching hands stretch into the void. It is as if emptiness were localized in our hands. Indeed, only the empty hand, like the beggar's hand, can receive. Emptiness is the condition by which our hands can be filled. Only because of remoteness can it make contact.

We understand that the phobic patient feels somewhat more comfortable by carrying something in his hand, maybe no more than a cane, an umbrella, or a bag. Does not each of us, if he alone is exposed to a group—e.g., as a speaker or an actor—like to put his hands on a chair or a desk or to fiddle with a pencil or notes? Finally, we may even surprise ourselves with gesticulations which help less to clarify our thoughts than to fill emptiness and cover distance. In such situations, we are only one step ahead of the embarrassed child who pulls his fingers, as if in doing this he could fill his empty hands.

All the variations of the expression of emptiness are related to upright posture. They are, it seems, a universal language. When Darwin prepared his book on expression (1910), he sent questionnaires to missionaries abroad in order to find out the distribution of gestures familiar to us in the western world. He was interested, among other things, in the gesture of shrugging the shoulders, an expression of the incapacity to advise or to help. Here, one again meets the empty hands. With the lifting of the shoulders, we also supinate our arms and demonstrate the empty hands. Shrugging the shoulders is an expression of fruitless endeavor. Darwin learned through his questionnaires that this expression is indigenous everywhere, not imported from other civilizations, not formed by more or less local conventions and customs. Its universality proves it to be autochthonous with the human race. It is a universal and spontaneous gesture of man, wherever and whenever he, with upright posture, experiences a distance from things and fellow-men.

Expansion of the Body Scheme by the Arms

In upright posture, the arms expand the body scheme. The arm motion circumscribes a sphere which surrounds the body as territorial waters surround the shores of a country. This constitutes a section of space that, like the three-mile zone, belongs to the central body and yet not completely. It is not an indisputable property but a variable possession. My intervening space is a medium between me and the world. As such, it has the greatest social significance; it mediates between the other and me. In this space, which is not completely my own, I can meet the other as the other, join him as my partner, arm in arm or hand in hand, and yet leave him in his integrity. Through this space, I hold the other at arm's length or let him come toward me and receive him with open arms. It is the space of the linking of arms or of embracing[10] but also of crossing the arms, a motion in which we keep distance, "circumwalling" ourselves in an attitude of defense or of fortification. It is also the space of handshaking. There are many nuances of handshaking, such as warm and strong or cool and hesitant. There can be spon-

[10] The etymological root of "embrace" is *brac*, as in *brachium*, the Latin word for arm.

taneous advance or a no less spontaneous containment—as by the hand of the schizophrenic. In a farewell, the hands hold each other, press each other, move on together; they will not part. In a handshake that seals a bargain, the hands meet each other halfway in a mutually firm grasp in which the motion is arrested, expressing final agreement. Even the formalized gesture signifies social acceptance. We pass through a reception line, and the hands stretched out toward us tell us that we are welcome and received into the group.

The "three-mile zone" is not static. It is a border with fluctuating frontiers. It expands or shrinks. The body scheme is not so much a concept or image that a person has of his own body as it is an ensemble of directions and demarcations—directions in which we reach out toward the world and demarcations that we encounter in contact with the world (Schilder, 1935). The body scheme is also experienced, therefore, as an I-world relation. Corresponding to our conation, space itself loses its static character, opens endlessly before us, and expands or represses us. The "de-pressed," with his head bent, his shoulders lowered, his arms fallen to his sides, and with his slow, short steps succumbs to the pressure that pushes him down. The Christian attitude of kneeling in prayer, of bending the head, and of interlacing the hands expresses humility, surrender to a higher power. The hands, withdrawn from the territorial space and joined at the midline in full symmetry—taking no sides—have renounced all action. The Moslem, in his pious prostration, goes to the extreme of fatalistic submission. The ancient Greek attitude of praying—upright, arms lifted and extended—opened and widened the body space in an enthusiastic gesture—"en-thus-iastic," indeed, because *entheos-iastic* means "to receive the God" or "to be possessed by him."

> Ah, but a man's reach should exceed his grasp,
> Or what's a heaven for?—Robert Browning

In pointing, also, man's reach exceeds his grasp. Upright posture enables us to see things in their distance without any intention of incorporating them. In the totality of this panorama that unfolds in front of us, the pointing finger singles out one detail. The arm constitutes intervening space as a medium which separates and connects. The pointing arm, hand, and finger share with the intervening space the dynamic functions of separating and connecting. The pointing hand directs the sight of another one to whom I show something, for pointing is a social gesture. I do not point for myself; I indicate something to someone else. To distant things, within the visible horizon, we are related by common experience. As observers, we are directed, although through different perspectives, to one and the same thing, to one and the same world. Distance creates new forms of communication.

The organization of action space is deeply imprinted on the memory. Even after the loss of a limb, it persists in the "phantom." As long as there is a phantom, there is also intervening space through which the illusive arm stretches to a distant world, with the illusive hand in a terminal position. It is a common experience that the phantom arm shrinks, that the phantom hand moves closer to the trunk, but it never disappears completely; it is preserved in its terminal position. The loss of the limb reduces the reach. It modifies the intervening space but does not annihilate it altogether.

The human arm owes its specific mobility to upright posture. Many factors contribute to its development and functions, but through all of them upright posture is at work. First to be mentioned is the change in proportions of the sagittal and transverse diameter of the chest. In quadrupeds, the sagittal diameter is relatively long, the curvature of the ribs flattened, the motions of the humerus in the shoulder joint restricted, and the flexibility of the elongated scapula limited. The humerus is kept in close contact with the trunk. The basic function of supporting the trunk prevails, and this imprints one definite general mark on the structure of the shoulder girdle, in spite of all the variations to be found in different species. With upright posture, the transverse diameter is increased. This change, together with the corresponding sharp, angular curvature of the ribs, gives to the human thorax its characteristic shape, which in turn permits the development of the shoulder girdle into a kind of superstructure. This superstructure, which tailors like to emphasize, moves the root of the arm upward very high and markedly to the side. Far from supporting the human body, the arm and the shoulder are themselves supported or, better, held in position by muscle action, especially by that of the trapezius. The arm, separated from the trunk in its full length, can swing from its elevated hub with the widest angle of excursions in the greatest variety of motions.

The arm, not designed for one specific task, has acquired the potentiality for a wide range of performance. The principle of growing indetermination, one of Hughlings Jackson's criteria of functional evolution (1932), is applicable to the comparative anatomy of the shoulder girdle.[11] One should not forget that the human arm neither supports the trunk nor has to hold up the body, a function still assigned to the forelimb of tree-inhabiting primates. Small but still significant changes ensue in the shape and position of scapula and clavicle, in the origin and insertion of the shoulder muscles, and in the configuration of the acromio-clavicular and the sterno-clavicular joints. All this together provides for maximum flexibility of the arm, aiding the display of the mechanisms of the scapulo-humeral articulation, where, because of the looseness of the capsule and the shallowness of the glenoid cavity, the humerus can move with great ease in all directions. In the hip joints, on the contrary, the head of the femur is deeply set in the socket of the acetabular cavity and the capsule is tight and reinforced by strong ligaments. While the primarily tectonic formation of the neck of the femur also somewhat extends the range of excursions, the emphasis in the hip is on stability, in the shoulder, on flexibility.

Language, obviously inspired by phenomenological observation, takes the arm as the prototype of the articulation of a limb and of its motions from the joint, for the root of the word "arm" is $\sqrt{ar}$ with the meaning "to fit, to join," the same root from which the Greek *ar-thros* and the evenly Latin *ar-ticulatio* stem.[12]

Within the totality of the new spatial dimensions acquired with upright posture, lateral space is perhaps most important. Through the mobility and action of arm and hand, lateral space becomes accessible

[11] The highest centers of the brain are, according to Jackson, the least organized, the most complex, and the most voluntary. Evolution is a passage from the most to the least organized, from the simple to the most complex, from the most automatic to the most voluntary (Jackson, 1932, pp. 46 ff.). The highest centers were not, or were little, accessible to direct experimentation in Jackson's time. Their functions were found by inference, reasoning backward from the observation of peripheral performances. The diverse functions of finger, hand, arm, and shoulder would tell something about the organization of the corresponding highest centers. Complexity of the brain centers must have and does have its exact counterpart in the organization of the limbs.

[12] In this paper, the writer has made frequent use of etymology, although it is not customary to introduce "linguistic evidence" in a biological discussion. However, because the history of a word represents the sedimentation of general psychological experience, it appears to the writer to be justified to refer to etymology as an auxiliary discipline.

and relevant for man. In this sector, most of the human crafts originated. Hammer and ax, scythe and sickle, the carpenter's saw, the weaver's shuttle, the potter's wheel, the mason's trowel, and the painter's brush all relate to lateral space. This list could be extended *ad libitum* but probably would never come to an end, for lateral space is the matrix of primitive and sophisticated skills: of spinning and sewing, stirring and ironing, sowing and husking, soldering and welding, fiddling and golfing, batting and discus-throwing.

The crafts of peace are followed, accompanied, or preceded by the techniques and weapons of war: club, sword, spear, bow, sling, and boomerang, to mention some elemental forms only. Lateral space makes action at a distance possible, as David successfully proved to Goliath.[13] Superiority has not always belonged to the light forces. Even so, the importance of action at a distance, for which throwing is the primordial and perennial model, remains undiminished and, with it, the importance of lateral space.

The development of primitive and elaborate weapons makes one wonder whether "arm" (the limb) and "arms" (the weapons) may have the same etymological root. To this question, the linguists answer both "yes" and "no." Their answer is "no" because arms, arming, and armament are historically related to the Latin root *arma*. The Romans' word for "arm" (the limb) is *brachium*, with another derivation and meaning. However, the root for *arma*, "weapon," is also $\sqrt{ar}$.

---

[13] In this Biblical legend, a situation permanently repeating itself is told as a unique event. The Bible takes great pains to describe Goliath's heavy armor (Sam I: 17). It also tells that Saul offered David his own sword, a "helmet of brass," and a "coat of mail." However, David, not trained in the use of these weapons, laid them down. We may not go far wrong if we assume that the Bible, in a poetical condensation, describes as a duel what is really a conflict of two civilizations and of two types of military tactics. Goliath, the Philistine, belonged to a settled, seafaring nation, advanced in the techniques of metal forgery; David, described as a shepherd, belonged to a small nomadic tribe that invaded the Philistine territory from the interior. The conflict of the two coexistent types of military tactics is this: Goliath, heavily armed—the Philistine "Maginot Line"—almost immobilized by the weight of his armor—someone has to carry his shield for him—can move only directly forward to a close fight, while David, a kind of guerilla fighter, finds his advantage in mobility, in dodging, and in sudden attacks. This conflict between fortified defense and mobile attack is found in all military history up to our own time.

In considering the phenomenon of throwing, one cannot pass over the remarkable difference in the manner of throwing of the two sexes. It seems the manifestation of a biological, not an acquired, difference. Gesell (Gesell *et al.*, 1940, pp. 85-89) illustrates the familiar facts with some good photographs. They show little girls of five and six and two boys of the same age throwing a ball. The girl of five does not make any use of lateral space. She does not stretch her arm sideward; she does not twist her trunk; she does not move her legs, which remain side by side. All she does in preparation for throwing is to lift her right arm forward to the horizontal and to bend the forearm backward in a pronate position. In the final motion, action is limited to the triceps and flexors of the hand. The excursion of her motion in the elbow joint does not exceed an angle of about 90°. The length of the lever from the fulcrum at the elbow to the palm of the hand coincides with the length of the forearm. The ball is released without force, speed, or accurate aim. It enters almost immediately the descending branch of a steep parabola. At the age of six, the girl tilts her right shoulder slightly and moves the left foot forward one small step, but shows no further progress. A boy of the same age, when preparing to throw, stretches his right arm sideward and backward; supinates the forearm;[14] twists, turns, and bends his trunk; and moves his right foot backward. From this stance, he can support his throwing almost with the full strength of his total motorium. The excursion of his final motion reaches an angle of 180°. It moves around the left standing leg as its central axis. The radius of this semicircle exceeds by far the full length of the arm. The ball leaves the hand with considerable acceleration; it moves toward its goal in a long flat curve.

As this difference appears in early childhood, it cannot result from the development of the female breast. While the legendary Amazons had the right breast removed to allow the use of bow and spear,[15] it seems certain that Nausicaa and all her companions threw a ball just like our Betty's, Mary's, and Susan's. How can we explain the difference? The little girl has no more difficulty in keeping her equilibrium than the boy. It is true that she is weaker in muscle power, but, therefore, one should expect her to compensate for this lack of strength with added preparatory excursion. Instead, we find her avoiding the

[14] Supination reaches its fullest and freest excursion with the horizontal abduction of the arm.

[15] Amazon means *a-mazos*, without breast.

turn into lateral space. Maybe the masculine way of throwing corresponds to masculine "eccentricity," while the feminine attitude reveals a deep-seated restraint and an inclination to circle around one's own center. The difference, then, would belong to the area of expression; it would not be a difference of strength and build but of a general psychological attitude in relation to the world and to space.

Thus far, lateral space has been discussed as if it were a unit, a single whole. Indeed, in many motions, we lift our arms symmetrically in surrounding space. However, even simultaneous movements need not be actually symmetrical. They appear symmetrical; they are not so in their intention. The arms can be stretched and the hands can point in opposite directions, to the right and to the left, at the same time. It is this contrast of directions that divides, articulates, and organizes lateral space, producing heteronymous, unequal parts. These can be reunited into an ordered whole where one half dominates the other. Spatial syntax cannot deviate from the general principle of taxis, which always demands a leading part to which the others are subordinated. The pair, right-left, is the true emodiment of unity, unfolding itself into opposites or, if we begin with the opposites, the unity of a contrasting manifold. Both aspects belong together. Practical discrimination between and coordination of right and left precede their conceptual distinction. The amazing cases of autotopagnosia demonstrate to what extent the organization of the body scheme, as a manifold of directions, dominates recognition. In the Gerstmann syndrome, we find (1) finger agnosia, (2) agraphia, and (3) acalculia, besides a right-left disturbance. Searching for a common denominator, we may find it in the loss of the capacity to organize opposite directions into one or to break the unit into opposite directions:

1. The fingers of the hand repeat, so to speak, the right-left scheme for one side. Thumb and little finger point in opposite directions. This maximum of divergency (the direct opposition) sets the pattern for the intermediary positions.

2. Writing, the spatial construction of letters, presupposes the same capacity to differentiate a scheme of varying directions and to establish them simultaneously in advance. The shape of the printed letters *b* and *d* illustrates this well.

3. Numbers follow the same principle. Two, the model of all numbers, is a unit of one plus one, which, while they become united, remain separate: one and one, or two. The figure "one" is unity, the "two," a

unit. It should therefore not be surprising that a child learns cardinal numbers a considerable time after mastering the ordinals. While he knows the series of numerals and enumerates the fingers of one hand, he is not able to sum them up into one unit of five. When he has reached the age when he can conceive of cardinal numbers, he is usually able to distinguish right and left.*

Upright Posture and the Formation of the Human Head

Upright posture has lifted eye and ear from the ground. In the family of senses, smell has lost the right of the first-born. Seeing and hearing have assumed dominion. Now, these really function as senses of distance. In every species, eye and ear respond to stimuli from remote objects, but the interest of animals is limited to the proximate. Their attention is caught by that which is within the confines of reaching or approaching. The relation of sight and bite distinguishes the human face from those of lower animals. Animal jaws, snoot, trunk, and beak—all of them organs acting in the direct contact of grasping and gripping—are placed in the "visor line" of the eyes. With upright posture, with the development of the arm, the mouth is no longer needed for catching and carrying or for attacking and defending. It sinks down from the "visor line" of the eyes, which now can be turned directly in a piercing, open look toward distant things and rest fully upon them, viewing them with the detached interest of wondering. Bite has become subordinated to sight.

Language expresses this relation in signifying the whole, the face, through its dominating part—the eyes, as in the English and French word "visage," in the German *Gesicht*, and in the Greek *prosopon*. While the origin of the Latin word *facies*—and therefore, also, of the English noun "face"—is uncertain, the verb "to face" reassumes, in a remarkable twist, the original phenomenological meaning: to look at things straight ahead and to withstand their thrust. Eyes that lead jaws and fangs to the prey are always charmed and spellbound by nearness. To eyes looking straight forward—to the gaze of upright posture—

---

* The section entitled "Neurophysiological Considerations" has been deleted. (Ed.)

things reveal themselves in their own nature. Sight penetrates depth; sight becomes insight.

Animals move in the direction of their digestive axis. Their bodies are expanded between mouth and anus as between an entrance and an exit, a beginning and an ending. The spatial orientation of the human body is different throughout. The mouth is still an inlet but no longer a beginning, the anus, an outlet but no longer the tail end. Man in upright posture, his feet on the ground and his head uplifted, does not move in the line of his digestive axis; he moves in the direction of his vision. He is surrounded by a world panorama, by a space divided into world regions joined together in the totality of the universe. Around him, the horizons retreat in an ever growing radius. Galaxy and diluvium, the infinite and the eternal, enter into the orbit of human interests.

The transformation of the animal jaws into the human mouth is an extensive remodeling: mandible, maxilla, and teeth are not the only parts recast. The mark of the jaws is brute force. The muscles that close the jaws, especially the masseter, are built for simple, powerful motions. Huge ridges and crests, which provide the chewing muscles with an origin appropriate to the development of power, encompass the skull of the gorilla. They disappear when the jaws are transformed into the mouth. The removal of these pinnacles permits the increase of the brain case while, at the same time, the reduction of the mighty chewing muscles permits the development of the subtle mimic and phonetic muscles.

The transformation of jaws into the mouth is a prerequisite for the development of language but only one of them. There are many other factors involved. In upright posture, the ear is no longer limited to the perception of noises—rustling, crackling, hissing, bellowing, roaring—as indicators of actual events, like warnings, threats, or lures. The external ear loses its mobility. While the ear muscles are preserved, their function of adapting the ear to actuality ceases. Detached from actuality, the ear can comprehend sounds in the sounds' own shape—in their musical or phonetic pattern. This capacity to separate the acoustical Gestalt from the acoustical material makes it possible to produce purposefully and to "re-produce" intentionally sounds articulated according to a preconceived scheme.

Just as the speaker produces his words—articulated sounds which function as symbols or carriers of meanings—these should be received and understood by the listener in exactly the same way. The articulated sound, the phoneme, has an obligatory shape. The phoneme itself is a universal. The relation which connects speech and speaker can be held in abeyance so that speech as such can be abstracted, written down, preserved, and repeated. Speech, while connecting speaker and listener, keeps them at the same time at a distance. The most intimate conversation is bound to common, strict rules of phonetics, grammar, and intended meanings. A spontaneous cry can never be wrong. The pronunciation of a word or the production of the phoneme is either right or wrong. The virtuosity acquired by the average person in expressing himself personally and individually in the general medium of language hides the true character of linguistic communication. It is rediscovered by reflection when disturbances of any kind interfere with the easy and prompt use of language or when the immediateness of contact does not tolerate linguistic distance, and the word dies in an angry cry, in tender babble, or in gloomy silence.

In conversation, we talk with one another about something. Conversation, therefore, demands distance in three directions: from the acoustical signs, so that the phoneme can be perceived in its pure form; from things, so that they can be the object of common discourse; from the other person, so that speech can mediate between the speaker and listener. Upright posture produces such distances. It lifts us from the ground, puts us opposite to things, and confronts us with one another.

The sensory organs cannot change without a corresponding change in the central nervous system. No part could be altered alone. With upright posture, there is a transformation of sensorium and motorium, of periphery and center, of form and function. While upright posture permits the formation of the human skull and, thereby, of the human brain, the maintenance of upright posture demands the development of the human nervous system. Who can say what comes first and what comes last—what is cause and what is effect? All these alterations are related to upright posture as their basic theme. "In man, everything converges into the form which he has now. In his history, everything is understandable through it, nothing without it" (Herder, 1784, p. 129).

The phenomenon of upright posture should not be neglected in favor of the lying man, or the man on the couch. To do this is to ignore facts that are obvious and undebatable, accessible without labyrinthine detours of interpretation, facts which exact consideration and permit proof and demonstration. It is true that sleep and rest, lying down and lying with someone, are essential functions; it is no less true that man is built for upright posture and gait and that upright posture, which is as original as any drive, determines his mode of being-in-the-world.

"The upright gait of man is the only natural one to him, nay, it is the organization for every performance of his species and his distinguishing character" (Herder, 1784, p. 128). Human physique reveals human nature.

References

Aristotle. *De anima*.

Asch, S., & H. Witkin. Studies in space perception. *J. exper. Psychol., 1948, 38*, 325-337, 435-477.

Browning, R. Andrea del Sarto.

Darwin, C. *The expression of the emotions* (1872). New York: Appleton, 1910.

Foerster, O. Die motorischen Bahnen und Felder. In O. Bumke & O. Foerster, *Handbuch der Neurologie*. Vol. VI. Berlin: Springer-Verlag, 1936.

Gesell, A. *et al. The first five years of life*. New York & London: Harper, 1940.

Gibson, E., & Mowrer, O. Determinants of the perceived vertical and horizontal. *Psychol. Rev.*, 1938, 45.

Goldstein, K. *Über Zeigen und Greifen*. Vol. 4. Berlin: Der Nervenarzt, 1931.

Gregory, W. K. *The humerus from fish to man*. American Museum Novitates, January 31, 1949.

Herder, G. W. *Ideen zur Philosophie der Geschichte der Menschheit*. Riga: 1784.

Jackson, H. *Selected writings*. . . . Vol. 2. London: J. Taylor, 1932.

Katz, D. *Der Aufbau der Tastwelt*. Leipzig: Engelman, 1925.

Kleist, K. *Gehirnpathologie*, Leipzig: 1934.

Minkowski, E. Les notions de distance vécue. *J. de Psychol.*, 1930, 27, 727-745.

Moskati, *Vom Koerperlichen Wesentlichen Unterschiede der Thiere und Menschen*. Goettingen: 1771.

Nielsen, N. J. *Agnosia, apraxia, aphasia*. (2nd ed.) New York & London: Hoeber, 1946.

Portmann, A. *Biologische Fragmente zu einer Lebre vom Menschen*. Basel: 1944.

Ramon y Cajal, S. *Histologie du système nerveux de l'homme et des vertébrés*. 1909.

Revesz, G. *Die menschliche Hand*. New York & Basel: Karger, 1944.

Schilder, P. The image and appearance of the human body. *Psychol. Monogr.*, 1935, No. 4.

Sherrington, Ch. *The integrative action of the nervous system*. (9th ed.) Cambridge: Cambridge Univ. Press, 1947.

Sittig, O. *Über Apraxie*. Berlin: S. Karger, 1931.

von Uexkuell, J. *Theoretical biology*. New York: Harcourt, Brace, 1926.

Weidenreich, F. *Apes, giants and man*. Chicago: Univ. of Chicago Press, 1946.

B. Sociality

JEAN-PAUL SARTRE (1905-

Born in France in 1905, Jean-Paul Sartre has become known as a primary figure associated with the existentialist movement. Although Sartre briefly held a position as a teacher of philosophy at the Lycée Condorcet, he has distinguished himself primarily as a writer and lecturer. Sartre studied phenomenology in Berlin, and his philosophical works include: *The Imagination* (1936), *Sketch for a Theory of the Emotions* (1948), and *Being and Nothingness* (1943).

CONCRETE RELATIONS WITH OTHERS*

The fundamental relation with the Other has enabled us to make explicit our body's three dimensions of being. And since the original bond with the Other first arises in connection with the relation between my body and the Other's body, it seemed clear to us that the knowledge of the nature of the body was indispensable to any study of the particular relations of my being with that of the Other. These particular relations, in fact, on both sides presuppose facticity; that is, our existence as body in the midst of the world. Not that the body is the instrument and the cause of my relations with others. But the body constitutes their meaning and marks their limits. It is as body-in-situation that I apprehend the Other's transcendence-transcended, and it is as body-in-situation that I experience myself in my alienation for the Other's benefit. Now we can examine these concrete relations since we are cognizant of what the body is. They are not simple specifications of the fundamental relation. Although each one of them includes within it the original relation with the Other as its essential structure and its foundation, they are entirely new modes of being on the part of the for-itself. In fact they represent

* By permission of Philosophical Library, Inc. From *Being and Nothingness* by Jean-Paul Sarte, Copyright © 1956, by Philosophical Library, Inc., New York. Inc., New York.

Also by permission of Methuen & Company, Ltd., London, England.

the various attitudes of the for-itself in a world where there are Others. Therefore each relation in its own way presents the bilateral relation: for-itself-for-others, in-itself. If then we succeed in making explicit the structures of our most primitive relations with the Other-in-the-world, we shall have completed our task. "What are the relations of the for-itself with the in-itself?" We have learned now that our task is more complex. There is a relation of the for-itself with the in-itself *in the presence of the Other*. When we have described this concrete fact, we shall be in a position to form conclusions concerning the fundamental relations of the three modes of being, and we shall perhaps be able to attempt a metaphysical theory of being in general.

The for-itself as the nihilation of the in-itself temporalizes itself as a *flight toward*. Actually it surpasses its facticity (i.e., to be either *given* or past or body) toward the in-itself which it would be if it were able to be its own foundation. This may be translated into terms already psychological—and hence inaccurate although perhaps clearer—by saying that the for-itself attempts to escape its factual existence (i.e., its being there, as an in-itself for which it is in no way the foundation) and that this flight takes place toward an impossible future always pursued where the for-itself would be an in-itself-for-itself—i.e., an in-itself which would be to itself its own foundation. Thus the for-itself is both a flight and a pursuit; it flees the in-itself and at the same time pursues it. The for-itself is a pursued-pursuing. But in order to lessen the danger of a psychological interpretation of the preceding remarks, let us note that the for-itself is not *first* in order to attempt *later* to attain being; in short we must not conceive of it as an existent which would be provided with tendencies as this glass is provided with certain particular qualities. This pursuing flight is not given which is added on to the being of the for-itself. The for-itself *is* this very flight. The flight is not to be distinguished from the original nihilation. To say that the for-itself is a pursued-pursuing, or that it is in the mode of having to be its being, or that it is not what it is and is what it is not—each of these statements is saying the same thing. The for-itself is not the in-itself and can not be it. But it is a relation to the in-itself. It is even the sole relation possible to the in-itself. Cut off on every side by the in-itself, the for-itself can not escape it because the for-itself is *nothing* and it is separated from the in-itself by *nothing*. The for-itself is the foundation of all negativity and of all relation. *The for-itself is relation*.

Such being the case, the upsurge of the Other touches the for-itself in its very heart. By the Other and for the Other the pursuing flight is fixed in in-itself. Already the in-itself was progressively recapturing it; already it was at once a radical negation of fact, an absolute positing of value and yet wholly paralyzed with facticity. But at least it was escaping by temporalization; at least its character as a totality detotalized conferred on it a perpetual "elsewhere." Now it is this very totality which the Other makes appear before him and which he transcends toward his own "elsewhere." It is this totality which is totalized. For the Other I am irremediably what I am, and my very freedom is a given characteristic of my being. Thus the in-self recaptures me at the threshold of the future and fixes me wholly in my very flight, which becomes a flight foreseen and contemplated, a *given* flight. But this fixed flight is never the flight which I am for myself; it is fixed *outside*. The objectivity of my flight I experience as an alienation which I can neither transcend nor know. Yet by the sole fact that I experience it and that it confers on my flight that in-itself which it flees, I must turn back toward it and assume *attitudes* with respect to it.

Such is the origin of my concrete relations with the Other; they are wholly governed by my attitudes with respect to the object which I am for the Other. And as the Other's existence reveals to me the being which I am without my being able either to appropriate that being or even to conceive it, this existence will motivate two opposed attitudes: First—The Other *looks* at me and as such he holds the secret of my being, he knows what I *am*. Thus the profound meaning of my being is outside of me, imprisoned in an absence. The Other has the advantage over me. Therefore in so far as I am fleeing the in-itself which I am without founding it, I can attempt to deny that being which is conferred on me from outside; that is, I can turn back upon the Other so as to make an object out of him in turn since the Other's object-ness destroys my object-ness for him. But on the other hand, in so far as the Other as freedom is the foundation of my being-in-itself, I can seek to recover that freedom and to possess it without removing from it its character as freedom. In fact if I could identify myself with that freedom which is the foundation of my being-in-itself, I should be to myself my own foundation. To transcend the Other's transcendence, or, on the contrary, to incorporate that transcendence within me without removing from it its character as transcendence—such are the two primitive attitudes which I assume confronting the Other. Here again we must understand the words exactly. It is not true that I first am and then later "seek" to make an object of the Other or to assimilate him; but to the extent that the upsurge of my being is an upsurge in the presence of the Other, to the extent that I am a pursuing flight and a pursued-pursuing, I am—at the very root of my being—the project of assimilating and making an object of the Other. I am the proof of the Other. That is the original fact. But this proof of the Other is in itself an attitude toward the Other; that is, I can not *be in the presence of the Other* without being that "in-the-presence" in the form of having to be it. Thus again we are describing the for-itself's structures of being although the Other's presence in the world is an absolute and self-evident fact, but a contingent fact—that is, a fact impossible to deduce from the ontological structures of the for-itself.

These two attempts which I am are opposed to one another. Each attempt is the death of the other; that is, the failure of the one motivates the adoption of the other. Thus there is no dialectic for my relations toward the Other but rather a circle—although each attempt is enriched by the failure of the other. Thus we shall study each one in turn. But it should be noted that at the very core of the one the other remains always present, precisely because neither of the two can be held without contradiction. Better yet, each of them is in the other and endangers the death of the other. Thus we can never get outside the circle. We must not forget these facts as we approach the study of these fundamental attitudes toward the Other. Since these attitudes are produced and destroyed in a circle, it is as arbitrary to begin with the one as with the other. Nevertheless since it is necessary to choose, we shall consider first the conduct in which the for-itself tries to assimilate the Other's freedom.

I. FIRST ATTITUDE TOWARD OTHERS:

LOVE, LANGUAGE, MASOCHISM

Everything which may be said of me in my relations with the Other applies to him as well. While I attempt to free myself from the hold of the Other, the Other is trying to free himself from mine; while I seek to enslave the Other, the Other seeks to enslave me. We are by no means dealing with unilateral relations with an object-in-itself, but with reciprocal and moving relations. The following descriptions of concrete behavior must therefore be envisaged within the perspective of *conflict*. Conflict is the original meaning of being-for-others.

If we start with the first revelation of the Other as a *look*, we must recognize that we experience our inapprehensible being-for-others in the form of a *possession*. I am possessed by the Other; the Other's look fashions my body in its nakedness, causes it to be born, sculptures it, produces it as it *is,* sees it as I shall never see it. The Other holds a se-cret—the secret of what I am. He makes me be and thereby he possesses me, and this possession is nothing other than the consciousness of possessing me. I in the recognition of my object-state have proof that he has this consciousness. By virtue of consciousness the Other is for me simultaneously the one who has stolen my being from me and the one who causes "there to be" a being which is my being. Thus I have a com-prehension of this ontological structure: I am responsible for my being-for-others, but I am not the foundation of it. It appears to me therefore in the form of a contingent given for which I am nevertheless responsi-ble; the Other founds my being in so far as this being is in the form of the "there is." But he is not responsible for my being although he founds it in complete freedom—in and by means of his free transcendence. Thus to the extent that I am revealed to myself as responsible for my being, I *lay claim to* this being which I am; that is, I wish to recover it, or, more exactly, I am the project of the recovery of my being. I want to stretch out my hand and grab hold of this being which is presented to me as *my being* but at a distance—like the dinner of Tantalus; I want to found it by my very freedom. For if in one sense my being-as-object is an unbearable contingency and the pure "possession" of myself by another, still in another sense this being stands as the indication of what I should be obliged to recover and found in order to be the foundation of myself. But this is conceivable only if I assimilate the Other's freedom. Thus my project of recovering myself is fundamentally a proj-ect of absorbing the Other.

Nevertheless this project must leave the Other's nature intact. Two consequences result: (1) I do not thereby cease to assert the Other—that is, to deny concerning myself that I am the Other. Since the Other is the foundation of my being, he could not be dissolved in me without my being-for-others disappearing. Therefore if I project the realization of unity with the Other, this means that I project my assimilation of the Other's Otherness as my own possibility. In fact the problem for me is to make myself be by acquiring the possibility of taking the Other's point of view on myself. It is not a matter of acquiring a pure, abstract faculty of knowledge. It is not the pure *category* of the Other which I project appropriating to myself. This category is not conceived nor even conceivable. But on the occasion of concrete experience with the Other, an experience suffered and realized, it is this concrete Other as an absolute reality whom in his otherness I wish to incorporate into myself. (2) The Other whom I wish to assimilate is by no means the Other-as-object. Or, if you prefer, my project of incorporating the Other in no way corresponds to a recapturing of my for-itself as myself and to a sur-passing of the Other's transcendence toward my own possibilities. For me it is not a question of obliterating my object-state by making an ob-ject of the Other, which would amount to *releasing* myself from my being-for-others. Quite the contrary, I want to assimilate the Other as the Other-looking-at-me, and this project of assimilation includes an augmented recognition of my being-looked-at. In short, in order to maintain before me the Other's freedom which is looking at me, I iden-tify myself totally with my being-looked-at. And since my being-as-object is the only possible relation between me and the Other, it is this being-as-object which alone can serve me as an instrument to effect my assimilation of the *other freedom*.

Thus as a reaction to the failure of the third ekstasis, the for-itself wishes to be identified with the Other's freedom as founding its own being-in-itself. To be other to oneself—the ideal always aimed at concretely in the form of being *this Other* to oneself—is the primary value of my rela-tions with the Other. This means that my being-for-others is haunted by the indication of an absolute-being which would be itself as other and other as itself and which by freely giving to itself its being-itself as other and its being-other as itself, would be the very being of the ontological proof—that is, God. This ideal can not be realized without my sur-mounting the original contingency of my relations to the Other; that is, by overcoming the fact that there is no relation of internal negativity between the negation by which the Other is made other than I and the negation by which I am made other than the Other. We have seen that this contingency is insurmountable; it is the *fact* of my relations with the Other, just as my body is the *fact* of my being-in-the-world. Unity with the Other is therefore *in fact* unrealizable. It is also unrealizable *in theory*, for the assimilation of the for-itself and the Other in a single transcendence would necessarily involve the disappearance of the char-acteristic of otherness in the Other. Thus the condition on which I project the identification of myself with the Other is that I persist in de-nying that I am the Other. Finally this project of unification is the source of *conflict* since while I experience myself as an object for the Other and while I project assimilating him in and by means of this ex-perience, the Other apprehends me as an object in the midst of the world and does not project identifying me with himself. It would

therefore be necessary—since being-for-others includes a double internal negation—to act upon the internal negation by which the Other
transcends my transcendence and makes me exist for the Other; that is,
to act upon the Other's freedom.

This unrealizable ideal which haunts my project of myself in the
presence of the Other is not to be identified with love in so far as love is
an enterprise; i.e., an organic ensemble of projects toward my own
possibilities. But it is the ideal of love, its motivation and its end, its u-
nique value. Love as the primitive relation to the Other is the ensemble of
the projects by which I aim at realizing this value.

These projects put me in direct connection with the Other's freedom.
It is in this sense that love is a conflict. We have observed that the
Other's freedom is the foundation of my being. But precisely because I
exist by means of the Other's freedom, I have no security; I am in
danger in this freedom. It moulds my being and *makes me be*, it confers
values upon me and removes them from me; and my being receives
from it a perpetual passive escape from self. Irresponsible and beyond
reach, this protean freedom in which I have engaged myself can in turn
engage me in a thousand different ways of being. My project of recovering my being can be realized only if I get hold of this freedom and
reduce it to being a freedom subject to my freedom. At the same time it
is the only way in which I can act on the free negation of interiority by
which the Other constitutes me as an Other; that is the only way in
which I can prepare the way for a future identification of the Other with
me. This will be clearer perhaps if we study the problem from a purely
psychological aspect. Why does the lover want to be *loved?* If Love
were in fact a pure desire for physical possession, it could in many cases
be easily satisfied. Proust's hero, for example, who installs his mistress
in his home, who can see her and possess her at any hour of the day,
who has been able to make her completely dependent on him eco-
nomically, ought to be free from worry. Yet we know that he is, on
the contrary, continually gnawed by anxiety. Through her consciousness Albertine escapes Marcel even when he is at her side, and that
is why he knows relief only when he gazes on her while she sleeps. It
is certain then that the lover wishes to capture a "consciousness." But
why does he wish it? And how?

The notion of "ownership," by which love is so often explained, is
not actually primary. Why should I want to appropriate the Other if it
were not precisely that the Other makes me be? But this implies precisely a certain mode of appropriation; it is the Other's freedom as such

that we want to get hold of. Not because of a desire for power. The tyrant scorns love, he is content with fear. If he seeks to win the love of his subjects, it is for political reasons; and if he finds a more economical way to enslave them, he adopts it immediately. On the other hand, the man who wants to be loved does not desire the enslavement of the beloved. He is not bent on becoming the object of passion which flows forth mechanically. He does not want to possess an automaton, and if we want to humiliate him, we need only try to persuade him that the beloved's passion is the result of a psychological determinism. The lover will then feel that both his love and his being are cheapened. If Tristan and Isolde fall madly in love because of a love potion, they are less interesting. The total enslavement of the beloved kills the love of the lover. The end is surpassed; if the beloved is transformed into an automaton, the lover finds himself alone. Thus the lover does not desire to possess the beloved as one possesses a thing; he demands a special type of appropriation. He wants to possess a freedom as freedom.

On the other hand, the lover can not be satisfied with that superior form of freedom which is a free and voluntary engagement. Who would be content with a love given as pure loyalty to a sworn oath? Who would be satisfied with the words, "I love you because I have freely engaged myself to love you and because I do not wish to go back on my word." Thus the lover demands a pledge, yet is irritated by a pledge. He wants to be loved by a freedom but demands that this freedom as freedom should no longer be free. He wishes that the Other's freedom should determine itself to become love—and this not only at the beginning of the affair but at each instant—and at the same time he wants this freedom to be captured by *itself*, to turn back upon itself, as in madness, as in a dream, so as to will its own captivity. This captivity must be a resignation that is both free and yet chained in our hands. In love it is not a determinism of the passions which we desire in the Other nor a freedom beyond reach; it is a freedom which *plays the role of* a determinism of the passions and which is caught in its own role. For himself the lover does not demand that he be the cause of this radical modification of freedom but that he be the unique and privileged occasion of it. In fact he could not want to be the cause of it without immediately submerging the beloved in the midst of the world as a tool which can be transcended. That is not the essence of love. On the contrary, in Love the Lover wants to be "the whole World" for the beloved. This means that he puts himself on the side of the world; he is the one who assumes and symbolizes the world; he is a *this* which includes all other *thises*. He is and consents to be an *object*. But on the other hand, he wants to be the object in which the Other's freedom consents to lose itself, the object in which the Other consents to find his being and his raison d'être as his second facticity—the object-limit of transcendence, that toward which the Other's transcendence transcends all other objects but which it can in no way transcend. And everywhere he desires the circle of the Other's freedom; that is, at each instant as the Other's freedom accepts this limit to his transcendence, this acceptance is *already* present as the motivation of the acceptance considered. It is in the capacity of an end already chosen that the lover wishes to be chosen as an end. This allows us to grasp what basically the lover demands of the beloved; he does not want to *act* on the Other's freedom but to exist a *priori* as the objective limit of this freedom; that is, to be given at one stroke along with it and in its very upsurge as the limit which the freedom must accept in order to be free. By this very fact, what he demands is a liming, a gluing down of the Other's freedom by itself; this limit of structure is in fact a *given*, and the very appearance of the given as the limit of freedom means that the freedom *makes itself exist* within the given by being its own prohibition against surpassing it. This prohibition is envisaged by the lover *simultaneously* as something lived— that is, something suffered (in a word, as a facticity) and as something freely consented to. It must be freely consented to since it must be effected only with the upsurge of a freedom which chooses itself as freedom. But it must be only what is lived since it must be an impossibility always present, a facticity which surges back to the heart of the Other's freedom. This is expressed psychologically by the demand that the free decision to love me, which the beloved formerly has taken, must slip in as a magically determining motivation *within* his present free engagement.

Now we can grasp the meaning of this demand: the facticity which is to be a factual limit for the Other in my demand to be loved and which is to result in being *his own* facticity—this is *my* facticity. It is in so far as I am the object which the Other makes come into being that I must be the inherent limit to his very transcendence. Thus the Other by his upsurge into being makes me be as unsurpassable and absolute, not as a nihilating For-itself but as a being-for-others-in-the-midst-of-the-world. Thus to want to be loved is to infect the Other with one's own facticity; it is to wish to compel him to recreate you perpetually as the condition of a freedom which submits itself and which is engaged; it is to wish both that freedom found fact and that fact have pre-eminence over freedom. If this end could be attained, it would result in the first place in my being *secure* within the Other's consciousness. First because the motive of my uneasiness and my shame is the fact that I apprehend and experience myself in my being-for-others as that which can always be surpassed towards something else, that which is the pure object of a value judgment, a pure means, a pure tool. My uneasiness stems from the fact that I assume necessarily and freely that being which another makes me be in an absolute freedom. "God knows what I am for him! God knows what he thinks of me!" This means "God knows what he makes me be." I am haunted by this being which I fear to encounter someday at the turn of a path, this being which is so strange to me and which is yet *my being* and which I know that I shall never encounter in spite of all my efforts to do so. But if the Other loves me then I become the *unsurpassable*, which means that I must be the absolute end. In this sense I am saved from *instrumentality*. My existence in the midst of the world becomes the exact correlate of my transcendence-for-myself since my independence is absolutely safeguarded. The object which the Other must make me be is an object-transcendence, an absolute center of reference around which all the instrumental-things of the world are ordered as pure *means*. At the same time, as the absolute limit of freedom—i.e., of the absolute source of all values—I am protected against any eventual devalorization. I am the absolute value. To the extent that I assume my being-for-others, I assume myself as value. Thus to want to be loved is to want to be placed beyond the whole system of values posited by the Other and to be the condition of all valorization and the objective foundation of all values. This demand is the usual theme of lovers' conversations, whether as in *La Porte Etroite*, the woman who wants to be loved identifies herself with an ascetic morality of self-surpassing and wishes to embody the ideal limit of this surpassing—or as more usually happens, the woman in love demands that the beloved in his acts should sacrifice traditional morality for her and is anxious to know whether the beloved would betray his friends for her, "would steal for her," "would kill for her," etc.

From this point of view, my being must escape the *look* of the beloved, or rather it must be the object of a look with another structure. I must no longer be seen on the ground of the world as a "this" among other "thises," but the world must be revealed in terms of me. In fact to the extent that the upsurge of freedom makes a world exist, I must be, as the limiting-condition of this upsurge, the very condition of the upsurge of a world. I must be the one whose function is to make trees and water exist, to make cities and fields and other men exist, in order to give them later to the Other who arranges them into a world, just as the mother in matrilineal communities receives titles and the family name not to keep them herself but to transfer them immediately to her children. In one sense if I am to be loved, I am the object through whose procuration the world will exist for the Other; in another sense I am the world. Instead of being a "this" detaching itself on the ground of the world, I am the ground-as-object on which the world detaches itself. Thus I am reassured; the Other's look no longer paralyzes me with finitude. It no longer fixes my being in *what I am*. I can no longer be *looked at* as ugly, as small, as cowardly, since these characteristics necessarily represent a factual limitation of my being and an apprehension of my finitude as finitude. To be sure, my possibles remain transcended possibilities, dead-possibilities; but I possess all possibles. I am all the dead-possibilities in the world; hence I cease to be the being who is understood from the standpoint of other beings or of its acts. In the loving intuition which I demand, I am to be given as an absolute totality in terms of which all its peculiar acts and all beings are to be understood. One could say, slightly modifying a famous pronouncement of the Stoics, that "the beloved can fail in three ways."[1] The ideal of the sage and the ideal of the man who wants to be loved actually coincide in this that both want to be an object-as-totality accessible to a global intuition which will apprehend the beloved's or the sage's actions in the world as partial structures which are interpreted in terms of the totality. Just as wisdom is proposed as a state to be attained by an absolute metamorphosis, so the Other's freedom must be absolutely metamorphosed in order to allow me to attain the state of being loved.

Up to this point our description would fall into line with Hegel's famous description of the Master and Slave relation. What the Hegelian Master is for the Slave, the lover wants to be for the beloved. But the analogy stops here, for with Hegel the master demands the Slave's freedom only laterally and, so to speak, implicitly, while the lover wants the beloved's freedom *first and foremost*. In this sense if I am to be loved by the Other, this means that I am to be freely chosen as beloved. As we know, in the current terminology of love, the beloved is often called *the chosen one*. But this choice must not be relative and contingent. The lover is irritated and feels himself cheapened when he thinks that the beloved has chosen him *from among others*. "Then if I had not

---

[1] Literally, "can tumble three times." Tr.

come into a certain city, if I had not visited the home of so and so, you would never have known me, you wouldn't have loved me?'' This thought grieves the lover; his love becomes one love among others and is limited by the beloved's facticity and by his own facticity as well as by the contingency of encounters. It becomes *love in the world*, an object which presupposes the world and which in turn can exist for others. What he is demanding he expresses by the awkward and vitiated phrases of "fatalism." He says, "We were made for each other," or again he uses the expression "soul mate." But we must translate all this. The lover knows very well that "being made for each other" refers to an original choice. This choice can be God's, since he is the being who is absolute choice, but God here represents only the farthest possible limit of the demand for an absolute. Actually what the lover demands is that the beloved should make of him an absolute choice. This means that the beloved's being-in-the-world must be a being-as-loving. The upsurge of the beloved must be the beloved's free choice of the lover. And since the Other is the foundation of my being-as-object, I demand of him that the free upsurge of his being should have his choice of *me* as his unique and absolute end; that is, that he should choose to be for the sake of founding my object-state and my facticity.

Thus my facticity is *saved*. It is no longer this unthinkable and insurmountable given which I am fleeing; it is that for which the Other freely makes himself exist; it is as an end which he has given to himself. I have infected him with my facticity, but as it is in the form of freedom that he has been infected with it, he refers it back to me as a facticity taken up and consented to. He is the foundation of it in order that it may be his end. By means of this love I then have a different apprehension of my alienation and of my own facticity. My facticity—as for-others—is no longer a fact but a right. My existence *is* because it is *given a name*. I am because I give myself away. These beloved veins on my hands exist—beneficently. How good I am to have eyes, hair, eyebrows and to lavish them away tirelessly in an overflow of generosity to this tireless desire which the Other freely makes himself be. Whereas before being loved we were uneasy about that unjustified, unjustifiable protuberance which was our existence, whereas we felt ourselves *"de trop,"* we now feel that our existence is taken up and willed even in its tiniest details by an absolute freedom which at the same time our existence conditions and which we ourselves will with our freedom. This is the basis for the joy of love when there is joy: we feel that our existence is justified.

By the same token if the beloved can love us, he is wholly ready to be assimilated by our freedom; for this being-loved which we desire is already the ontological proof applied to our being-for-others. Our objective essense implies the existence of the Other, and conversely it is the Other's freedom which founds our essence. If we could manage to interiorize the whole system, we should be our own foundation.

Such then is the real goal of the lover in so far as his love is an enterprise—i.e., a project of himself. This project is going to provoke a conflict. The beloved in fact apprehends the lover as one Other-as-object among others; that is, he perceives the lover on the ground of the world, transcends him, and utilizes him. The beloved is a *look*. He can not therefore employ his transcendence to fix an ultimate limit to his surpassings, nor can he employ his freedom to captivate itself. The beloved can not will to love. Therefore the lover must seduce the beloved, and his love can in no way be distinguished from the enterprise of seduction. In seduction I do not try to reveal my subjectivity to the Other. Moreover I could do so only by *looking* at the other; but by this look I should cause the Other's subjectivity to disappear, and it is exactly this which I want to assimilate. To seduce is to risk assuming my object-state completely for the Other; it is to put myself beneath his look and to make him look at me; it is to risk the danger of *being-seen* in order to effect a new departure and to appropriate the Other in and by means of my object-ness. I refuse to leave the level on which I make proof of my object-ness; it is on this level that I wish to engage in battle by making myself a *fascinating object*. In Part Two we defined fascination as a state. It is, we said, the non-thetic consciousness of being *nothing* in the presence of being. Seduction aims at producing in the Other the consciousness of his state of nothingness as he confronts the seductive object. By seduction I aim at constituting myself as a fullness of being and at making myself *recognized as such*. To accomplish this I constitute myself as a meaningful object. My acts must *point* in two directions: On the one hand, toward that which is wrongly called subjectivity and which is rather a depth of objective and hidden being; the act is not performed for itself only, but it points to an infinite, undifferentiated series of other real and possible acts which I give as constituting my objective, unperceived being. Thus I try to guide the transcendence which transcends me and to refer it to the infinity of my dead-possibilities precisely in order to be the unsurpassable and to the exact extent to which the only unsurpassable is the infinite. On the other hand, each of my acts tries to point to the great density of possible-world and must present me as bound to the vastest regions of the world. At the same time I *present* the world to the beloved, and I try to constitute myself as the necessary intermediary between her and the world; I manifest by my acts infinitely varied examples of my power over the world (money, position, "connections," etc.). In the first case I try to constitute myself as an infinity of depth, in the second case to identify myself with the world. Through these different procedures I propose myself as unsurpassable. This proposal could not be sufficient in itself; it is only a besieging of the Other. It can not take on value as fact without the consent of the Other's freedom, which I must capture by making it recognize itself as nothingness in the face of my plenitude of absolute being.

Someone may observe that these various attempts at expression *presuppose* language. We shall not disagree with this. But we shall say rather that they are language or, if you prefer, a fundamental mode of language. For while psychological and historical problems exist with regard to the existence, the learning and the use of *a particular* language, there is no special problem concerning what is called the discovery or invention of language. Language is not a phenomenon added on to being-for-others. It *is* originally being-for-others; that is, it is the fact that a subjectivity experiences itself as an object for the Other. In a universe of pure objects language could under no circumstances have been "invented" since it presupposes an original relation to another subject. In the intersubjectivity of the for-others, it is not necessary to invent language because it is already given in the recognition of the Other. I *am* language. By the sole fact that whatever I may do, my acts freely conceived and executed, my projects launched toward my possibilities have outside of them a meaning which escapes me and which I experience. It is in this sense—and in this sense only— that Heidegger is right in declaring that *I am what I* say.[2] Language is not an instinct of the constituted human creature, nor is it an invention of our subjectivity. But neither does it need to be referred to the pure "being-outside-of-self" of the *Dasein*. It forms part of the *human condition*; it is originally the proof which a for-itself can make of its being-

---

[2] This formulation of Heidegger's position is that of A. de Waehlens. *La Philosophie de Martin Heidegger*. Louvain, 1942, p. 99. *Cf*. also Heidegger's text, which he quotes: "Diese Bezeugung meint nicht hier einen nachträglichen und bei her laufenden Ausdruck des Menschseins, sonder sie macht das Dasein des Menschen mit usw. (*Hölderlin und das Wesen der Dichtung*, p. 6.)

("This affirmation does not mean here an additional and supplementary expression of human existence, but it does in the process make plain the existence of man." Douglas Scott's translation. *Existence and Being*, Chicago: Henry Regnery. 1949, p. 297.)

for-others, and finally it is the surpassing of this proof and the utilization of it toward possibilities which are my possibilities; that is, toward
my possibilities of being this or that for the Other. Language is therefore not distinct from the recognition of the Other's existence. The
Other's upsurge confronting me as a look makes language arise as the
condition of my being. This primitive language is not necessarily seduction; we shall see other forms of it. Moreover we have noted that there
is another primitive attitude confronting the Other and that the two succeed each other in a circle, each implying the other. But conversely
seduction does not presuppose any earlier form of language; it is the
complete realization of language. This means that language can be revealed entirely and at one stroke by seduction as a primitive mode of
being of expression. Of course by language we mean all the phenomena
of expression and not the articulated word, which is a derived and
secondary mode whose appearance can be made the object of an
historical study. Especially in seduction language does not *aim* at *giving
to be known* but at causing to experience.

But in this first attempt to find a fascinating language I proceed
blindly since I am guided only by the abstract and empty form of my object-state for the Other. I can not even conceive what effect my gestures
and attitudes will have since they will always be taken up and founded
by a freedom which will surpass them and since they can have a meaning only if this freedom confers one on them. Thus the "meaning" of my
expressions always escapes me. I never know exactly if I signify what I
wish to signify nor even if I *am* signifying anything. It would be
necessary that at the precise instant I should read in the Other what on
principle is inconceivable. For lack of knowing what I actually express
for the Other, I constitute my language as an incomplete phenomenon
of flight outside myself. As soon as I express myself, I can only guess at
the meaning of what I express—i.e., the meaning of what I am—since
in this perspective to express and to be are one. The Other is always
there, present and experienced as the one who gives to language its
meaning. Each expression, each gesture, each word is on my side a
concrete proof of the alienating reality of the Other. It is only the
psychopath who can say, "someone has stolen my thought"—as in
cases of psychoses of influence, for example.[3] The very fact of ex-

[3] Furthermore the psychosis of influence, like the majority of psychoses, is a
special experience translated by myths, of a great metaphysical fact—here the fact
of alienation. Even a madman in his own way realizes the human condition.

pression is a stealing of thought since thought needs the cooperation of an alienating freedom in order to be constituted as an object. That is why this first aspect of language—in so far as it is I who employ it for the Other—is *sacred*. The sacred object is an object which is in the world and which points to a transcendence beyond the world. Language reveals to me the freedom (the transcendence) of the one who listens to me in silence.

But at the same moment I remain for the Other a meaningful object—that which I have always been. There is no path which departing from my object-state can lead the Other to my transcendence. Attitudes, expressions, and words can only indicate to him other attitudes, other expressions, and other words. Thus language remains for him a simple property of a magical object—and this magical object itself. It is an action at a distance whose effect the Other exactly knows. Thus the word is *sacred* when I employ it and *magic* when the Other hears it. Thus I do not know my language any more than I know my body for the Other. I can not hear myself speak nor see myself smile. The problem of language is exactly parallel to the problem of bodies, and the description which is valid in one case is valid in the other.

Fascination, however, even if it were to produce a state of being-fascinated in the Other could not by itself succeed in producing love. We can be fascinated by an orator, by an actor, by a tightrope-walker, but this does not mean that we love him. To be sure we can not take our eyes off him, but he is still raised on the ground of the world, and fascination does not posit the fascinating object as the ultimate term of the transcendence. Quite the contrary, fascination *is* transcendence. When then will the beloved become in turn the lover?

The answer is easy: when the beloved projects being loved. By himself the Other-as-object never has enough strength to produce love. If love has for its ideal the appropriation of the Other qua Other (i.e., as a subjectivity which is looking at an object) this ideal can be projected only in terms of my encounter with the Other-as-subject, not with the Other-as-object. If the Other tries to seduce me by means of his object-state, then seduction can bestow upon the Other only the character of a *precious* object "to be possessed." Seduction will perhaps determine me to risk much to conquer the Other-as-object, but this desire to appropriate an object in the midst of the world should not be confused with love. Love therefore can be born in the beloved only from the proof which he makes of his alienation and his flight toward the Other.

Still the beloved, if such is the case, will be transformed into a lover only if he projects being loved; that is, if what he wishes to overcome is not a body but the Other's subjectivity as such. In fact the only way that he could conceive to realize this appropriation is to make himself be loved. Thus it seems that to love is in essence the project of making oneself be loved. Hence this new contradiction and this new conflict: each of the lovers is entirely the captive of the Other inasmuch as each wishes to make himself loved by the Other to the exclusion of anyone else; but at the same time each one demands from the other a love which is not reducible to the "project of being-loved." What he demands in fact is that the Other without originally seeking to make himself be loved should have at once a contemplative and affective intuition of his beloved as the objective limit of his freedom, as the ineluctable and chosen foundation of his transcendence, as the totality of being and the supreme value. Love thus exacted from the other could not *ask* for anything; it is a pure engagement without reciprocity. Yet this love can not exist except in the form of a demand on the part of the lover.

The lover is held captive in a wholly different way. He is the captive of his very demand since love is the demand to be loved; he is a freedom which wills itself a body and which demands an outside, hence a freedom which imitates the flight toward the Other, a freedom which qua freedom lays claim to its alienation. The lover's freedom, in his very effort to make himself be loved as an object by the Other, is alienated by slipping into the body-for-others; that is, it is brought into existence with a dimension of flight toward the Other. It is the perpetual refusal to posit itself as pure selfness, for this affirmation of self as itself would involve the collapse of the Other as a look and the upsurge of the Other-as-object—hence a state of affairs in which the very possibility of being loved disappears since the Other is reduced to the dimension of objectivity. This refusal therefore constitutes freedom as dependent on the Other; and the Other as subjectivity becomes indeed an unsurpassable limit of the freedom of the for-itself, the goal and supreme end of the for-itself since the Other holds the key to its being. Here in fact we encounter the true ideal of love's enterprise: alienated freedom. But it is the one who wants to be loved who by the mere fact of wanting someone to love him alienates his freedom.

My freedom is alienated in the presence of the Other's pure subjectivity which founds my objectivity. It can never be alienated before the Other-as-object. In this form in fact the beloved's alienation, of which the lover dreams, would be contradictory since the beloved can found the being of the lover only by transcending it on principle toward other objects of the world; therefore this transcendence can constitute the object which it surpasses both as a transcended object and as an object limit of all transcendence. Thus each one of the lovers wants to be the object for which the Other's freedom is alienated in an original intuition; but this intuition which would be love in the true sense is only a contradictory ideal of the for-itself. Each one is alienated only to the exact extent to which he demands the alienation of the other. Each one wants the other to love him but does not take into account the fact that to love is to want to be loved and that thus by wanting the other to love him, he only wants the other to want to be loved in turn. Thus love relations are a system of indefinite reference—analogous to the pure "reflection-reflected" of consciousness—under the ideal standard of the *value* "love;" that is, in a fusion of consciousnesses in which each of them would preserve his otherness in order to found the other. This state of affairs is due to the fact that consciousnesses are separated by an insurmountable nothingness, a nothingness which is both the internal negation of the one by the other and a factual nothingness between the two internal negations. Love is a contradictory effort to surmount the factual negation while preserving the internal negation. I demand that the Other love me and I do everything possible to realize my project; but if the Other loves me, he radically deceives me by his very love. I demanded of him that he should found my being as a privileged object by maintaining himself as pure subjectivity confronting me; as soon as he loves me he experiences me as subject and is swallowed up in his objectivity confronting my subjectivity.

The problem of my being-for-others remains therefore without solution. The lovers remain each one for himself in a total subjectivity; nothing comes to relieve them of their duty to make themselves exist each one for himself; nothing comes to relieve their contingency nor to save them from facticity. At least each one has succeeded in escaping danger from the Other's freedom—but altogether differently than he expected. He escapes not because the Other makes him be as the object-limit of his transcendence but because the Other experiences him as subjectivity and wishes to experience him only as such. Again the gain is perpetually compromised. At the start, each of the consciousnesses can at any moment free itself from its chains and suddenly contemplate the other as an *object*. Then the spell is broken; the Other becomes one mean among means. He is indeed an object-for-others as the lover desires but an object-as-tool, a perpetually transcended object. The illusion, the game of mirrors which makes the concrete reality of love, suddenly ceases. Later in the experience of love each consciousness seeks to shelter its being-for-others in the Other's freedom. This supposes that the Other is beyond the world as pure subjectivity, as the absolute by which the world comes into being. But it suffices that the lovers should be *looked at* together by a third person in order for each one to experience not only his own objectivation but that of the other as well. Immediately the Other is no longer for me the absolute transcendence which founds me in my being; he is a transcendence-transcended, not by me but by another. My original relation to him—i.e., my relation of being the beloved for my lover, is fixed as a dead-possibility. It is no longer the experienced relation between a limiting object of all transcendence and the freedom which founds it; it is a love-as-object which is wholly alienated toward the third. Such is the true reason why lovers seek solitude. It is because the appearance of a third person, whoever he may be, is the destruction of their love. But factual solitude (*e.g.* we are alone in my room) is by no means a theoretical solitude. Even if nobody sees us, we exist for *all* consciousnesses and we are conscious of existing for all. The result is that love as a fundamental mode of being-for-others holds in its being-for-others the seed of its own destruction.

We have just defined the triple destructibility of love: in the first place it is, in essence, a deception and a reference to infinity since to love is to wish to be loved, hence to wish that the Other wish that I love him. A preontological comprehension of this deception is given in the very impulse of love—hence the lover's perpetual dissatisfaction. It does not come, as is so often said, from the unworthiness of being loved but from an implicit comprehension of the fact that the amorous intuition is, as a fundamental-intuition, an ideal out of reach. The more I am loved, the more I lose my *being*, the more I am thrown back on my own responsibilities, on my own power to be. In the second place the Other's awakening is always possible; at any moment he can make me appear as an object—hence the lover's perpetual insecurity. In the third place love is an absolute which is perpetually made *relative* by others. One would have to be alone in the world with the beloved in order for love to preserve its character as an absolute axis of reference—hence the lover's perpetual shame (or pride—which here amounts to the same thing).

Thus it is useless for me to have tried to lose myself in objectivity; my passion will have availed me nothing. The Other has referred me to my own unjustifiable subjectivity—either by himself or through others. This result can provoke a total despair and a new attempt to realize the identification of the Other and myself. Its ideal will then be the opposite of that which we have just described; instead of projecting the absorbing of the Other while preserving in him his otherness, I shall project causing myself to be absorbed by the Other and losing myself in his subjectivity in order to get rid of my own. This enterprise will be expressed concretely by the *masochistic* attitude. Since the Other is the foundation of my being-for-others, if I relied on the Other to make me exist, I should no longer be anything more than a being-in-itself founded in its being by a freedom. Here it is my own subjectivity which is considered as an obstacle to the primordial act by which the Other would found me in my being. It is my own subjectivity which above all must be denied by *my own freedom*. I attempt therefore to engage myself wholly in my being-as-object. I refuse to be anything more than an object. I rest upon the Other, and as I experience this being-as-object in shame, I will and I love my shame as the profound sign of my objectivity. As the Other apprehends me as object by means of *actual desire*, I wish to be desired, I make myself in shame an object of desire.

This attitude would resemble that of love if instead of seeking to exist for the Other as the object-limit of his transcendence, I did not rather insist on making myself be treated as one object among others, as an instrument to be used. Now it is *my* transcendence which is to be denied, not his. This time I do not have to project capturing his freedom; on the contrary I hope that this freedom may be and *will* itself to be radically free. Thus the more I shall feel myself surpassed toward other ends, the more I shall enjoy the abdication of my transcendence. Finally I project being nothing more than an *object*; that is, radically an *in-itself*. But inasmuch as a freedom which will have absorbed mine will be the foundation of this in-itself, my being will become again the foundation of itself. Masochism, like sadism, is the assumption of guilt. I am guilty due to the very fact that I am an object, I am guilty toward myself since I consent to my absolute alienation. I am guilty toward the Other, for I furnish him with the occasion of being guilty—that is, of radically missing my freedom as such. Masochism is an attempt not to fascinate the Other by means of my objectivity but to cause myself to be fascinated by my objectivity-for-others; that is, to cause myself to be constituted as an object by the Other in such a way that I non-thetically apprehend my subjectivity as a *nothing* in the presence of the in-itself which I represent to the Other's eyes. Masochism is characterized as a species of vertigo, vertigo not before a precipice of rock and earth but before the abyss of the Other's subjectivity.

But masochism is and must be itself a failure. In order to cause myself to be fascinated by my self-as-object, I should necessarily have to be able to realize the intuitive apprehension of this object such as it is *for the Other*, a thing which is on principle impossible. Thus I am far from being able to be fascinated by this alienated Me, which remains on principle inapprehensible. It is useless for the masochist to get down on his knees, to show himself in ridiculous positions, to cause himself to be used as a simple lifeless instrument. It is *for the Other* that he will be obscene or simply passive, for the Other that he will *undergo* these postures; for himself he is forever condemned to *give them to himself*. It is in and through his transcendence that he disposes of himself as a being to be transcended. The more he tries to taste his objectivity, the more he will be submerged by the consciousness of his subjectivity— hence his anguish. Even the masochist who pays a woman to whip him is treating her as an instrument and by this very fact posits himself in transcendence in relation to her.

Thus the masochist ultimately treats the Other as an object and transcends him toward his own objectivity. Recall, for example, the tribulations of Sacher Masoch, who in order to make himself scorned, insulted, reduced to a humiliating position, was obliged to make use of the great love which women bore toward him; that is, to act upon them just in so far as they experienced themselves as an object for him. Thus in every way the masochist's objectivity escapes him, and it can even happen—in fact usually does happen—that in seeking to apprehend his own objectivity he finds the Other's objectivity, which in spite of himself frees his own subjectivity. Masochism therefore is on principle a failure. This should not surprise us if we realize that masochism is a "vice" and that vice is, on principle, the love of failure. But this is not the place to describe the structures peculiar to vice. It is sufficient here to point out that masochism is a perpetual effort to *annihilate* the subject's subjectivity by causing it to be assimilated by the Other; this effort is accompanied by the exhausting and delicious consciousness of failure so that finally it is the failure itself which the subject ultimately seeks as his principal goal.[4]

---

[4] Consistent with this description, there is at least one form of exhibitionism which ought to be classed among masochistic attitudes. For example, when Rousseau exhibits to the washerwomen "not the obscene object but the ridiculous object." Cf. *Confessions*, ch. III.

EMMANUEL LEVINAS

Emmanuel Levinas was one of the first French philosophers to study phenomenology. It was through Levinas that Jean-Paul Sartre first became interested, and through Sartre, Maurice Merleau-Ponty found his interest. Levinas studied with both Husserl and Heidegger and currently is a professor of philosophy at the University of Paris. His contributions include: *Théorie de l'intuition dans la phénoménologie de Husserl* (1930) and *Totality and Infinity* (1961).

DISCOURSE AND ETHICS*

Can objectivity and the universality of thought be founded on discourse? Is not universal thought of itself prior to discourse? Does not a mind in speaking evoke what the other mind already thinks, both of them participating in common ideas? But the community of thought ought to have made language as a relation between beings impossible. Coherent discourse is one. A universal thought dispenses with communication. A reason cannot be other for a reason. How can a reason be an I or an other, since its very being consists in renouncing singularity?

European thought has always combated, as skeptical, the idea of man as measure of all things, although this idea contributes the idea of atheist separation and one of the foundations of discourse. For it the sentient I could not found Reason; the I was defined by reason. Reason speaking in the first person is not addressed to the other, conducts a monologue. And, conversely, it would attain to veritable personality, would recover the sovereignty characteristic of the autonomous person, only by becoming universal. Separated thinkers become rational only in the measure that their personal and particular acts of thinking figure as moments of this unique and universal discourse. There would be reason in the thinking individual only in the measure that he would himself enter into his own discourse, that thought would, in the etymological sense of the term, comprehend the thinker—that it would include him.

* By permission of Duquesne University Press. From Emmanuel Levinas, *Totality and Infinity*, Duquesne University Press, Pittsburgh, Pennsylvania, 1969.

But to make of the thinker a moment of thought is to limit the revealing function of language to its coherence, conveying the coherence of concepts. In this coherence the unique I of the thinker volatilizes. The function of language would amount to suppressing "the other," who breaks this coherence and is hence essentially irrational. A curious result: language would consist in suppressing the other, in making the other agree with the same! But in its expressive function language precisely maintains the other—to whom it is addressed, whom it calls upon or invokes. To be sure, language does not consist in invoking him as a being represented and thought. But this is why language institutes a relation irreducible to the subject-object relation: the *revelation* of the other. In this revelation only can language as a system of signs be constituted. The other called upon is not something represented, is not a given, is not a particular, through one side already open to generalization. Language, far from presupposing universality and generality, first makes them possible. Language presupposes interlocutors, a plurality. Their commerce is not a representation of the one by the other, nor a participation in universality, on the common plane of language. Their commerce, as we shall show shortly, is ethical.

Plato maintains the difference between the objective order of truth, that which doubtlessly is established in writings, impersonally, and reason *in* a living being, "a living and animated discourse," a discourse "which can defend itself, and knows when to speak and when to be silent."[1] This discourse is therefore not the unfolding of a prefabricated internal logic, but the constitution of truth in a struggle between thinkers, with all the risks of freedom. The relationship of language implies transcendence, radical separation, the strangeness of the interlocutors, the revelation of the other to me. In other words, language is spoken where community between the terms of the relationship is wanting, where the common plane is wanting or is yet to be constituted. It takes place in this transcendence. Discourse is thus the experience of something absolutely foreign, a *pure* "knowledge" or "experience," a *traumatism of astonishment*.

The absolutely foreign alone can instruct us. And it is only man who could be absolutely foreign to me—refractory to every typology, to every genus, to every characterology, to every classification—and consequently the term of a "knowledge" finally penetrating beyond the object. The strangeness of the Other, his very freedom! Free beings alone

[1] *Phaedrus*, 276a.

can be strangers to one another. Their freedom which is "common" to them is precisely what separates them. As a "pure knowledge" language consists in the relationship with a being that in a certain sense is not by relation to me, or, if one likes, that is in a relationship with me only inasmuch as he is wholly by relation to himself [2] καθ'αὐτό, a being that stands beyond every attribute, which would precisely have as its effect to qualify him, that is, to reduce him to what is common to him and other beings—a being, consequently, completely naked.

The things are naked, by metaphor, only when they are without adornments: bare walls, naked landscapes. They have no need of adornment when they are absorbed in the accomplishment of the function for which they are made: when they are subordinated to their own finality so radically that they disappear in it. They disappear beneath their form. The perception of individual things is the fact that they are not entirely absorbed in their form; they then stand out in themselves, breaking through, rending their forms, are not resolved into the relations that link them up to the totality. They are always in some respect like those industrial cities where everything is adapted to a goal of production, but which, full of smoke, full of wastes and sadness, exist also for themselves. For a thing nudity is the surplus of its being over its finality. It is its absurdity, its uselessness, which itself appears only relative to the form against which it contrasts and of which it is deficient. The thing is always an opacity, a resistance, an ugliness. Thus the Platonic conception of the intelligible sun situated outside of the eye that sees and the object it illuminates describes with precision the perception of things. Objects have no light of their own; they receive a borrowed light.

Beauty then introduces a new finality, an internal finality, into this naked world. To disclose by science and by art is essentially to clothe the elements with signification, to go beyond perception. To disclose a thing is to clarify it by forms: to find for it a place in the whole by apperceiving its function or its beauty.

The work of language is entirely different: it consists in entering into relationship with a nudity disengaged from every form, but having meaning by itself, καθ'αὐτό, signifying before we have projected light upon it, appearing not as a privation on the ground of an ambivalence of values (as good or evil, as beauty or ugliness), but as an *always positive value*. Such a nudity is the face. The nakedness of the face is not what is presented to me because I disclose it, what would therefore be presented to me, to my powers, to my eyes, to my perceptions, in a light exterior to it. The face has turned to me—and this is its very nudity. It *is* by itself and not by reference to a system.

To be sure nakedness can have still a third meaning, outside of the absurdity of the thing losing its system or the signification of the face breaking through all form: the nudity of the body felt in modesty, appearing to the Other in repulsion and desire. But this nudity always refers in one way or other to the nakedness of the face. Only a being absolutely naked by his face can also denude himself immodestly.

But the difference between the nakedness of the face that turns to me and the disclosure of the thing illuminated by its form does not simply separate two modes of "knowledge." The relation with the face is not an object-cognition. The transcendence of the face is at the same time its absence from this world into which it enters, the exiling [dépaysement] of a being, his condition of being stranger, destitute, or proletarian. The strangeness that is freedom is also strangeness-destitution [étrangeté-misère]. Freedom presents itself as the other to the same, who is always the autochthon of being, always privileged in his own residence. The other, the free one, is also the stranger. The nakedness of his face extends into the nakedness of the body that is cold and that is ashamed of its nakedness. Existence καθ'αὐτό is, in the world, a destitution. There is here a relation between me and the other beyond rhetoric.

This gaze that supplicates and demands, that can supplicate only because it demands, deprived of everything because entitled to everything, and which one recognizes in giving (as one "puts the things in question in giving")—this gaze is precisely the epiphany of the face as a face. The nakedness of the face is destituteness.[3] To recognize the Other is to recognize a hunger. To recognize the Other is to give. But it is to give to the master, to the lord, to him whom one approaches as "You"[4] in a dimension of height.

It is in generosity that the world possessed by me—the world open to enjoyment—is apperceived from a point of view independent of the egoist position. The "objective" is not simply the object of an impassive

[3] "La nudité du visage est dénûment."
[4] "Vous"—the "you" of majesty, in contrast with the "thou" of intimacy.—Trans.

contemplation. Or rather impassive contemplation is defined by gift, by the abolition of inalienable property. The presence of the Other is equivalent to this calling into question of my joyous possession of the world. The conceptualization of the sensible arises already from this incision in the living flesh of my own substance, my home, in this suitability of the mine for the Other, which prepares the descent of the things to the rank of possible merchandise. This initial dispossession conditions the subsequent generalization by money. Conceptualization is the first generalization and the condition for objectivity. Objectivity coincides with the abolition of inalienable property—which presupposes the ephiphany of the other. The whole problem of generalization is thus posed as a problem of objectivity. The problem of the general and abstract idea cannot presuppose objectivity as constituted: the general object is not a sensible object that would, however, be thought in an intention of generality and ideality. For the nominalist critique of the general and abstract idea is not yet overcome thereby; it is still necessary to say what this intention of ideality and generality signifies. The passage from perception to the concept belongs to the constitution of the objectivity of the perceived object. We must not speak of an intention of ideality investing perception, an intention in which the solitary being of the subject, identifying itself in the same, directs itself toward the transcendent world of the ideas. The generality of the Object is correlative with the generosity of the subject going to the Other, beyond the egoist and solitary enjoyment, and hence making the community of the goods of this world break forth from the exclusive property of enjoyment.

To recognize the Other is therefore to come to him across the world of possessed things, but at the same time to establish, by gift, community and universality. Language is universal because it is the very passage from the individual to the general, because it offers things which are mine to the Other. To speak is to make the world common, to create commonplaces. Language does not refer to the generality of concepts, but lays the foundations for a possession in common. It abolishes the inalienable property of enjoyment. The world in discourse is no longer what it is in separation, in the being at home with oneself where everything is given to me; it is what I give: the communicable, the thought, the universal.

Thus conversation is not a pathetic confrontation of two beings absenting themselves from the things and from the others. Discourse is not love. The transcendence of the Other, which is his eminence, his height, his lordship, in its concrete meaning includes his destitution, his exile [dépaysement], and his rights as a stranger. I can recognize the gaze of the stranger, the widow, and the orphan only in giving or in refusing; I am free to give or to refuse, but my recognition passes necessarily through the interposition of things. . . . The relationship between the same and the other, my welcoming of the other, is the ultimate fact, and in it the things figure not as what one builds but as what one gives.

ETHICS AND THE FACE

The face resists possession, resists my powers. In its epiphany, in expression, the sensible, still graspable, turns into total resistance to the grasp. This mutation can occur only by the opening of a new dimension. For the resistance to the grasp is not produced as an insurmountable resistance, like the hardness of the rock against which the effort of the hand comes to naught, like the remoteness of a star in the immensity of space. The expression the face introduces into the world does not defy the feebleness of my powers, but my ability for power.[5] The face, still a thing among things, breaks through the form that nevertheless delimits it. This means concretely: the face speaks to me and thereby invites me to a relation incommensurate with a power exercised, be it enjoyment or knowledge.

And yet this new dimension opens in the sensible appearance of the face. The permanent openness of the contours of its form in expression imprisons this openness which breaks up form in a caricature. The face at the limit of holiness and caricature is thus still in a sense exposed to powers. In a sense only: the depth that opens in this sensibility modifies the very nature of power, which henceforth can no longer take, but can kill. Murder still aims at a sensible datum, and yet it finds itself before a datum whose being can not be *suspended* by an appropriation. It finds itself before a datum absolutely non-neutralizable. The "negation" effected by appropriation and usage remained always partial. The grasp that contests the independence of the thing preserves it "for me." Neither the destruction of things, nor the hunt, nor the extermination of living beings aims at the face, which is not of the world. They still belong to labor, have a finality, and answer to a need. Murder alone lays claim to total negation. Negation by labor and usage, like negation

---

[5] "Mon pouvoir de pouvoir."

by representation, effect a grasp or a comprehension, rest on or aim at affirmation; they can. To kill is not to dominate but to annihilate; it is to renounce comprehension absolutely. Murder exercises a power over what escapes power. It is still a power, for the face expresses itself in the sensible, but already impotency, because the face rends the sensible. The alterity that is expressed in the face provides the unique "matter" possible for total negation. I can wish to kill only an existent absolutely independent, which exceeds my powers infinitely, and therefore does not oppose them but paralyzes the very power of power. The Other is the sole being I can wish to kill.

But how does this disproportion between infinity and my powers differ from that which separates a very great obstacle from a force applied to it? It would be pointless to insist on the banality of murder, which reveals the quasi-null resistance of the obstacle. This most banal incident of human history corresponds to an exceptional possibility—since it claims the total negation of a being. It does not concern the force that this being may possess as a part of the world. The Other who can sovereignly say *no* to me is exposed to the point of the sword or the revolver's bullet, and the whole unshakeable firmness of his "for itself" with that intransigent *no* he opposes is obliterated because the sword or the bullet has touched the ventricles or auricles of his heart. In the contexture of the world he is a quasi-nothing. But he can oppose to me a struggle, that is, oppose to the force that strikes him not a force of resistance, but the very *unforeseeableness* of his reaction. He thus opposes to me not a greater force, an energy assessable and consequently presenting itself as though it were part of a whole, but the very transcendence of his being by relation to that whole; not some superlative of power, but precisely the infinity of his transcendence. This infinity, stronger than murder, already resists us in his face, is his face, is the primordial *expression*, is the first word: "you shall not commit murder." The infinite paralyses power by its infinite resistance to murder, which, firm and insurmountable, gleams in the face of the Other, in the total nudity of his defenceless eyes, in the nudity of the absolute openness of the Transcendent. There is here a relation not with a very great resistance, but with something absolutely *other:* the resistance of what has no resistance—the ethical resistance. The epiphany of the face brings forth the possibility of gauging the infinity of the temptation to murder, not only as a temptation to total destruction, but also as the purely ethical impossibility of this temptation and attempt. If the resistance to murder were not ethical but real, we would have a *percep-*

tion of it, with all that reverts to the subjective in perception. We would remain within the idealism of a *consciousness* of struggle, and not in relationship with the Other, a relationship that can turn into struggle, but already overflows the consciousness of struggle. The epiphany of the face is ethical. The struggle this face can threaten *presupposes* the transcendence of expression. The face threatens the eventuality of a struggle, but this threat does not exhaust the epiphany of infinity, does not formulate its first word. War presupposes peace, the antecedent and non-allergic presence of the Other; it does not represent the first event of the encounter.

The impossibility of killing does not have a simply negative and formal signification; the relation with infinity, the idea of infinity in us, conditions it positively. Infinity presents itself as a face in the ethical resistance that paralyses my powers and from the depths of defenceless eyes rises firm and absolute in its nudity and destitution. The comprehension of this destitution and this hunger establishes the very proximity of the other. But thus the epiphany of infinity is expression and discourse. The primordial essence of expression and discourse does not reside in the information they would supply concerning an interior and hidden world. In expression a being presents itself; the being that manifests itself attends its manifestation and consequently appeals to me. This attendance is not the *neutrality* [*le neutre*] of an image, but a solicitation that concerns me by its destitution and its Height. To speak to me is at each moment to surmount what is necessarily plastic in manifestation. To manifest oneself as a face is to *impose oneself* above and beyond the manifested and purely phenomenal form, to present oneself in a mode irreducible to manifestation, the very straight-forwardness of the face to face, without the intermediary of any image, in one's nudity, that is, in one's destitution and hunger. In *Desire* are conjoined the movements unto the Height and unto the Humility of the Other.

Expression does not radiate as a splendor that spreads unbeknown to the radiating being—which is perhaps the definition of beauty. To manifest oneself in attending one's own manifestation is to invoke the interlocutor and expose oneself to his response and his questioning. Expression does not impose itself as a true representation or as an action. The being offered in true representation remains a possibility of appearance. The world which invades me when I engage myself in it is powerless against the "free thought" that suspends that engagement, or even refuses it interiorly, being capable of living hidden. The being that expresses itself imposes itself, but does so precisely by appealing to me with its destitution and nudity—its hunger—without my being able to be deaf to that appeal. Thus in expression the being that imposes itself does not limit but promotes my freedom, by arousing my goodness. The order of responsibility, where the gravity of ineluctable being freezes all laughter, is also the order where freedom is ineluctably invoked. It is thus the irremissible weight of being that gives rise to my freedom. The ineluctable has no longer the inhumanity of the fateful, but the severe seriousness of goodness.

This bond between expression and responsibility, this ethical condition or essence of language, this function of language prior to all disclosure of being and its cold splendor, permits us to extract language from subjection to a preexistent thought, where it would have but the servile function of translating that preexistent thought on the outside, or of universalizing its interior movements. The presentation of the face is not true, for the true refers to the non-true, its eternal contemporary, and ineluctably meets with the smile and silence of the skeptic. The presentation of being in the face does not leave any logical place for its contradictory. Thus I cannot evade by silence the discourse which the epiphany that occurs as a face opens, as Thrasymachus, irritated, tries to do, in the first book of the *Republic* (moreover without succeeding). "To leave men without food is a fault that no circumstance attenuates; the distinction between the voluntary and the involuntary does not apply here," says Rabbi Yochanan.[6] Before the hunger of men responsibility is measured only "objectively"; it is irrecusable. The face opens the primordial discourse whose first word is obligation, which no "interiority" permits avoiding. It is that discourse that obliges the entering into discourse, the commencement of discourse rationalism prays for, a "force" that convinces even "the people who do not wish to listen"[7] and thus founds the true universality of reason.

Preexisting the disclosure of being in general taken as basis of knowledge and as meaning of being is the relation with the existent that expresses himself; preexisting the plane of ontology is the ethical plane.

<hr>

[6] Treatise *Synhedrin,* 104 b.
[7] Plato, *Republic,* 327 b.

ALFRED SCHUTZ (1899-1959)

Alfred Schutz was born in Vienna in 1899. His early studies were in the fields of law and sociology. But from the start he also mantained interest in philosophy. He gained the Dr. Juris degree from the University of Vienna. After moving to the United States, Alfred Schutz was for many years professor of sociology and philosophy at the New School for Social Research in New York. His philosophical writings include: *The Phenomenology of the Social World* (1932), *Reflections on the Problem of Relevance* (1970) and *Collected Papers* (1962).

COMMON-SENSE AND SCIENTIFIC INTERPRETATION OF HUMAN ACTION*

I. INTRODUCTION: CONTENT OF EXPERIENCE AND THOUGHT OBJECTS

1) *The constructs of common-sense and of scientific thinking*

"Neither common sense nor science can proceed without departing from the strict consideration of what is actual in experience." This statement by A. N. Whitehead is at the foundation of his analysis of the Organization of Thought.[1] Even the thing perceived in everyday life is more than a simple sense presentation.[2] It is a thought object, a construct of a highly complicated nature, involving not only particular forms of time-successions in order to constitute it as an object of one

* By permission of Philosophy and Phenomenological Research Quarterly. From Alfred Schutz, "Common Sense and Scientific Interpretation of Human Action," Volume XIV, No. 1, September, 1953.

[1] Alfred North Whitehead: *The Organization of Thought,* London, 1917, now partially republished in *The Aims of Education,* New York, 1929, also as "Mentor-Book," New York, 1949. The quotations refer to this edition. For the first quotation see p. 110.

[2] *Ibid.,* Chapter 9, "The Anatomy of Some Scientific Ideas, I Fact, II Objects."

single sense, say of sight,[3] and of space relations in order to constitute it as a sense-object of several senses, say of sight and touch,[4] but also a contribution of imagination of hypothetical sense presentations in order to complete it.[5] According to Whitehead, it is precisely the last-named factor, the imagination of hypothetical sense presentation, "which is the rock upon which the whole structure of common-sense thought is erected"[6] and it is the effort of reflective criticism "to construe our sense presentation as actual realization of the hypothetical thought object of perceptions."[7] In other words, the so-called concrete facts of common-sense perception are not so concrete as it seems. They already involve abstractions of a highly complicated nature, and we have to take account of this situation lest we commit the fallacy of misplaced concreteness.[8]

Science always, according to Whitehead, has a twofold aim: First, the production of a theory which agrees with experience, and second, the explanation of common-sense concepts of nature at least in their outline; this explanation consists in the preservation of these concepts in a scientific theory of harmonized thought.[9] For this purpose physical science (which, in this context, is alone of concern to Whitehead) has to develop devices by which the thought objects of common-sense perception are superseded by the thought objects of science.[10] The latter, such as molecules, atoms, and electrons have shed all qualities capable of direct sense presentation in our consciousness and are known to us only by the series of events in which they are implicated, events, to be sure, which are represented in our consciousness by sense presentations. By this device a bridge is formed between the fluid vagueness of sense and the exact definition of thought.[11]*

*   *   *

[3] *Ibid.*, p. 128f. and 131.
[4] *Ibid.*, p. 131 and 136.
[5] *Ibid.*, p. 133.
[6] *Ibid.*, p. 134.
[7] *Ibid.*, p. 135.
[8] Alfred North Whitehead: *Science and the Modern World*, New York, 1925, reprinted as "Mentor-Book," New York, 1948, p. 52 ff.
[9] *The Aims of Education*, p. 126.
[10] *Ibid.*, p. 135.
[11] *Ibid.*, p. 136.
* Material deleted includes footnotes 12-16. (Eds.)

All our knowledge of the world, in common-sense as well as in scientific thinking, involves constructs, i.e., a set of abstractions, generalizations, formalizations, idealizations specific to the respective level of thought organization. Strictly speaking, there are no such things as facts, pure and simple. All facts are from the outset facts selected from a universal context by the activities of our mind. They are, therefore, always interpreted facts, either facts looked at as detached from their context by an artificial abstraction or facts considered in their particular setting. In either case, they carry along their interpretational inner and outer horizon. This does not mean that, in daily life or in science, we are unable to grasp the reality of the world. It just means that we grasp merely certain aspects of it, namely those which are relevant to us either for carrying on our business of living or from the point of view of a body of accepted rules of procedure of thinking called the method of science.

2) Particular structure of the constructs of the social sciences

If, according to this view, all scientific constructs are designed to supersede the constructs of common-sense thought, then a principal difference between the natural and the social sciences becomes apparent. It is up to the natural scientists to determine which sector of the universe of nature, which facts and events therein, and which aspects of such facts and events are topically and interpretationally relevant to their specific purpose. These facts and events are neither preselected nor preinterpreted; they do not reveal intrinsic relevance structures. Relevance is not inherent in nature as such, it is the result of the selective and interpretative activity of man within nature or observing nature. The facts, data, and events with which the natural scientist has to deal are just facts, data, and events within his observational field but this field does not "mean" anything to the molecules, atoms, and electrons therein.

But the facts, events, and data before the social scientist are of an entirely different structure. His observational field, the social world, is not essentially structureless. It has a particular meaning and relevance structure for the human beings living, thinking, and acting therein. They have preselected and preinterpreted this world by a series of common-sense constructs of the reality of daily life, and it is these thought objects which determine their behavior, define the goal of their action, the means available for attaining them—in brief, which help them to find their bearings within their natural and socio-cultural environment and to come to terms with it. The thought objects constructed by the social scientists refer to and are founded upon the thought objects constructed by the common-sense thought of man living his everyday life among his fellow-men. Thus, the constructs used by the social scientist are, so to speak, constructs of the second degree, namely constructs of the constructs made by the actors on the social scene, whose behavior the scientist observes and tries to explain in accordance with the procedural[17] rules of his science.

* * *

II. CONSTRUCTS OF THOUGHT OBJECTS IN COMMON-SENSE THINKING

1) The individual's common-sense knowledge of the world is a system of constructs of its typicality

Let us try to characterize the way in which the wide-awake[18] grown-up man looks at the intersubjective world of daily life within which and upon which he acts as a man amidst his fellow-men. This world existed before our birth, experienced and interpreted by others, our predecessors, as an organized world. Now it is given to our experience and interpretation. All interpretation of this world is based on a stock of previous experiences of it, our own or those handed down to us by parents or teachers; these experiences in the form of "knowledge at hand" function as a scheme of reference.

To this stock of knowledge at hand belongs our knowledge that the world we live in is a world of more or less well circumscribed objects with more or less definite qualities, objects among which we move, which resist us and upon which we may act. Yet none of these objects is perceived as insulated. From the outset it is an object within a horizon of familiarity and pre-acquaintanceship which is, as such, just taken for granted until further notice as the unquestioned, though at any time

---

[17] On the concept of procedural rules, see Felix Kaufmann, *Methodology of the Social Sciences,* New York, 1944, esp. Chs. III and IV; on the divergent views of the relationship between the natural and the social sciences, *ibid.,* Ch. X.

[18] As to the precise meaning of this term, see "On Multiple Realities," in: Alfred Schutz, *Collected Papers*, Vol. I, ed. by Maurice Natanson (The Hague, Martinus Nijhoff, 1962), p. 213.

questionable stock of knowledge at hand. The unquestioned pre-experiences are, however, also from the outset, at hand as *typical*, that is, as carrying open horizons of anticipated similar experiences. For example, the outer world is not experienced as an arrangement of individual unique objects, dispersed in space and time, but as "mountains," "trees," "animals," "fellow-men." I may have never seen an Irish setter but if I see one, I know that it is an animal and in particular a dog, showing all the familiar features and the typical behavior of a dog and not, say, of a cat. I may reasonably ask: "What kind of dog is this?" The question presupposes that the dissimilarity of this particular dog from all other kinds of dogs which I know stands out and becomes questionable merely by reference to the similarity it has to my unquestioned experiences of typical dogs. In the more technical language of Husserl, whose analysis of the typicality of the world of daily life we have tried to sum up,[19] what is experienced in the actual perception of an object is apperceptively transferred to any other similar object, perceived merely as to its type. Actual experience will or will not confirm my anticipation of the typical conformity with other objects. If confirmed, the content of the anticipated type will be enlarged; at the same time the type will be split up into sub-types; on the other hand the concrete real object will prove to have its individual characteristics, which, nevertheless, have a form of typicality.

Now, and this seems to be of special importance, I *may* take the typically apperceived object as an *exemplar* of the general type and allow myself to be led to this concept of the type, but I do not *need* by any means to think of the concrete dog as an exemplar of the general concept of "dog." "In general" my Irish setter Rover shows all the characteristics which the type "dog," according to my previous experience, implies. Yet exactly what he has in common with other dogs is of no concern to me. I look at him as my friend and companion Rover, as such distinguished from all the other Irish setters with which he shares certain typical characteristics of appearance and behavior. I am, without a special motive, not induced to look at Rover as a mammal, an animal, an object of the outer world, although I know that he is all this too.

Thus, in the natural attitude of daily life we are concerned merely

[19] Edmund Husserl, *Erfahrung und Urteil*, Secs. 18-21 and 82-85; cf. also "Language, Language Disturbances and the Texture of Consciousness," in *Collected Papers*, I, *op. cit.*, pp. 277-283.

with certain objects standing out over against the unquestioned field of pre-experienced other objects, and the result of the selecting activity of our mind is to determine which particular characteristics of such an object are individual and which typical ones. More generally, we are merely concerned with some aspects of this particular typified object. Asserting of this object S that it has the characteristic property p, in the form "S is p," is an elliptical statement. For S, taken without any question as it appears to me, is not merely p but also q and r and many other things. The full statement should read: "S is, among many other things, such as q and r, also p." If I assert with respect to an element of the world as taken for granted: "S is p," I do so because under the prevailing circumstances I am interested in the p-being of S, disregarding as not relevant its being also q and r. [20]

The terms "interest" and "relevant" just used are, however, merely headings for a series of complicated problems which cannot be elaborated upon within the frame of the present discussion.* We have to restrict ourselves to a few remarks.

Man finds himself at any moment of his daily life in a biographically determined situation, that is, in a physical and sociocultural environment as defined by him, [21] within which he has his position, not merely his position in terms of physical space and outer time or of his status and role within the social system but also his moral and ideological position. [22] To say that this definition of the situation is biographically determined is to say that it has its history; it is the sedimentation of all man's previous experiences, organized in the habitual possessions of his stock of knowledge at hand, and as such his unique possession, given to him and to him alone. This biographically determined situation includes certain possibilities of future practical or theoretical activities which shall be briefly called the "purpose at hand."

[20] See literature referred to in Footnote 19.

* See Alfred Schutz, *Reflections on the Problem of Relevance,* ed., annotated and introd. R. M. Zaner (New Haven, Yale Univ. Press, 1970).

[21] As to the concept of "Defining the Situation," see the various pertinent papers of W. I. Thomas, now collected in the volume, *Social Behavior and Personality, Contributions of W. I. Thomas to Theory and Social Research,* ed. by Edmund H. Volkart, New York, 1951. Consult index and the valuable introductory essay by the editor.

[22] Cf. Maurice Merleau-Ponty, *Phénoménologie de la perception,* Paris, 1945, p. 158.

It is this purpose at hand which defines those elements among all the others contained in such a situation which are relevant for this purpose. This system of relevances in turn determines what elements have to be made a substratum of generalizing typification, what traits of these elements have to be selected as characteristically typical, and what others as unique and individual, that is, how far we have to penetrate into the open horizon of typicality. . . .

2) The intersubjective character of common-sense knowledge and its implication

In analyzing the first constructs of common-sense thinking in everyday life we proceeded, however, as if the world were my private world and as if we were entitled to disregard the fact that it is from the outset an intersubjective world of culture. It is intersubjective because we live in it as men among other men, bound to them through common influence and work, understanding others and being understood by them. It is a world of culture because, from the outset, the world of everyday life is a universe of significance to us, that is, a texture of meaning which we have to interpret in order to find our bearings within it and come to terms with it. This texture of meaning, however—and this distinguishes the realm of culture from that of nature—originates in and has been instituted by human actions, our own and our fellow-men's, contemporaries and predecessors. All cultural objects—tools, symbols, language systems, works of art, social institutions, etc.—point back by their very origin and meaning to the activities of human subjects. For this reason we are always conscious of the historicity of culture which we encounter in traditions and customs. This historicity is capable of being examined in its reference to human activities of which it is the sediment. For the same reason I cannot understand a cultural object without referring it to the human activity from which it originates. For example, I do not understand a tool without knowing the purpose for which it was designed, a sign or symbol without knowing what it stands for in the mind of the person who uses it, an institution without understanding what it means for the individuals who orient their behavior with regard to its existence. Here is the origin of the so-called postulate of subjective interpretation of the social sciences which will call for our attention later on.

Our next task is, however, to examine the additional constructs which emerge in common-sense thinking if we take into account that this world is not my private world but an intersubjective one and that, therefore, my knowledge of it is not my private affair but from the outset intersubjective or socialized. For our purpose we have briefly to consider three aspects of the problem of the socialization of knowledge:

a) The reciprocity of perspectives or the structural socialization of knowledge;
b) The social origin of knowledge or the genetic socialization of knowledge;
c) The social distribution of knowledge.

a) The reciprocity of perspectives

In the natural attitude of common-sense thinking in daily life I take it for granted that intelligent fellow-men exist. This implies that the objects of the world are, as a matter of principle, accessible to their knowledge, i.e., either known to them or knowable by them. This I know and take for granted beyond question. But I know also and take for granted that, strictly speaking, the "same" object must mean something different to me and to any of my fellow-men. This is so because

i) I, being "here," am at another distance from and experience other aspects as being typical of the objects than he, who is "there." For the same reason, certain objects are out of my reach (of my seeing, hearing, my manipulatory sphere, etc.) but within his, and vice versa.
ii) My and my fellow-man's biographically determined situations, and therewith our respective purposes at hand and our respective systems of relevances originating in such purposes, must differ, at least to a certain extent.

Common-sense thinking overcomes the differences in individual perspectives resulting from these factors by two basic idealizations:

i) The idealization of the interchangeability of the standpoints: I take it for granted—and assume my fellow-man does the same—that if I change places with him so that his "here" becomes mine, I shall be at the same distance from things and see them with the same typicality as he actually does;

moreover, the same things would be in my reach which are actually in his. (The reverse is also true.)

ii) The idealization of the congruency of the system of relevances: Until counterevidence I take it for granted—and assume my fellow-man does the same—that the differences in perspectives originating in our unique biographical situations are irrelevant for the purpose at hand of either of us and that he and I, that "We" assume that both of us have selected and interpreted the actually or potentially common objects and their features in an identical manner or at least an "empirically identical" manner, i.e., one sufficient for all practical purposes.

It is obvious that both idealizations . . . are typifying constructs of objects of thought which supersede the thought objects of my and my fellow-man's private experience. By the operation of these constructs of common-sense thinking it is assumed that the sector of the world taken for granted by me is also taken for granted by you, my individual fellow-man, even more, that it is taken for granted by "Us." But this "We" does not merely include you and me but "everyone who is one of us," i.e., everyone whose system of relevances is substantially (sufficiently) in conformity with yours and mine. . . .

We must interpret the terms "objects" and "aspect of objects" in the broadest possible sense as signifying objects of knowledge taken for granted. If we do so, we shall discover the importance of the constructs of intersubjective thought objects, originating in the structural socialization of knowledge just described, for many problems investigated, but not thoroughly analyzed, by eminent social scientists. What is supposed to be known in common by everyone who shares our system of relevances is the way of life considered to be the natural, the good, the right one by the members of the "in-group";[23] as such, it is at the origin of the many recipes for handling things and men in order to come to terms with typified situations, of the folkways and mores, of "traditional behavior," in Max Weber's sense,[24] of the "of-course state-

[23] William Graham Sumner, *Folkways, A Study of the Sociological Importance of Manners, Customs, Mores and Morals,* New York, 1906.

[24] Max Weber, *The Theory of Social and Economic Organization,* translated by A. M. Henderson and Talcott Parsons, New York, 1947, pp. 115ff; see also Talcott Parsons, *The Structure of Social Action,* New York, 1937, Ch. XVI.

ments'' believed to be valid by the in-group in spite of their inconsistencies,[25] briefly, of the "relative natural aspect of the world."[26] All these terms refer to constructs of a typified knowledge of a highly socialized structure which supersede the thought objects of my and my fellow-man's private knowledge of the world as taken for granted. Yet this knowledge has its history, it is a part of our "social heritage," and this brings us to the second aspect of the problem of socialization of knowledge, its genetic structure.

b) The social origin of knowledge

Only a very small part of my knowledge of the world originates within my personal experience. The greater part is socially derived, handed down to me by my friends, my parents, my teachers and the teachers of my teachers. I am taught not only how to define the environment (that is, the typical features of the relative natural aspect of the world prevailing in the in-group as the unquestioned but always questionable sum total of things taken for granted until further notice), but also how typical constructs have to be formed in accordance with the system of relevances accepted from the anonymous unified point of view of the in-group. This includes ways of life, methods of coming to terms with the environment, efficient recipes for the use of typical means for bringing about typical ends in typical situations. The typifying medium *par excellence* by which socially derived knowledge is transmitted is the vocabulary and the syntax of everyday language. The vernacular of everyday life is primarily a language of named things and events, and any name includes a typification and generalization referring to the relevance system prevailing in the linguistic in-group which found the named thing significant enough to provide a separate term for it. The pre-scientific vernacular can be interpreted as a treasure house

[25] Robert S. Lynd, *Middletown in Transition*, New York, 1937, Ch. XII, and *Knowledge for What?*, Princeton, 1939, pp. 38-63.
[26] Max Scheler, *Die Wissensformen und die Gesellschaft, Probleme einer Soziologie des Wissens*, Leipzig, 1926, pp. 58ff. Cf. Howard Becker and Helmut Dahlke, "Max Scheler's Sociology of Knowledge," *Philosophy and Phenomenological Research*, Vol. II, 1942, pp. 310-22, esp. 315.

of ready made pre-constituted types and characteristics, all socially derived and carrying along an open horizon of unexplored content.[27]

c) The social distribution of knowledge

Knowledge is socially distributed. The general thesis of reciprocal perspectives, to be sure, overcomes the difficulty that my actual knowledge is merely the potential knowledge of my fellow-men and vice versa. But the stock of *actual* knowledge at hand differs from individual to individual, and common-sense thinking takes this fact into account. Not only *what* an individual knows differs from what his neighbor knows, but also *how* both know the "same" facts. Knowledge has manifold degrees of clarity, distinctness, precision, and familiarity. To take as an example William James'[28] well known distinction between "knowledge of acquaintance" and "knowledge-about," it is obvious that many things are known to me just in the dumb way of mere acquaintance, whereas *you* have knowledge "about" what makes them what they are and vice versa. I am an "expert" in a small field and "layman" in many others, and so are you.[29] Any individual's stock of knowledge at hand is at any moment of his life structured as having zones of various degrees of clarity, distinctness and precision. This structure originates in the system of prevailing relevances and is thus biographically determined. The knowledge of these individual differences is itself an element of common-sense experience: I know whom and under what typical circumstances I have to consult as a "competent" doctor or lawyer. In other words, in daily life I construct types of the Other's field of acquaintance and of the scope and texture of his knowledge. In doing so, I assume that he will be guided by certain relevance structures, expressing themselves in a set of constant motives leading to a particular pattern of action and even co-determining his personality. But this statement anticipates the analysis of the common-sense constructs related to the understanding of our fellow-men, which is our next task.

[27] See "Language, Language Disturbances, and the Texture of Consciousness", *Collected Papers,* I, *op. cit.,* p. 285f.

[28] William James, l.c., Vol. I, p. 221f.

[29] Alfred Schutz, "The Well-Informed Citizen, an Essay on the Social Distribution of Knowledge," *Social Research,* Vol. 13, 1946, pp. 463-472.

3) *The structure of the social world and its typification by common-sense constructs*

I, the human being, born into the social world, and living my daily life in it, experience it as built around my place in it, as open to my interpretation and action, but always referring to my actual biographically determined situation. Only in reference to me does a certain kind of my relations with others obtain the specific meaning which I designate with the word "We"; only with reference to "Us," whose center I am, do others stand out as "You," and in reference to "You," who refer back to me, third parties stand out as "They." In the dimension of time there are with reference to me in my actual biographical moment "contemporaries," with whom a mutual interplay of action and reaction can be established; "predecessors," upon whom I cannot act, but whose past actions and their outcome are open to my interpretation and may influence my own actions; and "successors," of whom no experience is possible but toward whom I may orient my actions in a more or less empty anticipation. All these relations show the most manifold forms of intimacy and anonymity, of familiarity and strangeness, of intensity and extensity.[30]

* * *

Among my contemporaries are some with whom I share, as long as the relation lasts, not only a community of time but also of space. We shall, for the sake of terminological convenience, call such contemporaries "consociates" and the relationship prevailing among them a "face-to-face" relationship, this term being understood in a sense other than that used by Cooley[31] and his successors; we designate by it merely a purely formal aspect of social relationship equally applicable

[30] Alfred Schutz, *Der sinnhafte Aufbau der sozialen Welt,* Vienna, 1932, 2nd edition 1960. [*Phenomenology of the Social World*, trans. by George Walsh and Frederick Lehnert (Evanston, Northwestern University Press, 1967.)] See also Alfred Stonier and Karl Bode, "A New Approach to the Methodology of the Social Sciences," *Economica,* Vol. V, November, 1937, pp. 406-424, esp. pp. 416ff.

[31] Charles H. Cooley, *Social Organization,* New York, 1909, Chs. III-V; and Alfred Schutz, "The Homecomer," *American Journal of Sociology,* Vol. 50, 1945, p. 371.

to an intimate talk between friends and the co-presence of strangers in a railroad car.

Sharing a community of space implies that a certain sector of the outer world is equally within the reach of each partner, and contains objects of common interest and relevance. For each partner the other's body, his gestures, his gait and facial expressions, are immediately observable, not merely as things or events of the outer world but in their physiognomical significance, that is, as symptoms of the other's thoughts. Sharing a community of time—and this means not only of outer (chronological) time, but of inner time—implies that each partner participates in the on-rolling life of the other, can grasp in a vivid present the other's thoughts as they are built up step by step. They may thus share one another's anticipations of the future as plans, or hopes or anxieties. In brief, consociates are mutually involved in one another's biography; they are growing older together; they live, as we may call it, in a pure We-relationship.

In such a relationship, fugitive and superficial as it may be, the Other is grasped as a unique individuality (although merely one aspect of his personality becomes apparent) in its unique biographical situation (although revealed merely fragmentarily). In all the other forms of social relationship (and even in the relationship among consociates as far as the unrevealed aspects of the Other's self are concerned) the fellow-man's self can merely be grasped . . . by forming a construct of a typical way of behavior, a typical pattern of underlying motives, of typical attitudes of a personality type, of which the Other and his conduct under scrutiny, both outside of my observational reach, are just instances or exemplars. We cannot here[32] develop a full taxonomy of the structuredness of the social world and of the various forms of constructs of course-of-action types and personality types needed for grasping the Other and his behavior. Thinking of my absent friend A, I form an ideal type of his personality and behavior based on my past experience of A as my consociate. Putting a letter in the mailbox, I expect that unknown people, called postmen, will act in a typical way, not quite intelligible to me, with the result that my letter will reach the addressee within typically reasonable time. Without ever having met a Frenchman or a German, I understand "Why France fears the rearmament of Germany." . . .

These are just a few examples but they are arranged according to the

[32] See footnote 30.

degree of increasing anonymity of the relationship among contemporaries involved and therewith of the construct needed to grasp the Other and his behavior. It becomes apparent that an increase in anonymity involves a decrease of fullness of content. The more anonymous the typifying construct is, the more detached it is from the uniqueness of the individual fellow-man involved and the fewer aspects of his personality and behavior pattern enter the typification as being relevant for the purpose at hand, for the sake of which the type has been constructed. If we distinguish between (subjective) personal types and (objective) course-of-action types, we may say that increasing anonymization of the construct leads to the superseding of the former by the latter. In complete anonymization the individuals are supposed to be interchangeable and the course-of-action type refers to the behavior of "whomsoever" acting in the way defined as typical by the construct.

Summing up, we may say that, except in the pure We-relation of consociates, we can never grasp the individual uniqueness of our fellow-man in his unique biographical situation. In the constructs of common-sense thinking the Other appears at best as a partial self, and he enters even the pure We-relation merely with a part of his personality. This insight seems to be important in several respects. It helped Simmel[33] to overcome the dilemma between individual and collective consciousness, so clearly seen by Durkheim[34]; it is at the basis of Cooley's[35] theory of the origin of the Self by a "looking glass effect"; it led George H.

[33] Georg Simmel: "Note on the Problem: How is Society Possible?" translated by Albion W. Small, *The American Journal of Sociology,* Vol. XVI, 1910, pp. 372-391; see also, *The Sociology of Georg Simmel,* translated, edited and with an introduction by Kurt H. Wolff, Glencoe, Ill. 1950, and consult Index under "Individual and Group".

[34] An excellent presentation of Durkheim's view in Georges Gurvitch, *La Vocation Actuelle de la Sociologie,* Paris, 1950, Ch. VI, pp. 351-409; see also Talcott Parsons, *The Structure of Social Action,* Ch. X; Emile Benoit-Smullyan: "The Sociologism of Emile Durkheim and his School," in Harry Elmer Barnes: *An Introduction to the History of Sociology,* Chicago, 1948, pp. 499-537, and Robert K. Merton: *Social Theory and Social Structure,* Glencoe, Ill. 1949, Ch. IV, pp. 125-150.

[35] Charles H. Cooley, *Human Nature and the Social Order,* rev. ed., New York, 1922, p. 184.

Mead[36] to his ingenious concept of the "generalized other"; it is, finally, decisive for the clarification of such concepts as "social functions," "social role," and, last but not least, "rational action."*

But this is merely half the story. My constructing the Other as a partial self, as the performer of typical roles or functions, has a corollary in the process of self-typification which takes place if I enter into interaction with him. I am not involved in such a relationship with my total personality but merely with certain layers of it. In defining the role of the Other I am assuming a role myself. In typifying the Other's behavior I am typifying my own, which is interrelated with his, transforming myself into a passenger, consumer, taxpayer, reader, bystander, etc. It is this self-typification which is at the bottom of William James'[37] and of George H. Mead's[38] distinction between the "I" and the "Me" in relation to the social self.

* * *

4) Course-of-action types and personal types

We have now briefly to investigate the pattern of action and social interaction which underlies the construction of course-of-action and personal types in common-sense thinking.

a) Action, project, motive

The term "action" as used in this paper shall designate human conduct devised by the actor in advance, that is, conduct based upon a preconceived project. The term "act" shall designate the outcome of this ongoing process, that is, the accomplished action. Action may be covert (for example, the attempt to solve a scientific problem mentally) or overt, gearing into the outer world; it may take place by commission or omission, purposive abstention from acting being considered an action in itself.

[36] George H. Mead: *Mind, Self, and Society,* Chicago, 1934, pp. 152-163.

* For critical clarification of this concept, see "The Problem of Rationality in the Social World", *Economica,* Vol. X, May 1943. (Eds.)

[37] William James, *op. cit.,* Vol. I, Ch. X.

[38] George H. Mead, *op. cit.,* pp. 173-175, 196-198, 203; "The Genesis of the Self," reprinted in *The Philosophy of the Present,* Chicago, 1932, pp. 176-195; "What Social Objects Must Psychology Presuppose?" *Journal of Philosophy,* Vol. X, 1913, pp. 374-380.

All projecting consists in anticipation of future conduct by way of phantasying, yet it is not the ongoing process of action but the phantasied act as having been accomplished which is the starting point of all projecting. I have to visualize the state of affairs to be brought about by my future action before I can draft the single steps of such future acting from which this state of affairs will result. Metaphorically speaking, I must have some idea of the structure to be erected before I can draft the blueprints. Thus I have to place myself in my phantasy at a future time, when this action *will* already *have been* accomplished. Only then may I reconstruct in phantasy the single steps which *will have* brought forth this future act. In the terminology suggested, it is not the future action but the future act that is anticipated in the project, and it is anticipated in the Future Perfect Tense, *modo futuri exacti*. This time perspective peculiar to the project has rather important consequences.

i) All projects of my forthcoming acts are based upon my knowledge at hand at the time of projecting. To this knowledge belongs my experience of previously performed acts which are typically similar to the projected one. Consequently all projecting involves a particular idealization, called by Husserl the idealization of "I-can-do-it-again,"[39] i.e., the assumption that I may under typically similar circumstances act in a way typically similar to that in which I acted before in order to bring about a typically similar state of affairs. It is clear that this idealization involves a construction of a specific kind. . . . The first action A' started within a set of circumstances C' and indeed brought about the state of affairs S'; the repeated action A'' starts in a set of circumstances C'' and is expected to bring about the state of affairs S''. By necessity C'' will differ from C' because the experience that A' succeeded in bringing about S' belongs to my stock of knowledge, which is an element of C'', whereas to my stock of knowledge, which was an element of C', belonged merely the empty anticipation that this would be the case. Similarly S'' will differ from S' as A'' will from A'. This is so because all the terms—C', C'', A', A'', S', S''—are as such unique and ir-

[39] Edmund Husserl, *Formale und transzendentale Logik,* Halle, 1929, Sec. 74, p. 167 [*Formal and Transcendental Logic*, trans. by Dorion Cairns (The Hague: Martinus Nijhoff, 1970)]; *Erfahrung and Urteil*, Sec. 24, Sec. 51b.

retrievable events. Yet exactly those features which make them unique and irretrievable in the strict sense are — to my common-sense thinking — eliminated as being irrelevant for my purpose at hand. When making the idealization of "I-can-do-it-again" I am merely interested in the typicality of A, C, and S, all of them without primes. The construction consists, figuratively speaking, in the suppression of the primes as being irrelevant, and this, incidentally, is characteristic of typifications of all kinds.

*   *   *

ii) The particular time perspective of the project sheds some light on the relationship between project and motive. In ordinary speech the term "motive" covers two different sets of concepts which have to be distinguished.

a) We may say that the motive of a murderer was to obtain the money of the victim. Here "motive" means the state of affairs, the end, which is to be brought about by the action undertaken. We shall call this kind of motive the "in-order-to motive." From the point of view of the actor this class of motives refers to the future. The state of affairs to be brought about by the future action, prephantasied in its project, is the in-order-to motive for carrying out the action.

b) We may say that the murderer has been motivated to commit his deed because he grew up in this or that environment, had these or those childhood experiences, etc. This class of motives, which we shall call "(genuine)[39a] because-motives" refers from the point of view of the actor to his past experiences which have determined him to act as he did. What is motivated in an action in the form of "because" is the project of the action itself (for instance, to satisfy his need for money by killing a man).

We cannot enter here[40] into a more detailed analysis of the theory of motives. But it should be pointed out that the actor who lives in his ongoing process of acting has merely the in-order-to motive of his ongoing action in view, that is, the projected state of affairs to be brought

---

[39a]Linguistically in-order-to motives may be expressed in modern languages also by "because"-sentences. Genuine because-motives, however, cannot be expressed by "in-order-to" sentences. . . .

[40] See footnote 30.

about. Only by turning back to his accomplished act or to the past initial phases of his still ongoing action or to the once established project which anticipates the act *modo futuri exacti* can the actor grasp retrospectively the because-motive that determined him to do what he did or what he projected to do. But then the actor is not acting any more; he is an observer of himself.

The distinction between the two kinds of motives becomes of vital importance for the analysis of human interaction to which we now turn.

b) Social interaction

Any form of social interaction is founded upon the constructs already described relating to the understanding of the Other and the action pattern in general. Take as an example the interaction of consociates involved in questioning and answering. In projecting my question, I anticipate that the Other will understand my action (for instance my uttering an interrogative sentence) as a question and that this understanding will induce him to act in such a way that I may understand his behavior as an adequate response. (I: "Where is the ink?" The Other points at a table.) The in-order-to motive of my action is to obtain adequate information which, in this particular situation, presupposes that the understanding of my in-order-to motive will become the Other's because-motive to perform an action in-order-to furnish me this information—provided he is able and willing to do so, which I assume he is. . . . Our example shows that even the simplest interaction in common life presupposes a series of common-sense constructs—in this case constructs of the Other's anticipated behavior—all of them based on the idealization that the actor's in-order-to motives will become because-motives of his partner and vice versa. We shall call this *idealization* that *of the reciprocity of motives.* It is obvious that this idealization depends upon the general thesis of the reciprocity of perspectives, since it implies that the motives imputed to the Other are typically the same as my own or that of others in typically similar circumstances; all this is in accordance with my genuine or socially derived knowledge at hand.

Suppose now that I want to find some ink in order to refill my fountain pen so that I can write this application to the fellowship committee which, if granted, will change my entire way of life. I, the actor (questioner), and I alone know of this plan of mine to obtain the fellowship which is the ultimate in-order-to motive of my actual action, the state of affairs to be brought about. Of course, this can be done merely by a series of steps (writing an application, bringing writing tools within my reach, etc.) each of them to be materialized by an "action" with its particular project and its particular in-order-to motive. Yet all these "sub-actions" are merely phases of the total action and all intermediary steps to be materialized by them are merely means for attaining my final goal as defined by my original project. It is the span of this original project which welds together the chain of sub-projects into a unit. . . .

In other words, only the actor knows "when his action starts and where it ends," that is, why it will have been performed. It is the span of his projects which determines the unit of his action. His partner has neither knowledge of the projecting preceding the actor's action nor of the context of a higher unit in which it stands. He knows merely that fragment of the actor's action which has become manifest to him, namely, the performed act observed by him or the past phases of the still ongoing action. If the addressee of my question were asked later on by a third person what I wanted from him he would answer that I wanted to know where to find some ink. That is all he knows of my projecting and its context, and he has to look at it as a selfcontained unit action. In order to "understand" what I, the actor, meant by my action he would have to start from the observed act and to construct from there my underlying in-order-to motive for the sake of which I did what he observed.

It is now clear that the meaning of an action is necessarily a different one (a) for the actor; (b) for his partner involved with him in interaction and having, thus, with him a set of relevances and purposes in common; and (c) for the observer not involved in such relationship. This fact leads to two important consequences: First, that in common-sense thinking we have merely a *chance* to understand the Other's action sufficiently for our purpose at hand; secondly that to increase this chance we have to search for the meaning the action has for the actor. Thus, the postulate of the "subjective interpretation of meaning," as the unfortunate term goes, is not a particularity of Max Weber's[41] sociology or of the methodology of the social sciences in general but a principle of

---

[41] Max Weber, *op. cit.*, pp. 9, 18, 22, 90, esp. p. 88: "In 'action' is included all human behavior when and insofar as the acting individual attaches a subjective meaning to it . . . Action is social insofar as, by virtue of the subjective meaning attached to it by the acting individual (or individuals), it takes account of the behavior of others and is thereby oriented in it course." See Talcott Parsons, *op. cit.*, esp. pp. 82ff, 345-47, and 484ff; Felix Kaufmann, *op. cit.*, pp. 166f.

constructing course-of-action types in common-sense experience.*

But subjective interpretation of meaning is merely possible by revealing the motives which determine a given course of action. By referring a course-of-action type to the underlying typical motives of the actor we arrive at the construction of a personal type. The latter may be more or less anonymous and, therewith, more or less empty of content. In the We-relationship among consociates the Other's course of action, its motives (insofar as they become manifest) and his person (insofar as it is involved in the manifest action) can be shared in immediacy and the constructed types, just described, will show a very low degree of anonymity and a high degree of fullness. In constructing course-of-action types of contemporaries other than consociates, we impute to the more or less anonymous actors a set of supposedly invariant motives which govern their actions. This set is itself a construct of typical expectations of the Other's behavior and has been investigated frequently in terms of social role or function or institutional behavior. In common-sense thinking such a construct has a particular significance for projecting actions which are oriented upon my contemporaries' (not my consociates') behavior. Its functions can be described as follows:

I) I take it for granted that my action (say putting a stamped and duly addressed envelope in a mailbox) will induce anonymous fellow-men (postmen) to perform typical actions (handling the mail) in accordance with typical in-order-to motives (to live up to their occupational duties) with the result that the state of affairs projected by me (delivery of the letter to the addressee within reasonable time) will be achieved. 2) I also take it for granted that my construct of the Other's course-of-action type corresponds substantially to his own self-typification and that to the latter belongs a typified construct of my, his anonymous partner's, typical way of behavior based on typical and supposedly invariant motives. ("Whoever puts a duly addressed and stamped envelope in the mailbox is assumed to intend to have it delivered to the addressee in due time.") 3) Even more, in my own self-typification—that is by assuming the role of a customer of the mail service—I have to project my action in such a typical way as I suppose the typical post office employee expects a typical customer to behave. Such a construct of mutually interlocked behavior patterns reveals itself as a construct of mutually interlocked in-order-to and because motives which are supposedly invariant. The

* Cf. "Concept and Theory Formation in the Social Sciences," *Collected Papers*, I, *op. cit.*, p. 56f (Eds.)

more institutionalized or standardized such a behavior pattern is, that is, the more typified it is in a socially approved way by laws, rules, regulations, customs, habits, etc., the greater is the chance that my own self-typifying behavior will bring about the state of affairs aimed at.

c) The observer

We have still to characterize the special case of the observer who is not a partner in the interaction patterns. His motives are not interlocked with those of the observed person or persons; he is "tuned in" upon them but not they upon him. In other words, the observer does not participate in the complicated mirror-reflexes involved by which in the interaction pattern among contemporaries, the actor's in-order-to motives become understandable to the partner as his own because motives and vice versa. Precisely this fact constitutes the so-called "disinterestedness" or detachment of the observer. He is not involved in the actor's hopes and fears whether or not they will understand one another and achieve their end by the interlocking of motives. Thus, his system of relevances differs from that of the interested parties and permits him to see at the same time more and less than what is seen by them. But under all circumstances, it is merely the manifested fragments of the actions of *both* partners that are accessible to his observation. In order to understand them the observer has to avail himself of his knowledge of typically similar patterns of interaction in typically similar situational settings and has to construct the motives of the actors from that sector of the course of action which is patent to his observation. The constructs of the observer are, therefore, different ones than those used by the participants in the interaction, if for no other reason than the fact that the purpose of the observer is different from that of the interactors and therewith the systems of relevances attached to such purposes are also different. There is a mere chance, although a chance sufficient for many practical purposes, that the observer in daily life can grasp the subjective meaning of the actor's acts. This chance increases with the degree of anonymity and standardization of the observed behavior. The scientific observer of human interrelation patterns, the social scientist, has to develop specific methods for the building of his constructs in order to assure their applicability for the interpretation of the subjective meaning the observed acts have for the actors. Among these devices we are here especially concerned with the constructs of models of so-called rational actions. Let us consider first the possible meaning of the term "rational action" within the common-sense experience of everyday life.

III. RATIONAL ACTION WITHIN
COMMON-SENSE EXPERIENCE

Ordinary language does not sharply distinguish among a sensible, a reasonable, and a rational way of conduct. We may say that a man acted sensibly if the motive and the course of his action is understandable to us, his partners or observers. This will be the case if his action is in accordance with a socially approved set of rules and recipes for coming to terms with typical problems by applying typical means for achieving typical ends. If I, if We, if "Anybody who is one of us" found himself in typically similar circumstances he would act in a similar way. Sensible behavior, however, does not presuppose that the actor is guided by insight into his motives and the means-ends context. A strong emotional reaction against an offender might be sensible and refraining from it foolish. If an action seems to be sensible to the observer and is, in addition, supposed to spring from a judicious choice among different courses of action, we may call it reasonable even if such action follows traditional or habitual patterns just taken for granted. Rational action, however, presupposes that the actor has clear and distinct insight into the end, the means, and the secondary results, which "involves rational consideration of alternative means to the end, of the relations of the end to other prospective results of employment of any given means and, finally, of the relative importance of different possible ends. Determination of action, either in affectual or in traditional terms, is thus incompatible with this type."[42]

These very preliminary definitions for sensible, reasonable, and ra-

---

[42] Max Weber, *op. cit.*, p. 117. The characterization of "rational action" follows Max Weber's definition of one of the two types of rational actions distinguished by him, (*op. cit.*, p. 115) namely, the so-called "*zweckrationales Handeln*" (rendered in Parsons' translation by "rational orientation to a system of discrete ends"). We disregard here Weber's second type of rational action, the "*wertrationales Handeln*" (rendered by "rational orientation to an absolute value") since the distinction between both types can be reduced in the terms of the present discussion to a distinction between two types of "because-motives" leading to the project of an action as such. . . .

tional actions are stated in terms of common-sense interpretations of other people's actions in daily life but, characteristically, they refer not only to the stock of knowledge taken for granted in the in-group to which the observer of this course of action belongs but also to the subjective point of view of the actor, that is, to his stock of knowledge at hand at the time of carrying out the action. This involves several difficulties. First, it is, as we have seen, our biographical situation which determines the problem at hand and, therewith, the systems of relevances under which the various aspects of the world are constructed in the form of types. Of necessity, therefore, the actor's stock of knowledge will differ from that of the observer. Even the general thesis of the reciprocity of perspectives is not sufficient to eliminate this difficulty because it presupposes that both the observed and the observer are sharing a system of relevances sufficiently homogeneous in structure and content for the practical purpose involved. If this is not the case, then a course of action which is perfectly rational from the point of view of the actor may appear as non-rational to the partner or observer and vice versa. . . .

Secondly, even if we restrict our investigation to the subjective point of view, we have to ascertain whether there is a difference in the meaning of the term "rational," in the sense of reasonable, if applied to my own past acts or to the determination of a future course of my actions. At first glance, it seems that the difference is considerable. What I did has been done and cannot be undone, although the state of affairs brought about by my actions might be modified or eliminated by countermoves. I do not have, with respect to past actions, the possibility of choice. Anything anticipated in an empty way in the project which had preceded my past action has been fulfilled or not by the outcome of my action. On the other hand, all future action is projected under the idealization of "I can do it again," which may or may not stand the test.

Closer analysis shows, however, that even in judging the reasonableness of our own past action we refer always to our knowledge at hand at the time of projecting such action. If we find, retrospectively, that what we had formerly projected as a reasonable course of action under the then known circumstances proved to be a failure, we may accuse ourselves of various mistakes: of an error in judgment if the then prevailing circumstances were incorrectly or incompletely ascertained; or of a lack of foresight if we failed to anticipate future developments, etc. We will, however, not say that we acted unreasonably.

Thus, in both cases, that of the past and of the future action, our judgment of reasonableness refers to the project determining the course of action and, still more precisely, to the choice among several projects of action involved. As has been shown elsewhere,[43] any projecting of future action involves a choice between at least two courses of conduct, namely, to carry out the projected action or to refrain from doing so.

Each of the alternatives standing to choice has, as Dewey says,[44] to be rehearsed in phantasy in order to make choice and decision possible. If this deliberation is to be strictly a rational one then the actor must have a clear and distinct knowledge of the following elements of each projected course-of-action standing to choice:

   a) of the particular state of affairs within which his projected action has to start. This involves a sufficiently precise definition of his biographical situation in the physical and sociocultural environment;

   b) of the state of affairs to be brought about by his projected action, that is, its end. Yet since there is no such thing as an isolated project or end (all my projects, present to my mind at a given time, being integrated into systems of projects, called my plans and all my plans being integrated into my plan of life), there are also no isolated ends. They are interconnected in a hierarchical order, and the attaining of one might have repercussions on the other. I have, therefore, to have clear and distinct knowledge of the place of my project within the hierarchical order of my plans (or the interrelationship of the end to be achieved with other ends), the compatibility of one with the other, and the possible repercussions of one upon another, briefly: of the secondary results of my future action, as Max Weber calls it;[45]

   c) of the various means necessary for attaining the established end, of the possibility of bringing them within my reach, of the degree of the expediency of their application, of the possible employment of these same means for the attainment of other potential ends, and of the compatibility of the selected means with other means needed for the materialization of other projects.

The complication increases considerably if the actor's project of a ra-

---

[43] "Choosing Among Projects of Action," *Collected Papers*, I, pp. 67-96.
[44] John Dewey, *Human Nature and Conduct,* Modern Library edition, p. 190.
[45] See quotation from Max Weber on p. 311.

tional action involves the rational action or reaction of a fellow-man, say of a consociate. Projecting rationally such a kind of action involves sufficiently clear and distinct knowledge of the situation of departure not only as defined by me but also as defined by the Other. Moreover, there has to be sufficient likelihood that the Other will be tuned in upon me and consider my action as relevant enough to be motivated in the way of because by my in-order-to motive. If this is the case, then there has to be a sufficient chance that the Other will understand me, and this means in the case of a rational interrelationship that he will interpret my action rationally as being a rational one and that he will react in a rational way. To assume that the Other will do so implies, however, on the one hand, that he will have sufficiently clear and distinct knowledge of my project and of its place in the hierarchy of my plans (at least as far as my overt actions make them manifest to him) and of my system of relevances attached thereto; and, on the other hand, that the structure and scope of his stock of knowledge at hand will be in its relevant portion substantially similar to mine and that his and my system of relevances will, if not overlap, be at least partially congruent. If, furthermore, I assume in my projecting that the Other's reaction to my projected action will be a rational one, I suppose that he, in projecting his response, knows all the aforementioned elements (a), (b), (c) of his reaction in a clear and distinct way. Consequently, if I project a rational action which requires an interlocking of my and the Other's motives of action to be carried out (e.g., I want the Other to do something for me), I must, by a curious mirror-effect, have sufficient knowledge of what he, the Other, knows (and knows to be relevant with respect to my purpose at hand), and this knowledge of his is supposed to include sufficient acquaintance with what I know. This is a condition of *ideally* rational interaction because without such mutual knowledge I could not "rationally" project the attainment of my goal by means of the Other's cooperation or reaction. Moreover, such mutual knowledge has to be clear and distinct; merely a more or less empty expectation of the Other's behavior is not sufficient.

It seems that under these circumstances rational social interaction becomes impracticable even among consociates. And yet we receive reasonable answers to reasonable questions, our commands are carried out, we perform in factories and laboratories and offices highly "rationalized" activities, we play chess together, briefly, we come conveniently to terms with our fellow-men. How is this possible?

Two different answers seem to offer themselves. First, if interaction among consociates is involved we may assume that the mutual participation in the consociate's onrolling life, the sharing of his anticipations so characteristic of the pure We-relation establishes the prerequisites for rational interaction just analyzed. Yet it is precisely this pure We-relation which is the irrational element of any interrelationship among consociates. The second answer refers not only to the interrelationship among consociates but among contemporaries in general. We may explain the rationality of human interaction by the fact that both actors orient their actions on certain standards which are socially approved as rules of conduct by the in-group to which they belong: norms, mores of good behavior, manners, the organizational framework provided for this particular form of division of labor, the rules of the chess game, etc. But neither the origin nor the import of the socially approved standard is "rationally" understood. Such standards might be traditionally or habitually accepted as just being taken for granted, and, within the meaning of our previous definitions, behavior of this kind will be sensible or even reasonable but not necessarily rational. At any rate, it will not be "ideally" rational, that is, meeting all the requirements worked out in the analysis of this concept.

We come, therefore, to the conclusion that "rational action" on the common-sense level is always action within an unquestioned and undetermined frame of constructs of typicalities of the setting, the motives, the means and ends, the courses of action and personalities involved and taken for granted. . . . Thus we may say that on this level actions are at best partially rational and that rationality has many degrees. For instance, our assumption that our fellow-man who is involved with us in a pattern of interaction knows its rational elements will never reach "empirical certainty" (certainty "until further notice" or "good until counterevidence")[46] but will always bear the character of plausibility, that is, of subjective likelihood (in contradistinction to mathematical probability). We always have to "take chances" and to "run risks," and this situation is expressed by our hopes and fears which are merely the subjective corollaries of our basic uncertainty as to the outcome of our projected interaction.

To be sure, the more standardized the prevailing action pattern is, the more anonymous it is, the greater is the subjective chance of conformity and, therewith, of the success of intersubjective behavior. Yet—and this is the paradox of rationality on the common-sense level—the more stand-

[46] Edmund Husserl, *Erfahrung und Urteil,* Sec. 77, p. 370.

ardized the pattern is, the less the underlying elements become analyzable for common-sense thought in terms of rational insight.

All this refers to the criterion of rationality as applicable to the thinking of everyday life and its constructs. Only on the level of models of interaction patterns constructed by the social scientist in accordance with certain particular requirements defined by the methods of his science does the concept of rationality obtain its full significance. In order to make this clear we have first to examine the basic character of such scientific constructs and their relationship to the "reality" of the social world, as such reality presents itself to the common-sense thought of everyday life.

IV. CONSTRUCTS OF THOUGHT OBJECTS BY THE SOCIAL SCIENCES

1) The postulate of subjective interpretation

. . . In the following pages we take the position that the social sciences have to deal with human conduct and its common-sense interpretation in the social reality, involving the analysis of the whole system of projects and motives, of relevances and constructs dealt with in the preceding sections. Such an analysis refers by necessity to the subjective point of view, namely, to the interpretation of the action and its settings in terms of the actor. Since this postulate of the subjective interpretation is, as we have seen, a general principle of constructing course-of-action types in common-sense experience, any social science aspiring to grasp "social reality" has to adopt this principle also.

Yet, at first glance, it seems that this statement is in contradiction to the well-established method of even the most advanced social sciences. Take as an example modern economics. . . . Does not the economist investigate successfully subject matters such as "savings," "capital," "business cycle," "wages" and "unemployment," "multipliers" and "monopoly" as if these phenomena were entirely detached from any activity of the economic subjects, even less without entering into the subjective meaning structure such activities may have for them? The achievements of modern economic theories would make it preposterous to deny that an abstract conceptual scheme can be used very successfully for the solution of many problems. . . . Closer investigation, however, reveals that this abstract conceptual scheme is nothing else than a kind of intellectual shorthand and that the underlying subjective elements of human actions involved are either taken for granted or deemed to be irrelevant with respect to the scientific purpose at hand . . . and are, therefore, disregarded. Correctly understood, the postulate of subjective interpretation as applied to economics as well as to all the other social sciences means merely that we always *can*—and for certain purposes *must*—refer to the activities of the subjects within the social world and their interpretation by the actors in terms of systems of projects, available means, motives, relevances, and so on.[47]

But if this is true, two other questions have to be answered. First, we have seen from the previous analyses that the subjective meaning an action has for an actor is unique and individual because it originates in the unique and individual biographical situation of the actor. How is it then possible to grasp subjective meaning scientifically? Secondly, the meaning context of any system of scientific knowledge is objective knowledge but accessible equally to all his fellow scientists and open to their control, which means capable of being verified, invalidated, or falsified by them. How is it, then, possible to grasp by a system of objective knowledge subjective meaning structures? Is this not a paradox?

Both questions can be satisfactorily met by a few simple considerations. As to the first question, we learned from Whitehead that all sciences have to construct thought objects of their own which supersede the thought objects of common-sense thinking.[48] The thought objects constructed by the social sciences do not refer to unique acts of unique individuals occurring within a unique situation. By particular methodological devices, to be described presently, the social scientist replaces the thought objects of common-sense thought relating to unique events and occurrences by constructing a model of a sector of the social world within which merely those typified events occur that are relevant to the scientist's particular problem under scrutiny. All the other happenings within the social world are considered as being irrelevant, as contingent "data," which have to be put beyond question by appropriate methodological techniques as, for instance, by the assumption "all other things being equal."[49] Nevertheless, it is possible to con-

---

[47] Ludwig Von Mises rightly calls his "Treatise on Economics" *Human Action,* New Haven, 1949. See also F. A. Hayek, *The Counter-Revolution of Science,* Glencoe, 1952, pp. 25-36.

[48] See above, pp. 292-93.

[49] On this concept see Felix Kaufman, *op. cit.*, pp. 84ff and 213ff, on the concept "scientific situation" p. 52 and 251 n. 4.

struct a model of a sector of the social world consisting of typical human interaction and to analyze this typical interaction pattern as to the meaning it might have for the personal types of actors who presumptively originated them.

The second question has to be faced. It is indeed the particular problem of the social sciences to develop methodological devices for attaining objective and verifiable knowledge of a subjective meaning structure. In order to make this clear we have to consider very briefly the particular attitude of the scientist to the social world.

2) *The social scientist as disinterested observer*

This attitude of the social scientist is that of a mere disinterested observer of the social world. He is not involved in the observed situation, which is to him not of practical but merely of cognitive interest. It is not the theater of his activities but merely the object of his contemplation. . . .

A word of caution is necessary here to prevent possible misunderstandings. Of course, in his daily life the social scientist remains a human being, a man living among his fellow-men, with whom he is interrelated in many ways. And, surely, scientific activity itself occurs within the tradition of socially derived knowledge, is based upon cooperation with other scientists, requires mutual corroboration and criticism and can only be communicated by social interaction. . . . Dealing with science and scientific matters within the social world is one thing, the specific scientific attitude which the scientist has to adopt toward his object is another, and it is the latter which we propose to study in the following.

. . . By resolving to adopt the disinterested attitude of a scientific observer—in our language, by establishing the life-plan for scientific work —the social scientist detaches himself from his biographical situation within the social world. What is taken for granted in the biographical situation of daily life may become questionable for the scientist, and vice versa; what seems to be of highest relevance on one level may become entirely irrelevant on the other. The center of orientation has been radically shifted and so has the hierarchy of plans and projects. By making up his mind to carry out a plan for scientific work governed by the disinterested quest for truth in accordance with preestablished rules, called the scientific method, the scientist has entered a field of preorganized knowledge, called the corpus of his science.[50] He has either to accept what is considered by his fellow-scientist as established knowledge or to "show cause" why he cannot do so. Merely within this frame may he select his particular scientific problem and make his scientific decisions. This frame constitutes his "being in a scientific situation" which supersedes his biographical situation as a human being within the world. It is henceforth the scientific problem once established which determines alone what is and what is not relevant to its solution, and thus what has to be investigated and what can be taken for granted as a "datum," and, finally, the level of research in the broadest sense, that is, the abstractions, generalizations, formalizations, idealizations, briefly, the constructs required and admissible for considering the problem as being solved. . . . It follows that any shifting of the problem under scrutiny and the level of research involves a modification of the structures of relevance and of the constructs formed for the solution of another problem or on another level; a great many misunderstandings and controversies, especially in the social sciences, originate from disregarding this fact.

3) Differences between common-sense and scientific constructs of action patterns

Let us consider very briefly (and very incompletely) some of the more important differences between common-sense constructs and scientific constructs of interaction patterns originating in the transition from the biographically determined to the scientific situation. Common-sense constructs are formed from a "Here" within the world which determines the presupposed reciprocity of perspectives. They take a stock of socially derived and socially approved knowledge for granted. The social distribution of knowledge determines the particular structure of the typifying construct, for instance, the assumed degree of anonymity of personal roles, the standardization of course-of-action patterns, and the supposed constancy of motives. Yet this social distribution itself depends upon the heterogeneous composition of the stock of knowledge at hand which itself is an element of common-sense experience. The concepts of "We," "You," "They," of "in-group" and "out-group," of consociates, contemporaries, predecessors, and successors, all of them with

---

[50] *Ibid.*, pp. 42 and 232.

their particular structurization of familiarity and anonymity are at least implied in the common-sense typifications or even co-constitutive for them. All this holds good not only for the participants in a social interaction pattern but also for the mere observer of such interaction who still makes his observations from his biographical situation within the social world. The difference between both is merely that the participant in the interaction pattern, guided by the idealization of reciprocity of motives, assumes his own motives as being interlocked with that of his partners, whereas to the observer merely the manifest fragments of the actors' actions are accessible. Yet both, participants and observer, form their common-sense constructs relatively to their biographical situation. In either case, these constructs have a particular place within the chain of motives originating in the biographically determined hierarchy of the constructor's plans.

The constructs of human interaction patterns formed by the social scientist, however, are of an entirely different kind. The social scientist has no "Here" within the social world or, more precisely, he considers his position within it and the system of relevances attached thereto as irrelevant for his scientific undertaking. His stock of knowledge at hand is the corpus of his science, and he has to take it for granted—which means, in this context, as scientifically ascertained—unless he makes explicit why he cannot do so. To this corpus of science belong also the rules of procedure which have stood the test, namely, the methods of his science, including the methods of forming constructs in a scientifically sound way. This stock of knowledge is of quite another structure than that which man in everyday life has at hand. To be sure, it will also show manifold degrees of clarity and distinctness. But this structurization will depend upon knowledge of problems solved, of their still hidden implications and open horizons of other still not formulated problems. The scientist takes for granted what he defines to be a datum, and this is independent of the beliefs accepted by any in-group in the world of everyday life.[51] The scientific problem, once established, determines alone the structure of relevances.

* * *

Thus, adopting the scientific attitude, the social scientist observes human interaction patterns or their results insofar as they are accessible to his observation and open to his interpretation. These interaction pat-

[51] We intentionally disregard the problems of the so-called sociology of knowledge here involved.

terns, however, he has to interpret in terms of their subjective meaning structure lest he abandon any hope of grasping "social reality."

In order to comply with this postulate, the scientific observer proceeds in a way similar to that of the observer of a social interaction pattern in the world of everyday life, although guided by an entirely different system of relevances.

4) The scientific model of the social world[52]

He begins to construct typical course-of-action patterns corresponding to the observed events. Thereupon he co-ordinates to these typical course-of-action patterns a personal type, a model of an actor whom he imagines as being gifted with consciousness. Yet it is a consciousness restricted to containing nothing but all the elements relevant to the performance of the course-of-action patterns under observation and relevant, therewith, to the scientist's problem under scrutiny. He ascribes, thus, to this fictitious consciousness a set of typical in-order-to motives corresponding to the goals of the observed course-of-action patterns and typical because-motives upon which the in-order-to motives are founded. Both types of motives are assumed to be invariant in the mind of the imaginary actor-model.

Yet these models of actors are not human beings living within their biographical situation in the social world of everyday life. Strictly speaking, they do not have any biography or any history, and the situation into which they are placed is not a situation defined by them but defined by their creator, the social scientist. He has created these puppets or homunculi to manipulate them for his purpose. A merely specious consciousness is imputed to them by the scientist, which is constructed in such a way that its presupposed stock of knowledge at hand (including the ascribed set of invariant motives) would make actions originating from it subjectively understandable, provided that these actions were performed by real actors within the social world. But the puppet and his artificial consciousness is not subjected to the ontological conditions of human beings. . . . Whereas man, as Simmel has clearly seen,[53] enters any social relationship merely with a part of his

---

[52] To this section cf. in addition to the literature mentioned in footnotes 30 and 43, Alfred Schutz: "The Problem of Rationality in the Social World," *Economica*, Vol. X, May 1943, pp. 130-149.

[53] See footnote 33 above.

self and is, at the same time, always within and outside of such a relationship, the homunculus, placed into a social relationship is involved therein in his totality. He is nothing else but the originator of his typical function because the artificial consciousness imputed to him contains merely those elements which are necessary to make such functions subjectively meaningful.

. . . It is he, the social scientist, who sets the stage, who distributes the roles, who gives the cues, who defines when an "action" starts and when it ends and who determines, thus, the "span of projects" involved. All standards and institutions governing the behavioral pattern of the model are supplied from the outset by the constructs of the scientific observer.

In such a simplified model of the social world pure rational acts, rational choices from rational motives are possible because all the difficulties encumbering the real actor in the everyday life-world have been eliminated. Thus, the concept of rationality in the strict sense already defined does not refer to actions within the common-sense experience of everyday life in the social world; it is the expression for a *particular* type of constructs of *certain specific* models of the social world made by the social scientist for certain specific methodological purposes.

Before discussing the particular functions of "rational" models of the social world, however, we have to indicate some principles governing the construction of scientific models of human action in general.

5) Postulates for scientific model constructs of the social world

We said before that it is the main problem of the social sciences to develop a method in order to deal in an objective way with the subjective meaning of human action and that the thought objects of the social sciences have to remain consistent with the thought objects of common sense, formed by men in everyday life in order to come to terms with social reality. The model constructs as described before fulfill these requirements if they are formed in accordance with the following postulates:

a) The postulate of logical consistency

The system of typical constructs designed by the scientist has to be established with the highest degree of clarity and distinctness of the conceptual framework implied and must be fully compatible with the principles of formal logic. Fulfillment of this postulate warrants the objective validity of the thought objects constructed by the social scientist, and their strictly logical character is one of the most important features by which scientific thought objects are distinguished from the thought objects constructed by common-sense thinking in daily life which they have to supersede.

b) The postulate of subjective interpretation

In order to explain human actions the scientist has to ask what model of an individual mind can be constructed and what typical contents must be attributed to it in order to explain the observed facts as the result of the activity of such a mind in an understandable relation. The compliance with this postulate warrants the possibility of referring all kinds of human action or their result to the subjective meaning such action or result of an action had for the actor.

c) The postulate of adequacy

Each term in a scientific model of human action must be constructed in such a way that a human act performed within the life-world by an individual actor in the way indicated by the typical construct would be understandable for the actor himself as well as for his fellow-men in terms of common-sense interpretation of everyday life. Compliance with this postulate warrants the consistency of the constructs of the social scientist with the constructs of common-sense experience of the social reality.

V. SCIENTIFIC MODEL CONSTRUCTS OF RATIONAL ACTION PATTERNS

All model constructs of the social world in order to be scientific have to fulfill the requirements of these three postulates. But is not any construct complying with the postulate of logical consistency, is not any scientific activity by definition a rational one?

This is certainly true but here we have to avoid a dangerous misunderstanding. We have to distinguish between rational constructs of models of human actions on the one hand, and constructs of models of rational human actions on the other. Science may construct rational models of irrational behavior, as a glance in any textbook of psychiatry shows. On the other hand, common-sense thinking frequently constructs irrational models of highly rational behavior, for example, in explaining economic, political, military and even scientific decisions by referring them to sentiments or ideologies presupposed to govern the behavior of the participants. The rationality of the construction of the model is one thing and in this sense all properly constructed models of the sciences—not merely of the social sciences—are rational; the construction of models of rational behavior is quite another thing. It would be a serious misunderstanding to believe that it is the purpose of model constructs in the social sciences or a criterion for their scientific character that irrational behavior patterns be interpreted as if they were rational.

In the following we are mainly interested in the usefulness of scientific—therefore rational—models of rational behavior patterns. It can easily be understood that the scientific construct of a perfect rational course-of-action type, of its corresponding personal type and also of rational interaction patterns is, as a matter of principle, possible. This is so because in constructing a model of a fictitious consciousness the scientist may select as relevant for his problem merely those elements which make rational actions or reactions of his homunculi possible. The postulate of rationality which such a construct would have to meet can be formulated as follows:

The rational course-of-action and personal types have to be constructed in such a way that an actor in the life-world would perform the typified action if he had a perfectly clear and distinct knowledge of all the elements, and only of the elements, assumed by the social scientist as being relevant to this action and the constant tendency to use the most appropriate means assumed to be at his disposal for achieving the ends defined by the construct itself.

The advantage of the use of such models of rational behavior in the social sciences can be characterized as follows:

I) The possibility of constructing patterns of social interaction under the assumption that all participants in such interaction act rationally within a set of conditions, means, ends, motives defined by the social scientist and supposed to be either common to all participants or distributed among them in a specific manner. By this arrangement standardized behavior such as so-called social roles, institutional behavior, etc., can be studied in isolation.

2) Whereas the behavior of individuals in the social life-world is not predictable unless in empty anticipations, the rational behavior of a constructed personal type is by definition supposed to be predictable,

within the limits of the elements typified in the construct. The model of rational action can, therefore, be used as a device for ascertaining deviating behavior in the real social world and for referring it to "problem-transcending data," that is, to non-typified elements.

3) By appropriate variations of some of the elements several models or even sets of models of rational actions can be constructed for solving the same scientific problem and compared with one another.

The last point, however, seems to require some comment. Did we not state earlier that all constructs carry along a "subscript" referring to the problem under scrutiny and have to be revised if a shift in the problem occurs? Is there not a certain contradiction between this insight and the possibility of constructing several competing models for the solution of one and the same scientific problem?

The contradiction disappears if we consider that any problem is merely a locus of implications which can be made explicit or, to use a term of Husserl's,[54] that it carries along its inner horizon of unquestioned but questionable elements.

In order to make the inner horizon of the problem explicit we may vary the conditions within which the fictitious actors are supposed to act, the elements of the world of which they are supposed to have knowledge, their assumed interlocked motives, the degree of familiarity or anonymity in which they are assumed to be interrelated, etc. . . .*

All these models are models of rational actions but not of actions performed by living human beings in situations defined by them. They are assumed to be performable by the personal types constructed by the economist within the artificial environment in which he has placed his homunculi.

VI. CONCLUDING REMARKS

The relationship between the social scientist and the puppet he has created reflects to a certain extent an age-old problem of theology and

[54] As to the concept of horizon, see Helmut Kuhn, "The Phenomenological Concept of Horizon" in *Philosophical Essays in Memory of Edmund Husserl*, edited by Marvin Farber, Cambridge, 1940, pp. 106-124 and Ludwig Landgrebe in Husserl, *Erfahrung und Urteil*, secs. 8-10.

* Footnote 55 left out; Schutz uses some examples from economics borrowed from Fritz Machlup, *The Economics of Seller's Competition Model Analysis of Seller's Conduct* (Baltimore, 1952), pp. 4 ff.

C. *Historicality*

metaphysics, that of the relationship between God and his creatures. The puppet exists and acts merely by the grace of the scientist; it cannot act otherwise than according to the purpose which the scientist's wisdom has determined it to carry out. Nevertheless, it is supposed to act as if it were not determined but could determine itself. A total harmony has been pre-established between the determined consciousness bestowed upon the puppet and the pre-constituted environment within which it is supposed to act freely, to make rational choices and decisions. This harmony is possible only because both, the puppet and its reduced environment, are the creation of the scientist. And by keeping to the principles which guided him, the scientist succeeds, indeed, in discovering within the universe, thus created, the perfect harmony established by himself.

WHAT IS CALLED THINKING?*

MARTIN HEIDEGGER

LECTURE
V

When we ask our question "What is called thinking?" in the second manner, it turns out that thinking is defined in terms of the λόγος. The basic character of thinking is constituted by propositions.

When we ask our question "What is called thinking?" in the first

---

* "Lecture" from *What is Called Thinking?* by Martin Heidegger, translated by Fred D. Wieck and J. Glenn Gray. Copyright © 1968 in the English translation by Harper & Row, Publishers, Inc. Originally published in German under the title *Was Heisst Denken?* Copyright, 1954 by Max Miemeyer Verlag, Tuebingen. Reprinted by permission of Harper & Row, Publishers, Inc.

manner, then the word "thinking" directs us to the essential sphere of memory, devotion, and thanks. In the two questions, thinking emerges from different sources of its essential nature. One might be tempted to explain the difference offhand in terms of linguistic designation. Among the Greeks, the name for the basic form of thinking, the proposition, is λόγος. Among ourselves, the name for the thing that is also concealed in the λόγος happens to be "thinking." Linguistically, the word is related to thought, memory, and thanks. But this explanation explains nothing so far, assuming any explanation could be fruitful here. The decisive question still remains this: why is it that for Greek thinking, hence Western and especially European thinking (and for us of today), thinking receives its essential character to this day from what in Greek is called λέγειν and λόγος? Just because at one time the calling into thought took place in terms of the λόγος, logistics today is developing into the global system by which all ideas are organized.

And why does the determination of the essence of thought not take place in terms of those things that are evoked in the sphere of these words *thanc*, "memory," "thanks"—particularly since what these words designate was in its essential profundity by no means unknown to the Greeks? The differences in the essential sources of thinking to which we have alluded do not, then, inhere in any way in the distinctive linguistic designations. Rather, the one and only thing that is decisive for what even still for us constitutes the basic character of thinking—the λέγειν of the λόγος, the proposition, the judgment—is that call by which thinking has been called, and is still being called, into its long-habituated nature.

When we raise the second question, what do we understand by thinking according to the prevailing doctrine, it looks at first as though we were merely seeking historical information about what view of the nature of thinking had come to predominate and is still in force. But if we ask the second question *qua* second question, that is, in the unitary context of the four modes of which we spoke, we then ask it ineluctably in the sense of the decisive fourth question. Then the question runs: what is the calling that has directed and is still directing us into thinking in the sense of the predicative λόγος?

This question is no longer historical—in the sense of narrative history—though it is an historic question. But it is not historic in the sense that it represents some occurrence as a chain of events in the course of which various things are brought about—among them this, that thinking after the manner of the λόγος achieved validity and currency. The question: "What call has directed the mode of thinking to the λέγειν of the λόγος?," is an historic, perhaps *the* historic question, though in the sense that it determines our destiny. It asks what it is that destines our nature to think according to the λόγος that directs it there, and there turns it to use, and thus implies many possible turns. Thus Plato's definition of the nature of thought is not identical with that of Leibniz, though it is the same. They belong together in that both reveal *one* basic nature, which appears in different ways.

But the fateful character of being destined to such thinking, and thus that destiny itself, will never enter our horizon so long as we conceive the historic from the start only as an occurrence, and occurrence as a causal chain of events. Nor will it do to divide the occurrences so conceived into those whose causal chain is transparent and comprehensible, and others that remain incomprehensible and opaque, what we normally call "fate." The call as destiny is so far from being incomprehensible and alien to thinking, that on the contrary it always is precisely what must be thought, and thus is waiting for a thinking that answers to it.

In order to be equal to the question what, by prevailing doctrine, is called "thinking," we simply have to risk *asking* the question. This implies: we must submit, deliver ourselves specifically to the calling that calls on us to think after the manner of the λόγος. As long as we ourselves do not set out from where we are, that is, as long as we do not open ourselves to the call and, with this question, get underway toward the call—just so long we shall remain blind to the mission and destiny of our nature. You cannot talk of colors to the blind. But a still greater ill than blindness is delusion. Delusion believes that it sees, and that it sees in the only possible manner, even while this its belief robs it of sight.

The destiny of our fateful-historic Western nature shows itself in the fact that our sojourn in this world rests upon thinking, even where this sojourn is determined by the Christian faith—faith which cannot be proved by thinking, nor is in need of proof because it is faith.

But this, that we hardly discern the destiny of our nature, and therefore pay no heed to the calling that has called us to thinking according to the λόγος, flows from still another source. The influence of that source is not up to us. But we are not for that reason excused from admitting that our understanding and explaining, our knowledge and our intelligence—that our thinking still remains totally without mission in terms of the destiny of its own being. The more completely our thinking regards itself merely in terms of its own comparative written history, and historical in *this* sense, the more decisively it will petrify in fatelessness, and the less it will arrive at the artless, fateful relation to the calling by which thinking has been directed to the basic character of the λόγος.

Our age rages in a mad, steadily growing craving to conceive history in terms of universal history, as an occurrence. Its frenzy is exacerbated and fed by the quick and easy availability of sources and means of presentation. This sounds like an exaggeration, but is a fact: the unexpressed archetype of the portrayal of all and everything in terms of universal history that is palatable today is the illustrated weekly. Universal history, operating with the most comprehensive means, assumes that a comparative portrayal of the most varied cultures, from ancient China to the Aztecs, can establish a relation to world history. This world history, however, is not the destiny of a world but rather the object established by conceiving world in terms of universal history, thus: the occurrence, to be presented from every angle, of every human achievement and failure that can in any way be found out.

World history, however, is the destiny whereby a world lays claim to us. We shall never hear that claim of the world's destiny while we are engaged on world-historic—which in this context always means universal-historical—voyages. We shall hear it only by giving heed to the simple calling of our essential mission, so that we may give it thought. The most precursory attempt to pay attention to this way is the question "What does call on us to think?" Note that we say: the question.

But even when we ask what the call to think according to the λόγος is—must we not even then go back to the early ages of Western thinking in order to comprehend what call directed this thinking to begin? This, too, seems to be only a narrative-historical and besides very risky question. After all, we know little about the early thinking of the Greeks, and that little only in fragments, and these fragments of disputed meaning. All we have left of the works of the decisive early thinkers can be put in a pamphlet of not more than thirty pages. What does that amount to, compared with the long shelves of voluminous tomes with which the works of later philosophers keep us occupied?

Inevitably it begins to look as though the attempt to ask the question "What is called thinking?" in the second manner also amounts to no more than a historical consideration of the beginnings of Western philosophy. We shall let it go at that, not because we are indifferent to that impression, but because it cannot be dispelled by talking about it instead of setting out on the way of our question.

What is that calling which commends our Western thinking to its own proper beginnings, and from there still directs even today's thinking on its way? The thinkers of the fateful beginnings of Western thought did not, of course, raise the question of the calling, as we are trying to do now. What distinguishes the beginning is rather that those thinkers experienced the claim of the calling by responding to it in thought. But with such a destiny, must they not also have come to comprehend explicitly the calling that starts their thinking on its way? We may assume so, simply because any thinking is sent out on its way only when it is addressed by that which gives food for thought as that which is-to-be-thought. In this address, however, the source of the call itself appears, though not in its full radiance nor under the same name. But before inquiring about the calling that encompasses all Western and modern European thinking, we must try to listen to an early saying which gives us evidence how much early thought generally responds to a call, yet without naming it, or giving it thought, as such. Perhaps we need no more than to recall this one testimony in order to give the fitting, that is, a restrained answer to that question of the initial calling.

The doctrine of thinking is called logic because thinking develops in the λέγειν of the λόγος. We are barely capable of comprehending that at one time this was not so, that a calling became "needful" in order to set thinking on the way of the λόγος into the λέγειν. A fragment of Parmenides, which has been given the number 6, begins with these words: " χρὴ τὸ λέγειν τε νοεῖν τ' ἐὸν ἔμμεναι ." The usual translation of the saying is: "One should both say and think that Being is."

Summary and Transition

The answer to the question "What is called thinking?" is, of course, a statement, but not a proposition that could be formed into a sentence with which the question can be put aside as settled. The answer to the question is, of course, an utterance, but it speaks from a correspondence. It follows the calling, and maintains the question in its problematic. When we follow the calling, we do not free ourselves of what is being asked.

The question cannot be settled, now or ever. If we proceed to the encounter of what is here in question, the calling, the question becomes in fact only more problematical. When we are questioning within this problematic, we are thinking.

Thinking itself is a way. We respond to the way only by remaining underway. To be underway on the way in order to clear the way—that is one thing. The other thing is to take a position somewhere along the road, and there make conversation about whether, and how, earlier and later stretches of the way may be different, and in their difference might even be incompatible—incompatible, that is, for those who never walk the way, nor ever set out on it, but merely take up a position outside it, there forever to formulate ideas and make talk about the way.

In order to get underway, we do have to set out. This is meant in a double sense: for one thing, we have to open ourselves to the emerging prospect and direction of the way itself; and then, we must get on the way, that is, must take the steps by which alone the way becomes a way.

The way of thinking cannot be traced from somewhere to somewhere like a well-worn rut, nor does it at all exist as such in any place. Only when we walk it, and in no other fashion, only, that is, by thoughtful questioning, are we on the move on the way. This movement is what allows the way to come forward. That the way of thought is of this nature is part of the precursoriness of thinking, and this precursoriness in turn depends on an enigmatic solitude, taking the word "solitude" in a high, unsentimental sense.

No thinker ever has entered into another thinker's solitude. Yet it is only from its solitude that all thinking, in a hidden mode, speaks to the thinking that comes after or that went before. The things which we conceive and assert to be the results of thinking, are the misunderstandings to which thinking ineluctably falls victim. Only they achieve publication as alleged thought, and occupy those who do *not* think.

To answer the question "What is called thinking?" is itself always to keep asking, so as to remain underway. This would seem easier than the intention to take a firm position; for adventurer-like, we roam away into the unknown. Nevertheless, if we are to remain underway we must first of all and constantly give attention to the way. The movement, step by step, is what is essential here. Thinking clears its way only by its own questioning advance. But this clearing of the way is curious. The way that is cleared does not remain behind, but is built into the next step, and is projected forward from it.

Now it always remains possible, of course, and very often actually is the case, that we dislike a way of this sort from the start, because we consider it hopeless or superfluous, or because we consider it foolishness. If that is our attitude, we should refrain from looking at the way even from outside. But perhaps it is not fitting anyhow to let the way be seen in public. With this hint, we shall break off our general remarks about ways of thinking.

We shall now try to walk the way of our question, by asking it in the sense of the decisive fourth, but in the mode of the second manner.

The initially proposed version of the second question ran: what do we understand by thinking according to traditional doctrine, logic? At first it appears that the question inquires historically what we have hitherto had in mind and taught about thinking. But now we ask:

"What is the call to which Western-European thinking is subject, the thinking whose roads we, too, follow as soon as we let ourselves get involved in thinking?"

But even so, the impression unavoidably remains that the question amounts to no more than a historical description of the beginnings of Western philosophy. The treatment of the question may retain this peculiarity, that it will remain forever implausible to the scholarly research in the history of philosophy and its principles of interpretation.

In the writings of Parmenides, a Greek thinker who lived around the turn of the sixth into the fifth century B.C., we read the saying:

" χρὴ τὸ λέγειν τε νοεῖν τ᾽ ἐὸν ἔμμεναι ."

According to the usual translations, this means:

"One should both say and think that Being is."

It would be most in keeping with the way on which we have set out with our question, if we were now to leave off all asides and warnings, and tried to trace in thought what the saying tells us. But today, when we know much too much and form opinions much too quickly, when we compute and pigeonhole everything in a flash—today there is no room at all left for the hope that the presentation of a matter might in itself be powerful enough to set in motion any fellow-thinking which, prompted by the showing of the matter, would join us on our way. We therefore need these bothersome detours and crutches that otherwise run counter to the style of thinking ways. This is the necessity to which we bow when we now attempt, by circumscribing the matter in ever narrower circles, to render possible the leap into what the saying tells us:

" χρὴ τὸ λέγειν τε νοεῖν τ᾽ ἐὸν ἔμμεναι ."

"One should both say and think that Being is."

HERMENEUTIC METHOD AND
REFLECTIVE PHILOSOPHY*

PAUL RICOEUR

THE RECOURSE OF SYMBOLS TO REFLECTION

I will begin by retracing the path of my own inquiry. It was as a requirement of lucidity, of veracity, of rigor, that I encountered what I called, at the end of *The Symbolism of Evil*, "the passage to reflection." Is it possible, I asked, to coherently interrelate the interpretation of symbols and philosophic reflection? My only answer to this question was in the form of a contradictory resolve: I vowed, on the one hand, *to listen* to the rich words of symbols and myths that precede my reflection, instruct and nourish it; and on the other hand to continue, by means of the philosophical exegesis of symbols and myths, the tradition of rationality of philosophy, of our western philosophy. Symbols give rise to thought, I said, using a phrase from Kant's *Critique of Judgment*. Symbols give, they are the gift of language; but this gift creates for me the duty to think, to inaugurate philosophic discourse, starting from what is always prior to and the foundation of that discourse. I did not conceal the paradoxical character of this promise; on the contrary, I accentuated it by affirming first that philosophy does not begin anything, since the fullness of language precedes it, and second that it begins from itself, since it is philosophy which inaugurates the question of meaning and of the foundation of meaning.

I was encouraged along these lines by what appeared to me to be a prephilosophical richness of symbols. Symbols, it seemed to me, call not only for interpretation . . . but for *philosophic reflection*. If this did not become apparent to us sooner, it is because we have restricted ourselves up to now to the semantic structure of symbols, that is, to the excess of meaning due to their "overdetermination."

That symbols call for reflection, however, is due to a second trait of symbols which we have left in the shadows; the purely semantic aspect is merely their most abstract aspect. Linguistic expressions are embodied not only in rituals and emotions . . . but also in myths, that is, in the great narratives about the beginning and the end of evil. I have studied four cycles of these myths: the myths of the primal chaos, the myths of the wicked god, the myths of the soul exiled in an evil body, and the myths concerning the historical fault of an individual who is both an ancestor and a prototype of humanity. New traits of symbol appear here, and with them new suggestions for a hermeneutics. First, these myths introduce exemplary personages—Prometheus, Anthropos, Adam—who begin to generalize human experience on the level of a universal concept or paradigm in which we can read our condition and destiny. Second, thanks to the structure of the narrative that tells of events that happened "once upon a time," our experience receives a temporal orientation, an *élan* extended between a beginning and an end; our present becomes charged with a memory and a hope. More profoundly still, these myths recount, after the manner of a transhistorical event, the irrational break, the absurd leap, which separates two views, one concerned with the innocence of coming-to-be, the other with the guilt of history. At this level symbols have not only an expressive value, as they do on the merely semantic level, but a heuristic value, since they confer universality, temporality and ontological import upon our self-understanding. Interpretation therefore does not consist simply in extricating the second intention, which is both given and masked in the literal meaning; it tries to thematize this universality, this temporality, this ontological exploration implied in myth. Thus, in their mythical form symbols themselves push toward speculative expression; symbols themselves are the dawn of reflection. The hermeneutic problem therefore is not imposed upon reflection from without, but proposed from within by the very movement of meaning, by the implicit life of symbols taken at their semantic and mythical level.

There is a third way in which the symbolism of evil calls for a science of interpretation, a hermeneutics. Semantically as well as mythically, the symbols of evil are always the obverse side of a greater symbolism, a symbolism of salvation. This is already true on the semantic level: to the impure there corresponds the pure; to the wandering of sin corresponds pardon in its symbol of the return; to the weight of sin, deliverance; and, more generally, to the symbolism of slavery, that of liberation. It is even clearer on the mythical level; the images of the beginning receive their true meaning from the images of the end. The symbolism of chaos constitutes the preface of a poem that celebrates the enthroning of Marduk; to the tragic god corresponds the purification of Apollo, the same Apollo who through his oracle called Socrates to "examine" other men; to the myth of the soul in exile corresponds the symbolism of deliverance through knowledge; to the figure of the first Adam correspond the successive figures of the King, the Messiah, the Just One who suffers, the Son of Man, the Lord, the Logos. The philosopher, qua philosopher, has nothing to say concerning the proclamation, the apostolic kerygma, according to which these figures are brought to fulfillment in the coming of the Christ Jesus; but he can and should reflect upon these symbols insofar as they are representations of the end of evil. What, then, does this one-to-one correspondence between the two symbolisms signify? It signifies, first, that the symbolism of evil receives its true meaning from the symbolism of salvation. The symbolism of evil is only a particular province within religious symbolism; thus the Christian *Credo* does not say "I believe in sin," but "I believe in the remission of sins." More fundamentally, however, the correspondence between a symbolism of evil and a symbolism of salvation signifies that we must cease being totally absorbed in a symbolism of evil that is severed from the rest of the symbolic and mythic universe and reflect upon the totality formed by these symbols of the beginning and the end. Thereby is suggested the architectonic task of reason, which has already been sketched in the interplay of the mythic correspondences; it is this totality, as such, which demands expression at the level of reflection and speculation.

Symbols themselves demand this speculative reflection. An interpretation of symbols that extricated their philosophical meaning would not be something superadded to them. Such an interpretation is required by the semantic structure of symbols, by the latent speculation of myths, and finally by the fact that each symbol belongs to a meaningful totality which furnishes the first schema of the system.

Though we do not yet know what privileged place[1] the symbols and myths of evil have within the empire of symbolism, we will here try to

---

[1] In giving precedence to the problem of method, we reduce the entire symbolism of evil to the rank of an example. We shall not regret doing so: one of the results of reflection will be precisely that the symbolism of evil is not one example out of many but a privileged example, perhaps even the native land of all symbolism, the birthplace of the hermeneutic conflict taken in its full extent. But this we shall understand only through the movement of reflection—a reflection that at first knows the symbols of evil merely as a given or arbitrarily chosen example.

pose the problem in its full generality by asking the question: How can a philosophy of reflection nourish itself at the symbolic source and become hermeneutic?

It must be admitted that the question seems quite perplexing. Traditionally—since Plato, that is—it is put in the following terms: What is the place of myth in philosophy? If myth calls for philosophy, is it true that philosophy calls for myth? Or, in the terms of the present work, does reflection call for symbols and the interpretation of symbols? This question precedes any attempt to move from mythical symbols to speculative symbols, whatever the symbolic area being dealt with. One must first make sure that the philosophic act, in its innermost nature, not only does not exclude, but requires something like an interpretation.

At first sight the question seems hopeless. Philosophy, born in Greece, introduced new demands in contrast to mythical thought; first and foremost it established the idea of a science, in the sense of the Platonic *epistêmê* or the *Wissenschaft* of German idealism. In view of this idea of philosophical science, the recourse to symbols has something scandalous about it.

In the first place, symbols remain caught within the diversity of languages and cultures and espouse their irreducible singularity. Why begin with the Babylonians, the Hebrews, the Greeks—be they tragic or Pythagorean? Because they nourish my memory? In that case I put my singularity at the center of my reflection; but does not philosophical science require that the singularity of cultural creations and individual memories be reabsorbed into the universality of discourse?

Secondly, philosophy as a rigorous science seems to require univocal significations. But symbols, by reason of their analogical texture, are opaque, nontransparent; the double meaning that gives them concrete roots weights them down with materiality. This double meaning is not accidental but constitutive, inasmuch as the analogous sense, the existential sense, is given only in and through the literal sense; in epistemological terms, this opacity can only mean equivocity. Can philosophy systematically cultivate the equivocal?

Thirdly, and this is the most serious point, the bond between symbol and interpretation, in which we have seen the promise of an organic connection between *mythos* and *logos*, furnishes a new motive for suspicion. Any interpretation can be revoked; no myths without exegesis, but no exegesis without contesting. The deciphering of enigmas is not a science, either in the Platonic, Hegelian, or modern sense of the word "science." Our preceding chapter gave a glimpse of the gravity of the problem: there we considered the most extreme opposition imaginable within the field of hermeneutics, the opposition between the phenomenology of religion, conceived as a remythicizing of discourse, and psychoanalysis, conceived as a demystification of discourse. By the same token our problem becomes graver in becoming more precise. The question now is not simply why an interpretation, but why *these* opposed interpretations? The task is not only to justify the recourse to some kind of interpretation, but to justify the dependence of reflection upon preconstituted hermeneutics that are mutually exclusive.

To justify the recourse to symbols in philosophy is ultimately to justify cultural contingency, equivocal language, and the war of hermeneutics within itself.

The solution of the problem hinges on showing that reflection, in principle, requires something like interpretation; starting from that requirement one can then justify, also in principle, the detour through the contingency of cultures, through an incurably equivocal language, and through the conflict of interpretations.

Let us begin at the beginning. Up to the present we have only been considering the recourse of symbols to reflection; what makes that recourse intelligible is reflection's recourse to symbols.

THE RECOURSE OF REFLECTION
TO SYMBOLS

When we say philosophy is reflection we mean, assuredly, self-reflection. But what does the Self signify? Do we know it any better than the words symbol and interpretation? No doubt we do, but with a knowledge that is abstract, empty, and vain. Let us start, then, by taking stock of this vain certitude. Perhaps it is symbolism that will save reflection from its vanity, while at the same time reflection will provide the structure for handling any hermeneutic conflict. Therefore, what does Reflection signify? What does the Self of self-reflection signify?

I assume here that the positing of the self is the first truth for the philosopher placed within that broad tradition of modern philosophy that begins with Descartes and is developed in Kant, Fichte, and the reflective stream of European philosophy. For this tradition, which we shall consider as a whole before setting its main representatives in opposition to one another, the positing of the self is a truth which posits itself; it can be neither verified nor deduced; it is at once the positing of a being and of an act; the positing of an existence and of an operation of thought: *I am, I think;* to exist, for me, is to think; I exist inasmuch as I think. Since this truth cannot be verified like a fact, nor deduced like a conclusion, it has to posit itself in reflection; its self-positing is reflection; Fichte called this first truth the *thetic judgment.* Such is our philosophical starting point.

But this first reference of reflection to the positing of the self, as existing and thinking, does not sufficiently characterize reflection. In particular, we do not yet understand why reflection requires a work of deciphering, an exegesis, and a science of exegesis or hermeneutics, and still less why this deciphering must be either a psychoanalysis or a phenomenology of the sacred. This point cannot be understood so long as reflection is seen as a return to the so-called evidence of immediate consciousness. We have to introduce a second trait of reflection, which may be stated thus: reflection is not intuition; or, in positive terms, reflection is the effort to recapture the Ego of the Ego Cogito in the mirror of its objects, its works, its acts. But why must the positing of the Ego be recaptured through its acts? Precisely because it is given neither in a psychological evidence, nor in an intellectual intuition, nor in a mystical vision. A reflective philosophy is the contrary of a philosophy of the immediate. The first truth—*I am, I think*—remains as abstract and empty as it is invincible; it has to be "mediated" by the ideas, actions, works, institutions, and monuments that objectify it. It is in these objects, in the widest sense of the word, that the Ego must lose and find itself. We can say, in a somewhat paradoxical sense, that a philosophy of reflection is not a philosophy of consciousness, if by consciousness we mean immediate self-consciousness. Consciousness, as we shall say later, is a task, but it is a task because it is not a given . . . No doubt I have an apperception of myself and my acts, and this apperception is a type of evidence. Descartes cannot be dislodged from this incontestable proposition: I cannot doubt myself without perceiving that I doubt. But what does this apperception signify? A certitude, certainly, but a certitude devoid of truth. As Malebranche well understood, in opposition to Descartes, this immediate grasp is only a feeling and not an idea. If ideas are light and vision, there is no vision of the Ego, nor light in apperception. I only sense that I exist and that I think; I sense that I am awake; such is apperception. In Kantian language, an apperception of the Ego may accompany all my representations, but this apperception is not knowledge of oneself, it cannot be transformed into an intuition of a substantial soul; the decisive critique Kant directs against any "rational psychology'' has definitively dissociated reflection from any so-called knowledge of self.[2]

This second thesis, that reflection is not intuition, enables us to glimpse the place interpretation has in the knowledge of oneself; that place is indirectly indicated by the difference between reflection and intuition.

A new step will bring us closer to the goal. Having opposed reflection and intuition to one another, with Kant and in opposition to Descartes, I would like to distinguish the task of reflection from a mere critique of knowledge; this new step leads us away from Kant in the direction of Fichte and Nabert. The basic limitation of a critical philosophy lies in its exclusive concern for epistemology; reflection is reduced to a single dimension: the only canonical operations of thought are those that ground the "objectivity" of our representations. This priority given to epistemology explains why in Kant, in spite of appearances, the practical philosophy is subordinated to the critical philosophy: the second critique, that of practical reason, in fact borrows all of its structures from the first, that of pure reason. A single question rules the critical philosophy: What is a priori and what is merely empirical in knowledge? This distinction is the key to the theory of objectivity; it is purely and simply transposed into the second critique; the objectivity of the maxims of the will rests on the distinction between the validity of duty, which is a priori, and the content of empirical desires. It is in opposition to this reduction of reflection to a simple critique that I say, with Fichte and his French successor, Jean Nabert, that reflection is not so much a justification of science and duty as a reappropriation of our effort to exist; epistemology is only a part of this broader task: we have to recover the act of existing, the positing of the self, in all the density of its works. Why must this recovery be characterized as appropriation and even as reappropriation? I must recover something which has first been lost; I make "proper to me" what has ceased being mine. I make "mine" what I am separated from by space or time, by distraction or "diversion," or because of some culpable forgetfulness. Appropriation signifies that the initial situation from which reflection proceeds is "forgetfulness." I am lost, "led astray" among objects and separated from the center of my existence, just as I am separated from others and as an enemy is separated from all men. Whatever the secret of this

---

[2] In Husserlian language: the Ego Cogito is apodictic, but not necessarily adequate.

"diaspora," of this separation, it signifies that I do not at first possess what I am. The truth that Fichte called the thetic judgment posits itself in a desert wherein I am absent to myself. That is why reflection is a task, an *Aufgabe*—the task of making my concrete experience equal to the positing of "I am." Such is the ultimate elaboration of our initial proposition that reflection is not intuition; we now say: the positing of self is not given, it is a task, it is not *gegeben*, but *aufgegeben*.

At this point one may wonder whether we have not overly stressed the practical and ethical side of reflection. Is this not a new limitation, like that of the epistemological stream of the Kantian philosophy? Moreover, are we not farther than ever from our problem of interpretation? I do not think so; the ethical stress put on reflection does not mark a limitation, if we take the notion of ethical in its wide sense, as in Spinoza, when he calls the total process of philosophy "ethical."

Philosophy is ethical to the extent that it leads from alienation to freedom and beatitude. In Spinoza this conversion is achieved when the knowledge of self is made equal to the knowledge of the unique substance; but this speculative process has an ethical significance, inasmuch as the alienated individual is transformed by the knowledge of the whole. Philosophy is ethics, but ethics is not simply morality. If we follow Spinoza's use of the word "ethical" we must say that reflection is ethical before becoming a critique of morality. Its goal is to grasp the Ego in its effort to exist, in its desire to be. This is where a reflective philosophy recovers and perhaps also saves the Platonic notion that the source of knowledge is itself *Eros*, desire, love, along with the Spinozistic notion that it is *conatus*, effort. Such effort is a desire, since it is never satisfied; but the desire is an effort since it is the affirmative positing of a singular being and not simply a lack of being. Effort and desire are the two sides of this positing of the self in the first truth: *I am*.

We are now in a position to complete our negative proposition—reflection is not intuition—by a positive proposition: *Reflection is the appropriation of our effort to exist and of our desire to be, through the works which bear witness to that effort and desire.* That is why reflection is more than a mere critique of knowledge and even more than a mere critique of moral judgment; prior to every critique of judgment it reflects upon the act of existing that we deploy in effort and desire.

This third step leads us to the threshold of our problem of interpretation: the positing or emergence of this effort or desire is not only devoid of all intuition but is evidenced only by works whose meaning remains doubtful and revocable. This is where reflection calls for an interpretation and tends to move into hermeneutics. The ultimate root of our problem lies in this primitive connection between the act of existing and the signs we deploy in our works; reflection must become interpretation because I cannot grasp the act of existing except in signs scattered in the world. That is why a reflective philosophy must include the results, methods, and presuppositions of all the sciences that try to decipher and interpret the signs of man.[3]

Such is, in its principle and widest generality, the root of the hermeneutic problem. The problem is posed both by the factual existence of symbolic language which calls for reflection and, conversely, by the indigence of reflection which calls for interpretation. In positing itself, reflection understands its own inability to transcend the vain and empty abstraction of the *I think* and the necessity to recover itself by deciphering its own signs lost in the world of culture. Thus reflection realizes it does not begin as science; in order to operate it must take to itself the opaque, contingent, and equivocal signs scattered in the cultures in which our language is rooted.

REFLECTION AND EQUIVOCAL LANGUAGE

By this placing the hermeneutic problem within the movement of reflection we are enabled to meet the objections that would seemingly invalidate a philosophy that presents itself as a hermeneutics. In the foregoing we have reduced these objections to three main ones: Can philosophy derive its universality from contingent cultural productions? Can it build its rigor upon equivocal significations? Can it subject its vow of coherence to the fluctuations of an indecisive conflict between rival interpretations?

The aim . . . is not so much to resolve the problems as to show their legitimacy when they are rightly posed, to assure ourselves that they are not meaningless but are inscribed in the nature of things and in the nature of language. That philosophical discourse achieves universality only by passing through the contingency of cultures, that its rigor is

---

[3] Cf. my article "Acte et signe dans la philosophie de Jean Nabert," *Etudes philosophiques* (1962-63).

dependent upon equivocal languages, that its coherence must traverse the war between hermeneutics—all this can and must be seen as the necessary pathway, as the triple *aporia* rightly formed and rightly posed . . . : the aporias of interpretation are those of reflection itself.

I will say very little here about the first difficulty, since I have discussed it in the introduction to *The Symbolism of Evil*. To start from a pregiven symoblism, I objected, is to give oneself something to think about; but at the same time a radical contingency is brought into discourse, the contingency of the cultures of one's acquaintance. My answer was that the philosopher does not speak from nowhere: every question he can pose rises from the depths of his Greek memory; the field of his investigation is thereby unavoidably oriented; his memory carries with it the opposition of the "near" and the "far." Through this contingency of historical encounters we have to discern reasonable sequences between scattered cultural themes. I should now add that it is only abstract reflection which speaks from nowhere. To become concrete, reflection must lose its immediate pretension to universality, to the extent of fusing together its essential necessity and the contingency of the signs through which it recognizes itself. This fusion can be achieved precisely in the movement of interpretation.

We must now come to grips with the more formidable objection, that the recourse to symbolism hands thought over to equivocal language and fallacious arguments that are condemned by a sound logic. The difficulty in avoiding this objection is increased by the fact that logicians have invented symbolic logic with the express aim of eliminating equivocation from our arguments. For the logician, the word "symbol" means precisely the contrary of what it means for us. The important status of symbolic logic obliges us to say something about this encounter, which at the very least constitutes a strange homonymy; the obligation is all the more pressing in view of the fact that we have constantly alluded to the duality of univocal and equivocal expressions and have implicitly assumed that the latter can have an irreplaceable philosophical function.

The only radical way to justify hermeneutics is to seek in the very nature of reflective thought the principle of a *logic of double meaning*, a logic that is complex but not arbitrary, rigorous in its articulations but irreducible to the linearity of symbolic logic. This logic is no longer a formal logic, but a transcendental logic established on the level of the conditions of possibility; not the conditions of objectivity of nature, but the conditions of the appropriation of our desire to be. Thus the logic of double meanings, which is proper to hermeneutics, is of a transcendental order.

We have now to establish this connection between the logic of double meaning and transcendental reflection.

If the advocate of hermeneutics does not carry the discussion to this level, he will soon be driven into an untenable position. Any effort to maintain the debate on the level of the semantic structure of symbols will be to no purpose. He may of course appeal, as we ourselves have done up to now, to the overdetermination of meaning in symbols and thus defend a theory of two types of symbolism whose respective fields of application must be kept from any overlapping.

But the idea that there can exist two logics on the same level is strictly untenable; a pure and simple juxtaposition can only lead to the elimination of hermeneutics by symbolic logic.

For what advantages can the hermeneutician adduce when faced with formal logic? To the artificiality of logical symbols, which can be written and read but not spoken, he will oppose an essentially oral symbolism, in each instance received and accepted as a heritage. The man who speaks in symbols is first of all a narrator; he transmits an abundance of meaning over which he has little command. This abundance, this density of manifold meaning, is what gives him food for thought and solicits his understanding; interpretation consists less in suppressing ambiguity than in understanding it and in explicating its richness. It may also be said that logical symbolism is empty, whereas symbolism in hermeneutics is full; it renders manifest the double meaning of worldly or psychical reality. This was suggested earlier when we said that symbols are bound: the sensible sign is bound by the symbolic meaning that dwells in it and gives it transparency and lightness; the symbolic meaning is in turn bound to its sensible vehicle, which gives it weight and opacity. One might add that this is also the way symbols bind us, viz. by giving thought a content, a flesh, a density.

These distinctions and oppositions are not false; they are merely unfounded. A confrontation which restricts itself to the symbolic texture of symbols and does not face the question of their foundation in reflection will soon prove embarrassing to the advocate of hermeneutics. For the artificiality and emptiness of logical symbolism are simply the counterpart and condition of the true aim of this logic, viz. to guarantee the nonambiguity of arguments; what the hermeneutician calls double meaning is, in logical terms, ambiguity, i.e. equivocity of words and amphiboly of statements. A peaceful juxtaposition of hermeneutics and symbolic logic is therefore impossible; symbolic logic quickly makes any lazy compromise untenable. Its very "intolerance" forces hermeneutics to radically justify its own language.

We must therefore understand this intolerance in order to arrive *a contrario* at the foundation of hermeneutics.

If the rigor of symbolic logic seems more exclusive than that of traditional formal logic, the reason is that symbolic logic is not a simple prolongation of the earlier logic. It does not represent a higher degree of formalization; it proceeds from a global decision concerning ordinary language as a whole; it marks a split with ordinary language and its incurable ambiguity; it questions the equivocal and hence fallacious character of the words of ordinary language, the amphibolous character of its constructions, the confusion inherent in metaphor and idiomatic expressions, the emotional resonance of highly descriptive language. Symbolic logic despairs of natural language precisely at the point where hermeneutics believes in its implicit "wisdom."

This struggle begins with the exclusion from the properly cognitive sphere of all language that does not give factual information. The rest of discourse is classified under the heading of the emotive and hortatory functions of language; that which does not give factual information expresses emotions, feelings, or attitudes, or urges others to behave in some particular way.

Reduced thus to the informative function, language still has to be divested of the equivocity of words and the amphiboly of grammatical constructions; verbal ambiguity must be unmasked so as to eliminate it from arguments and to employ coherently the same words in the same sense within the same argument. The function of definition is to explain meaning and thereby eliminate ambiguity: the only definitions that succeed in doing this are scientific ones. These are not content with pointing out the meaning words already have in usage, independently of their definition; instead they very strictly characterize an object in light of a scientific theory (for example, the definition of force as the product of mass and acceleration in the context of Newtonian theory).

But symbolic logic goes further. For it, the price of univocity is the creation of a symbolism with no ties to natural language. This notion of symbol excludes the other notion of symbol. The recourse to a completely artificial symbolism introduces in logic a difference not only of degree but of nature; the symbols of the logician intervene precisely at the point where the arguments of classical logic, formulated in ordinary language, run into an invincible and, in a way, residual ambiguity. Thus the logical disjunction sign v eliminates the ambiguity of words that express disjunction in ordinary language (Eng., or; Ger., *oder;* Fr., *ou*); v expresses only the partial meaning common to the inclusive disjunction (the sense of the Latin *vel*) according to which at least one of the terms of the disjunction is true although both may be true, and to the exclusive disjunction (the sense of the Latin *aut*) according to which at least one is true and at least one is false; v resolves the ambiguity by formulating the inclusive disjunction as the part common to the two modes of disjunction. Likewise the symbol $\mid\supset$ resolves the ambiguity inherent in the notion of implication (which may denote formal implication, either logical, definitional, or causal); the symbol $\mid\supset$ formulates the common partial meaning, namely, that any hypothetical statement with a true antecedent and a false consequent must be false; the symbol is thus an abbreviation of a longer symbolism which expresses the negation of the conjunction of the truth value of the antecedent and the falsity of the consequent: $\sim (p \sim q)$.

Thus the artificial language of logical symbolism enables one to determine the validity of arguments in all cases where a residual ambiguity can be ascribed to the structure of ordinary language. The precise point where symbolic logic cuts across and contests hermeneutics, therefore, is this: verbal equivocity and syntactical amphiboly—in short, the ambiguity of ordinary language—can be overcome only at the level of a language whose symbols have a meaning completely determined by the truth table whose construction they allow. Thus the sense of the symbol v is completely determined by its truth function, inasmuch as it serves to safeguard the validity of the disjunctive syllogism; likewise the sense of the symbol $\mid\supset$ completely exhausts its meaning in the construction of the truth table of the hypothetical syllogism. These constructions guarantee that the symbols are completely unambiguous, while the nonambiguity of the symbols assures the universal validity of arguments.

As long as the logic of multiple meaning is not grounded in its reflective function, it necessarily falls under the blows of formal and symbolic logic. In the eyes of the logician, hermeneutics will always be suspected of fostering a culpable complacency toward equivocal meanings, of surreptitiously giving an informative function to expressions that have merely an emotive or hortatory function. Hermeneutics thus falls under the fallacies of relevance which a sound logic denounces.

The only thing that can come to the aid of equivocal expressions and truly ground a logic of double meaning is the problematic of reflection.

The only thing that can justify equivocal expressions is their a priori role in the movement of self-appropriation by self which constitutes reflective activity. This a priori function pertains not to a formal but to a transcendental logic, if by transcendental logic is meant the establishing of the conditions of possibility of a domain of objectivity in general. The task of such a logic is to extricate by a regressive method the notions presupposed in the constitution of a type of experience and a corresponding type of reality. Transcendental logic is not exhausted in the Kantian a priori. The connection we have established between reflection upon the *I think, I am* qua act, and the signs scattered in the various cultures of that act of existing, opens up a new field of experience, objectivity, and reality. This is the field to which the logic of double meaning pertains—a logic we have qualified above as complex but not arbitrary, and rigorous in its articulations. The principle of a limitation to the demands of symbolic logic lies in the structure of reflection itself. If there is no such thing as the transcendental, there is no reply to the intolerance of symbolic logic; but if the transcendental is an authentic dimension of discourse, then new force is found in the reasons that can be opposed to the requirement of logicism that all discourse be measured by its treatise of arguments. These reasons, which seemed to us to be left hanging in air for want of a foundation, are as follows:

1. The requirement of univocity holds only for discourse that presents itself as *argument:* but reflection does not argue, it draws no conclusion, it neither deduces nor induces; it states the conditions of possibility whereby empirical consciousness can be made equal to thetic consciousness. Hence, "equivocal" applies only to those expressions that ought to be univocal in the course of a single "argument" but are not; in the reflective use of multiple-meaning symbols there is no fallacy of ambiguity: to reflect upon these symbols and to interpret them is one and the same act.

2. The understanding developed by reflection upon symbols is not a weak substitute for definition, for reflection is not a type of thinking that defines and thinks according to "classes." This brings us back to the Aristotelian problem of the "many meanings of being." Aristotle was the first to see clearly that philosophical discourse is not subject to the logical alternative of univocal-equivocal, for being is not a "genus"; and yet, being is said; but it "is said in many ways."

3. Let us go back to the very first alternative considered above: a statement that does not give factual information, we said, expresses

only the emotions or attitudes of a subject. Reflection, however, falls outside this alternative; that which makes possible the appropriation of the *I think, I am* is neither the empirical statement nor the emotive statement, but something other than either of these.

This case for interpretation rests entirely on the reflective function of interpretative thought. If the double movement of symbols toward reflection and of reflection toward symbols is valid, interpretative thought is well grounded. Hence it may be said, at least negatively, that such thought is not measured by a logic of arguments; the validity of philosophical statements cannot be arbitrated by a theory of language conceived as syntax; the semantics of philosophy is not swallowed up by a symbolic logic.

These propositions concerning philosophic discourse do not enable us, however, to say positively what a philosophical statement is; such an affirmation could be fully justified only by its actually being said. At least we can affirm that the indirect, symbolic language of reflection *can* be valid, not *because* it is equivocal, but *in spite of* its being equivocal.

REFLECTION AND THE
HERMENEUTIC CONFLICT

But the reply of hermeneutics to the objections of symbolic logic is liable to be an empty victory. The challenge comes not only from without, it is not only the voice of the "intolerant" logician; it comes from within, from the internal inconsistency of hermeneutics, torn by contradiction. As we already know, not one but several interpretations have to be integrated into reflection. Thus the hermeneutic conflict itself is what nourishes the process of reflection and governs the movement from abstract to concrete reflection. Is this possible without "destroying" reflection?

In our attempt to justify the recourse to hermeneutics that are already constituted—that of the phenomenology of religion and that of psychoanalysis—we suggested that their conflict might well be not only a crisis of language but, deeper still, a crisis of reflection: to destroy the idols, to listen to symbols—are not these, we asked, one and the same enterprise? Indeed, the profound unity of the demystifying and the remythicizing of discourse can be seen only at the end of an ascesis of reflection, in the course of which the debate dramatizing the hermeneutic field shall have become a discipline of thinking.

One trait of this discipline is already clear to us: the two enterprises which we at first opposed to one another—the reduction of illusions and the restoration of the fullness of meaning—are alike in that they both shift the origin of meaning to another center which is no longer the immediate subject of reflection: "consciousness"—the watchful ego, attentive to its own presence, anxious about self and attached to self. Thus hermeneutics, approached from its most opposed poles, represents a challenge and a test for reflection, whose first tendency is to identify itself with immediate consciousness. To let ourselves be torn by the contradiction between these divergent hermeneutics is to give ourselves up to the wonder that puts reflection in motion: it is no doubt necessary for us to be separated from ourselves, to be set off center, in order finally to know what is signified by the *I think, I am.*

We thought we had resolved the antinomy of myth and philosophy by appealing to interpretation itself for the mediation between myth and philosophy or, in a broader sense, between symbols and reflection. But that mediation is not given, it is to be constructed.

It is not given like a ready-made solution. The dispossession of the ego, which psychoanalysis more than any other hermeneutics demands of us, is the first achievement of reflection that reflection does not understand. But the phenomenological interpretation of the sacred, to which psychoanalysis seems to be diametrically opposed, is no less foreign to the style and fundamental intention of the reflective method; does it not oppose a method of transcendence to the method of immanence of reflective philosophy? Does not the sacred, manifested in its symbols, seem to pertain to revelation rather than to reflection? Whether one looks back to the will to power of the Nietzschean man, to the generic being of the Marxist man, to the libido of the Freudian man, or whether one looks ahead to the transcendent home of signification which we designate here by the vague term the "sacred," the home of meaning is not consciousness but something other than consciousness.

Both hermeneutics pose therefore the same crucial question: Can the dispossession of consciousness to the profit of another home of meaning be understood as an act of reflection, as the first gesture of reappropriation? This is the question that remains in suspense; it is more radical than the question of the coexistence of several styles of interpretation, or the whole crisis of language in which the hermeneutic conflict is set.

We suspect that these three "crises"—crisis of language, crisis of interpretation, crisis of reflection—can only be overcome together. In order to become concrete, i.e. equal to its richest contents, reflection must become hermeneutic; but there exists no general hermeneutics. This aporia sets us in movement: would it not be one and the same thing to arbitrate the war of hermeneutics *and* to enlarge reflection to the dimensions of a critique of interpretations? Is it not by one and the same movement that reflection can become concrete reflection *and* that the rivalry between interpretations can be comprehended, in the double sense of the term: justified by reflection and embodied in its work?

For the moment our perplexity is great. What is offered to us is a three-term relation, a figure with three heads: reflection, interpretation understood as restoration of meaning, interpretation understood as reduction of illusion. No doubt we shall have to penetrate quite deeply into the conflict between interpretations before we see appear, as a requirement of the very war of hermeneutics, the means of grounding the three together in reflection. But in its turn reflection will no longer be the positing, as feeble as it is peremptory, as sterile as it is irrefutable, of the *I think, I am:* it will have become concrete reflection; and its concreteness will be due to the harsh hermeneutic discipline.

THE ORIGIN OF GEOMETRY*[1]

EDMUND HUSSERL

The interest that propels us in this work makes it necessary to engage first of all in reflections which surely never occurred to Galileo. We must focus our gaze not merely upon the ready-made, handed-down geometry and upon the manner of being which its meaning had in his thinking; it was no different in his thinking from what it was in that of all the late inheritors of the older geometric wisdom, whenever they were at work, either as pure geometers or as making practical applica-

* By permission of Northwestern University Press. From *The Crisis of European Science*, Appendix VI: The Origin of Geometry by Edmund Husserl, translated by David Carr, Copyright © 1970, Northwestern University Press, Evanston, Illinois.

[1] This manuscript was written in 1936 and was edited and published (beginning with the third paragraph) by Eugen Fink in the *Revue internationale de philosophie*, Vol. I, No. 2 (1939) under the title "Der Ursprung der Geometrie als intentional-historisches Problem." It appears in Biemel's edition of the *Crisis* as "Beilage III," pp. 365-86. The first paragraphs suggest it was meant for inclusion in the *Crisis*.

tions of geometry. Rather, indeed above all, we must also inquire back into the original meaning of the handed-down geometry, which continued to be valid with this very same meaning—continued and at the same time was developed further, remaining simply "geometry" in all its new forms. Our considerations will necessarily lead to the deepest problems of meaning, problems of science and of the history of science in general, and indeed in the end to problems of a universal history in general; so that our problems and expositions concerning Galilean geometry take on an exemplary significance.

Let it be noted in advance that, in the midst of our historical meditations on modern philosophy, there appears here for the first time with Galileo, through the disclosure of the depth-problems of the meaning-origin of geometry and, founded on this, of the meaning-origin of his new physics, a clarifying light for our whole undertaking: namely, [the idea of] seeking to carry out, in the form of historical meditations, self-reflections about our own present philosophical situation in the hope that in this way we can finally take possession of the meaning, method, and beginning of philosophy, the *one* philosophy to which our life seeks to be and ought to be devoted. For, as will become evident here, at first in connection with one example, our investigations are historical in an unusual sense, namely, in virtue of a thematic direction which opens up depth-problems quite unknown to ordinary history, problems which, [however,] in their own way, are undoubtedly historical problems. Where a consistent pursuit of these depth-problems leads can naturally not yet be seen at the beginning.

The question of the origin of geometry (under which title here, for the sake of brevity, we include all disciplines that deal with shapes existing mathematically in pure space-time) shall not be considered here as the philological-historical question, i.e., as the search for the first geometers who actually uttered pure geometrical propositions, proofs, theories, or for the particular propositions they discovered, or the like. Rather than this, our interest shall be the inquiry back into the most original sense in which geometry once arose, was present as the tradition of millennia, is still present for us, and is still being worked on in a lively forward development;* we inquire into that sense in which it appeared in history for the first time—in which it had to appear, even though we

* So also for Galileo and all the periods following the Renaissance, continually being worked on in a lively forward development, and yet at the same time a tradition.

know nothing of the first creators and are not even asking after them. Starting from what we know, from our geometry, or rather from the older handed-down forms (such as Euclidean geometry), there is an inquiry back into the submerged original beginnings of geometry as they necessarily must have been in their "primally establishing" function. This regressive inquiry unavoidably remains within the sphere of generalities, but, as we shall soon see, these are generalities which can be richly explicated, with prescribed possibilities of arriving at particular questions and self-evident claims as answers. The geometry which is ready-made, so to speak, from which the regressive inquiry begins, is a tradition. Our human existence moves within innumerable traditions. The whole cultural world, in all its forms, exists through tradition. These forms have arisen as such not merely causally; we also know already that tradition is precisely tradition, having arisen within our human space through human activity, i.e., spiritually, even though we generally know nothing, or as good as nothing, of the particular provenance and of the spiritual source that brought it about. And yet there lies in this lack of knowledge, everywhere and essentially, an implicit knowledge, which can thus also be made explicit, a knowledge of unassailable self-evidence. It begins with superficial commonplaces, such as: that everything traditional has arisen out of human activity, that accordingly past men and human civilizations existed, and among them their first inventors, who shaped the new out of materials at hand, whether raw or already spiritually shaped. From the superficial, however, one is led into the depths. Tradition is open in this general way to continued inquiry; and, if one consistently maintains the direction of inquiry, an infinity of questions opens up, questions which lead to definite answers in accord with their sense. Their form of generality—indeed, as one can see, of unconditioned general validity—naturally allows for application to individually determined particular cases, though it determines only that in the individual that can be grasped through subsumption.

Let us begin, then, in connection with geometry, with the most obvious commonplaces that we have already expressed above in order to indicate the sense of our regressive inquiry. We understand our geometry, available to us through tradition (we have learned it, and so have our teachers), to be a total acquisition of spiritual accomplishments which grows through the continued work of new spiritual acts into new acquisitions. We know of its handed-down, earlier forms, as those from which it has arisen; but with every form the reference to an earlier one is repeated. Clearly, then, geometry must have arisen out of a *first* acquisition, out of first creative activities. We understand its persisting manner of being: it is not only a mobile forward process from one set of acquisitions to another but a continuous synthesis in which all acquisitions maintain their validity, all make up a totality such that, at every present stage, the total acquisition is, so to speak, the total premise for the acquisitions of the new level. Geometry necessarily has this mobility and has a horizon of geometrical future in precisely this style; this is its meaning for every geometer who has the consciousness (the constant implicit knowledge) of existing within a forward development understood as the progress of knowledge being built into the horizon. The same thing is true of every science. Also, every science is related to an open chain of the generations of those who work for and with one another, researchers either known or unknown to one another who are the accomplishing subjectivity of the whole living science. Science, and in particular geometry, with this ontic meaning, must have had a historical beginning; this meaning itself must have an origin in an accomplishment: first as a project and then in successful execution.

Obviously it is the same here as with every other invention. Every spiritual accomplishment proceeding from its first project to its execution is present for the first time in the self-evidence of actual success. But when we note that mathematics has the manner of being of a lively forward movement from acquisitions as premises to new acquisitions, in whose ontic meaning that of the premises is included (the process continuing in this manner), then it is clear that the *total* meaning of geometry (as a developed science, as in the case of every science) could not have been present as a project and then as mobile fulfillment at the beginning. A more primitive formation of meaning necessarily went before it as a preliminary stage, undoubtedly in such a way that it appeared for the first time in the self-evidence of successful realization. But this way of expressing it is actually overblown. Self-evidence means nothing more than grasping an entity with the consciousness of its original being-itself-there [*Selbst-da*]. Successful realization of a project is, for the acting subject, self-evidence; in this self-evidence, what has been realized is there, *originaliter*, as itself.

But now questions arise. This process of projecting and successfully realizing occurs, after all, purely within the *subject* of the inventor, and thus the meaning, as present *originaliter* with its whole content, lies exclusively, so to speak, within his mental space. But geometrical existence is not psychic existence; it does not exist as something personal within the personal sphere of consciousness; it is the existence of what is objectively there for "everyone" (for actual and possible geometers, or those who understand geometry). Indeed, it has, from its primal establishment, an existence which is peculiarly supertemporal and which—of this we are certain—is accessible to all men, first of all to the actual and possible mathematicians of all peoples, all ages; and this is true of all its particular forms. And all forms newly produced by someone on the basis of pregiven forms immediately take on the same objectivity. This is, we note, an "ideal" objectivity. It is proper to a whole class of spiritual products of the cultural world, to which not only all scientific constructions and the sciences themselves belong but also, for example, the constructions of fine literature.* Works of this class do not, like tools (hammers, pliers) or like architectural and other such products, have a repeatability in many like exemplars. The Pythagorean theorem, [indeed] all of geometry, exists only once, no matter how often or even in what language it may be expressed. It is identically the same in the "original language" of Euclid and in all "translations"; and within each language it is again the same, no matter how many times it has been sensibly uttered, from the original expression and writing-down to the innumerable oral utterances or written and other documentations. The sensible utterances have spatiotemporal individuation in the world like all corporeal occurrences, like everything embodied in bodies as such; but this is not true of the spiritual form itself, which is called an "ideal object" [*ideale Gegenständlichkeit*]. In a certain way ideal objects do exist objectively in the world, but it is only in virtue of these two-leveled repetitions and ultimately in virtue of sensibly embodying repetitions. For language itself, in all its particularizations (words, sentences, speeches), is, as can easily be seen from the grammatical point of view, thoroughly made up of ideal objects; for example, the word *Löwe* occurs only once in the German language; it is identical throughout its innumerable utterances by any given persons. But the idealities of geometrical words, sentences, theories—considered purely as linguistic structures—are not the idealities that make up what is ex-

---

* But the broadest concept of literature encompasses them all; that is, it belongs to their objective being that they be linguistically expressed and can be expressed again and again; or, more precisely, they have their objectivity, their existence-for-everyone, only as signification, as the meaning of speech. This is true in a peculiar fashion in the case of the objective sciences: for them the difference between the original language of the work and its translation into other languages does not remove its identical accessibility or change it into an inauthentic, indirect accessibility.

pressed and brought to validity as truth in geometry; the latter are ideal geometrical objects, states of affairs, etc. Wherever something is asserted, one can distinguish what is thematic, that about which it is said (its meaning), from the assertion, which itself, during the asserting, is never and can never be thematic. And what is thematic here is precisely ideal objects, and quite different ones from those coming under the concept of language. Our problem now concerns precisely the ideal objects which are thematic in geometry: how does geometrical ideality (just like that of all sciences) proceed from its primary intrapersonal origin, where it is a structure within the conscious space of the first inventor's soul, to its ideal objectivity? In advance we see that it occurs by means of language, through which it receives, so to speak, its linguistic living body [Sprachleib]. But how does linguistic embodiment make out of the merely intrasubjective structure the *objective* structure which, e.g., as geometrical concept or state of affairs, is in fact present as understandable by all and is valid, already in its linguistic expression as geometrical speech, as geometrical proposition, for all the future in its geometrical sense?

Naturally, we shall not go into the general problem which also arises here of the origin of language in its ideal existence and its existence in the real world grounded in utterance and documentation; but we must say a few words here about the relation between language, as a function of man within human civilization, and the world as the horizon of human existence.

Living wakefully in the world we are constantly conscious of the world, whether we pay attention to it or not, conscious of it as the horizon of our life, as a horizon of "things" (real objects), of our actual and possible interests and activities. Always standing out against the world-horizon is the horizon of our fellow men, whether there are any of them present or not. Before even taking notice of it at all, we are conscious of the open horizon of our fellow men with its limited nucleus of our neighbors, those known to us. We are thereby coconscious of the men on our external horizon in each case as "others"; in each case "I" am conscious of them as "my" others, as those with whom I can enter into actual and potential, immediate and mediate relations of empathy; [this involves] a reciprocal "getting along" with others; and on the basis of these relations I can deal with them, enter into particular modes of community with them, and then know, in a habitual way, of my being so related. Like me, every human being—and this is how he is understood by me and everyone else—has his fellow men and, always counting himself, civilization in general, in which he knows himself to be living.

It is precisely to this horizon of civilization that common language belongs. One is conscious of civilization from the start as an immediate and mediate linguistic community. Clearly it is only through language and its far-reaching documentations, as possible communications, that the horizon of civilization can be an open and endless one, as it always is for men. What is privileged in consciousness as the horizon of civilization and as the linguistic community is mature normal civilization (taking away the abnormal and the world of children). In this sense civilization is, for every man whose we-horizon it is, a community of those who can reciprocally express themselves, normally, in a fully understandable fashion; and within this community everyone can talk about what is within the surrounding world of his civilization as objectively existing. Everything has its name, or is namable in the broadest sense, i.e., linguistically expressible. The objective world is from the start the world for all, the world which "everyone" has as world-horizon. Its objective being presupposes men, understood as men with a common language. Language, for its part, as function and exercised capacity, is related correlatively to the world, the universe of objects which is linguistically expressible in its being and its being-such. Thus men as men, fellow men, world—the world of which men, of which we, always talk and can talk—and, on the other hand, language, are inseparably intertwined; and one is always certain of their inseparable relational unity, though usually only implicitly, in the manner of a horizon.

This being presupposed, the primally establishing geometer can obviously also express his internal structure. But the question arises again: How does the latter, in its "ideality," thereby become objective? To be sure, something psychic which can be understood by others [*nachverstehbar*] and is communicable, as something psychic belonging to this man, is *eo ipso* objective, just as he himself, as concrete man, is experienceable and namable by everyone as a real thing in the world of things in general. People can agree about such things, can make common verifiable assertions on the basis of common experience, etc. But how does the intrapsychically constituted structure arrive at an intersubjective being of its own as an ideal object which, as "geometrical," is anything but a real psychic object, even though it has arisen psychically? Let us reflect. The original being-itself-there, in the immediacy [*Aktualität*] of its first production, i.e., in original "self-evidence," results in no persisting acquisition at all that could have objective existence. Vivid self-evidence passes—though in such a way that the activity immediately turns into the passivity of the flowingly fading consciousness of what-has-just-now-been. Finally this "retention" disappears, but the "disappeared" passing and being past has not become nothing for the subject in question: it can be reawakened. To the passivity of what is at first obscurely awakened and what perhaps emerges with greater and greater clarity there belongs the possible activity of a recollection in which the past experiencing [*Erleben*] is lived through in a quasi-new and quasi-active way. Now if the originally self-evident production, as the pure fulfillment of its intention, is what is renewed (recollected), there necessarily occurs, accompanying the active recollection of what is past, an activity of concurrent actual production, and there arises thereby, in original "coincidence," the self-evidence of identity: what has now been realized in original fashion is the same as what was previously self-evident. Also coestablished is the capacity for repetition at will with the self-evidence of the identity (coincidence of identity) of the structure throughout the chain of repetitions. Yet even with this, we have still not gone beyond the subject and his subjective, evident capacities; that is, we still have no "objectivity" given. It does arise, however—in a preliminary stage—in understandable fashion as soon as we take into consideration the function of empathy and fellow mankind as a community of empathy and of language. In the contact of reciprocal linguistic understanding, the original production and the product of one subject can be *actively* understood by the others. In this full understanding of what is produced by the other, as in the case of recollection, a present coaccomplishment on one's own part of the presentified activity necessarily takes place; but at the same time there is also the self-evident consciousness of the identity of the mental structure in the productions of both the receiver of the communication and the communicator; and this occurs reciprocally. The productions can reproduce their likenesses from person to person, and in the chain of the understanding of these repetitions what is self-evident turns up as the same in the consciousness of the other. In the unity of the community of communication among several persons the repeatedly produced structure becomes an object of consciousness, not as a likeness, but as the one structure common to all.

Now we must note that the objectivity of the ideal structure has not yet been fully constituted through such actual transferring of what has been originally produced in one to others who originally reproduce it. What is lacking is the *persisting existence* of the "ideal objects" even during periods in which the inventor and his fellows are no longer wakefully so related or even are no longer alive. What is lacking is their continuing-to-be even when no one has [consciously] realized them in self-evidence.

The important function of written, documenting linguistic expression is that it makes communications possible without immediate or mediate personal address; it is, so to speak, communication become virtual. Through this, the communalization of man is lifted to a new level. Written signs are, when considered from a purely corporeal point of view, straightforwardly, sensibly experienceable; and it is always possible that they be intersubjectively experienceable in common. But as linguistic signs they awaken, as do linguistic sounds, their familiar significations. The awakening is something passive; the awakened signification is thus given passively, similarly to the way in which any other activity which has sunk into obscurity, once associatively awakened, emerges at first *passively* as a more or less clear memory. In the passivity in question here, as in the case of memory, what is passively awakened can be transformed back,* so to speak, into the corresponding activity: this is the capacity for reactivation that belongs originally to every human being as a speaking being. Accordingly, then, the writing-down effects a transformation of the original mode of being of the meaning-structure, [e.g.,] within the geometrical sphere of self-evidence, of the geometrical structure which is put into words. It becomes sedimented, so to speak. But the reader can make it self-evident again, can reactivate the self-evidence.**

There is a distinction, then, between passively understanding the expression and making it self-evident by reactivating its meaning. But there also exist possibilities of a kind of activity, a thinking in terms of things that have been taken up merely receptively, passively, which deals with significations only passively understood and taken over, without any of the self-evidence of original activity. Passivity in general is the realm of things that are bound together and melt into one another associatively, where all meaning that arises is put together passively.

* This is a transformation of which one is conscious as being in itself patterned after [what is passively awakened].

** But this is by no means necessary or even factually normal. Even without this he can understand; he can concur "as a matter of course" in the validity of what is understood without any activity of his own. In this case he comports himself purely passively and receptively.

What often happens here is that a meaning arises which is apparently possible as a unity—i.e., can apparently be made self-evidence through a possible reactivation—whereas the attempt at actual reactivation can reactivate only the individual members of the combination, while the intention to unify them into a whole, instead of being fulfilled, comes to nothing; that is, the ontic validity is destroyed through the original consciousness of nullity.

It is easy to see that even in [ordinary] human life, and first of all in every individual life from childhood up to maturity, the originally intuitive life which creates its originally self-evident structures through activities on the basis of sense-experience very quickly and in increasing measure falls victim to the *seduction of language*. Greater and greater segments of this life lapse into a kind of talking and reading that is dominated purely by association; and often enough, in respect to the validities arrived at in this way, it is disappointed by subsequent experience.

Now one will say that in the sphere that interests us here—that of science, of thinking directed toward the attainment of truths and the avoidance of falsehood—one is obviously greatly concerned from the start to put a stop to the free play of associative constructions. In view of the unavoidable sedimentation of mental products in the form of persisting linguistic acquisitions, which can be taken up again at first merely passively and be taken over by anyone else, such constructions remain a constant danger. This danger is avoided if one not merely convinces oneself ex post facto that the particular construction can be reactivated but assures oneself from the start, after the self-evident primal establishment, of its capacity to be reactivated and enduringly maintained. This occurs when one has a view to the univocity of linguistic expression and to securing, by means of the most painstaking formation of the relevant words, propositions, and complexes of propositions, the results which are to be univocally expressed. This must be done by the individual scientist, and not only by the inventor but by every scientist as a member of the scientific community after he has taken over from the others what is to be taken over. This belongs, then, to the particulars of the scientific tradition within the corresponding community of scientists as a community of knowledge living in the unity of a common responsibility. In accord with the essence of science, then, its functionaries maintain the constant claim, the personal certainty, that everything they put into scientific assertions has been said "once and for all," that it "stands fast," forever identically repeatable with self-evidence and usable for further theoretical or practical ends—as indubitably reactivatable with the identity of its actual meaning.*

However, two more things are important here. First: we have not yet taken into account the fact that scientific thinking attains new results on the basis of those already attained, that the new ones serve as the foundation for still others, etc.—in the unity of a propagative process of transferred meaning.

In the finally immense proliferation of a science like geometry, what has become of the claim and the capacity for reactivation? When every researcher works on his part of the building, what of the vocational interruptions and time out for rest, which cannot be overlooked here? When he returns to the actual continuation of work, must he first run through the whole immense chain of groundings back to the original premises and actually reactivate the whole thing? If so, a science like our modern geometry would obviously not be possible at all. And yet it is of the essence of the results of each stage not only that their ideal ontic meaning in fact comes later [than that of earlier results] but that, since meaning is grounded upon meaning, the earlier meaning gives something of its validity to the later one, indeed becomes part of it to a certain extent. Thus no building block within the mental structure is self-sufficient; and none, then, can be immediately reactivated [by itself].

This is especially true of sciences which, like geometry, have their thematic sphere in ideal products, in idealities from which more and more idealities at higher levels are produced. It is quite different in the so-called descriptive sciences, where the theoretical interest, classifying and describing, remains within the sphere of sense-intuition, which for it represents self-evidence. Here, at least in general, every new proposition can by itself be "cashed in" for self-evidence.

How, by contrast, is a science like geometry possible? How, as a systematic, endlessly growing stratified structure of idealities, can it

---

* At first, of course, it is a matter of a firm direction of the will, which the scientist establishes in himself, aimed at the certain capacity for reactivation. If the goal of reactivatability can be only relatively fulfilled, then the claim which stems from the consciousness of being able to acquire something also has its relativity; and this relativity also makes itself noticeable and is driven out. Ultimately, objective, absolutely firm knowledge of truth is an infinite idea.

maintain its original meaningfulness through living reactivatability if its cognitive thinking is supposed to produce something new without being able to reactivate the previous levels of knowledge back to the first? Even if this could have succeeded at a more primitive stage of geometry, its energy would ultimately have been too much spent in the effort of procuring self-evidence and would not have been available for a higher productivity.

Here we must take into consideration the peculiar "logical" activity which is tied specifically to language, as well as to the ideal cognitive structures that arise specifically within it. To any sentence structures that emerge within a merely passive understanding there belongs essentially a peculiar sort of activity best described by the word "explication."[2] A passively emerging sentence (e.g., in memory), or one heard and passively understood, is at first merely received with a passive ego-participation, taken up as valid; and in this form it is already our meaning. From this we distinguish the peculiar and important activity of explicating our meaning. Whereas in its first form it was a straightforwardly valid meaning, taken up as unitary and undifferentiated—concretely speaking, a straightforwardly valid declarative sentence—now what in itself is vague and undifferentiated is actively explicated. Consider, for example, the way in which we understand, when superficially reading the newspaper, and simply receive the "news"; here there is a passive taking-over of ontic validity such that what is read straightway becomes our opinion.

But it is something special, as we have said, to have the intention to explicate, to engage in the activity which articulates what has been read (or an interesting sentence from it), extracting one by one, in separation from what has been vaguely, passively received as a unity, the elements of meaning, thus bringing the total validity to active performance in a new way on the basis of the individual validities. What was a passive meaning-pattern has now become one constructed through active production. This activity, then, is a peculiar sort of self-evidence; the structure arising out of it is in the mode of having been originally produced. And in connection with this self-evidence, too, there is communalization. The explicated judgment becomes an ideal object capable of being passed on. It is this object exclusively that is meant by logic when it speaks of sentences or judgments. And thus the *domain of logic* is universally designated; this is universally the sphere of being to which

---

[2] *Verdeutlichung*, i.e., making explicit.

logic pertains insofar as it is the theory of the sentences [or propositions] in general.

Through this activity, now, further activities become possible—self-evident constructions of new judgments on the basis of those already valid for us. This is the peculiar feature of logical thinking and of its purely logical self-evidences. All this remains intact even when judgments are transformed into assumptions, where, instead of ourselves asserting or judging, we think ourselves into the position of asserting or judging.

Here we shall concentrate on the sentences of language as they come to us passively and are merely received. In this connection it must also be noted that sentences give themselves in consciousness as reproductive transformations of an original meaning produced out of an actual, original activity; that is, in themselves they refer to such a genesis. In the sphere of logical self-evidence, deduction, or inference in forms of consequence, plays a constant and essential role. On the other hand, one must also take note of the constructive activities that operate with geometrical idealities which have been explicated but not brought to original self-evidence. (Original self-evidence must not be confused with the self-evidence of "axioms"; for axioms are in principle already the results of original meaning-construction and always have this behind them.)

Now what about the possibility of complete and genuine reactivation in full originality, through going back to the primal self-evidences, in the case of geometry and the so-called "deductive" sciences (so called, although they by no means merely deduce)? Here the fundamental law, with unconditionally general self-evidence, is: if the premises can actually be reactivated back to the most original self-evidence, then their self-evident consequences can be also. Accordingly it appears that, beginning with the primal self-evidences, the original genuineness must propagate itself through the chain of logical inference, no matter how long it is. However, if we consider the obvious finitude of the individual and even the social capacity to transform the logical chains of centuries, truly in the unity of one accomplishment, into originally genuine chains of self-evidence, we notice that the [above] law contains within itself an idealization: namely, the removal of limits from our capacity, in a certain sense its infinitization. The peculiar sort of self-evidence belonging to such idealizations will concern us later.

These are, then, the general essential insights which elucidate the whole methodical development of the "deductive" sciences and with it the manner of being which is essential to them.

These sciences are not handed down ready-made in the form of documented sentences; they involve a lively, productively advancing formation of meaning, which always has the documented, as a sediment of earlier production, at its disposal in that it deals with it logically. But out of sentences with sedimented signification, logical "dealing" can produce only other sentences of the same character. That all new acquisitions express an actual geometrical truth is certain a priori under the presupposition that the foundations of the deductive structure have truly been produced and objectified in original self-evidence, i.e., have become universally accessible acquisitions. A continuity from one person to another, from one time to another, must have been capable of being carried out. It is clear that the method of producing original idealities out of what is prescientifically given in the cultural world must have been written down and fixed in firm sentences prior to the existence of geometry; furthermore, the capacity for translating these sentences from vague linguistic understanding into the clarity of the reactivation of their self-evident meaning must have been, in its own way, handed down and ever capable of being handed down.

Only as long as this condition was satisfied, or only when the possibility of its fulfillment was perfectly secured for all time, could geometry preserve its genuine, original meaning as a deductive science throughout the progression of logical constructions. In other words, only in this case could every geometer be capable of bringing to mediate self-evidence the meaning borne by every sentence, not merely as its sedimented (logical) sentence-meaning but as its actual meaning, its truth-meaning. And so for all of geometry.

The progress of deduction follows formal-logical self-evidence; but without the actually developed capacity for reactivating the original activities contained within its fundamental concepts, i.e., without the "what" and the "how" of its prescientific materials, geometry would be a tradition empty of meaning; and if we ourselves did not have this capacity, we could never even know whether geometry had or ever did have a genuine meaning, one that could really be "cashed in."

Unfortunately, however, this is our situation, and that of the whole modern age.

The "presupposition" mentioned above has in fact never been fulfilled. How the living tradition of the meaning-formation of elementary concepts is actually carried on can be seen in elementary geometrical instruction and its textbooks; what we actually learn there is how to deal with *ready-made* concepts and sentences in a rigorously methodical way. Rendering the concepts sensibly intuitable by means of drawn figures is substituted for the actual production of the primal idealities. And the rest is done by success—not the success of actual insight extending beyond the logical method's own self-evidence, but the practical successes of applied geometry, its immense, though not understood, practical usefulness. To this we must add something that will become visible further on in the treatment of historical mathematics, namely, the dangers of a scientific life that is completely given over to logical activities. These dangers lie in certain progressive transformations of meaning * to which this sort of scientific treatment drives one.

By exhibiting the essential presuppositions upon which rests the historical possibility of a genuine tradition, true to its origins, of sciences like geometry, we can understand how such sciences can vitally develop throughout the centuries and still not be genuine. The inheritance of propositions and of the method of logically constructing new propositions and idealities can continue without interruption from one period to the next, while the capacity for reactivating the primal beginnings, i.e., the sources of meaning for everything that comes later, has not been handed down with it. What is lacking is thus precisely what had given and had to give meaning to all propositions and theories, a meaning arising from the primal sources which can be made self-evident again and again.

Of course, grammatically coherent propositions and concatenations of propositions, no matter how they have arisen and have achieved validity—even if it is through mere association—have in all circumstances their own logical meaning, i.e., their meaning that can be made self-evident through explication; this can then be identified again and again as the same proposition, which is either logically coherent or incoherent, where in the latter case it cannot be executed in the unity of an actual judgment. In propositions which belong together in one domain and in the deductive systems that can be made out of them we have a realm of ideal identities; and for these there exist easily understandable possibilities of lasting traditionalization. But propositions, like other cultural structures, appear on the scene in the form of tradition; they claim, so to speak, to be sedimentations of a truth-meaning that can be made originally self-evident; whereas it is by no means necessary that they [actually] have such a meaning, as in the case of

---

* These work to the benefit of logical method, but they remove one further and further from the origins and make one insensitive to the problem of origin and thus to the actual ontic and truth-meaning of all these sciences.

associatively derived falsifications. Thus the whole pregiven deductive science, the total system of propositions in the unity of their validities, is first only a claim which can be justified as an expression of the alleged truth-meaning only through the actual capacity for reactivation.

Through this state of affairs we can understand the deeper reason for the demand, which has spread throughout the modern period and has finally been generally accepted, for a so-called "epistemological grounding" of the sciences, though clarity has never been achieved about what the much-admired sciences are actually lacking.*

As for further details on the uprooting of an originally genuine tradition, i.e., one which involved original self-evidence at its actual first beginning, one can point to possible and easily understandable reasons. In the first oral cooperation of the beginning geometers, the need was understandably lacking for an exact fixing of descriptions of the prescientific primal material and of the ways in which, in relation to this material, geometrical idealities arose together with the first "axiomatic" propositions. Further, the logical superstructures did not yet rise so high that one could not return again and again to the original meaning. On the other hand, the possibility of the practical application of the derived laws, which was actually obvious in connection with the original developments, understandably led quickly, in the realm of praxis, to a habitually practiced method of using mathematics, if need be, to bring about useful things. This method could naturally be handed down even without the ability for original self-evidence. Thus mathematics, emptied of meaning, could generally propagate itself, constantly being added to logically, as could the methodics of technical application on the other side. The extraordinarily far-reaching practical usefulness became of itself a major motive for the advancement and appreciation of these sciences. Thus also it is understandable that the lost original truth-meaning made itself felt so little, indeed, that the need for the corresponding regressive inquiry had to be reawakened. More than this: the true sense of such an inquiry had to be discovered.

Our results based on principle are of a generality that extends over all the so-called deductive sciences and even indicates similar problems and investigations for all sciences. For all of them have the mobility of sedimented traditions that are worked upon, again and again, by an activity of producing new structures of meaning and handing them down.

* What does Hume do but endeavor to inquire back into the primal impressions of developed ideas and, in general, scientific ideas?

Existing in this way, they extend enduringly through time, since all new acquisitions are in turn sedimented and become working materials. Everywhere the problems, the clarifying investigations, the insights of principle are *historical*. We stand within the horizon of human civilization, the one in which we ourselves now live. We are constantly, vitally conscious of this horizon, and specifically as a temporal horizon implied in our given present horizon. To the one human civilization there corresponds essentially the one cultural world as the surrounding life-world with its [peculiar] manner of being; this world, for every historical period and civilization, has its particular features and is precisely the tradition. We stand, then, within the historical horizon in which everything is historical even though we may know very little about it in a definite way. But is has its essential structure that can be revealed through methodical inquiry. This inquiry prescribes all the possible specialized questions, thus including, for the sciences, the inquiries back into origin which are peculiar to them in virtue of their historical manner of being. Here we are led back to the primal materials of the first formation of meaning, the primal premises, so to speak, which lie in the prescientific cultural world. Of course, this cultural world has in turn its own questions of origin, which at first remain unasked.

Naturally, problems of this particular sort immediately awaken the total problem of the universal historicity of the correlative manners of being of humanity and the cultural world and the a priori structure contained in this historicity. Still, questions like that of the clarification of the origin of geometry have a closed character, such that one need not inquire beyond those prescientific materials.

Further clarifications will be made in connection with two objections which are familiar to our own philosophical-historical situation.

In the first place, what sort of strange obstinacy is this, seeking to take the question of the origin of geometry back to some undiscoverable Thales of geometry, someone not even known to legend? Geometry is available to us in its propositions, its theories. Of course we must and we can answer for this logical edifice to the last detail in terms of self-evidence. Here, to be sure, we arrive at first axioms, and from them we proceed to the original self-evidence which the fundamental concepts make possible. What is this, if not the "theory of knowledge," in this case specifically the theory of geometrical knowledge? No one would think of tracing the epistemological problem back to such a supposed Thales. This is quite superfluous. The presently available concepts and propositions themselves contain their own meaning, first as nonself-evident opinion, but nevertheless as true propositions with a meant but still hidden truth which we can obviously bring to light by rendering the propositions themselves self-evident.

Our answer is as follows. Certainly the historical backward reference has not occurred to anyone; certainly theory of knowledge has never been seen as a peculiarly historical task. But this is precisely what we object to in the past. The ruling dogma of the separation in principle between epistemological elucidation and historical, even humanistic-psychological explanation, between epistemological and genetic origin, is fundamentally mistaken, unless one inadmissibly limits, in the usual way, the concepts of "history," "historical explanation," and "genesis." Or rather, what is fundamentally mistaken is the limitation through which precisely the deepest and most genuine problems of history are concealed. If one thinks over our expositions (which are of course still rough and will later of necessity lead us into new depth-dimensions), what they make obvious is precisely that what we know—namely, that the presently vital cultural configuration "geometry" is a tradition and is still being handed down—is not knowledge concerning an external causality which effects the succession of historical configurations, as if it were knowledge based on induction, the presupposition of which would amount to an absurdity here; rather, to understand geometry or any given cultural fact is to be conscious of its historicity, albeit "implicitly." This, however, is not an empty claim; for quite generally it is true for every fact given under the heading of "culture," whether it is a matter of the lowliest culture of necessities or the highest culture (science, state, church, economic organization, etc.), that every straight-forward understanding of it as an experiential fact involves the "coconsciousness" that it is something constructed through human activity. No matter how hidden, no matter how merely "implicitly" coimplied this meaning is, there belongs to it the self-evident possibility of explication, of "making it explicit" and clarifying it. Every explication and every transition from making explicit to making self-evident (even perhaps in cases where one stops much too soon) is nothing other than historical disclosure; in itself, essentially, it is something historical, and as such it bears, with essential necessity, the horizon of its history within itself. This is of course also to say that the whole of the cultural present, understood as a totality, "implies" the whole of the cultural past in an undetermined but structurally determined generality. To put it more precisely, it implies a continuity of pasts which imply one another, each in itself being a past cultural present. And this whole continuity is a *unity* of traditionalization up to the present, which is our present *as* [a process of] traditionalizing itself in flowing-static vitality. This is, as has been said, an undetermined generality, but it has in principle a structure which can be much more widely explicated by proceeding from these indications, a structure which also grounds, "implies," the possibilities for every search for and determination of concrete, factual states of affairs.

Making geometry self-evident, then, whether one is clear about this or not, is the disclosure of its historical tradition. But this knowledge, if it is not to remain empty talk or undifferentiated generality, requires the methodical production, proceeding from the present and carried out as research in the present, of differentiated self-evidences of the type discovered above (in several fragmentary investigations of what belongs to such knowledge superficially, as it were). Carried out systematically, such self-evidences result in nothing other and nothing less than the universal a priori of history with all its highly abundant component elements.

We can also say now that history is from the start nothing other than the vital movement of the coexistence and the interweaving of original formations and sedimentations of meaning.

Anything that is shown to be a historical fact, either in the present through experience or by a historian as a fact in the past, necessarily has its *inner structure of meaning*; but especially the motivational interconnections established about it in terms of everyday understanding have deep, further and further-reaching implications which must be interrogated, disclosed. All [merely] factual history remains incomprehensible because, always merely drawing its conclusions naïvely and straightforwardly from facts, it never makes thematic the general ground of meaning upon which all such conclusions rest, has never investigated the immense structural a priori which is proper to it. Only the disclosure of the essentially general structure* lying in our present and then in every past or future historical present as such, and, in totality, only the disclosure of the concrete, historical time in which we live, in which our total humanity lives in respect to its total, essentially general structure—only this disclosure can make possible historical inquiry [*Historie*] which is truly understanding, insightful, and in the genuine sense scientific. This is the concrete, historical a priori which encompasses everything that exists as historical becoming and having-become or exists in its essential being as tradition and handing-down. What has been said was related to the total form "historical present in general," historical time generally. But the particular configurations of culture, which find their place within its coherent historical being as tradition and as vitally handing themselves down, have within this totality only relatively self-sufficient being in traditionality, only the being of nonself-sufficient components. Correlatively, now, account would have to be taken of the subjects of historicity, the persons who create cultural formations, functioning in totality: creative personal civilization.**

In respect to geometry one recognizes, now that we have pointed out the hiddenness of its fundamental concepts, which have become inaccessible, and have made them understandable as such in first basic outlines, that only the consciously set task of [discovering] the historical origin of geometry (within the total problem of the a priori of historicity in general) can provide the method for a geometry which is true to its origins and at the same time is to be understood in a universal-historical way; and the same is true for all sciences, for philosophy. In principle, then, a history of philosophy, a history of the particular sciences in the style of the usual factual history, can actually render nothing of their subject matter comprehensible. For a genuine history of philosophy, a genuine history of the particular sciences, is noth-

---

* The superficial structure of the externally "ready-made" men within the social-historical, essential structure of humanity, but also the deeper [structures] which disclose the inner historicities of the persons taking part. ["Structures" is Biemel's interpolation.]

** The historical world is, to be sure, first pregiven as a social-historical world. But it is historical only through the inner historicity of the individuals, who are individuals in their inner historicity, together with that of other communalized persons. Recall what was said in a few meager beginning expositions about memories and the constant historicity to be found in them [pp. 355f., above].

ing other than the tracing of the historical meaning-structures given in the present, or their self-evidences, along the documented chain of historical back-references into the hidden dimension of the primal self-evidences which underlie them.* Even the very problem here can be made understandable only through recourse to the historical a priori as the universal source of all conceivable problems of understanding. The problem of genuine historical explanation comes together, in the case of the sciences, with "epistemological" grounding or clarification.

We must expect yet a second and very weighty objection. From the historicism which prevails extensively in different forms [today] I expect little receptivity for a depth-inquiry which goes beyond the usual factual history, as does the one outlined in this work, especially since, as the expression "a priori" indicates, it lays claim to a strictly unconditioned and truly apodictic self-evidence extending beyond all historical facticities. One will object: what naïveté, to seek to display, and to claim to have displayed, a historical a priori, an absolute, super-temporal validity, after we have obtained such abundant testimony for the relativity of everything historical, of all historically developed world-apperceptions, right back to those of the "primitive" tribes. Every people, large or small, has its world in which, for that people, everything fits well together, whether in mythical-magical or in European-rational terms, and in which everything can be explained perfectly. Every people has its "logic" and, accordingly, if this logic is explicated in propositions, "its" a priori.

However, let us consider the methodology of establishing historical facts in general, thus including that of the facts supporting the objection; and let us do this in regard to what such methodology presupposes. Does not the undertaking of a humanistic science of "how it really was" contain a presupposition taken for granted, a validity-ground never observed, never made thematic, of a strictly unassailable [type of] self-evidence, without which historical inquiry would be a meaningless enterprise? All questioning and demonstrating which is in the usual sense historical presupposes history [*Geschichte*] as the universal horizon of questioning, not explicitly, but still as a horizon of implicit certainty which, in spite of all vague background-indeterminacy, is the presup-

* But what counts as primal self-evidence for the sciences is determined by an educated person or a sphere of such persons who pose new questions, new historical questions, questions concerning the inner depth-dimension as well as those concerning an external historicity in the social-historical world.

position of all determinability, or of all intention to seek and to establish determined facts.

What is historically primary in itself is our present. We always already know of our present world and that we live in it, always surrounded by an openly endless horizon of unknown actualities. This knowing, as horizon-certainty, is not something learned, not knowledge which was once actual and has merely sunk back to become part of the background; the horizon-certainty had to be already there in order to be capable of being laid out thematically; it is already presupposed in order that we can seek to know what we do not know. All not-knowing concerns the unknown world, which yet exists in advance for us *as* world, as the horizon of all questions of the present and thus also all questions which are specifically historical. These are the questions which concern men, as those who act and create in their communalized coexistence in the world and transform the constant cultural face of the world. Do we not know further—we have already had occasion to speak of this—that this historical present has its historical pasts behind it, that it has developed out of them, that historical past is a continuity of pasts which proceed from one another, each, as a past present, being a tradition producing tradition out of itself? Do we not know that the present and the whole of historical time implied in it is that of a historically coherent and unified civilization, coherent through its generative bond and constant communalization in cultivating what has already been cultivated before, whether in cooperative work or in reciprocal interaction, etc.? Does all this not announce a universal "knowing" of the horizon, an implicit knowing that can be made explicit systematically in its essential structure? Is not the resulting great problem here the horizon toward which all questions tend, and thus the horizon which is presupposed in all of them? Accordingly, we need not first enter into some kind of critical discussion of the facts set out by historicism; it is enough that even the claim of their factualness presupposes the historical a priori if this claim is to have a meaning.

But a doubt arises all the same. The horizon-exposition to which we recurred must not bog down in vague, superficial talk; it must itself arrive at its own sort of scientific discipline. The sentences in which it is expressed must be fixed and capable of being made self-evident again and again. Through what method do we obtain a universal and also fixed a priori of the historical world which is always originally genuine? Whenever we consider it, we find ourselves with the self-evident capacity to reflect—to turn to the horizon and to penetrate it in an expository way. But we also have, and know that we have, the capacity of complete freedom to transform, in thought and phantasy, our human historical existence and what is there exposed as its life-world. And precisely in this activity of free variation, and in running through the conceivable possibilities for the life-world, there arises, with apodictic self-evidence, an essentially general set of elements going through all the variants; and of this we can convince ourselves with truly apodictic certainty. Thereby we have removed every bond to the factually valid historical world and have regarded this world itself [merely] as one of the conceptual possibilities. This freedom, and the direction of our gaze upon the apodictically invariant, results in the latter again and again—with the self-evidence of being able to repeat the invariant structure at will—as what is identical, what can be made self-evident *originaliter* at any time, can be fixed in univocal language as the essence constantly implied in the flowing, vital horizon.

Through this method, going beyond the formal generalities we exhibited earlier, we can also make thematic that apodictic [aspect] of the prescientific world that the original founder of geometry had at his disposal, that which must have served as the material for his idealizations.

Geometry and the sciences most closely related to it have to do with space-time and the shapes, figures, also shapes of motion, alterations of deformation, etc., that are possible within space-time, particularly as measurable magnitudes. It is now clear that even if we know almost nothing about the historical surrounding world of the first geometers, this much is certain as an invariant, essential structure: that it was a world of "things" (including the human beings themselves as subjects of this world); that all things necessarily had to have a bodily character— although not all things could be mere bodies, since the necessarily co-existing human beings are not thinkable as mere bodies and, like even the cultural objects which belong with them structurally, are not exhausted in corporeal being. What is also clear, and can be secured at least in its essential nucleus through careful a priori explication, is that these pure bodies had spatiotemporal shapes and "material" [*stoffliche*] qualities (color, warmth, weight, hardness, etc.) related to them. Further, it is clear that in the life of practical needs certain particularizations of shape stood out and that a technical praxis always [aimed at][3] the production of particular preferred shapes and the im-

---

[3] Biemel's interpolation.

provement of them according to certain directions of gradualness.

First to be singled out from the thing-shapes are surfaces—more or less "smooth," more or less perfect surfaces; edges, more or less rough or fairly "even"; in other words, more or less pure lines, angles, more or less perfect points; then, again, among the lines, for example, straight lines are especially preferred, and among the surfaces the even surfaces; for example, for practical purposes boards limited by even surfaces, straight lines, and points are preferred, whereas totally or partially curved surfaces are undesirable for many kinds of practical interests. Thus the production of even surfaces and their perfection (polishing) always plays its role in praxis. So also in cases where just distribution is intended. Here the rough estimate of magnitudes is transformed into the measurement of magnitudes by counting the equal parts. (Here, too, proceeding from the factual, an essential form becomes recognizable through a method of variation.) Measuring belongs to every culture, varying only according to stages from primitive to higher perfections. We can always presuppose some measuring technique, whether of a lower or higher type, in the essential forward development of culture, [as well as] the growth of such a technique, thus also including the art of design for buildings, of surveying fields, pathways, etc.;[4] such a technique is always already there, already abundantly developed and pregiven to the philosopher who did not yet know geometry but who should be conceivable as its inventor. As a philosopher proceeding from the practical, finite surrounding world (of the room, the city, the landscape, etc., and temporally the world of periodical occurrences: day, month, etc.) to the theoretical world-view and world-knowledge, he has the finitely known and unknown spaces and times as finite elements within the horizon of an open infinity. But with this he does not yet have geometrical space, mathematical time, and whatever else is to become a novel spiritual product out of these finite elements which serve as material; and with his manifold finite shapes in their space-time he does not yet have geometrical shapes, the phoronomic shapes; [his shapes, as] formations developed out of praxis and thought of in terms of [gradual] perfection, clearly serve only as bases for a new sort of praxis out of which similarly named new constructions grow.

It is evident in advance that this new sort of construction will be a

----

[4] I have reverted to the original version of this sentence as given in the critical apparatus; I can make no sense of the emended version given in the text. (Tr.)

product arising out of an idealizing, spiritual act, one of "pure" thinking, which has its materials in the designated general pregivens of this factual humanity and human surrounding world and creates "ideal objects" out of them.

Now the problem would be to discover, through recourse to what is essential to history [*Historie*], the historical original meaning which necessarily was able to give and did give to the whole becoming of geometry its persisting truth-meaning.

It is of particular importance now to bring into focus and establish the following insight: Only if the apodictically general content, invariant throughout all conceivable variation, of the spatiotemporal sphere of shapes is taken into account in the idealization can an ideal construction arise which can be understood for all future time and by all coming generations of men and thus be capable of being handed down and reproduced with the identical intersubjective meaning. This condition is valid far beyond geometry for all spiritual structures which are to be unconditionally and generally capable of being handed down. Were the thinking activity of a scientist to introduce something "time-bound" in his thinking, i.e., something bound to what is merely factual about his present or something valid for him as a merely factual tradition, his construction would likewise have a merely time-bound ontic meaning; this meaning would be understandable only by those men who shared the same merely factual presuppositions of understanding.

It is a general conviction that geometry, with all its truths, is valid with unconditioned generality for all men, all times, all peoples, and not merely for all historically factual ones but for all conceivable ones. The presuppositions of principle for this conviction have never been explored because they have never been seriously made a problem. But it has also become clear to us that every establishment of a historical fact which lays claim to unconditioned objectivity likewise presupposes this invariant or absolute a priori.

Only [through the disclosure of this a priori][5] can there be an a priori science extending beyond all historical facticities, all historical surrounding worlds, peoples, times, civilizations; only in this way can a science as *aeterna veritas* appear. Only on this fundament is based the secured capacity of inquiring back from the temporarily depleted self-evidence of a science to the primal self-evidences.

[5] Biemel's interpolation.

Do we not stand here before the great and profound problem-horizon of reason, the same reason that functions in every man, the *animal rationale*, no matter how primitive he is?

This is not the place to penetrate into those depths themselves.

In any case, we can now recognize from all this that historicism, which wishes to clarify the historical or epistemological essence of mathematics from the standpoint of the magical circumstances or other manners of apperception of a time-bound civilization, is mistaken in principle. For romantic spirits the mythical-magical elements of the historical and prehistorical aspects of mathematics may be particularly attractive; but to cling to this merely historically factual aspect of mathematics is precisely to lose oneself to a sort of romanticism and to overlook the genuine problem, the internal-historical problem, the epistemological problem. Also, one's gaze obviously cannot then become free to recognize that facticities of every type, including those involved in the [historicist] objection, have a root in the essential structure of what is generally human, through which a teleological reason running throughout all historicity announces itself. With this is revealed a set of problems in its own right related to the totality of history and to the full meaning which ultimately gives it its unity.

If the usual factual study of history in general, and in particular the history which in most recent times has achieved true universal extension over all humanity, is to have any meaning at all, such a meaning can only be grounded upon what we can here call internal history, and as such upon the foundations of the universal historical a priori. Such a meaning necessarily leads further to the indicated highest question of a universal teleology of reason.

If, after these expositions, which have illuminated very general and many-sided problem-horizons, we lay down the following as something completely secured, namely, that the human surrounding world is the same today and always, and thus also in respect to what is relevant to primal establishment and lasting tradition, then we can show in several steps, only in an exploratory way, in connection with our own surrounding world, what should be considered in more detail for the problem of the idealizing primal establishment of the meaning-structure "geometry."